BORDER WAR

BORDER WAR

A Yankee Family in Civil War Missouri

Marilyn Ferris Motz

UNIVERSITY PRESS OF MISSISSIPPI / JACKSON

The University Press of Mississippi is the scholarly publishing agency of
the Mississippi Institutions of Higher Learning: Alcorn State University,
Delta State University, Jackson State University, Mississippi State University,
Mississippi University for Women, Mississippi Valley State University,
University of Mississippi, and University of Southern Mississippi.

www.upress.state.ms.us

The University Press of Mississippi is a member
of the Association of University Presses.

This work depicts actual events as truthfully as recollection permits
and/or can be verified by research. The names and identifying details of
some individuals may have been changed to respect their privacy.

Any discriminatory or derogatory language or hate speech regarding race,
ethnicity, religion, sex, gender, class, national origin, age, or disability
that has been retained or appears in elided form is in no way an endorsement
of the use of such language outside a scholarly context.

Copyright © 2025 by University Press of Mississippi
All rights reserved
Manufactured in the United States of America

∞

Publisher: University Press of Mississippi, Jackson, USA
Authorized GPSR Safety Representative: Easy Access System Europe -
Mustamäe tee 50, 10621 Tallinn, Estonia, gpsr.requests@easproject.com

Library of Congress Control Number: 2025948084

Hardback ISBN 978-1-4968-6003-3 | Paperback ISBN 978-1-4968-6005-7
Epub single ISBN 978-1-4968-6009-5 | Epub institutional ISBN 978-1-4968-6012-5
PDF single ISBN 978-1-4968-6013-2 | PDF institutional ISBN 978-1-4968-6014-9

British Library Cataloging-in-Publication Data available

For my husband,
Timothy Allen Motz

CONTENTS

Acknowledgments ix
Abbreviations xi

Introduction 3

Part I: Schoolcraft, Michigan, and Maumee, Ohio, 1853
Chapter One: Love And Work 15
Chapter Two: Leisure And Literacy 36

Part II: From Michigan to Missouri, 1854–1861
Chapter Three: Family And Nation 59
Chapter Four: Yankees And Pioneers 79
Chapter Five: Loyalties And Lies 108

Part III: Montevallo, Missouri, 1862
Chapter Six: Henry's Civil War 135
Chapter Seven: Harriet's Civil War 157
Chapter Eight: Refugees 180
Conclusion 203

Notes 211
Index 271

ACKNOWLEDGMENTS

I am indebted to the archivists of the Archives and Regional History Collections at the Zhang Legacy Collections Center at Western Michigan University and the University of Michigan's Bentley Historical Library for preserving and cataloging the family collections of diaries, correspondence, and other documents that made this research possible. I want to thank the Smith-Barney family for making this rich trove of material available to researchers by donating their papers to university archives. The Missouri Secretary of State's Digital Heritage website is an invaluable resource that provides online access to extensive databases and documents in Missouri archives. I also appreciate the detailed information that local historical societies, genealogists, and other researchers in Vernon County, Missouri, and Schoolcraft, Michigan, share online.

    I am grateful to my colleagues in the Department of Popular Culture at Bowling Green State University for sustaining an open-minded interdisciplinary environment for exploring the culture of everyday life. My understanding of the role of popular culture and folklore in processes of political, economic, and social change grew through conversations with Chris Geist, Jack Santino, Angela Nelson, Jeff Brown, Jeremy Wallach, Becca Cragin, Montana Miller, Kristin Rudisill, Rebecca Kinney, Esther Clinton, Matt Donahue, Chuck Coletta, Dan Shoemaker, and others. Discussions with Susana Peña, Director of the School of Cultural and Critical Studies at BGSU, expanded my awareness of the cultural construction of whiteness and its intersection with identities of gender and social class. Many years ago, historians Marcella Bush and Lewie Reece provided expert research assistance on 1850s Michigan political campaigns and daily life, and students, notably Larry Nelson, Sally Myers, and Vida Penezic, contributed to my understanding of the cultural and social life Harriet Smith experienced in Maumee, Ohio, in 1853.

    I want to thank Susanne Bunkers, Dan Ben-Amos, and especially Batsheva Ben-Amos for helpful feedback on my discussion of the Smith diaries in articles included in their edited volumes on diaries. At the University Press of Mississippi, Director Craig Gill and Editor-in-Chief Katie Keene enabled me to prune an overgrown manuscript to reveal the contours of this book. I also appreciate Katie Turner's assistance in navigating the manuscript preparation process. The suggestions made by two anonymous readers helped me tighten the book's focus and strengthen my analysis of the complex identities and loyalties the Smith family experienced in southwest Missouri during the early years of the Civil War.

I want to thank my son, Christopher Motz, for sharing his expertise in tracing ancient Roman social networks and information channels. My greatest debt is to my husband, Timothy Motz, for his encouragement and support, and his willingness to take on more than his share of the tasks of everyday life. His expertise with computers, visual images, and project management has been invaluable, and our conversations continue to provide inspiration and insights that shape my thinking and writing.

ABBREVIATIONS

21st GA	*Journal of the House*, 21st General Assembly, 1861, General Assembly, Record Group 550, MSA
BHL	Bentley Historical Library, University of Michigan
HVC	*History of Vernon County, Missouri* (St. Louis, 1887)
LC	Library of Congress, Washington, DC
MDH	Missouri Digital Heritage (https://www.sos.mo.gov/mdh/)
MHC	*Michigan Historical Collections* (Michigan Pioneer and Historical Society)
MSA	Missouri State Archives, Jefferson City
NARA	National Archives Records Administration, Washington, DC
OR	*The War of the Rebellion: A Compilation of the Official Records of the Union and Confederate Armies*, Series 1 (Washington, DC, 1883)
PM	Union Provost Marshals' File of Papers Related to Two or More Civilians, Microcopy 416, National Archives Microfilm Publications, MSA (MDH: https://www.sos.mo.gov/archives/provost/provostPDF)
"Reminiscences"	Isa H. Smith, "Reminiscences of Missouri" (unpublished manuscript, 1904), Isa Smith Essays 1904-1909 Folder, Box 5, SBSC
SBSC	Stanley Barney Smith Collection, A-88, Archives and Regional History Collections, Zhang Legacy Collections Center, Western Michigan University
US Census	US Census Bureau, Manuscript Census
"Young Pioneer"	H. P. Smith, "Reminiscences of the Life of a Young Pioneer," *Pioneer Day Exercises* (Schoolcraft, MI, 1898), non-paginated, BHL

BORDER WAR

INTRODUCTION

Henry Parker Smith's gravestone in the Schoolcraft Township Cemetery stands out among markers inscribed with names and dates, and sometimes places, of birth and death. After stating the facts of Henry Smith's birth in Petersburg, Virginia, on May 16, 1826, and death in Schoolcraft, Michigan, on June 24, 1898, his epitaph continues:

> In loving remembrance of his many virtues and kindly spirit, this stone has been erected by his friends and the church to whom his mellow notes were so long familiar.

In contrast to the lengthy personal tribute on the upright polished monument Henry's friends provided, a small flat headstone marks his wife's grave. As she probably preferred, her marker is inscribed simply:

> Harriet A. Johnson
> Wife of Henry P Smith
> 1832–1924.

Neither gravestone suggests the dramatic events of the couple's wartime experiences. Near the end of his life, Henry submitted biographical information for a book honoring "Prominent and Representative Citizens" of three counties in southwest Michigan. After describing Henry's early life and marriage to Harriet, the entry notes that the family moved to Vernon County, in southwest Missouri, where Henry farmed and taught school: "He mingled in the political life of the county, and held the office of County Judge for a few years. He was also appointed Probate Judge, but, immediately after his appointment, received a communication stating that should he accept, he would be summarily dealt with. For his own good and that of his family, he decided to leave the county. Accordingly, in the fall of 1862, Mr. Smith returned to Schoolcraft."

For the next thirty years, the entry continues, Henry Smith operated a dairy farm in Michigan and "took an active part in public affairs" as a "strong Republican."[1] Readers of this 1892 biographical sketch who had followed newspaper coverage of the Civil War probably would understand that Confederate guerrillas had threatened Henry's life if he accepted a judicial appointment that confirmed his loyalty to the Union. However, the *History of Vernon County, Missouri*, published in 1888, reports that the county court could not meet in July 1861 because County Judge H. P. Smith and other officials were in "Gen. Price's army" defending Missouri against federal troops.[2] Henry and Harriet Smith's diaries and correspondence paint a more complex picture of their wartime allegiances and activities than either of these apparently contradictory accounts indicates. In recent decades, historians have shown that loyalty to the Union or Confederacy was more complicated and regional identifications more fluid than the binary North versus South conflict constructed by postwar historical memory.[3] Studies that focus on a community or individual provide insight into the complex, multiple, sometimes incompatible identities and allegiances challenged by the experience of civil war.[4] In regions like southwestern Missouri, where the raids, chases, ambushes, and skirmishes of guerrilla fighting occurred in isolated villages, farms, and creek beds, the civilian population often became unwilling participants. The personal writing of Harriet and Henry Smith offers a window into one family's shifting and ambiguous relationships, identities, and loyalties on the border of the North and South.

By the time Henry and Harriet moved to Missouri in 1858, they had begun to consider themselves Yankees, an identity that was political and cultural as well as geographic. Growing up on the southwest Michigan prairie, Henry participated in the transition from frontier agriculture to commercial farming. As a young man, he observed the growth of industrial production in Seneca Falls, New York, and became part of the local and traveling sales force that linked Midwestern rural consumers and eastern manufacturers. In the daily journal he began at age twenty-one, Henry recorded his recreational and political activities. In rural Michigan, he played the fiddle in dance halls on Saturdays and sang in church choirs on Sundays. In Seneca Falls, Henry attended commercial productions by P. T. Barnum and other touring entertainment, met feminist Elizabeth Cady Stanton, and listened to abolitionist lecturers, including Frederick Douglass. After returning to Michigan, Henry participated in the development of the Republican Party and praised Abraham Lincoln's campaign speech for presidential candidate John Fremont. Harriet had fewer opportunities to engage in public cultural and political activities, but as the daughter of a Baptist minister in New

England and northern Ohio, she grew to adulthood under the influence of religious revivals, reform movements, and the cult of domesticity, enhanced by the proliferation of popular literature. She had dreamed of becoming an author and practiced her craft by writing letters and keeping a diary. In 1852, twenty-year-old Harriet Johnson was teaching on the Michigan prairie when she met Henry Smith, a handsome twenty-six-year-old dry-goods clerk. When she married Henry in 1854, Harriet not only gave up her goal of becoming a published author; she set aside her private diary as well, leaving Henry to chronicle the family's daily life.

After struggling for three years to gain a financial foothold in Michigan, Henry decided to look for farmland further west. In the letters he exchanged with Harriet in 1857, the couple envisioned a home that would embody the Yankee domestic ideal advocated by current magazines. Harriet and their young daughter arrived at the log house Henry built on the southwest Missouri prairie to face a financial panic, followed by a devastating drought, followed by the ruthless violence of civil war. Immobilized by the imminent birth of their third child in 1861, Henry and Harriet played reluctant host to the succession of guerrilla bands, Jayhawkers, Union forces, and Confederate troops who swarmed back and forth along the road that ran past the family's farm near the Kansas border. In the complex dynamics of a community with divided and shifting loyalties, Henry was drawn gradually into the conflict as he tried to help his neighbors and protect his family. Throughout the turmoil, Henry maintained the daily journal he kept hidden in a hollow log. In 1862, Harriet resumed the diary she had set aside eight years earlier. Their daily entries describe the social networks of a rural community that intersected with the guerrilla bands, Confederate partisans, and Union occupation troops wrestling for control of the region. They explain the circumstances and the moral reasoning that led Harriet and Henry to distrust federal authorities and provide assistance to insurgents.

When I ran across these hand-written diaries in the Henry Parker Smith Papers in the Bentley Historical Library at the University of Michigan decades ago, I was fascinated by their accounts of romance in 1853 and guerrilla warfare in 1862. The diaries Henry and Harriet wrote were tantalizing fragments of a story, but important parts were missing. Years later, I discovered some of the missing pieces. Harriet and Henry saved trunks full of family letters, account books, and other documents. Their grandson, Classics Professor Stanley Barney Smith, recognized the potential historical value of this documentation of daily life. He and his wife, Edna M. Smith, donated the material to the Archives and Regional History Collections at Western Michigan University.[5] As I read letter after letter, the outlines of the story began to emerge as the voices of friends and relatives joined those of Harriet and Henry to fill the gaps left by the diaries. Now, as government records are digitized and databases created, even more parts of the puzzle fall into place. Interwoven with a story of coming of age, of survival, and of personal growth are experiences unique to the tumultuous decade leading into the Civil War. In the diaries and letters they left behind, Harriet and Henry Smith provide an intimate view of the ways one family responded to, participated in, and made sense of a pivotal period in American history when the United States was determining its future demographic, geographic and political shape, creating its own forms of popular culture, developing a capitalist industrialized economy, forging a national identity, and constructing social formations of race, gender, region, and social class. Their writing reveals how cultural experiences intersected with economics, politics, religion, and personal relationships in the everyday lives of a Midwestern farm family and how the shock of a civil war disrupted those lives.

In *The Practice of Everyday Life*, Michel de Certeau argues that both statistical analysis in the social sciences and textual analysis in the humanities examine only data that can be removed from their contexts, erasing the creative process through which individuals use available cultural resources in specific situations of everyday life: their "ways of using things or words according to circumstances" with the "dispersed, tactical, and make-shift creativity of groups or individuals already caught in the nets of 'discipline'" described by Michel Foucault.[6] He suggests that by tracing the trajectories of individuals as they negotiate pathways through time and space, examining the details of their experiences in multiple facets of everyday life, and identifying the resources and constraints within which they operate, we can gain insight into their historical circumstances. In practice, de Certeau's ethnographic research team relied on previously published statistical studies to situate the perspectives of individuals within broader patterns of attitudes and behavior.[7] Growing interest in the varied range of experiences of everyday life in the antebellum and Civil War eras has produced a rich trove of scholarship that illuminates the complex choices Americans faced in the 1850s and 1860s. In the context of this body of work, examining Henry and Harriet Smiths' diaries and letters with the biographical attention often paid to the lives of famous people enables us to follow the labyrinth of personal responses and motivations that shaped their lives. We can gain a hint of how they made sense of their culture and participated in its creation. When Harriet and Henry decided against an abortion, moved west to Missouri, or hid the horses of Confederate guerrillas fleeing from Union troops, they were among the numerous Americans who were simultaneously or sequentially

Whigs, Know-Nothings, Republicans, Yankees, guerrilla supporters, temperance advocates, the reading public, settlers of the West, followers of the cult of domesticity, and members of the emerging middle class. They were also Baptists, farmers, teachers, and, in Henry's case, a Mason, fiddler, salesman, and local office-holder. The Smiths' personal writings reveal the complex interconnections among various identities, ideological positions, cultural experiences, and life choices.

Studying the everyday practices of individuals within their networks of social relationships makes it possible to see how their subjectivity—their sense of who they are and where they fit in the world—develops, operates, and changes over time.[8] Viewed in their historical context, the diaries and letters written by one person over a period of years or during a time of crisis can provide insight into this process of change in individual subjectivity. People write letters and diaries to define events, assign meanings, and construct a self in relation to others, but these documents are not transparent windows into the experiences or feelings of their authors.[9] Books, magazines, teachers, parents, and friends provide models of writing that influence the content and form of correspondence and diaries. A writer always selects which events and issues to include. Based on expectations of privacy and a sense of propriety, diarists may omit personal or controversial matters, and any account is limited by its author's knowledge and understanding. While a diarist may or may not expect the diary to be read by others, the author of a personal letter always writes within the context of a relationship that determines the subject matter, style, and rhetorical purpose of the correspondence. Collections of personal papers rarely provide a complete record: over time, documents are lost, damaged, or discarded. Despite these limitations, personal writings can reveal the ways an individual interweaves multiple aspects of culture into a consciousness of self, integrating the countless bits of information and varied experiences of everyday life.[10]

Maintaining a diary helps literate men and women create the narrative of their own life stories.[11] Historians have noted a convergence of the development of literary forms such as the novel with new modes of subjectivity and changing structures of social organization in family, workplace, and nation.[12] Forms of personal writing, such as diaries and correspondence, enabled literate men and women to trace the unifying thread that constituted a personal identity, constructing a self whose religious and political views, personal life, work practices, and consumption of goods represented a set of compatible values and perspectives.[13] Mastery of the technique of penmanship and knowledge of the rules of spelling and grammar enabled Henry and Harriet Smith to describe their observations, identify their emotions, and express their opinions. Understanding of rhetorical principles and the use of punctuation marks provided the grammatical flexibility to compare options, make evaluations, and use irony and metaphor.[14] This facility with written language allowed them to envision the future, weigh alternatives, and explore potential consequences. They could trace their personal growth and place themselves in the context of their community and the broader world. They described what Katherine Morrissey calls the "mental territory" they inhabited: the natural and built environment, the mapped and governed terrain, the social networks and communities, and the pathways of travel that constituted the geography of a region as understood by its inhabitants. The future they envisioned for themselves was linked to the future they anticipated for their community and region.[15]

The story I tell here, like the Smiths' personal narratives, focuses on three moments in time when the life course of the couple intersected with fundamental transformations in American society. The first moment of crisis both Harriet and Henry identified was their decision to marry. In Part I, the diaries Henry and Harriet wrote during their courtship in 1853 reveal their gendered expectations of married life. Chapter One: Love and Work examines the intersection of family and work in an industrializing economy as Harriet and Henry considered whether to assume the responsibilities of marriage. Chapter Two: Leisure and Literacy discusses their consumption of manufactured products and participation in recreational activities, as well as the practices of reading and writing that shaped their identity and influenced their perception of the world. As they looked ahead to their future married life, Harriet and Henry expected to experience predictable growth through the course of their own life cycle in the context of gradual national progress in scientific discovery, technological innovation, moral enlightenment, and civic achievement. To this end, Henry and Harriet monitored their daily use of time as an investment in their future success and happiness within a stable local community.

The second choice the couple faced was the decision to move west to Missouri. Part II tells the story of the Smith family during the nine years from the time Harriet set her diary aside to prepare for her marriage in 1854 to the time she resumed her daily entries in 1862. These chapters are based on Henry's diaries as well as the letters the couple wrote to one another and those they received from friends and family. Chapter Three: Family and Nation examines how the couple's adjustment to marriage and parenthood and Henry's increasing participation in politics led them to see moving west as an opportunity to realize the life they had envisioned. Chapter Four: Yankees and Pioneers explores Henry's attempts to build a house in western Missouri that would meet Harriet's expectations for a Yankee home within the constraints of the terrain and climate and the cultural traditions of his new neighbors. Chapter Five: Loyalties and Lies describes the hardships the couple faced as they adapted to the harsh environment, established friendships in the community, and watched the region slide into chaos as the Civil War broke out. The chapters in Part II trace Harriet and Henry's growing awareness of a fragile nation defined by geography. They began to see themselves as part of an imagined community of progressive, literate, enlightened Yankees who would establish northern middle-class customs and moral standards as the national norm.

The third crisis the couple faced was the intensification of Confederate guerrilla activity when Union forces asserted control over Missouri's civilian population. In Part III, the diary entries Henry and Harriet wrote in 1862 provide differing perspectives on their increasing involvement in the conflict. Chapter Six: Henry's War discusses Henry's conflicting loyalties and responsibilities to his family, friends, and community as he tried to maintain credibility with both guerrilla bands and Union officials. Chapter Seven: Harriet's War examines how Harriet's concepts of gender, class, religion, morality, and nation shifted as she questioned her identity as a Yankee. In Chapter Eight: Refugees, Harriet and Henry narrate the family's desperate journey back to Michigan through territory devastated by war and describe their ambivalent feelings as they return to their former home. The three chapters of Part III discuss how Henry and Harriet abandoned expectations for the future to focus on imminent dangers. Isolated from the world outside their rural Missouri community, Harriet and Henry drew on remembered cultural resources to situate themselves in a new moral order as their allegiance shifted from abstract patriotism to a nation into personal loyalty to a local community and finally to ensuring the survival of their own family.

Harriet and Henry Smith told the story of their lives in various narrative contexts: diaries, letters to each other as well as to family and friends, essays, letters published in a magazine, and petitions to government and military officials. In these writing acts, they adopted various narrative templates, rhetorical strategies, and authorial positions to represent themselves and others, envision possibilities, consider options, apply abstract principles to specific situations, and make sense of their experiences. The story I tell, overlaid on the Smiths' narratives, explores how they drew on available resources to assess the experiences of everyday life, interpret cultural texts, and build relationships with other people as they faced the increasing responsibilities of adulthood and the crises brought by civil war. I approach the story from a family background that is similar to theirs in many ways.

As a child in southern Michigan, I listened to my grandparents' stories of growing up in rural Vermont. Family papers in my attic include those of a great-grandfather who was four years younger than Harriet. Like Harriet, he was born to a revivalist preacher in Massachusetts and raised in Vermont. I knew that some of my father's family, like Henry's, had moved to Vermont from Massachusetts, but I was surprised to discover recently that Henry's ancestors and mine were among about twenty households that formed a frontier town in mid-seventeenth-century Massachusetts, where they served together in local government.[16] Although the record is less clear, it appears that my sixth-great-grandfather and Henry's third-great-grandfather married cousins, suggesting that Henry and I shared common ancestors in colonial Massachusetts. In annual childhood visits to my mother's parents in southern Ohio, I learned that my mother's grandfather fought in the Civil War and that five of her great-uncles died in the army, fighting "to preserve the Union," my grandmother explained. I discovered much later that these Ohio farm families, like Henry and Harriet's Missouri neighbors, were more southern than Yankee in heritage and culture. Some came to southern Ohio from South Carolina, and some moved further west to settle in Missouri.

Regional identities and national allegiances were especially ambiguous in Civil War Missouri, which shared only its southern border with another slave state and was represented in the legislatures of both the Confederacy and the Union. Since 1989, when Michael Fellman published his account of guerrilla conflict in Missouri, several studies have explored Confederate guerrilla bands and their interactions with civilians and Union occupation forces in the prosperous region surrounding the Missouri River.[17] Joseph Beilein's *Bushwhackers* examines the family networks that supported this guerrilla activity. LeeAnn Whites explores the essential role of female family members who created domestic supply lines to provide food and clothing. Andrew Fialko's mapping of movements of guerrilla bands reveals the spatial organization of these support systems.[18] Jeremy Neely's *The Border Between Them* and Matthew Stith's *Extreme Civil War* examine the less populated and less affluent regions of southwestern Missouri along the border with Kansas.[19] Henry and Harriet Smith's home in Montevallo, in southeastern Vernon County, was located at the southeastern corner of the region examined by Neely and the northern edge of southwestern Missouri included in Stith's study. The Smith family's diaries and letters illuminate an aspect of the conflict that has received little attention. There are accounts written by and about guerrilla leaders, their victims, and the Union troops who fought them. The civilians who provided assistance to the guerrillas are as silent and elusive in the historical record as they were to the federal soldiers who searched for them. In addition to kinship networks, guerrillas depended on the cooperation of other local residents to provide emergency food, shelter, and medical care for themselves and their horses, as well as information, transmission of messages, storage of goods, and other assistance.[20] They also needed trustworthy allies able to communicate with federal authorities and submit credible affidavits and petitions on their behalf. The documents from Harriet and Henry Smith's trunks provide a glimpse into these broader community networks and the process that led a Yankee family to participate in them. The story they tell begins in southern Michigan in 1853.

PART I

Schoolcraft, Michigan, and Maumee, Ohio, 1853

Chapter One

LOVE AND WORK

"Thank God I have found a good and true heart at last"[1]

In the stifling heat of the empty store on a Sunday afternoon in 1853, Henry Smith let his mind wander as his hands marked the goods that had arrived the previous day. As soon as he finished, he would harness Old George to his buggy and drive Miss Johnson back to Gourdneck prairie so she could open her schoolhouse Monday morning. Henry hoped this trip would be as pleasant as the one two weeks earlier when Miss Johnson had asked him to take her to Kalamazoo to have her watch repaired. Was it a coincidence that Miss Johnson was visiting her friends in Schoolcraft again? Or that she had come into the store on Saturday? It would be a small sacrifice to give up the bachelor pleasures of fiddling and dancing, card playing, and cigar smoking for cozy evenings in a home of his own. It was frustrating to be a dry-goods clerk at the age of twenty-seven, sleeping in the backroom behind the store, but he had a chance to buy a few acres of land that he could clear for farming. Miss Johnson was an intelligent and sincere woman who would make a suitable wife for a man of modest means. Later that night, Henry wrote in his diary: "Towards sundown called for Miss J– and *we* enjoyed the moonlight ride vastly. . . . The only thing of importance that happened during my long, short ride was that I proposed to my fair companion to become Mrs Smith. Required no answer until she considers this insignificant change in her life. . . . Came home late . . . and threw myself upon my bed to consider what I had done. . . . Feel a little curious to know how Hattie passed the same hours and what were her thoughts."[2] Harriet Johnson recorded her thoughts in her diary: "I am so quietly happy—so full of serene hope. . . . I have heard to-night no wild, romantic declarations, such as would captivate the youthful fancy—I have not been called an angel, and invested with all the graces of a divinity—no, no, but I have been addressed as every high-souled man *should* talk to a *true hearted* woman, who is human & imperfect like himself."[3] The following day, however, Harriet questioned whether she was ready for marriage: "I can scarcely realiize my new position—the scenes of the past night seem so *dreamlike*—so *visionary*! My mind has been very serious to-day—somewhat apprehensive & anxious—What *will* my father say to such a state of things? What *is duty*? Am I old & staid enough to marry? Would it not be wiser for me to defer such a step until *entirely* sated by the vanities that crowd the path of young 'single' *blesseds*?"[4] Harriet may have remembered the advice her older married sister had given her two years earlier. "Don't think of getting married yet," Edelia had written her eighteen-year-old sister. "There will be time enough for the sober realities of married life after you have enjoyed the freedom of youth for a few years." Harriet's father had concurred: "Wait, at least *six years* longer, and then if you should perchance get a *good* husband, you would not regret waiting so long, and if you should get a *bad* one, you would have long time enough to live with him."[5] He had warned Harriet recently: "Be *prudent*, be *cautious*: think more than once before you consent to yoke up with an unbeliever."[6] Although Henry attended church regularly and sang in the Methodist choir, he did not share the Johnson family's long-standing Baptist affiliation or their opposition to alcoholic beverages, tobacco, gambling, card games, and dancing.[7]

Growing up as the daughter of a Baptist preacher during the religious revivals known as the Second Great Awakening, Harriet had learned to monitor her behavior. Her parents carefully nurtured a conscience that would provide moral guidance throughout her life. When Harriet was three years old, her father wrote in his diary that Harriet lied to her stepmother, who told her she was "naughty and wicked" and had broken God's commandments. After Harriet spent nearly an hour alone in a bedroom, "conscious guilt and the dread of God's displeasure made her exceedingly unhappy," her father wrote, and she was willing to pray for forgiveness, "after which Harriet appeared satisfied."[8] From early childhood, Harriet had learned to align her thoughts and actions with her family and religious community, backed by the authority of God. "May the *path* of duty be made plain to me, that in its discharge I may secure a peaceful conscience, whatever else betide," Harriet wrote as she considered Henry's marriage proposal.[9]

The following Saturday, after a fishing outing she had arranged with Henry and mutual friends, Harriet contemplated her "strange, contradictory feelings & struggling hopes & fears."[10] Her thoughts wandered from the path of duty into the emotional landscape of romantic love as she described her relationship with Henry in the language of popular fiction:

> How much my mind has been rocked by useless fears & suspicions—how little have I dreamed of the real interest he has felt, and in my ignorance, I strove sedulously to conceal my own feelings thus leading us both into all the mazes of doubt & distrust. How we have both doubted—both feared and both been *true* & alike, perhaps, interested. I wonder that H– could ever love one so plain—so utterly devoid of attraction as myself, and perhaps it is equally strange for me to become so thoroughly "in love" with one so entirely different from all my imagination has ever pictured—but such seems to have been our *fate*—& I suppose we must submit to the *painful necessity* of loving each other.[11]

Two months earlier, Harriet had confided in her diary that she was "in love" with Henry: "a doubter, an unbeliever—a fiddler—a dancer—a cardplayer—a *horse*-racer!!!"[12] Regardless of her feelings for Henry, Harriet expressed anxiety about marriage: "I wish I knew *just* what course to pursue—Sometimes I feel an almost unconquerable shrinking from such a position—I feel that I *dare* not become the *wife* of any one. . . . I am restless, uneasy tonight—full of anxious fears—H– has never expressed so much interest—his manner has never been to me, so gentle, and full of tenderness, and my own heart has never responded more fully." Facing conflicting emotions, Harriet returned to the concept of moral duty to guide her decision. "O that I might be willing to sacrifice *self* upon the altar of *right*—that my eyes might be open to see the true path of rectitude—and my heart willing to keep it, though beset by thorny brambles and untold trials!" she wrote.[13]

Two days later, Harriet further defined her ambivalence as a contest between two emotions:

> When *shall* I cease to be the sport of that baleful *power Pride*? Here I am at the mercy of two strong, mighty passions. I cannot yield to either, and still they both exercise almost unlimited control over me—At one moment *Pride* seems to gain the mastery, and I sit calm and unmoved, defying the worst that Fate can do, & scorning all the weaker, softer impulses of the heart. Another and I'm all weakness—the pliant subject of that rival passion, *Love*: willing to sacrifice *all*, everything upon its alter—fame, genius—station—all, *all* for one true,

loving heart—one sure friend whose affections were all my own, & upon whom I might lavish the pent-up tenderness of my soul, unrepulsed & unrejected—one who could fully requite the life-long devotion of *such* a love as mine can be, as mine *is*—but alas, alas! I dare not indulge such feelings—Pride—Pride—ever ruling—ever tyrannical, still burns like a raging fire—and I much fear me, that its potent influence will be my present future, and eternal ruin—I cannot resist its overwhelming power.[14]

Capitalizing the words "Pride" and "Love" emphasizes their representation of universal passions and suggests a tradition of religious allegory that could define experiences and guide decisions. Harriet labeled her desire for achievement, recognition, and independence as "Pride," one of the seven deadly sins. Like Baptist preachers who warned against pride and against ambition for wealth or status, Harriet worried that "Pride" would be her "present, future and eternal ruin."[15] Although she portrayed herself as choosing between ideal romantic love and potential fame as an author, the real choice Harriet faced was between marriage to Henry and her life as an unmarried woman teaching in a one-room rural schoolhouse, her fifth school in four years, and living with families that took turns housing the teacher, sometimes in a shared bed.[16] By casting her deliberations in terms of overcoming her pride, Harriet could define as a moral duty her desire to marry a handsome and sociable young man of dubious reputation and uncertain financial prospects.

The next day, Harriet identified an underlying fear of sacrificing her "*own self*," noting her tendency to "forget or lose sight of [her] *own* character" in trying to please others.[17] In a composition she wrote three years earlier, Harriet defended women's inherent human rights: "Woman, with all the dignity of outraged humanity, has asserted her rights, and defied the power of man, usurping man, who has so long ground her down to an ignominious servitude." Harriet's father had added his critical comment: "But to think that woman who should be a model of harmonious consistency should [raise] contentions about certain imaginary rights which have an existence only in her diseased and inflammable brain."[18] By the time Harriet contemplated marriage to Henry, she described a "skeptical" former Baptist who "advocated the, so called, women's rights": "She is a strong 'hen's rights hen,' and enters, I should judge, fully into all the measures pursued by that class of females who are so anxious to sound abroad the trumpet of their fame.... priding themselves upon the arrogant assumption of mentle powers, which they would fain believe were invincible."[19] As Harriet struggled to overcome

Henry P. Smith, daguerreotype. Box 1, Stanley Barney Smith Collection, A-88, Archives and Regional History Collections, Zhang Legacy Collections Center, Western Michigan University.

her own pride in her intellectual ability, she reframed her literary ambition as a desire to "bring about important results long after this frame has turned to dust." She reassured herself that, as domestic advice literature promised, she had a lasting influence on other people. "I am responsible—I am accountable—I have an influence which is being constantly exerted," she wrote.[20]

Two days later, Harriet again discussed her ambition to become a famous author: "We had been talking about talent or genius beside a true, affectionate heart, and all my old, and as I hoped smothered, pride & ambition upon that subject revived—It seemed that I could sacrifice all the love of my soul at the shrine of genius & fame—Are these useless dreams ever to disturb my peace. Was I destined to be forever tossed upon the wild, raging sea of Ambition? Oh God *save me*!!"[21] The following day, Harriet brought into sharper focus her fear that her future life would consist of either "unloved solitude" as a single woman or "household drudgery" as a wife:

> My mind has been restless and unsettled. I feel that I love Henry, and yet I dare not *yield*—There is such a shrinking from the thought of marriage—of binding myself indissolubly—of *forever* pledging myself to him—I cannot—O I *cannot*! I cannot forego all the proud hopes that have bouyed my spirit from my youth up—I cannot

become one of your homespun, common-place characters, & settle down to household drudgery—No, no—I *cannot*, and yet I cannot cast from me a true, noble heart that loves me—I cannot resign myself to an unloved solitude—I cannot & I *will* not sacrifice all the strong love, that is even now gushing from my heart, upon the altar of selfish, worldly *pride!*[22]

Harriet's use of dashes, underlining, exclamation points and repetition suggests an oral performance in the tradition of religious or secular oratory.[23] Addressing an imagined audience by posing questions and interjecting exclamations, Harriet described one untenable option and then contrasted an equally undesirable alternative. This rhetorical strategy allowed Harriet to express her dissatisfaction with the choices she faced and assert the right to refuse both domestic drudgery and unloved solitude. Merging the language of religion with that of romantic fiction, Harriet made a leap of faith: "No, unyielding and stubborn as thou hast been, the time has come when thou must submit to a power more potent than any which has ever cast its all conquering spell over thy perverse nature. Yes, proud, boastful heart thou *must* submit. Love can vanquish the most mighty, and thou canst never hope to escape, though encased in a shield of adamants, thy hour has come, and another will claim thee. *Thy Allegiance is already given.*"[24] Shifting pronouns from "I" to "thou," Harriet directed herself to "submit" to the powerful "conquering spell" of love.

The following day, Harriet and Henry shared their diary entries with one another. "As I reveal more of my own feelings she seems dearer to me," Henry had written a week earlier. "Perhaps she will think less of me when she knows more but it is not my wish to conceal anything from her."[25] After reading Henry's diary, Harriet "felt better acquainted with his heart—and loved him all the more for the knowledge."[26] Reading one another's diaries established a greater degree of emotional intimacy and mutual trust.[27] That evening, Henry formally proposed marriage. He wrote:

This was one of the happiest rides I ever experienced. We talked long and freely and as we halted in front of widow W–s little cottage I asked her simply if she would be mine with the consent of her father. She did not answer very promptly, but it came at last. Twas *Yes Mr Smith*, yes *Henry* I will; whereupon I sealed the compact in a becoming manner and we went into the house. I feel that this is the most eventful period of the early life and dont know whether tis for the best or not: yet I pray God it is and will try very hard to make it so.

If I am decieved in her I would be a thousand times more liable to in any other woman I ever saw.[28]

Like many couples, Henry and Harriet valued honesty in discussing their expectations as they looked ahead to what Harriet described as "the serious responsibilities of marriage."[29] Henry tried to follow the advice he had noted years earlier: "Let courting be done in the day time with an open heart and in your every day clothes."[30] Although Harriet still felt "a shrinking dread; an almost shuddering fear" at realizing there was "*so* much at stake," she began to envision a future married life with Henry. "I will *try* to fit myself for the sphere of a *good wife*," she wrote.[31] Both Harriet and Henry approached the decision to marry with rational calculation as well as romantic enthusiasm. They promised to try to meet the expectations of a wife and husband as defined by their families and friends, their local communities, and the larger society they encountered through printed texts.

Boundaries of race and ethnicity were so strongly drawn that Henry and Harriet had not even considered crossing them in their choice of marriage partner. These constraints appeared to be the natural order of society, defined and reinforced by schools and churches as well as popular media. In addition to their identity as white Protestants of British ancestry, Harriet and Henry shared a New England cultural heritage. Although Harriet and Henry did not use the term "Yankee" to describe themselves or their communities, they were part of the cultural region historians and geographers have called the "Yankee West" or "Yankeeland," stretching from the New England states through upstate New York, across northern Ohio and southern Michigan, and eventually through northern Illinois and Indiana and into southern Wisconsin and Minnesota.[32] Settlers from New England predominated in southwest Michigan, including the village of Schoolcraft in Kalamazoo County.[33]

Although Henry was born in Virginia and grew up in Michigan, he was raised in a family with deep ties to New England. In the late eighteenth century, Henry's grandparents had moved to Cavendish, Vermont, with their relatives and neighbors from Middlesex County, Massachusetts, where their families had lived since the mid-seventeenth century.[34] Henry's parents, Thaddeus Smith and Eliza Parker, grew up in Cavendish. When Eliza was thirteen years old, her widowed mother sent her to live with her uncle, Jabez Parker, a Massachusetts native who was a merchant in Richmond, Virginia. Eight years later, Eliza married Thaddeus Smith, who had moved from Cavendish to Richmond as a young man. After their dry-goods store near Richmond failed, Thaddeus and Eliza returned to Vermont with their two-year-old son Henry.[35] Two years later, in 1830, the family moved to the

Michigan frontier. Like other New England settlers, Henry's family wanted to create a community that was, in historian Susan E. Gray's words, "more of the same, only better."[36] Relatives and former neighbors from Vermont joined them in Schoolcraft.[37] By the time Henry proposed to Harriet, his grandmother, four aunts and uncles, and four of his mother's cousins had moved from Vermont to Kalamazoo County.

Harriet had lived in Michigan for only two years when she accepted Henry's marriage proposal. She was a native of New England, born in Massachusetts and raised in Vermont. By the age of fourteen, she was living in the Western Reserve region of northern Ohio, surrounded by families from New York and New England. In contrast to Henry's childhood in Schoolcraft, Harriet had lived in eight communities, moving every few years as her father established or revived Baptist churches.[38] Harriet had little contact with her extended family. Her grandparents died before she was born. When Harriet was two years old, her mother died and her father remarried: she never met her mother's brothers and sisters.[39] Except for an uncle in Ohio, Harriet knew little about her father's family, who were deeply embedded in a network of evangelical Baptists that stretched westward from New England.[40] When Harriet met Henry, she was teaching at Cedar Falls Academy, a Baptist school in Schoolcraft.[41] Harriet may not have known that her great-grandfather, Solomon Johnson, left the established Congregational church to become a Baptist preacher and then disappeared after the Revolutionary War, leaving his wife and children in Cornwall, Connecticut.[42] A few years later, his oldest son, also named Solomon, married Rebecca Payne, whose father, Abraham, was a Separatist preacher during the First Great Awakening of the mid-eighteenth century, as were several of his outspoken uncles and cousins.[43] Solomon and Rebecca moved near Hamilton, New York, where Rebecca's brothers, parents, and other Connecticut families established a Baptist church.[44] Solomon became a Baptist preacher like his absent father.[45] His youngest son, Wakeman G. Johnson, married Betsey Lamson, daughter of Solomon's predecessor as pastor in Lorraine, New York.[46] Wakeman Johnson, Harriet's father, graduated from the seminary that his uncles, Elisha and Samuel Payne, helped establish in Hamilton to educate Baptist ministers and missionaries.[47] Harriet's older brother, Solomon, was ordained after earning a degree in Theology from Madison University, successor of the seminary his father attended. The American Baptist Home Mission Society sent Solomon to rejuvenate Baptist churches in Iowa and Missouri and supplemented the salary Harriet's father received from his Baptist congregation in Yorkville, Michigan.[48] Harriet's father participated in local and regional associations that supported the network of ministers, missionaries, and teachers who attempted to extend Baptist religious beliefs, cultural practices, and moral standards from New England and New York to western states and territories.[49] Baptists in southern states formed a separate organization in 1845 after the American Baptist Home Mission Society refused to fund missionaries who were slaveholders.[50]

Henry and Harriet accepted their families' assumption that their racial, ethnic, religious, and regional heritage was morally and culturally superior. Against this backdrop of secure identity, they negotiated the more uncertain recognition of their middle-class social position and the related expectations of manhood and womanhood. Courtship brought into focus the expanding range of options open to native-born Protestant white Americans in industrializing northern states. The decision to marry intersected with other choices, including denominational affiliation, occupation, leisure activities, and gender roles. Even in a small village like Schoolcraft, Michigan, young men and women could not assume that a potential spouse would share their expectations about how a husband or wife should act, which forms of entertainment were appropriate, what type of housing was desirable, or what moral principles should guide their behavior. Karen Lystra's examination of courtship letters in nineteenth-century America reveals that couples negotiated more malleable gender roles than advice literature of the time would suggest. She argues that concepts of gender formed a "complex repertoire" of "values, beliefs, images, and rules" that a couple could draw upon in a "dynamic and creative fashion."[51] In sermons, books, newspapers, lectures, songs, and conversations, young men and women encountered various models for gendered behavior. Although ideals of manhood and womanhood were contested, the binary differentiation of gender roles was central to the nineteenth-century concept of gendered identity. Male or female identity, assigned at birth, provided both a filter through which to sift experiences and a template on which to base future actions. Gender distinctions saturated all aspects of life: work, leisure, religion, politics, families, friendships, personal appearance, and demeanor. Ellen Rothman argues that the "definition of gender differences" was important in determining "how young men and women experienced the transition to marriage."[52] An engaged couple needed to reach an agreement on what sort of husband and wife they would become. In courtship, the realm of love merged with that of work, and gender intertwined with social class. For middle-class women, marriage meant leaving the workplace. Women knew that their choice of spouse would determine their future economic and social status.[53] For men, marriage required establishing the ability to support a family.[54] Both men and women contemplating marriage assessed their financial goals and considered the likelihood of attaining them with a potential spouse. Economic status was not an abstract concept to a couple considering marriage: it would determine the type of home in which they would live, the clothes they would wear, their social standing, and their financial security.

Although Henry believed that it was possible for a young man like himself to become financially independent, he had not been able to accumulate the capital he needed to start a business or buy an established farm near Schoolcraft.[55] After he reached the age of twenty-one in 1847, Henry no longer owed his labor to his father. Like many young men in Kalamazoo County, Henry continued to work on the family farm but kept his share of the profits.[56] He earned additional money from the fees he collected as constable and as a fiddler and dance teacher.[57] In 1849, Henry took over the bookkeeping for the forty-acre family farm. He concluded that the family would no longer buy anything on credit because they were "very poor & owe a great deal."[58] The absence of reliable transportation and banking systems, compounded by fluctuations in crop prices and the inherent risks of farming, created a financially precarious situation for many Kalamazoo County farmers. With little cash circulating in the community, they turned to private loans to fund operating expenses, relying on sales of the fall harvest to pay their debts.[59] By the summer of 1850, Henry was employed as a clerk in a Schoolcraft store.[60] He paid $450 to clear his father's debts and promised to contribute an additional $175 to ensure that the family would keep possession of their farm, which was valued at $1,000. In return for Henry's investment of more than a year's wages, his father gave him a deed to the farm, which Henry agreed to rent to his father at $1.50 per year for life.[61]

In October, Henry accepted a position as a clerk in a store in the larger and more industrial town of Seneca Falls in upstate New York, where he hoped to find better employment and cultural opportunities. The Michigan village of Schoolcraft served the surrounding rural area with a store where farmers could purchase essential staples on credit and a few skilled craftsmen who met local needs for harnesses, wagons, guns, barrels, and furniture. Nearby, a distillery, a flour mill, and a lumber mill transformed corn, wheat, and timber into whiskey, flour, and lumber. A plank road would soon link the thousand residents of Schoolcraft Township to the larger village of Kalamazoo, the western terminus of a rail line that provided farmers with access to eastern markets for their crops.[62] In Seneca Falls, New York, with a population of three thousand, about three hundred employees worked in fifty factories and mills, primarily in flour and woolen mills and in pump and agricultural implement factories.[63] Canals and railroads connected Seneca Falls to New York City to the south and Lake Erie to the north.

Seneca Falls, New York (downstream), ca. 1850, daguerreotype. 1994.91.231, Smithsonian American Art Museum, purchase from Charles Isaacs Collection made possible by Luisita L. and Franz H. Denghausen Endowment.

By 1850, Seneca Falls businessmen looked to the growing western frontier as a market for their manufactured products.[64] Production for a national market opened up salaried jobs for young men like Henry as clerks, salesmen, and managers.

In Seneca Falls, Henry observed that he never was satisfied with his current situation, but was always trying for his big chance and always falling short. He lamented: "As fast as I am situated right to prosper I kick over the dish by some new scheme to get rich or happy quicker. When will I be contented to take things as they come."[65] Mary Ryan found that fewer than thirty percent of the clerks working in stores and offices in the upstate New York town of Utica in 1850 owned their own businesses two decades later. By 1870, twenty percent were still working as clerks, and more than a third were employed in bookkeeping, accounting, sales, and related occupations.[66] Despite the odds against them, many urban clerks expected to become successful businessmen.[67] By the middle of the nineteenth century, E. Anthony Rotundo argues, northern white middle-class men derived their personal identity as well as their social status from their achievement in the workplace. Believing that "free competition would reward the best man," these young men focused on "self-improvement, self-control, self-interest, self-advancement" as the means to financial success.[68]

According to Rotundo, the choice of occupation was "a decision about what *sort* of a man one wished to be."[69] After he moved to Seneca Falls, Henry complained about "how hard it is to get along in the world & prosper without having a disposition to fight everything."[70] He contrasted merchants in Seneca Falls with farmers in Schoolcraft, noting that he had the "blessed privalige of being taught dishonesty that could not be learned at home." "There is no fashionable employment that is better calculated for making devils incarnate of men that are naturally honest than this lying thieving trade," he continued. "It makes gentlemen that have no human feelings from naturally honest men & gallows birds of the common herd." Henry added that others "go along easy & happy, thinking of but one person on earth & paying all the attention in the world to him. I am a fool and unlucky for [I] know it better than others."[71] From Henry's perspective, in order to become "gentlemen" situated in a "fashionable" occupation as merchants, "naturally honest" young men needed to become unfeeling, dishonest, selfish, and disputatious. Henry rejected this entrepreneurial behavior, which was defined more positively as individualistic, competitive, ambitious, and businesslike. Scott Sandage argues that an energetic, risk-tolerant "go-ahead" attitude was considered essential for financial success in the antebellum era.[72] Henry recognized that his awareness of the personal cost of this capitalist mode of manliness made it difficult for him to succeed in business. After six months as a clerk in a Seneca Falls store, Henry learned that he was "not *sharp* enough" to please his employers, although he adapted to the new expectations well enough to be hired for an additional year.[73]

Henry's mother urged him to come home, at least for a visit. She reminded him that his father's "inability to manage horses will ever make him dependent on some one while he works on the farm." Henry agreed that he could save more of what he earned in Schoolcraft. However, he concluded that he "could do better" in Seneca Falls if he "was dependent on a salary."[74] Henry had fallen in love with a young milliner in Seneca Falls but worried that she was "too feble to be a farmer wife, neither does her taste seem suitable to it." Although Henry realized that Sophia was engaged to a more affluent man and "never can be a suitable wife for my poor means any way I can fix it," he proposed marriage.[75] In the meantime, Henry's employer had become a partner in a company that manufactured pumps, tools, and stove parts. He offered Henry a position as a traveling salesman for the growing company.[76] In addition to taking orders and collecting payments, Henry would advise the company on the needs and preferences of western farm families.[77] Henry saw an opportunity to increase his income as well as spend time with his family. For five months, he traveled through Michigan, Ohio, Indiana, and Illinois, first by stagecoach, train, and canal boat, and then by horse and buggy.[78] Sophia wavered between her two suitors: she wrote Henry that she would marry him only if he agreed to live in Seneca Falls.[79] When he realized Sophia was still "in doubt whether she loves me more than somebody else," Henry "very delicately wrote her a farewell letter" in October but agreed to continue the correspondence.[80] In November, Henry returned to Schoolcraft to spend the winter with his family while he negotiated the terms of his employment as a sales agent and considered whether to move back to Seneca Falls.[81]

Two weeks after Henry arrived in Schoolcraft, he met two "young ladies now teaching at the seminary, very pleasant & intelligent, one pretty." He "escorted the plain one," Harriet Johnson, home.[82] A month later, Henry confirmed his decision not to marry Sophia: "I never could live with her unless I was rich and that I am not so I have made up my mind to take life as it comes. Who knows what will turn up!"[83] After spending two more months in Schoolcraft, Henry wrote that he wanted to marry "someone adapted to my situation in life."[84] He described "Miss Johnson": "She is a good girl or I cannot read the heart. I wish I did not fancy her quite as much as I do for it will avail nothing in the end. If she is what she appears to be she is too good for me and if not I will be sorry to be deceived in her. How much more suitable to my tastes and condition is she than S."[85] In April, Henry decided that working on commission as a traveling salesman involved too much financial risk.[86] On May 6, Henry visited "Miss J." at her school, where he "had the pleasure of witnessing her in the performance of her duties." He wrote: "She certainly possesses the rarest of womanly qualities. For decision promptness of character, connected with a clear active mind she is unsurpassed within the range of my acquaintance. Can she fill the wifes place as well I wonder. Could she love, bear and forbear, and meet every vicisitude in life as well as in her present station."[87] While Henry was assessing Harriet's character and wondering whether she could "fill the wife's place," Harriet's thoughts also turned to marriage. On her twenty-first birthday, the day before Henry's visit, Harriet wrote in her diary that she would "at last welcome the sober matronly duties of the wife & mother—welcome all their unaspiring hopes, and unassuming responsibilities." "How some of my 'Dear five hundred friends' would laugh to hear such quaint, old fashioned notions," she continued. "To think of my being willing to settle down to the humdrum life of married folks and mending coats & patching breetches."[88] In late May, Henry accepted a position as a clerk in a Schoolcraft store and looked at land to purchase for a farm.[89] A month later, he proposed to Harriet. While Harriet debated whether to accept his offer of marriage, Henry bought land for a stock farm near Schoolcraft.[90]

As Harriet considered Henry's proposal, she turned to her older unmarried cousin for advice. Cynthia replied that she hoped Harriet could have "a home, and a kind companion who will love and cherish you even more than himself, one who will prove true under all circumstances, and be ever ready to administer to your varied wants in sickness and health." She agreed with Harriet's father that ideally it "would be very desirable to have a companion who could advise council and lead you along in the devine life." However, she introduced the ideal of romantic love as an alternative basis for marriage: "If you believe as many others do, that every spirit, has a kindred one created by God, perhaps Mr S is *thee* man." Cynthia suggested ways Harriet could assess her feelings: "You think you like him well enough to say yes to his proposals. Could you have said the same of any of your former beautiful offers that you have slighted?" Cynthia reminded Harriet that she would "never find any one without imperfections or who will fill all your fancies" and advised her to "not say no at present." She urged Harriet to consider her decision carefully: "You must act your own judgment, realizing that it is for life, and upon your decision will depend your future happiness for time. If you had a suitable companion your happiness, and usefulness, might be greatly increased and if *Mr S is the one* say yes. This you can decide, better than any one else."[91] Cynthia outlined two concepts of marriage that can be traced to different strains of Protestant religious practices that Richard Rabinowitz identifies as prevalent in everyday life in nineteenth-century New England. In the moralist outlook Harriet's father advocated, daily habits revealed an individual's character.[92] A man's reputation for consistent moral behavior indicated his ability to assume the duties of a husband. In this moralist concept of the self, taking on a new social role represented a real and lasting change in personal identity. A couple approaching marriage expected to be transformed, in feelings as well as actions, into a married man and woman. When Henry proposed marriage, Harriet asked herself: "Can I be a counselor—a never failing friend—in short a faithful, devoted, loving wife? *Can I?* Until I feel that strength will be given me to *become* all this, I shall never assume the *name*."[93] The assumption of a new identity brought with it the problem of maintaining a consistent sense of self that would survive the transition.[94] The devotionalist approach to religion that Rabinowitz describes provided a solution to this dilemma. Devotionalism valued personal spiritual experience over proper public behavior. The lifelong core self, revealed only in the privacy of intimate relationships, performed various social roles with different expectations for behavior.[95] Lystra describes this "inner identity that transcended all roles the individual filled" as a "romantic self" that was enhanced by courtship.[96] The measure of romantic love was the intensity of feeling: falling in love with a kindred spirit who understood one's genuine self.⁹⁷ In practice, men and women considering marriage often balanced the emotional experience of romantic love with the rational assessment of character traits.⁹⁸

Harriet received Cynthia's letter on July 4, the day after she accepted Henry's proposal. "I begin to realize my situation & to shrink from it. Dim, dreary, heart-crushing fears weigh my spirit down," she wrote that night. Henry described how he spent Independence Day: "I celebrated it [in] a wise manner during the day by attending to my every day affairs in the store. I worked hard saw H once in the morning as she came in with Mrs W– to do a little shopping. In the evening I made a fiddler of myself to please the young folks that could not get a chance to dance at Vicksburg (1.50 couple there)."⁹⁹ The next day, he noted: "Sleepy and dull. How little a compensation is the miseries of a day like this for what little pleasure derive from a ball. What is H– thinking of just now." Harriet recorded in her diary exactly what she was thinking:

> Last evening about nine o'clock, after I had written in my journal, and was nearly ready to retire, some one rapped at the door and asked for Mr Moore—We were considerably startled supposing there must have been some accident—but no, *Henry Smith* had sent for him as an *associate fiddler* for a small company at one of the Schoolcraft Hotels!! And is it so? Am I to be linked with a common ball-room *fiddler*? Never—no **never**! How my heart *does* ache! I can but believe that H– engages in this just to please others—but should he not possess sufficient firmness & independence to refuse?¹⁰⁰

On July 3, Henry had shown Harriet the July 1 diary entry describing his "faint efforts to live a better life" by giving up dances: "Ball at the Schoolcraft house and I am one of the managers but I did not go neare[r] them than to listen to Hulls and Arnolds sweet music a few moments as it came to me from the open windows across the street." Henry's lapse from this path of reform would have given Harriet cause to question his ability to resist temptation and his commitment to her moral standards. Harriet explained why she would refuse to marry "a common ball-room fiddler": "I cannot brook the idea of his wasting time, health and even reputation for a set of giddy frolickers, whose heads & hearts are not fit to be thought of with his—No no *we* can never harmonize if *such* are his habits and tastes and it were better, for both, to separate *now*. . . . I can never bring myself to tolerate many practices, which to him, doubtless, appear harmless, and if we cannot agree respecting them, we had better by far, have never met."¹⁰¹ Harriet's alarm at the prospect of being "linked with a common ball-room fiddler" implies that fiddling was not merely a recreational activity. Being a fiddler summarized Henry's character, his reputation and his identity. Harriet's use of the term "common" suggests a lack of refined taste as well as a moral stigma.

Based on her Baptist upbringing, Harriet could not tolerate Henry playing the fiddle to accompany dancing, especially in the public venue of a hotel ballroom.[102] From a moralist point of view, Henry's fiddle playing was hazardous because leisure activities shaped as well as expressed moral standards.[103] Several years earlier, Harriet's father had reminded her of the wisdom of the saying: "A man is known by the company he keeps." He explained that "moral taste and character are formed in a great measure by association."[104] A hotel dance hall filled with "giddy frolickers" was not conducive to moral or economic advancement. In the emerging business economy, employment opportunities and financial credit were offered to men who demonstrated their good character and reputation through the consistent practice of morally sound habits.[105] A wife's comfort, prosperity, and social standing depended on her husband's reliable behavior. Authors of popular novels and advice books warned that one bad habit could lead to another, and a husband who spent his leisure time in public places of amusement risked falling prey to drunkenness and gambling, jeopardizing the family's safety and financial security.[106] Complicating these practical considerations was the romantic ideal of finding a compatible companion and soulmate.[107] For many reasons, it was crucial to Harriet that she and Henry "harmonize" in "habits and tastes," but she decided to "postpone further judgement" until she talked to Henry.

When Henry wrote on July 4 that he "made a fiddler" of himself, he implied that "fiddler" was a role he assumed temporarily. In Henry's mind, after a hard day's work, it was a generous act to "please the young folks that could not get a chance to dance at Vicksburg." He wanted to provide these couples with the pleasures enjoyed by their more affluent neighbors who could afford carriages and admission fees. In Henry's family, dancing and fiddling were an accepted part of daily life, a sociable punctuation to the week's farm work. Henry's married and unmarried sisters attended dances, and his dance school attracted several "little girls."[108] The music Henry played for dances included traditional reels popular in rural communities, and his knowledge of the new dance forms of polkas and cotillions probably brought him status among the "young folks."[109] Within his circle of family and friends, fiddling provided Henry with social approval as well as artistic pleasure. However, Henry's employer in Seneca Falls had made him aware of the social stigma attached to playing the fiddle at dances.[110] Henry understood that respectability and economic success might require giving up "what little pleasure derive from a ball."[111] He hoped Harriet could guide his efforts to reform his behavior and refine his taste.

Two days after Harriet expressed alarm about Henry's fiddle playing, her "dear old instructor and fellow teacher M. A. Page," principal of the Union School in Maumee City, Ohio, offered her a teaching position.[112] Teaching in a school with five hundred pupils in the northern Ohio town commonly called Maumee would provide cultural and social opportunities not available to a teacher in a rural one-room school in western Michigan. Harriet could live in town in her aunt and uncle's comfortable home instead of boarding with her students' families on Gourdneck prairie. The salary would enable her to pay her debts and replenish her wardrobe before her marriage.[113] Harriet weighed the advantages of returning to Maumee, where she had attended high school and taught previously, against the disadvantages of a separation from Henry. She quickly decided to accept Mr. Page's offer. Henry described Harriet's plans as a "blow to my heart for an instant in spite of myself."[114] He felt reassured after driving her back to Gourdneck two days later. "I read in her journal more than I was permitted to before and find it a mutual feeling from the first," he wrote. "I can confidently call her *mine now* though we may be separated a long time. Thank God I have found a good and true heart at last."[115] For the first time, Harriet expressed confidence in her commitment to Henry:

> H– and I are now firmly engaged, as much so as we can be before receiving my father's approval. I have no higher earthly aim than to become a true hearted wife for him—I would not wish to lose my own identity, and settle down into one of your dull characterless persons—who have no original thoughts—in short, a mere *nonentity*—no—no I'd sooner spill my heart's blood than live at *such* a feeble "poor dying rate." I want to progress mentally & morally—I want to influence those around me to good. I want, in a husband one who will be a willing helper that we may mutually assist—I felt more confidence, to night, in looking forward to a happy future than ever before.[116]

Harriet began to envision a relationship based on mutual respect and assistance. Delaying marriage for a year provided time to know one another more fully, to confirm their decision, and to make practical arrangements for setting up a new household.[117] "If our love will not survive such a test, it surely cannot endure a *lifelong* trial," Harriet wrote.[118] Six weeks later, after Harriet's father gave his approval of the marriage, Henry helped Harriet board the stagecoach headed toward Maumee. He watched until the stage disappeared from view.[119]

As the stagecoach pulled away from Schoolcraft, Harriet drew her veil and settled into her seat. She would travel south about thirty miles over the rough road that linked the rural village to the rail line. The eastbound train would take her across Michigan, then south to Toledo, Ohio, where she would board a stagecoach for the last ten miles of her journey to Maumee.[120] When Harriet was sixteen years old, she came to Maumee to live with her father's brother, Solomon, and his wife, Abigail, while she attended high school in the new five-room public school.[121] After returning to Bedford, Ohio, for a year, she moved back to Maumee to teach at the school she previously attended. A year later, she rejoined her parents, who had moved to Kalamazoo County, Michigan. When the stagecoach finally rattled into Maumee, Harriet recognized the familiar surroundings she had left behind two years earlier. But when her aunt greeted her as a stranger, Harriet realized how much her own appearance and circumstances had changed: now she was a twenty-one-year-old engaged woman. After she unpacked her belongings in her "old room," Harriet picked up her diary and pen: "What changes have the last two years wrought in my circumstances, feelings and character. Twenty-four months ago I had formed no decisive plans—my mind was restless, unsettled. . . . I had no other prospect but a lifetime spent amid the unappreciated cares & trials of a schoolroom—with *such* views—such prospects I left Maumee. . . . Now I can enter upon my old duties in this Maumee School with a *heart* at rest—an ultimate object in view—a *something* to live for—to labor for—to *love!*"[122] The circumstances of Maumee had changed also. When Harriet had first arrived in 1848, the town was the county seat, a thriving center of shipping and shipbuilding on the Maumee River, linked to the system of canals that connected the Ohio River at the southern boundary of the state with Lake Erie on Ohio's northern border. From Maumee, passengers and cargo could travel by boat either southwest to the Ohio River and then west to the Mississippi River or east across Lake Erie to Buffalo, New York, where the Erie Canal provided a connection to the Hudson River and the Atlantic coast at New York City. Nearly four thousand canal boats passed through Maumee in 1848.[123] Water released from the locks provided power for large mills and small manufacturing facilities. By the time Harriet returned in 1853, the canals had been supplanted by railroads that bypassed the town. Toledo had replaced Maumee as the transportation hub and had recovered its position as the county seat. Maumee remained a prosperous town whose population of nearly 1,500 supported numerous stores, churches, mills, and manufacturing operations. The two-story Union School served five hundred students from primary grades through high school.[124]

"Over sixty bright, merry-eyed children have conspired to harrass & distract me to-day," Harriet wrote after her first day of teaching. The next day brought some improvement, she reported, but "each little roguish-eyed urchin, busies his active brain in conjuring up mischievous capers—taxing his ingenuity in manufacturing paper balls & all sorts of offhand toys."[125] Two weeks later, when Harriet kept some of her students after school to complete an assignment, one student's father threatened to prosecute her. The next day, the older brother of another student Harriet had detained drew a knife on Mr. Page, the principal.[126] Harriet complained that teachers had been issued "inquisatorial instruments of torture, in the shape of long, savage strips of leather."[127] Harriet wanted to "pursue a milder course of moral, & physical tactics." She explained: "I am *so* tired of the eternal ding, ring of merciless stripes which fall upon the cringing backs of our galley-slave pupils, with all the ferocity of a southern overseer. There we stand, our faces distorted into an expression of fierceness, well becoming a modern Nero; frowns must become habitual—sharp, harsh tones must destroy the music of our woman voices— we must guard against all approach to tenderness—the slightest inroad upon our regal authorities must be checked by the savage lash—no matter what the offense, one universal penalty prevails—one universal response to our oft repeated requests for counsel; 'put on the strap! put on the strap!'"[128] Harriet conflated scenes of inhumane whipping depicted by reformers who advocated abolishing slavery, outlawing the flogging of sailors, and ending corporal punishment in schools.[129] Intimidation and physical punishment contradicted the ideals of womanhood and child-rearing practices Harriet had experienced in her evangelical New England family.

Harriet recognized that teachers, like overseers, were hired to maintain order and impose discipline as surrogates for their employers while their own social position remained marginal.[130] In addition to parents and members of the school's Board of Directors, many local residents and their out-of-town guests visited Harriet's classroom to observe her teaching, sometimes offering criticism and suggestions. Although some visitors were interested in "the manner of giving instruction" and "the method of bringing science to bear upon the mind," others were concerned only with "the mere physical organization & control of the school."[131] During the seven months Harriet taught in Maumee, her class had 130 visits from sixty-five different people, an average of four or five visits per week. About a third were supportive visits from Harriet's friends and family or from other teachers. Seventeen visitors were out-of-town guests brought by local residents. The remaining visitors were merchants, attorneys, clergy, and other prominent citizens, or their wives, who felt a personal responsibility for the tax-supported public school that taught community values as well as basic skills in literacy and arithmetic. Following the model for educational reform introduced by Horace Mann in Massachusetts and widely implemented in northern states, residents of Maumee had voted to implement a graded school with a standardized curriculum supervised by an elected board of local citizens.[132]

As the term progressed, Harriet struggled to apply the teaching methods she learned in the annual Teachers' Institute and weekly teachers' meetings. She tried to motivate her students by "guiding and directing the youthful mind" without "discouraging its aspirations, & misdirecting its aims."[133] By Thanksgiving, Harriet's class had grown to ninety-seven children.[134] She wrote: "Completely hemmed in on all sides by miniature men & women, you cannot look upon any spot, but what *eyes* are staring boldly, viciously or sportively at you—eyes, eyes, all eyes—one wide, glittering, twinkling sea of eyes.... Work, work, **work**, **work**!"[135] The Board of Directors agreed to hire an additional teacher, and Harriet's class was divided. A month later, when the term ended, some students were promoted to the next grade.[136] All the remaining students returned to Harriet's class, leaving her again in "sole charge" of more than seventy children.[137] The following day, two members of the Board of Directors visited Harriet's classroom. Harriet noted that although the men were "wealthy merchants" and "most respectable citizens," their "ideas of school are dated back to the time when they went to a 'district' schoolhouse." "Their minds have been a little too much cramped within the narrow precincts of those old school-houses to expand to the broader views and more benevolent plans of the present age," she concluded.[138] During the following month, board members observed Harriet's class seven times after an influential parent objected to his child's seat assignment and the noise level in the classroom.[139] Harriet complained in her diary about "interfering parents whose little *darlings* must *each* be the special favorite."[140] She threatened to resign rather than "sacrifice" her "independence to a servile submission to the contemptible 'powers that be.'"[141] Two weeks later, at the end of the term, Harriet submitted her resignation.[142] Personal as well as professional considerations influenced Harriet's decision. She had accomplished her goal of paying off her debts before her wedding, and Henry's visit to Maumee a month earlier had reinforced her commitment to marriage and increased her desire to return to Schoolcraft.[143]

Back in Michigan, Henry continued to work as a store clerk and bookkeeper and earned additional income as a constable. As he assumed a more active role in managing the family farm, he concluded: "Our family is very large, we buy *everything*, have too much stock for the little farm and our income is a small one indeed."[144] Like other farmers in Kalamazoo County, Henry and his father grew wheat and corn as cash crops, supplementing their income by raising sheep for wool production and local sale. A few hogs and milk cows, a garden, and fruit trees provided food for the family.[145] After selling three wagonloads of wheat in October, Henry was able to pay for the construction of a barn, settle all of his father's debts, and pay off his own loan for the land he had purchased.[146] He noted: "The farm is now my own and I am thus far independent." "I shall be able to pay all the debts this fall and a *little* more," he added.[147] As he considered his situation, Henry wrote: "I believe it is impossible for a poor man to dig himself into a competency without being very selfish. I begrudge everybody their *just dues* even, when it comes from my pocket."[148] Henry realized that attaining the modest goal of competency, which for farmers meant the ownership of sufficient land to support a family, required the financial discipline and self-interest he had criticized in Seneca Falls merchants.[149] He devoted his available time to hauling timber for a barn and improving his new property by clearing fields for farming. The forty acres Henry had purchased in June adjoined a forty-acre plot his father acquired in May with a military bounty warrant for service as a musician in the Michigan Militia during the Black Hawk War.[150] Henry traded the buggy he had purchased as a traveling salesman and had used in courting Harriet for a lumber wagon.[151] In April, Henry was elected Township Clerk, a position previously held by his uncle, Seneca Smith, who served as Henry's deputy.[152] On his twenty-eighth birthday, Henry noted that he felt "more of a *man*." "I am a man and can bear responsibilities I never dared to before," he wrote in his diary.[153] Henry had achieved the benchmarks of manhood in Schoolcraft: he was a property owner and an office holder, and soon he would be a married man.

Chapter Two

LEISURE AND LITERACY

"Exciting scenes and frivolous amusement"[1]

In spite of the challenges she faced as a teacher, Harriet had savored the freedom of her "last year of 'single blessedness.'"[2] In the relative independence of her life in Maumee, she considered how her choices of leisure activities and consumer goods intersected with her work, personal relationships, and social status, as well as her religious beliefs and moral principles. Harriet established or renewed friendships with several young women who often "spent the evening," "took tea," or "called upon" friends together.[3] With her aunt and uncle, she joined the Reynolds family and Mr. and Mrs. Page for holiday dinners, frequent casual visits, and occasional tea parties with invited guests.[4] Two generations of the Reynolds, Page, and Johnson families were linked by friendship and marriage in Jefferson County, New York, and Maumee.[5] Catherine E. Kelly describes the development in antebellum New England of a "provincial middle class" who adapted urban upper-class customs of formal social calls, teas, dinner parties, and weddings to the more inclusive sociability of smaller communities.[6] When Harriet joined the household of her aunt and uncle in Maumee, she entered a similar provincial social environment. Harriet's uncle, Solomon Johnson, was a carpenter who owned a house in Maumee.[7] Harriet and another teacher, Miss Gorrill, paid "board and lodging" for a shared bedroom and the meals Harriet's aunt, Abigail Johnson, prepared.[8] When Abigail invited ten guests to tea with a visitor from Jefferson County, New York, she improvised a tea party without the servants and tableware of an upper-class urban household.[9] Harriet wrote that she and Miss Gorrill "dressed," met the guests, and "waited upon them at tea." They then "had rather a merry time in taking our own supper, as Mr and Mrs Page and Mrs Holmes waited upon us." Harriet helped her aunt "in doing up the work" after the guests left.[10]

Harriet distinguished acquaintances' brief formal "calls" from informal visiting among close friends. She wrote: "After school I found Mrs. Reynolds at uncle's visiting and Mrs. J. W. Forsyth calling."[11] On New Year's Eve, she noted: "The Miss Carpenters called this afternoon & we went out '*calling*.'"[12] While casual visits from friends often incorporated household tasks, formal calls required participants' full attention. By decorating her parlor, grooming and clothing her body, and scripting her movements and speech, a woman who aspired to middle-class status demonstrated her taste and established her place in society.[13] After making eight social calls with her aunt one afternoon, Harriet described the effort this performance of feminine gentility required: "And now our calls are over & I can act myself—this smiling & talking smooth things is *so* fatiguing to rough nature. Yet I have enjoyed the afternoon much, but as a whole I do detest these formal calls, where one must sit just so, & go just through the same ceremony at every house, speaking of the weather, & your great anxiety to call before, hoping they will remember you, &c. &c. One learns the lesson well before getting through the long list of 'dear five hundred friends.'"[14] Harriet had been raised in a religious tradition that valued honesty of expression: she wanted her appearance and actions to reflect her genuine feelings. Yet she realized that standards of ladylike behavior required that she hide her emotions beneath a veneer of conventional manners.[15] She complained about the similar emotional labor required of a teacher: "to smother every true, natural impulse, and *act* a *studied* part . . . before my scholars, no sombre clouds must rest upon my brow—smiles, smiles, eternal smiles & sunshine."[16] Looking back at her childhood, Harriet identified the early constraints on her behavior: "I *had no childhood*—like other children. I never gave way to the unrestrained joyousness of the youthful heart, but with a methodical *form* and *government*—I laughed just so—and played *just so!*"[17] With her aunt's guidance, Harriet learned to smile and "sit just so," as she had "*laughed just so*—and played *just so*" as the young daughter of a Baptist preacher in Vermont.

Although she reluctantly practiced "smiling and talking smooth things" herself, Harriet criticized other women for hypocritical politeness and social pretense: "Miss J was as polite and *soft soaping* as of yore & apologised wonderfully for her neglect & of course I'm bound to believe *all*. Her youthful charms retain their freshness miraculously. The ladies were all very much dressed & none of them *too* well supplied with brains—just enough *dash*, select becoming velvets & ribbons &c. Bah! these *fashionable* humiliations, with their cringing servilities, 'white lies' and artificial smiles are enough to sicken one."[18] Harriet interpreted simple clothing and restrained manners as indicative of warmth and sincerity.[19] After she attended a friend's wedding, Harriet contrasted the "sincere wishes" she unobtrusively conveyed by quietly squeezing the bride's hand to the "cold formal nothings of gay butterflies" and the "greetings & congratulations" of "idle flatterers & heartless fashionables."[20] Thinking of her upcoming wedding, Harriet wrote: "When life's most solemn step is taken I'd have it done in a quiet, dignified manner without ostentation."[21] Using the vocabulary of evangelical preachers and popular writers, Harriet criticized "fashionable" women who tried to appear younger, wealthier and more charming by wearing fancy clothes and engaging in frivolous conversation.[22] She described the wife of a prominent attorney as a "trifler" who "affects youthful frivolities." "I am not pleased with her and her privileged affectations—priveleged because her *station* is high," she explained." *Wealth* 'covers a multitude of sins,' and inconsistencies to say nothing of imprudencies."[23] Like many Americans, Harriet saw herself as morally superior to people with greater wealth and higher social status.[24]

Harriet also disapproved of people who were poorly dressed and unfamiliar with genteel social rituals. She described a Baptist couple who arrived in Maumee expecting "to get their support by the hospitality of their 'brethren in the Lord.'"[25]

> Found, upon my arrival at uncle's, an old rickety wagon, with an old rickety horse, and an old rickety man with his awkward, wife, at the gate. . . . Her dress was a dingy white sunbonnet, a small, faded, thin blanket shawl, and a calico dress that looked as though it was of antedeluvian memory. . . . After they retired for the night we had quite a discussion relative to the positions such people should occupy—my opinion is that persons should keep the sphere for which nature and education, have fitted them—not that I would discourage laudable effort to rise above degradation, and progress in moral intellectual and social improvement. No, no. I care not how much one struggles to overcome natural defects & hindrances, but I *do* care when coarse, vulgar people aspire to terms of familiarity with the educated and refined.[26]

The woman's unfashionable clothes and the couple's arrival in "an old rickety wagon" rather than a buggy revealed their rural poverty. Harriet struggled to align her belief in the potential for self-improvement with her assumption that clothing, speech, and etiquette indicated social status and moral worth.[27] Despite her own financial insecurity, Harriet placed herself among the "educated and refined" who had mastered the nuances of manners and dress that signified taste and respectability.[28] Houses and yards also marked social status. Harriet described her visit to "a poor family whose boy has been absent some time from school." In this rural home on "the other side of the canal," a cow and a puppy shared the yard, and a pile of wood stood by the door. Although the door had no latch, Harriet knocked and waited to be greeted as if she were paying a formal social call in town. The boy's German father, who spoke little English and smelled of tobacco and "perhaps whiskey," called out to her to enter the house. "Oh! What miserable homes these swarms of children, which daily flock around us, come from," she wrote.[29] Animals in the yard and a woodpile by the door violated the urban middle-class norm of presenting a decorative facade to visitors. Lacking even a latch for privacy, the house embodied its occupant's ignorance of the social practice that kept guests at the door until formally admitted.

Harriet envisioned herself as situated in an ideal middle ground between the fashionable and frivolous social elites and the "coarse and vulgar" rural poor and recent immigrants.[30] Members of this middle class demonstrated their virtue and respectability by the refined taste they displayed in their clothing, speech, and posture, as well as their choice of leisure activities.[31] Growing up as the daughter of a Baptist preacher in Vermont, Harriet had learned that personal appearance and behavior publicly displayed a private resolve to follow moral standards.[32] In Maumee, she recognized that any perceived moral lapse on her part could jeopardize her reputation and end her employment as a teacher.[33] On her meager salary, Harriet attempted to follow principles of neatness and cleanliness in her grooming and clothing. She relied on a line of credit at the local store to buy the fabrics she needed to sew an acceptable wardrobe.[34] "I must be a little cautious and not incur more expense than is absolutely necessary," she wrote after purchasing cotton cloth and a pair of rubber boots.[35] These attitudes were part of a broader concept of morality that accompanied the growth of the market economy in the New England states. Evangelical churches, public schools, print publications, and voluntary organizations reinforced values of self-control and self-improvement. The emerging middle class preferred to spend money on products rather than on socializing and valued leisure activities situated in the home rather than in public places.[36] Residents of New England who moved west through northern New York and Ohio and into southern Michigan brought these attitudes with them.[37] They monitored the efficient use of time as well as money.[38] Time wasted in frivolous pursuits was time taken away from productive activities. Harriet had avoided "exciting scenes & frivolous amusement" in Schoolcraft on the Fourth of July, but she regretted the time she had wasted when she "read, lounged, talked, *sauntered*, laughed, drank lemonade &c" with her friend Mary Tyrell. She wrote: "How trifling has been the manner in which I have spent this day—not *one* act can I point to and say it was a useful one—I have merely lived for my own gratification—just to '*kill* time,' for which one day I shall sigh in vain."[39] The day after a "large, fashionable & quite pleasant party" in Maumee, Harriet realized that she could "feel the effects of late hours, school not quite so blithe as usual." She concluded that she "must not attend parties if I hope to do justice by my charge."[40] Such social activities not only wasted her own time; they also cheated her employer and students.

Harriet more emphatically opposed activities she found morally objectionable: drinking, dancing, and any form of gambling, including card games, horse races, and even fund-raising lotteries for charity.[41] Parlor games and amateur dramatic and musical performances provided a genteel alternative to dancing and card playing.[42] At the parties Harriet attended in Maumee homes, entertainment included a "melodrama" and guessing games such as Proverbs and Twenty Questions.[43] Harriet especially enjoyed hearing Mrs. Page and other friends play the guitar and sing sentimental songs that "awakened old emotions" and evoked memories of "absent loved ones."[44] "H– sings some of these songs very sweetly," she remembered, "& I *do* believe I shall want him to do nothing but sing, until we 'make a swanlike end, fading in music.'"[45] After singing with friends on a moonlit evening, Harriet felt "a heavenly influence" in the "elevating notes of music."[46] Popular songs distributed through commercially produced sheet music elicited an emotional response by interweaving religious beliefs about heaven with secular ideals of romantic love, family, and home.[47] From Harriet's viewpoint, religious principles, moral standards, status distinctions, and gender roles intersected in leisure activities as they did in social interactions and personal appearance. In the choices she made as she looked forward to her impending marriage and in her evaluation of the choices other women made, Harriet demonstrated the taste, self-control, and cultural knowledge that established her identity as a respectable woman who avoided the moral hazards of both wealth and poverty. She accepted without question that Baptist principles and New England cultural traditions provided the criteria for appropriate behavior.

A week after she arrived in Maumee, Harriet attended a temperance meeting.[48] Two days later, she read "an interesting temperance story entitled 'The Senator's Son; or The Maine Law a Last Refuge' by Metta Fuller," advocating legislation modeled on an 1851 Maine law that prohibited the sale of alcoholic beverages.[49] A "poor drunken man" who "reeled up to the window" of Harriet's school embodied the debilitating effects of alcohol, leading Harriet to write: "Oh may the day soon come when the *Law* will do its own work &

stop the wholesale murderer of *human souls*! There was a temperance mass meeting out in the country, for the purpose of creating a feeling that will result in the establishment of the 'Maine Law.'"[50] A few weeks later, Harriet's uncle read *The Senator's Son* aloud to Harriet and her aunt.[51] When Harriet's father visited Maumee, she asked him to deliver a copy of *The Senator's Son*, which she had bought for Henry. She noted: "I hope it will interest him as it did me. Oh! May we always harmonize in tastes and pursuits."[52] Harriet knew that Michigan voters had approved legislation prohibiting the sale of alcohol the previous summer, so her gift was not intended to influence the way Henry voted.[53] *The Senator's Son* depicted the disastrous impact of a man's drinking on his wife and children.[54] Two months earlier, Harriet's older brother had warned her against "throwing herself away upon a 'drunken gambler.'" "Were Henrie *that*, I should very soon discard him," she had replied.[55] Henry's ambivalence about temperance had led both the advocates and the opponents of prohibition to nominate him as Schoolcraft's delegate to select representatives to Michigan's 1850 constitutional convention.[56] Although Henry played and sang at temperance meetings Harriet attended, his earlier diary entries mentioned occasional beer consumption.[57] By asking her father to deliver a copy of *The Senator's Son* to Henry, Harriet made her own position clear to both men. She wanted to confirm Henry's commitment to standards of behavior she and her family viewed as essential to her future well-being.

During her first two weeks in Maumee, Harriet read two recently published books in addition to *The Senator's Son*. In *The Last Leaf from Sunny Side*, "The Country Cousins" tells the story of two rural young women who find work in Boston: pious and frugal Ruth is contrasted with carefree and extravagant Lucy, whose husband later deserts the family.[58] Harriet also read "one of T. S. Arthur's little moral tales, called, 'The Two Wives; or Lost & Won.'" A merchant's diligent wife pays her alcoholic husband's gambling debt with money she saved, inspiring him to reform, while another wife's lavish spending leaves the family in poverty. "Many good hints are contained in this volume for all the votaries of Hymen," Harriet concluded.[59] Both books advised young women that their management of the household budget determined the comfort, financial security, and social standing of their families.[60] The formulaic nature of these moral fables, where good choices bring happiness and bad choices result in suffering, outlined the moral landscape of industrializing northern states.[61] During the months after she read these books, Harriet assessed the moral implications of the behavior and clothing of married women she met in Maumee, sometimes explicitly comparing good and bad consumer choices. After an afternoon of social calls with her aunt, Harriet praised a "youthful bride, who ... would prefer quiet, home sort of folks, to your aristocratic *dashers*," comparing her favorably to another woman who "met us at the gate, all tricked out in fanciful regalia." Harriet noted "some difference between the two *step mothers*—the one young & pretty but unadorned, the other past the first bloom of youth & beauty but mightily 'fixed up.'"[62] As she approached marriage, Harriet looked to popular literature and her observation of other women for models to guide her own behavior.[63]

Michael Denning argues that popular literature helped readers "name the characters and map the terrain of the social world."[64] T. S. Arthur's *The Lady at Home; or Happiness in the Household* attributes the poverty and illness of the families of an Irish seamstress and a Black laundress to the negligence of their affluent employers.[65] In contrast to *The Senator's Son*, which showed the need for reform legislation, both of Arthur's books locate the causes and solutions of social problems in the behavior of individual women.[66] Arthur's suggestion that "the lady at home" should pay her domestic workers on time and provide charitable assistance in emergencies ignores underlying income inequality based on social class, ethnicity, and race.[67] However, his depiction of virtuous workers and callous employers maps a social terrain for readers to explore.[68] While the merchants' families in *Two Wives* could solve their financial problems by reforming their spending and leisure habits, no amount of diligence and virtue could overcome the obstacles faced by the Black and Irish laborers Arthur describes. Harriet, who sewed and washed her own clothes, did not anticipate becoming either a domestic worker or an employer. She agreed that "were there better mistresses, there would be better servants," but drew a more fundamental moral lesson from the scenes Arthur presented. "Human beings, black or white, should be treated as such," she concluded.[69]

The books Harriet read reflected the values of a reading community that shared her family's northern evangelical Baptist beliefs.[70] Harriet reminisced about reading aloud with her friend, Mary Tyrell, a fellow teacher at the Baptist academy in Schoolcraft.[71] In Maumee, Harriet borrowed books from Mr. and Mrs. Page and their Baptist preacher, Elder Prentice.[72] She spent many evenings listening to her uncle, a Baptist Elder, read aloud from books like *Heroines of the Crusades* and Horace Mann's *A Few Thoughts on the Powers and Duties of Woman*.[73] Missionaries and reform advocates used advances in printing technology and transportation networks to publish and distribute inexpensive popular literature that illustrated the consequences of moral and immoral behavior.[74] Harriet appreciated the "sound sense" of eighteenth-century British evangelist Hannah More's "Two Wealthy Farmers," which contrasts the unhappiness of Mr. Bragwell, whose house was designed for ostentatious display, with the happiness Mr. Worthy finds in a modest but cozy home.[75] Like book reviews in popular magazines, Harriet evaluated books by their impact on readers' behavior.[76] When Harriet's aunt returned from a prayer meeting to find Harriet and her uncle "deeply absorbed with the thickening plot of the interesting story" that Harriet called "Home and Its Influences," she criticized them for staying home to read a novel. Harriet replied that "judging from *effects*, the *novel* had produced the best *influence*."[77] Several books Harriet read warned about the dangers of sensational fiction. In T. S. Arthur's *The Two Wives*, the errant wife rejects her husband's offers to read aloud from Prescott's *History of Mexico*, preferring instead to silently read a French novel.[78] In contrast, in *The Shady Side*, a minister's wife prepares to discuss theology and literature with her husband by "perusing,—not the latest novelette, but the October number of a well-known quarterly, the *Spectator*."[79] The heroine of "The Country Cousins" loses interest in "sober and profitable reading" after her "feelings were excited by sickly sentiment" from "worthless, cheap stories."[80] In Hannah More's "The Two Farmers," the virtuous daughters of Mr. Worthy avoid reading anything that could excite extravagant desires, while the spoiled daughters of Mr. Bragwell read sentimental novels that glorify romantic love, leading them to marry deceitful husbands.

Harriet occasionally indulged in the type of fiction these evangelical authors warned against. She criticized "N. P. Willis' stories, entitled, 'People That I Have Met'" as "nothing more than mere love trash—about angelic beauties & gallant heroes."[81] Emerson Bennett's *Leni-Leoti; or Adventures in the Far West* held Harriet's attention for over a hundred pages.[82] "I cannot feel that this was a profitable way of spending time," Harriet commented after finishing the book, "but as is ever the case, when I begin to indulge I become fascinated."[83] Two weeks later, Harriet confided in her diary: "I have done one wicked thing. I accidentally came across a pamphlet called 'The History of Charles Moore & his associations with Emma Mucherly,' and I sat down and read it through. This was wrong—such books of crime, murder & punishment are never profitable, but upon the Sabbath they are certainly pernicious. The only commendable thing I did was to consign it to the flames—but notwithstanding, two or three hours were spent in this sinful manner & I knew it was wrong all the time."[84] Exciting fiction, like alcohol, was addictive: reformers recommended total abstinence from both. They warned young readers to avoid the transgressive reading practices Harriet described: reading alone, at night, quickly, and for excessive periods of time.[85] When Harriet was fourteen years old, her older sister explained why she had not sent "the sequel of that foolish love-story written by some brain-cracked plagairist who had read just enough of romance to glean here and there an idea that jumbled together formed the web of his story." She continued:

> Now Harriet, have you not memory and imagination sufficient to regale yourself quite as well from the store-house of your own mind as to depend upon other fiction-loving skulls? Fie, fie Harriet, how many sleepless nights have you had sympathizing with the "poor nun" and wondering what became of her, and conjuring up all kinds of imaginings respecting the fate of the good lovers that so kindly interested themselves in her welfare. Well I dont see but you *must* remain satisfied with such information for I cannot get a paper to send you (*ours never came*). Dont be grieved at this announcement, for I am quite sure you can find as good reading somewhere else.

Edelia chastised Harriet for adopting the effusive tone of such fiction in her own correspondence: "You say unless *I* come my husband shall be branded as cruel and myself disowned by father and mother and cast off from the affections of sisters and brothers.... I verily believe Harriet your mind was bewildered in its fruitless wanderings after the poor lovers... or you would not have made such wild calculations."[86] Several years later, Edelia congratulated Harriet on her first teaching position, employment she viewed as preferable to "the fading unsatisfying earth-confined renown of those ephemeral authors that flash *weekly* before our mental vision and then disappear without producing aught save a momentary amusement."[87] Despite her sister's warnings and her own sense of guilt, these tales of romance and adventure joined the moralistic accounts of virtuous wives in shaping Harriet's perception of the world.

Stories Harriet read supplied the vocabulary and rhetorical strategies that enabled her to create a narrative of her own struggles, with herself in the role of heroine.[88] In her diary, Harriet described a situation familiar to many nineteenth-century readers: a plain and misunderstood young woman finds happiness with the handsome and charming man she marries despite his poverty. Harriet portrayed herself as trading her literary ambitions for a marriage based on equality and respect. In the style of sentimental fiction, Harriet wrote: "But few know how to handle the delicate chords of a sensitive spirit—but few can sympathize with the very refinement of anguish such a spirit endures at the first rough, careless touch—but few can fathom the depths of such a nature—& probe its wounds with a skillful hand—Such souls are made for happiness the most perfect, or misery the most exquisite.

If cast amid uncongenial minds the latter *must* be their fate. Thank God, I have one true genial heart to cast my writhing, wounded spirit upon in trust!"[89] Harriet's description summarizes a plight common to lonely fictional heroines. After gaining confidence and financial independence, she could choose to marry a man who understood her sensitive nature.[90]

Harriet grew up in a family that placed a high value on literacy. When Harriet was ten years old, her older sister wrote her: "Improve your time sis in study and *writing* that you become wiser and better as life wears away."[91] Her father's letters reveal his mastery of vocabulary and grammar, if not always of spelling. He reminded Harriet of the "great privilege it is, that we who are larened, and know how to spel a word, and hold a pen, can write our feelins to one another."[92] Formal education for clergy was a controversial issue among Baptists.[93] In her diary, Harriet criticized a preacher in Maumee for using "*elegant & refined* expressions; such as 'have did,' and 'they was.'" "Such sermons are not fit for 'ears polite,'" she explained.[94] Harriet viewed proper grammar as an essential marker of middle-class respectability. Shortly before she moved to Maumee, Harriet criticized a prosperous but illiterate Michigan family: "What do *such* people live for—no intellectual gratifications—nothing but the selfish indulgence of mere animal desires, whose aspirations reach no farther than a good meal of victuals, a fine house, racing horses and gold rings &c. &c."[95] She saw the "intellectual gratifications" of literacy as preferable to "selfish indulgence" in luxuries.[96]

The lyceum organization that was founded shortly after Harriet arrived in Maumee relied on widespread literacy among public school graduates. In 1852, the Governor of Ohio urged the legislature to fund lyceums and literary societies as desirable forms of public entertainment. While some lyceums invited paid speakers, many featured debates and lectures by residents.[97] The Maumee lyceum programs consisted of a paper, read aloud by its author, followed by editorials and discussion. This format required Harriet and her neighbors to take a position on an issue and express their opinions in writing. The oral presentation and ensuing discussion enabled women to speak in public about broadly political issues.[98] Although Harriet had opposed an elocution club two years earlier, she confidently read her paper to the lyceum audience on January 6.[99] One Maumee lyceum session addressed the topic: "Is the hope of a reward a greater incentive to action than the fear of punishment?"[100] Another considered whether "wealth and prosperity exert a good influence upon the *morals* of a Nation."[101] Both topics posed questions related to a developing market economy in which workers labored for wages while wealth was concentrated in the hands of a few. By participating in lyceums, people like Harriet learned how to form an argument, present evidence, draw conclusions, and assess ideas, entering a public sphere of debate about local and national issues.

Literate women could express their views in print for a national readership as well as in lyceum papers for a local audience.[102] A few years earlier, a friend had written Harriet that she earned three dollars per week by "doing some writing for Esqr Leslie."[103] Another friend had approved of Harriet's suggestion that they choose a topic about which to write back and forth. "*Who knows but we may write for the Press*," she added.[104] Harriet's younger brother compared her to Ohio author Harriet Beecher Stowe, whose phenomenally successful book, *Uncle Tom's Cabin*, was published in 1852. "Hattie you have got talents and if you was a mind to you might w[r]ite as good and maybe better book than that of Mrs Stowes," he wrote.[105] Harriet described a magazine published in Cincinnati to promote regional literature: "Have been reading this evening in a new magazine—'The Genius of the West.' It contains tolerable good pieces—many of them evidently by young writers. There are so many aspirants for literary fame that its honors cannot be awarded to all. *My* ambition has turned into an humbler sphere, & now I'm content with the reward of a quiet, virtuous life in the society of a true & loving heart."[106] Although she had given up her ambition of becoming a published author, Harriet defended her right to maintain a private diary.[107] She wrote that her aunt referred to her writing "*penchant*" with "contempt" and thought she should spend her time "to better advantage than in *scribbling* so much."[108] She heard her aunt comment: "Harriet's talents will never raise her in society, or amount to any thing."[109] Harriet responded in her diary: "I really think I'd render a home, [in] spite of my writing propensity, quite as agreeable to a husband."[110] The family life Harriet envisioned featured reading together in the cozy domestic setting described in popular literature.[111]

Fortunately, Henry shared Harriet's enthusiasm for both reading and writing. He had regularly kept a diary for several years. While Harriet usually read stories about domestic life, Henry preferred tales of adventure and travel.[112] Unlike the books Harriet read, much of Henry's reading questioned inequalities of power and wealth and challenged conventional moral standards. In the two and a half years before he moved to Seneca Falls in 1850, Henry mentioned reading only a few books. One day, when rain prevented him from working on the farm, Henry commented: "Did nothing but read the 7 deadly sins. Eugene Sue Esq is the author of it. It begins well as all of his stories do but he will kick it all over before he finishes it."[113] The French author's descriptions of sins and empathy with the sinners scandalized critics and shocked authors of the moralistic tales Harriet preferred.[114] Henry also read Bulwer-Lytton's *Earnest Maltrevers*, which was criticized for its sympathetic portrayal of an unmarried mother.[115] Maria Edgeworth's *Helen* explores the dilemma of a young wife whose husband discovers letters from her previous courtship. Henry commented: "I have about finished Helen by Mrs Edgworth & it is decidedly the best novel I have read in five years. The moral of it is worth every Lecture on Morality that has been delivered since Adam."[116] Like Harriet, Henry accepted the critical consensus that the measure of a novel's quality was the appropriateness of its moral message.[117]

Henry read ten books during the year and a half he lived in Seneca Falls, six of them in the four months between two courtships. Dinner table conversations with his employer, S. S. Gould, and Mrs. Gould may have exposed Henry to a wider range of literature and literary criticism than he had encountered previously.[118] In addition to James Fenimore Cooper's *The Last of the Mohicans*, Frederika Bremer's *The Neighbors*, Phillip Bailey's narrative poem *Festus*, and Bayard Taylor's account of adventures in California, Henry read three novels by Frederick Marryat and three by Charles Dickens.[119] About six weeks after he began boarding with the Gould family, Henry wrote: "Finished Barnaby Rudge last night. I think I never read a more capable work in many respects than that is. Boz can depict the worst of human passion better than any man of his age but he is not equal to Shakespeare [or] Thackery in drawing from nature." In contrast to his earlier comments on Edgeworth and Sue, Henry had learned how to phrase his evaluation in the language of contemporary literary criticism and compare Dickens to other authors.[120] After reading *David Copperfield*, Henry described two men he observed outside his window, contrasting the strong moral character he attributed to the poorly dressed man with the undesirable traits he assigned to the well-dressed stranger.[121] It was while he was reading Dickens that Henry had commented on the greed of merchants and the moral hazards of economic competition.[122] Henry could easily identify with David Copperfield's naive but sincere attempts to make his way in a community in which he was friendless and subject to exploitation. Marryat's *Jacob Faithful* tells the story of a poor orphan who becomes wealthy, although "the only capital with which he embarked was a good education and good principles." Marryat's *Mr. Midshipman Easy* details the humorous adventures of an ingenuous young sailor searching for a society that practices perfect equality.[123] Like Dickens' *David Copperfield* and *Martin Chuzzlewit*, these books describe the adventures of young white men forced to rely on their wits and abilities to surmount numerous obstacles before settling safely into employment and marriage. They formed a male counterpoint to the books Harriet read to prepare for married life.

Soon after he returned to Schoolcraft, Henry read Ik Marvell's *Bachelor's Reveries* aloud to his parents and sister. Now that he had rejoined his family, reading was no longer a solitary occupation. He appreciated the humorous sketches anticipating the misfortunes of a married man. "How very very appropriate they are to my situation now, & how true they *draw lifes* likeness as I see it," Henry wrote. "Bachelorhood is the happy life to live after all."[124] A week later, Henry met Harriet Johnson, and his thoughts turned again to marriage. Henry understood that in order to meet Harriet's expectations, he would need to give up many of the pastimes his family and friends enjoyed. In contrast to Harriet's childhood in New England and northern Ohio towns, Henry had grown up in an isolated frontier community. When his parents, Eliza and Thaddeus Smith, arrived in southwest Michigan with their four-year-old son in 1830, they built a log house on the wooded edge of the Prairie Ronde, where they sold liquor, cloth, and household supplies shipped west by sailing vessel, river barge, and wagon.[125] Local Potawatomi women often spent the day with Henry's mother, who became fluent in their language.[126] As a young child, Henry had watched the women trade berries, maple syrup, and produce for manufactured goods, following Potawatomi expectations for fair exchange and cordial relations. Henry later remembered that Chief Sagamaw "was a personal friend of the Smith family and used to make us weekly visits with his family, staying from one to two days" and often bringing Henry baby animals.[127] A few years later, after complicated and contested treaty negotiations, the government forced the families Henry remembered as their "most numerous customers and neighbors" to move from the Prairie Ronde Potawatomi village surrounded by their cultivated fields and burial grounds to the Nottawaseepe Reservation.[128] Henry's father sold his interest in the store to Eliza's cousin, E. L. Brown, for eighty acres of land and a frame house on lots that would become part of the village of Schoolcraft.[129] Brown later wrote that his extended family and friends from Vermont, along with several other New England families, joined earlier settlers who were primarily "plain, uneducated men, from Ohio, Kentucky, and Virginia." He noted that the Virginians and the Vermonters, who were all Whigs, "always fraternized."[130] Henry remembered that most local men hunted and trapped in addition to farming and that "Saturdays were always devoted to fun, such as horse-racing, wrestling and jumping, target shooting, etc." "Whiskey was the only luxury," he recalled decades later, "Everyone drank it to keep out cold, heat, pain of every kind; as an antidote against ague and a bond of sociability."[131] In 1840, armed federal troops "gathered up" Henry's Potawatomi neighbors and escorted them, mostly on foot, to Kansas: many resisted this forcible relocation by escaping to Canada or northern Michigan, and some returned, bought land, and re-established native communities.[132]

In 1847, when Henry reached the age of twenty-one, he entered fully into the social world of rural male citizens. Henry and his friends entertained themselves by playing card games and tossing pennies, "pitching coppers for a stick of candy a game."[133] Henry also enjoyed hunting geese, squirrels, and deer.[134] He attended a local fair to see livestock and bet on his friend Hurley's horse in the races.[135] The absence of rail or boat transportation and the rough condition of the few existing roads limited the community's access to entertainment.[136] An annual circus was one of the few commercial performances that visited Schoolcraft. In 1848, Henry described the arrival of thirty horses, two trained dogs, and a clown: "Hurrah! for the circus.... Welch & Delenans & Nathans circus shows here this afternoon & evening. They come in, in great style with thirty beautiful horses driven by one man. Their chariot had some of the prettiest paintings I ever saw on it. Their band was a good one. They had one fiddler that beat any thing ever I saw. Their performance was first rate. Nathans his two boys, Mr Dunbar and the [G]erman [with] his two dogs were right. The clown was rather vulgar & somewhat bawdy for ladies to be present."[137] That summer, a touring group, probably a minstrel show with white performers wearing blackface make-up, sang "negro melodies."[138] Six months later, Henry and five other young men went to Kalamazoo to see a theater company from Detroit perform "Damon & Pythius," followed by a comedy, "The Loan of a Lover." A week later, they returned for a performance of "Brigand." "Don't I wish I was in that line sometime," Henry remarked.[139] Henry wrote that he and "some of the bohoys" were at the store "talking about the recent nomination of Gen Taylor for president by our party; one thing brought on another" until they "gave the neighboring Lasses a Salute allround with an anvil and seven or eight guns."[140] The urban Bowery B'hoy had become a familiar figure in popular culture, identifiable by his mode of dress, cigar, body language, and speech patterns.[141] Elliott Gorn describes this New York City subculture of young working-class men who turned to "the strut and swagger of leisure-time activities" to provide a sense of accomplishment, identity, status, and belonging.[142] As Henry's use of the term "bohoys" suggests, his male peers in Schoolcraft exhibited similar bravado and rowdiness. In rural as well as urban contexts, political parties provided both a sense of individual identity and a feeling of belonging to a larger group, as did fraternal organizations. When Henry was elected as a delegate to a county convention in Kalamazoo to select representatives to revise the state constitution, he visited the Masonic lodge in the evening.[143]

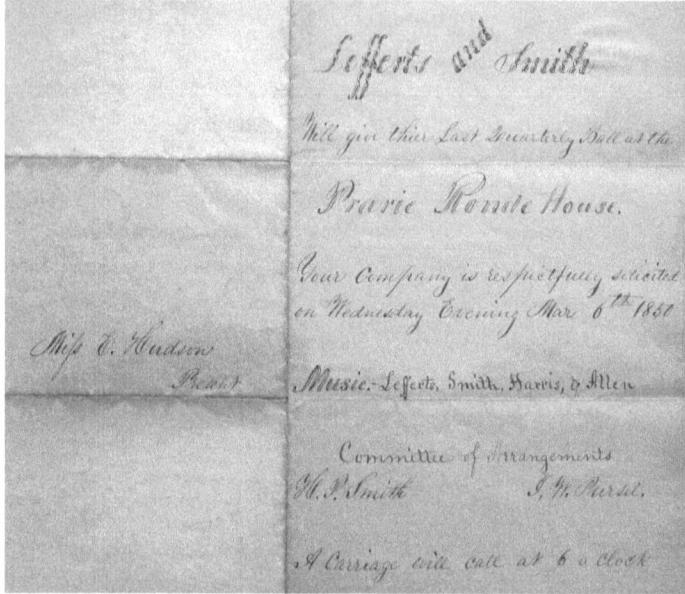

Henry Smith was a manager and fiddler for a ball at the Prairie Ronde House, March 6, 1850. Leffert & Smith, hand-lettered ball invitation. Box 4, Stanley Barney Smith Collection, A-88, Archives and Regional History Collections, Zhang Legacy Collections Center, Western Michigan University.

Hull and Arnold Quadrille Band, Constantine, Michigan, ca. 1875. Object 64.219, Kalamazoo Valley Museum.

Henry occasionally played the fiddle at parties held in local homes, including a quilting bee, and he and his friends sometimes provided music for dances the young men organized.[144] Henry participated in both the musical tradition of fiddling for contradances, in which musicians improvised their parts, and the new style of playing that relied on reading published sheet music to accompany the cotillions that were the forerunners of square dances. Round dances such as the polka and the schottische had also become popular. By 1849, Henry knew the Jenny Lind polka, which New York dance teacher Allen Dodworth had published in 1846.[145] Since the new cotillions and round dances required formal instruction, Henry offered dance lessons for local children in 1849.[146] On New Year's Day, the Fourth of July, and other holidays, unmarried men and women and young married couples gathered at a local dance hall for an evening "ball," often paying an admission charge to listen to a hired band.[147]

During the 1850s, cotillion bands with a regional reputation replaced the local fiddlers who had accompanied contradances. The cotillion bandleader, a fiddler, played the melody and called the figures, accompanied by the second fiddler and two or three other musicians playing clarinet, cornet, trombone, or bass viol.[148] Henry heard two fiddlers play with a post horn and a trombone at the Christmas ball in 1848.[149] On Independence Day in 1850, he hired a lumber wagon to take young men and women from Schoolcraft to a nearby community where they danced to a band consisting of "3 fiddles & a clarinet all playing at one part while one man had a bass viol and just sawed away with all his might never touching a string with any thing but the bow no matter what the key was."[150] Henry was more satisfied with the New Year's Day ball, where the regionally renowned Hull and Arnold's Quadrille Band, including a clarinet, cornet, trombone, and fiddle, played arrangements created from published piano scores.[151]

When Henry was hired as a clerk in the larger upstate New York town of Seneca Falls in 1850, he slept above the store but took his meals with his employer's family, whom he described as "Aristocrats of the first order."[152] The Gould household, with a cook and a housekeeper, introduced Henry to a more affluent lifestyle and more stratified social class distinctions than he had known in Michigan. Mr. and Mrs. Gould criticized Henry for fiddling for hire at a dance hall. "I never was so ashamed of my profession before," he wrote. The next day, Henry "had the blues thinking of [his] fiddling scrape." He wrote: "I would give $5.00 dollars rather than bear the stigma that will be attached to my name for this one foolish act."[153] Henry found more acceptable musical venues by singing in a Glee Club and an Episcopal choir and by joining informal serenade bands that played and sang at night under the windows of young women.[154] Nicholas Tawa notes that vocal and instrumental serenading was a common pastime for young men.[155] Since serenades required only a passive audience, they allowed a newcomer like Henry to express interest in a woman without a formal introduction. According to

Henry, these musical tributes were well received by young women and their parents. When Henry and other young men played the violin, accordion, bugle, and guitar under the window of a young woman, she dropped flowers to them, and a man brought out a pie.[156] Another evening, "the serenade band was out making noises under windows and recieving in return gloves, thanks, apples, invitations to walk in &c until most midnight."[157] One serenade included a fiddle, flute, accordion, triangle, and tambourine.[158]

Daniel Cavicchi describes a transition from playing music to attending concerts as the dominant musical experience for men who aspired to middle-class respectability, especially for young clerks who moved from rural to urban locations.[159] The transportation networks of canals and railroads that supported manufacturing in Seneca Falls also brought touring performers as part of a circuit of entertainment events promoted by entrepreneurs and funded by ticket sales.[160] Henry heard an organ for the first time, attended a performance by Swiss bell ringers, and enjoyed a "Druid" concert that featured cow horns and "Mons Herr Somebody & his violin."[161] He regretted that he could not afford to hear the famous singer Jenny Lind and mentioned that he caught sight of "the renowned Dodge," who had paid $625 for a ticket to her concert as a publicity stunt.[162] The following year, Henry attended a harp and violin concert and traveled to a nearby town to hear the Riley family sing.[163] Although these performances featured costumes and instruments that Henry found exotic, the musical traditions were familiar ones from northern Europe. Concert organizers attempted to control audience behavior to avoid the stigma of rowdiness associated with the circus, theater, and dance hall.[164] When Henry began attending concerts, he bought a silk hat that he worried he would "be afraid to wear now I have it."[165] Henry also attended three circus parades in Seneca Falls in 1851, including the Dan Rice circus and the Turner & Co Circus and Caravan.[166] The highlight of the season was P. T. Barnum's Great Asiatic Caravan, Museum and Menagerie. Henry wrote: "There was a vast concern of people to see Barnum's Museum which was like all other men[a]geries except the great tent, eight Elephants, including a calf & Barnum's name to make it popular."[167] Barnum's use of the term "museum" conveys an aura of cultural authority and suggests a collection of specimens displayed to highlight their difference from the local and the everyday.[168] Barnum's shows were unabashedly commercial operations. The price of admission guaranteed the right to gaze at the objects, animals, and even people presented as exotic.[169] Henry also attended a hot-air balloon ascent.[170] Like Barnum's exhibits, the hot-air balloonists provided an entertaining spectacle that allowed spectators to imagine themselves transported to distant places, exploring the boundaries of the natural world and testing the limits of human potential.

Challenges to norms of appearance and behavior were more easily accepted in traveling performances than when encountered unexpectedly on the street. In an 1851 series of illustrated editorials in her Seneca Falls newspaper, *Lily* editor Amelia Bloomer suggested that women replace their voluminous skirts with gathered trousers in the interest of health, safety, and cleanliness, as well as comfort and mobility. Another Seneca Falls resident, Elizabeth Cady Stanton, who in 1848 had convened the path-breaking Woman's Rights Convention, worked with Bloomer to construct garments modeled on the trousers Stanton's cousin had worn at a European spa.[171] Henry criticized the onlookers who stared and laughed when Mrs. Stanton wore a knee-length skirt over long "breeches": "How they gaze at her as she passes hardly repressing the broad grin within their wondering faces. Oh! What an infernal stuck-up world this is."[172] Although Stanton's "breeches" violated European-American gender norms, they reminded Henry of a familiar alternative, the leggings worn by the "neat" Potawatomi women he had known as a child.[173] Describing a woman's appearance as "neat" was a compliment that indicated tidiness, cleanliness, and respectability.[174] By spring, several Seneca Falls women appeared in similar trousers. Newspapers and magazines across the country commented on this challenge to the physical and symbolic constraints embodied by fashionable women's clothing. Although editorials and cartoons lampooned the new style, it quickly gained advocates based on its health benefits as well as the freedom of movement it offered. The women who wore these trousers, as well as the garments themselves, became known as "bloomers."[175] In November, Henry wrote: "There came into the store this morning one of the bloomers if I ever saw one. Her dress was bl[ac]k velvet, pants and all with a white hat on her head that looked in shape like a wilted cabbage stuck on the back of her head. She was ridiculous in the extreme."[176] By this time, Henry associated "bloomers" with feminist advocates of dress reform. He dismissed this woman's attire as ridiculous, in contrast to his approval of the trousers worn by the Gould family's friend, Mrs. Stanton, several months earlier.[177]

Public lectures also challenged expectations of gender and race. In Seneca Falls, Henry heard several prominent abolitionists. He "went to hear Thomson the great Abolition lecturer who was not there, consequently had to sit & hear Abby Kelly." Henry climbed over other members of the audience and returned home to read *David Copperfield*.[178] A few weeks later, Henry attended a lecture by Gerrit Smith, cousin of feminist activist Elizabeth Cady Stanton.[179] The evening before he left Seneca Falls, Henry heard Frederick Douglass give a lecture advocating the abolition of slavery. Henry wrote that he had "not heard a man speak on any subject to please me as much [as] he did since I have lived here." He added, "He is the only specimen of an educated negro I ever saw. What an iron willed man he is though."[180] Henry's use of the term "specimen" suggests that Douglass provided evidence of a new social category: "an educated negro." Douglass addressed northern white men by arguing that slavery denied enslaved men their inherent manhood.[181] Henry's expression of admiration for Douglass as "an iron willed man" suggests that he understood and accepted this rhetorical appeal to a shared masculine identity that transcended racial distinctions.

Henry's experiences in Seneca Falls continued to shape his perceptions even after he moved back to Michigan. When Henry briefly returned to Schoolcraft in the summer of 1852, he attended a horse race. "Many a brawny hand I shook that would have made me blush had my Seneca Falls friends seen me," he observed.[182] Henry recognized the social distance separating the suntanned farmers at the Michigan horse race from his merchant associates in upstate New York. After he moved back to Schoolcraft in November, Henry began to question some of the activities he had once enjoyed. The following April, as he was beginning to court Harriet, Henry expressed misgivings about enjoying a horserace: "In the afternoon I attended the races, had some fun and something else & mus[t] confess I did not spend the time very profitably."[183] Shortly before he proposed to Harriet, Henry distanced himself from racing fans. "Horse race in town but I saw nothing of them except as they came out opposite the store," Henry noted in his diary. "The tavern was crowded with drunken ragged wretches that should never be allowed to roam at large," he added.[184] After he became engaged to Harriet, Henry wrote emphatically: "A *horse race* comes off this afternoon and a more drunken filthy, scurvy crowd, I never saw together."[185] The rural entertainment of amateur horseracing, closely associated with betting and drinking, epitomized the rowdy male street culture that Harriet found objectionable.[186]

Henry turned to genteel musical activities that Harriet, like his Seneca Falls friends, would find acceptable. He listened as his friend Hurley's sister "discoursed sweet music on the piano" and planned to take guitar lessons from her.[187] In addition to singing the popular songs Harriet later remembered, Henry joined a church choir and a Sunday evening singing school.[188] In a more public performance, he sang and played at an annual exhibition at the seminary where Harriet taught.[189] Henry attended house parties, donation parties for pastors, oyster suppers, picnics, and ice cream parties.[190] He played euchre with his male friends, backgammon with his grandmother or a female friend, and whist with groups of men and women that sometimes included his sisters.[191] While Harriet was living in Maumee, Henry continued to participate in musical activities and social gatherings.[192] In deference to Harriet, he passed up the opportunity to attend a ball at the Schoolcraft House and played the fiddle only at Hurley's house and, on November 20, "all alone" at home.[193] As New Year's Day approached, he wondered: "What Hattie would think to hear of my attending balls." "I believe I will dance once more if there is a good respectable one near us," he concluded.[194] Two months later, Henry joined his sisters and boyhood friends at an "oyster party" at the Schoolcraft House, where he danced until two o'clock.[195]

While Harriet held fast to the principles of her New England Baptist upbringing, Henry cultivated the ability to blend in with diverse social groups. He learned to feel at home among the merchants of Seneca Falls as well as the farmers of Schoolcraft. Henry also learned to redefine his activities to make them more socially acceptable, turning a dance at the Schoolcraft House into a genteel oyster party. Henry and Harriet understood that their performance of the roles of husband and wife would be defined in part by the leisure activities they pursued and the goods they purchased. These personal choices would link them to broader cultural systems of fashion, morality, social class, and gender. They used their skills in reading and writing to envision themselves as married adults, but the models provided by literature fell short of reality. Although Harriet reassured Henry that she would be happy in any home he provided, she assumed that they would live in comfortable circumstances. Shortly before she left Maumee, Harriet visited a family who had "moved into an old, leaky, dirty log house." "Wonder if I could ever be contented in such a spot—I fear not yet *hope* will do wonders," she speculated.[196] She little suspected that living in an "old, leaky, dirty log house" would prove to be the least of the challenges she and Henry would face.

PART II

From Michigan to Missouri, 1854–1861

Chapter Three

FAMILY AND NATION

"This stormy sea of matrimony"[1]

"It is *decided*; we are to be married soon *very* soon. I'm dizzy with thoughts that come tearing into my head," Henry wrote in his diary on May 25, 1854. "I am not prepared for this step [and] neither is she, but we cannot be much better prepared three months hence; She is willing to take it now while her brothers & sister are with her and I am too happy that it may be so."[2] Harriet stopped writing in her diary when she moved from Maumee to her parents' new home in White Pigeon, Michigan, but Henry continued his daily entries. On June 1, he wished he could hear the visiting musician Kanderbeck play. The next day, Henry wrote that he was "urged so strongly by Pike to help the young aristocracy get up music for them to *dance* to, I (being under obligation to him for a buggy to go with *Monday* and that the only covered one in town) went and pledged myself to Kanderbeck & wife that they should receive 15$ to play." Henry attended the dance with his sister and cousin, danced until after one o'clock, and "paid the music which was the best I ever heard."[3] Having secured the use of the only covered buggy in Schoolcraft by paying the visiting musicians, Henry drove to White Pigeon, where he and Harriet would be married in her family's home. The next morning, Henry arose early and "waited nervously for the hour which was to be at 8 A M. before breakfast."[4] He described the ceremony: "The time came as all such do at last and I stood up before her father and pledged myself to love, cherish and shean her from the dangers of this stormy sea of matrimony as long as I lived and she pledged herself in like manner to fulfill her duties to me as the wife & we were to take the word of God as our guide and we were *husband & wife*."[5] Henry and Harriet drove back to Schoolcraft in the borrowed buggy to spend the evening with "quite a company of young people" at Mr. Allen's house.[6] The next day, Henry went back to work at the dry goods store while he and Harriet stayed with his family. A month later, Harriet returned to White Pigeon to complete a quilt and purchase household items while Henry finished his home renovations.[7] He had decided that rather than building a new house, he would enlarge the Smith family home to make "a separate home for two families."[8] Henry hired a carpenter and mason to extend the front of the three-room frame house, replace the chimney, add a new kitchen, and enclose a porch.[9]

A week after she left Schoolcraft, Harriet wrote Henry: "Do not be disappointed if I send a miserably poor letter, for my head is reeling & my hand tremulous. I am not well though no serious malady afflicts. This faint, oppressive weather deadens all life & I have hardly enough to take my customary meals."[10] In the last few lines of an eight-page letter she mailed three weeks later, Harriet alluded to the cause of her lack of energy. "Henrie dear," she wrote, "nothing but an unforseen accident can prevent the realization of our fears. Now there seems no doubt as to the termination. My health is pretty good [but] suffer a little from *nausea* headache &c."[11] In his diary, Henry expressed his anxiety about the dangers of childbirth: "Rec'd dear Hatties letter, a long, loving & trusting one. That which we would have shunned and hoped to avoid has already come upon her. Why did I not know the consequences; It was the sin of ignorance for which I may lose my gentle wife."[12] Henry's sister had almost died the previous year from "childbed fever," a bacterial infection that claimed the lives of many women after childbirth.[13] Apparently, Henry and Harriet had attempted to avoid pregnancy without the use of birth control devices. Popular advice books calculated a woman's least fertile time to be exactly the days on which she was most likely to conceive.[14] In attempting to plan the size and timing of their family, Harriet and Henry were in step with many other couples of their generation. The ratio of young children to women of childbearing age in the United States fell by thirty percent from 1800 to 1860.[15] The letters and diaries Sylvia Hoffert examined reveal that in the mid-nineteenth century, many northern middle-class couples attempted to limit the size of their families, although they seldom specified the methods they used.[16]

In a letter to Harriet in early August, Henry referred to "what *can* be done to throw a shade over what *has been* done." Two weeks later, after Harriet's second reference to an "accident," he assured her that he was "quite reconciled" to the pregnancy and was "satisfied that it is *much more safe* to let nature have its course and *guard against* accident." He urged Harriet to "take good care *against* accidents for the danger is *greater* to your health unless nature takes her own course."[17] Henry and Harriet approached the termination of pregnancy as a medical rather than a moral decision. The rate of abortions rose sharply in the second quarter of the nineteenth century when self-induced early-term abortions became common among married as well as unmarried women of all classes. Religious publications paid little attention to the practice. There was no reliable test to confirm pregnancy, and it was commonly assumed that life began with quickening, when the first fetal movement was detected several months after conception.[18] Harriet soon became resigned to the reality of her pregnancy. She wrote Henry: "Sometimes I have a dread, shrinking from the future & many of its *feared* responsibilities—Henrie I have hoped against hope & now nothing is left but to wait the result. Accident *may* befriend—nothing else *can*. And now what can be done but to quietly submit & *enjoy* the *congratulations* of our 'dear five hundred friends.'"[19] Henry also seemed to accept his new status. "To be sure," he wrote Harriet, "were it in my power to live over the few weeks that we have been husband & wife, I would *diverge* a trifle from the course I have taken, but I cannot help it now, and only trust that you may have sufficient strength to bear up under all."[20] Henry informed Harriet that he had turned down a position as a traveling salesman in Michigan, Iowa, and Illinois. He explained: "Perseverance and economy will enable us to *progress* slowly but happily, and however humble we may live we try to be respected by others."[21] Harriet replied that Henry's current job was "wasting his best energies in a service that affords so poor a remuneration & furnishes little hope of advancement." She assured Henry that she would be willing to live apart while he earned enough to put his new farmland into "prosperous condition" so that they could live in their "*own* pleasant home free from harassing cares & the anxieties consequent upon *debt*."[22] A few weeks later, Harriet and Henry moved into their new room in the house they would share with Henry's parents and sister in Schoolcraft.

The previous October, while Harriet was teaching in Maumee, Henry and his father had made enough profit from the wheat crop on the family farm to pay off all their debts. Henry had purchased forty acres of land, with payments due over a two-year period, and had been optimistic about his ability to establish a farm. However, hot weather and drought during the summer of 1854 threatened farm crops. As the market economy had encompassed agriculture, farmers had come to rely on a cycle of debt. They bought seed on credit each year and paid off the loans when they harvested and sold their crops.[23] Crop failure meant inability to repay debts. Investment in farm equipment and land incurred additional debt, especially for a young farmer. In November, Harriet's brother Joseph, a druggist in St. Louis, invited Henry to join his business venture. Henry explained his situation: "I am not able

In 1854, the Smith home in Schoolcraft consisted of the front half of the house shown in this later photograph. RHC Photographs P-4668, Stanley Barney Smith Collection, A-88, Archives and Regional History Collections, Zhang Legacy Collections Center, Western Michigan University.

to go into any business that requires capital (rather an essential in the drug business) as my all is in land and home. If I were to sell out my parents would go mourning the rest of their lives; besides it is my duty to provide for them."[24] Henry was heavily invested in the family farm that he would inherit as the only son, and he felt responsible for his parents as well as his wife and child. Although working as a clerk provided Henry with a steady income, he felt frustrated by his subservient position. In January, he wrote: "I am afraid I shall lose my identity here and cease to be other than somebodies *clerk* unless I do some kind of business for myself. If it were not for the fetters which debt binds about me I *could* do something."[25] Henry came to realize that while borrowing money allowed a young man without capital to establish himself in business or farming, debt meant trading dependence on an employer for dependence on a lender.[26]

Henry looked to party politics to alleviate the difficulties he faced. The rhetoric of political debate provided a way to comprehend the obstacles to success that became even more apparent as Henry considered his new responsibilities. He translated his earlier resentment of wealthy merchants into a belief that he could join with others like himself to redress the imbalance of power and wealth in society. In 1854, Henry was the town clerk and school inspector, and he ran unsuccessfully for county clerk.[27] Henry's participation in politics at the local level drew him into a realignment of national parties that transformed the American political landscape: the demise of the Whig Party, the rise and fall of the Know-Nothings, and the creation of the Republican Party. In May 1854, the Kansas-Nebraska Act allowed western territories to decide by popular vote whether to allow slavery. In northern states, opponents of the extension of slavery into the western territories formed "fusion" coalitions to elect anti-slavery candidates in state elections in the summer and fall of 1854. Michigan leaders of the Whig Party and the Free Soil Party negotiated to form a new state party. At a convention held in Jackson on July 6, the coalition adopted the name "Republican," accepted a platform opposed to the extension of slavery, and selected a slate of candidates for the November election, including Henry's neighbor and relative, E. Lakin Brown, for state senator.[28] Henry, who had supported the Whigs since he became eligible to vote, was a delegate to the state Whig convention in October.[29] Delegates who supported the Republican fusion ticket overruled delegates who tried to nominate a slate of candidates to run as Whigs, effectively dissolving the Whig Party in Michigan. On October 17, Henry used a numerical code to indicate that he and other men had organized a local Know-Nothing society. The Know-Nothings had begun organizing in Michigan during the summer to influence the selection of Know-Nothing members as Republican candidates.[30] The Know-Nothings followed the model of a fraternal organization, with local lodges that voted on the admission of members and practiced initiation rituals, oaths, and secret signs. From June to October of 1854, Know-Nothing membership grew from about fifty thousand to over one million nationwide, including disillusioned former Whigs and Democrats as well as new voters.[31]

The Whig philosophy relied on the premise that a man of good character who demonstrated self-discipline could borrow money on the strength of his personal reputation.[32] Policies that enhanced the availability of credit and supported construction of railroads and canals would allow men like Henry to become property owners and entrepreneurs, providing independence and respect as well as financial security. These political and economic assumptions were interwoven with ideals of masculinity that made manhood contingent on autonomy in the workplace as well as on financial success. For Henry, the Whig program of self-improvement and self-control had not paid the promised rewards. His modest salary as a dry-goods clerk seemed to announce that he was unworthy of the confidence of his community. Like the Whigs, the Know-Nothings espoused individualism and equality for native-born white men. However, according to the Know-Nothings, the economic failure of hard-working and honest men was not due to their lack of diligence or character. Northern Know-Nothings argued that corrupt politicians, backed by wealthy men who profited from slavery or the liquor trade, influenced Catholic immigrants to vote for legislation harmful to Protestant native-born workers. They promised to remove the obstacles hampering the aspiring self-made man (assuming he was white, Protestant, and native-born) by curtailing the rights of immigrants to vote and hold office, controlling the sale of alcohol, and preventing the extension of slavery into the western territories.[33]

Two days after Henry assisted his father with the difficult delivery of a stillborn calf, he wrote: "Hattie feels that her time is drawing near. I feel anxious about it, sometimes fear trouble to come but I will trust in the all powerful arm of Providence as we see it exerted in nature, and try to behave myself as a man should and make myself of some use instead of folding my hands and saying Gods will be done, I cannot help it."[34] Henry's recent observation of birth in the natural world would hardly have been reassuring. He stumbled over the theological question of whether events were determined by the will of God, but he understood the ideal of masculinity that required a man to meet emergencies with stoic fortitude and an ability to provide practical assistance. After a few days without recording any diary entries, Henry described the birth of his daughter: "Wednesday evening Father called for me to go to the house to assist them and it was with doubt & misgiving that I went but I did go and stood by my own dear wife through her great trial. She gave birth to a girl weighing 9 1/2 pounds, about half past eight in the evening after which we (Aunt Jane & Mary the Doctor & I) took our supper with a relish, while mother was dressing the child."[35] Doctors often presided at births by midcentury, but female relatives and neighbors also provided help and advice, and a husband's presence was not unusual.[36] Henry participated in Isa's daily care, at least for a few weeks. He wrote that it was humorous to see "us change her diapers" since "we are *very* awkward to be sure." Henry's mother stayed with the family for several nights after Isa's birth. The first night Henry and Harriet were alone with Isa, they felt overwhelmed by the task of caring for the baby. Henry wrote: "I looked up and saw Hattie in tears, whereupon we both cried." Henry held Isa in his arms all night, and the feelings of tenderness he experienced overcame his frustration.[37]

A few weeks later, Isa developed colic, causing her to cry inconsolably for hours every day. "What trials these young mothers have," Henry wrote, "especially those who have never thought or [been] educated [to] have the care of a home, without means to keep servants."[38] By the 1850s, affluent middle-class families customarily hired an experienced monthly nurse to care for a newborn baby, supervise the mother's recovery, and provide advice on infant care.[39] These mothers often spent the first week after childbirth in bed, gradually increasing their activity until they were able to leave the house at the end of the month.[40] Henry could not afford to hire a nurse to help Harriet, who was inexperienced in housekeeping as well as childcare. He envisioned a time when his family would exemplify an ideal of rural domesticity: "I shall be glad when I can have a little more time to devote to my family and when the baby gets old enough to help itself some and not have the colic and when Hattie gets strong and a return of buoyant spirits and we are forehanded enough to live in a little cottage of our own an[d] 'a little farm well tilled' and able to hire a girl &c &c &c."[41] As prospects for a good crop faded after a heavy frost in June, Henry became even more discouraged. He wrote: "Heaven seems to have stamped its seal of disapprobation upon our crops, my labors here are hard enough because they confine me so closely, and the salary is not enough to more than support my family. Where will the money come from to pay my debts!"[42] Henry realized that he could assert some control over his financial condition by limiting the size of his family. About two months after Isa's birth, Henry received a letter from his cousin, Charley Wheeler: "I enclose herewith the fine 'patent safety fuse' which was mentioned. [H]ope the *article* will give satisfaction. [T]is not quite as good as I wanted to send you, but will get some better when I go to Boston. You are probably posted in the use of them, being a man of *some experience*. When you wish to use it soften in water or olive oil, and you will find it will work to admiration. You have my best wishes for the success of the '*Enter*-prise.'"[43] In the market economy, a small family was advantageous, a factor sometimes taken into account by the bankers who would decide whether to extend credit for a farm or business.[44] Henry resented the higher social status and financial success of some of his neighbors. He wrote: "I now regret very much that I had not the opportunities when young to get a good thorough education. When I look upon the world and take in its attributes as *I* do I wish I could put it upon paper that others may see it also. How I would like to hold a mirror before a certain class in this community."[45] Henry recognized the power of written language to persuade others and bring about social change. He also realized his limited ability to make himself heard. Although Henry expressed a vague awareness that his personal circumstances were linked to the transformation to a wage-based economy, he blamed his difficulties on his own low salary and lack of educational opportunities rather than on the structure of society.

In mid-summer, four-month-old Isa had to be "taken from her mother's breast" when Harriet suffered the intermittent fever, chills, and weakness of malaria, a common illness in swampy southern Michigan.[46] In addition to looking after his sick wife, Henry struggled to care for a baby who had to be weaned abruptly to cow's milk and fed with a spoon or baby bottle.[47] Within a few days, Henry wrote that he "was up with Isa, poor thing most of the night."[48] The next day, he explained: "Isa finds her cows milk rather a poor substitute for her own food and she fails under it some." Henry continued to worry about his financial situation: "Hope to be out of debt again soon and when once out I will not jump in again very soon." The following day, Henry again felt overwhelmed. As temperatures fluctuated from almost one hundred degrees to below freezing, he confided in his journal: "I feel discouraged and hardly know which way to turn; Isa is almost sick from being taken from her mother or taking her disease, the store demands my time and I must devote every minute I have to spare to my family. Perhaps this is but a shadow of my future connubial bliss; if so may God take me from this sphere soon."[49]

Within a few days, Henry's spirits rose as Harriet's health began to improve, and Isa acted like "the best baby in the world."[50] Harriet's father wrote to express his regret that "already has insatiate disease, drunk up or poison'd the nutricious pool which nature provided, and the little sufferer is compelled to embrace a cold unfeeling *bottle*, instead of a warmhearted affectionate mother." He criticized Henry for the tone of the letter Henry had written to inform him of Harriet's illness: "Henrie! what means that complaining, faultfinding spirit breath'd forth in your letter! [D]o you think that in the eye of the *Great Eternal*, your little family is all the world? What if the wheel of providence in its constant motion, should crush the *idols* of your heart[:] have you a right to complain, and charge God with injustice or cruelty?"[51]

After reading the letter from his father-in-law, Henry again associated manliness with the ability to cope with adversity and the physical suffering of others. "I get the blues as soon as they are sick," he wrote in his journal, "wish I was a little more of the *man*."[52] By autumn, Isa also suffered from the symptoms of malaria. Henry stayed awake all night as she moaned with a high fever. "How I felt lying beside her until the long night wore away," he wrote, "none can tell but the father of just such another babe." The next evening, Henry anxiously rushed home. He described his relief: "I found her sleeping quietly and when I took her up in my arms to retire she put her little face to mine and nestled a little then sank to repose again."[53] As Henry struggled to meet his new obligations, he imagined finding both validation of his manliness and a more ideal life for his family in the West.

"I feel a hankering for the west," Henry wrote, "and the more I see of this rotten tottering village the less hopes I have of its ever becoming any better."[54] Two days later, he mused: "How I would like to wander about in the new countries of the west beyond the boundaries of civilization. If Hattie was only tough we would all go."⁵⁵ Relocation was a common solution for young men looking for greater financial success.⁵⁶ Henry's father had moved west to the frontier of Michigan as a young man after his business failed. Susan Gray describes the Yankee settlement of southwestern Michigan by young men who left areas where land had become expensive to settle further west, where land prices were lower.⁵⁷ As the price of farmland around Schoolcraft rose rapidly during the 1850s, Henry looked to the west to replicate the experience of his parents and neighbors. By early spring of 1856, Henry had switched his party affiliation again, this time abandoning the Know-Nothings for the Republican Party.⁵⁸ The Know-Nothings had dropped the practice of secret endorsements in order to operate as a national party and nominate a presidential candidate. At the party's national convention in February, delegates split over whether the Kansas-Nebraska Act should be repealed. When New York delegates joined with the southern wing of the party to endorse popular sovereignty, many northern voters who opposed the extension of slavery in the West left the Know-Nothings for the Republican Party.⁵⁹ Republicans denounced the Kansas-Nebraska Act as part of a plan to exclude free labor from the western territories and enhance the power of southern enslavers at the expense of northern voters.⁶⁰ On February 23, 1856, Henry attended a lecture on Kansas, where he probably heard arguments against the Kansas-Nebraska Act and accounts of turmoil on the Kansas-Missouri border.⁶¹ When organized groups of anti-slavery settlers moved to Kansas Territory, they came into conflict with pro-slavery residents of Kansas and Missouri. Northern politicians, religious leaders, and newspapers amplified the resulting political unrest and physical violence.⁶²

The newly formed Republican Party tried to attract northern rural young men like Henry.⁶³ Like the Whigs, the Republican Party emphasized the importance of property ownership in enabling a young man to become independent. Like the Know-Nothings, they suggested that a man's financial failure might not be his own fault and could be rectified through access to land in the West. Eric Foner argues that the Republicans appealed to the belief that any man who worked hard and maintained his good character should be able to raise his economic and social status. They claimed that the extension of slavery threatened northern white men's opportunity to achieve manly independence and economic security.⁶⁴ On April 2, Henry complained about his employment as a store clerk: "I shall be glad when I am my own man again. This service is not congenial to my sweet disposition & injures my health."⁶⁵ On April 4, Henry gained the nomination of the township Republican Caucus for the position of School Inspector. The next day, he explained: "Whigs are truly no more; I would willingly take side with fanatics but I must do something and that shall never be with Loco foco Slave owners and extentionists."⁶⁶ With the Whig party no longer an option, Henry chose the Republican Party, whose members included abolitionists, often labeled as fanatics, over the American (Know-Nothing) Party that was supported by former Democrats (derisively called Loco focos), enslavers, and men who wanted to extend slavery to the western territories.⁶⁷ He was receptive to the argument that the extension of slavery in the West would close off opportunities that might otherwise be available to him.

Henry was becoming disillusioned with Harriet as well as with his job and his financial prospects. He described his irritation at Harriet's assertion of independence during a visit from her cousin:

> This morning when I came to breakfast Hattie proposed to take Cynthia to uncle Johns to visit & bring Grandmother home with them & I remonstrated because George had not been out of the stable since last sabbath & I was afraid he might run away with them. Hattie answered me rather unkindly I thought, said there was always an *excuse* to prevent her riding when she proposed to, so I concluded *not* to make any more excuses on that score but as soon as I could swallow my breakfast [I] brought the horse & buggy to the door for them. They are now gone & I trust no accident may happen to them, but I never will offer her another *excuse* of that kind while I live. They arrived at nine oclock this evening *safe*.⁶⁸

Harriet rebuffed Henry's attempt to act as her protector and challenged his assumption that he was better able to handle a spirited horse. Henry complained at the end of July: "I am afraid there is no help for me in the future. I cannot get a situation that will pay better than this nor can I go into business for myself."⁶⁹ The following day, Henry's friend Hurley returned to Schoolcraft as Second Lieutenant Orlando H. Moore, with a US Army salary of sixty-five dollars per month. Henry lamented: "While I have been laboring & aspiring to better times he has done no labor & walked right up the ladder to a round where he is secure from want & which has no objection to my eyes even except the necessity to go wherever and whenever ordered to live as long as his superior officers say. Success to Hurley say I."⁷⁰ A few days later, Henry wrote: "I do not feel very well to day & have the blues the worst way. It seems that everything goes against my ever having an independent home & business that I can hold my head above water and look every man in the face & feel at least as independent as they."⁷¹ Two years earlier, when Hurley was a portrait painter and fiddler, Henry and Harriet had regarded him as irresponsible; now they watched Hurley achieve the recognition and financial security that Henry had labored unsuccessfully to attain.[72]

While Henry monitored his diminishing prospects for success, he became active in the local campaign for the Republican presidential candidate. On June 19, Henry announced: "Got the news of Fremonts nomination as candidate for president upon the Republican ticket. How earnestly we hope he may be elected."[73] In July, Henry traveled to Kalamazoo to consult with the local Republican headquarters. He participated in a meeting of the Fremont club on August 22 to plan a rally in Kalamazoo and attended a pole raising and speeches on August 25 in preparation for the event.[74] Harriet persuaded Henry to take her to the Fremont rally instead of accompanying his male friends. On August 27, he described the event:

> Did not go as I had intended with our banner wagon but as Hattie wanted to go I took her, left Isa with Cynthia and drove very comfortably and got there before the multitude commenced pouring in[:] we stopped upon the corner of Portage & some other street under the shade of some oaks and saw our delegation come up which was over two miles long & then went up near the ground for speaking and attempted to count the number of teams that drove past and after going up to 250 they came pouring in so fast that we gave up in despair.

They retired to the home of Harriet's friends and former colleagues, Mr. and Mrs. Page, who had moved from Maumee to Kalamazoo in 1854 when Mr. Page was appointed Professor of Rhetoric and History at Kalamazoo College.[75] Henry returned to the rally, as he recorded in his diary: "I left Hattie & the horse, went to ground where there were four or five tables spread with the staples of the land[:] bread meat cheese &c. The tables were about 15 rods long and every few rods were set barrels of ice water with tin cups attached. I commenced at one end of a table and ate my way *through*." Harriet returned with the Pages to hear the political speeches. Although women were not eligible to vote, Fremont's presidential campaign encouraged women's participation in parades and rallies.[76] Henry continued: "Mr Lincoln Blair Bingham Bates Jones Kellogg and many other distinguished speakers were there. They occupied four different stands at once and the crowd was so dense at every one of them that we could not listen with much satisfaction. After awhile I found Hattie who had come with Mr Ps family and we wandered about until tired out[:] listened to Mr Bates the longest and liked him much but Lincoln is the man for me."[77] Henry and Harriet heard one of the few speeches Abraham Lincoln, then a relatively unknown politician, gave outside of Illinois.

Lincoln's speech in support of Fremont was transcribed by a reporter and published in the Detroit *Daily Advertiser*. Lincoln framed the Kansas-Nebraska Act as the central issue of the election: "The question is simply this: Shall slavery be into new territories, or not?" Lincoln explained why this question was important to voters in the northern states:

> Have we no interest in the free Territories of the United States—that they should be kept open for the homes of free white people? As our Northern States are growing more and more in wealth and population, we are continually in want of an outlet, through which it may pass out to enrich our country. In this we have an interest—a deep and abiding interest. . . . We stand at once the wonder and admiration of the whole world, and we must enquire what it is that has given us so much prosperity, and we shall understand that to give up that one thing, would be to give up all future prosperity. This cause is that every man can make himself.

Lincoln refuted the claims of southern newspapers that "their slaves are far better off than northern freemen": "What a mistaken view do these men have of Northern laborers! They think that men are always to remain laborers here—but there is no such class. The man who labored for another last year, this year labors for himself, and next year he will hire others to labor for him. These men don't understand when they think in this manner of Northern free labor. When these reasons can be introduced, tell me not that we have no interest in keeping the territories free for the settlement of free laborers." Lincoln continued:

> Slavery is to be made a ruling element in our government. The question can be avoided in but two ways. By the one, we must submit, and allow slavery to triumph, or by the other, we must triumph over the black demon. We have chosen the latter manner. If you of the North wish to get rid of this question, you must decide between these two ways—submit and vote for Buchanan, submit and vote that slavery is a just and good thing, and immediately get rid of the question; or unite with us, and help to triumph.[78]

Lincoln's argument resonated with Henry. Since land in the West would no longer be affordable to men like Henry if slavery were allowed there, it was slavery rather than the conditions of wage labor that stood in the way of the white worker's ability to own his own business or farm.[79]

Campaign events created a sense of belonging to a local group that was part of a larger movement: competition with supporters of a rival political party enhanced the feeling of affinity with like-minded citizens.[80] Henry described the contingent of Democrats that gathered in Schoolcraft to travel to Kalamazoo for their state party convention: "As they passed here to some attempt at a tune by their excuse of a band they presented a dreary, drizzly mournful crowd of 230 including boys of which there were as many as men and girls a goodly number and eleven dogs."[81] The following day, he reported: "Find by various reports that there could not have been more than two thirds as many at the meeting yesterday as at ours and about one third of them were Fremont men."[82] A few days later, Henry wrote: "Took passage aboard a 6 horse waggon with 24 others for Centerville to attend a St. Joseph Co[unty] Republican meeting. We were join[ed] on the road by a delegation & band from Kalamazoo & about 100 horsemen in blue blouses."[83] Henry hoped his work for the party would lead to a political appointment if Fremont won the election.[84] "Wonder if the firm do not intend dispensing with my services whether Fremont is elected or not," he wrote. "Well I do hope he will be whether I get an appointment or not."[85] Henry attended a caucus to select delegates to "send to the representative convention," helped "raise a Republican pole," and heard a speech from the Honorable Mr. Walbridge.[86] A few weeks later Henry attended another Republican lecture "which was as good as I ever heard."[87] Henry submitted his "list of republicans for the poll clerk" two days before the election.[88]

As Election Day approached, the fervor intensified: political gatherings provided entertainment and generated excitement.[89] The day before the election, Henry attended another Republican pole raising, with "167 horsemen in blue denims, band from Kalamazoo and the town litterally crammed with muddy republicans." "All went off right," he wrote. "Father uncle Seneca & [Uncle] Foster & Mr Allen & Underwood gave them martial music all day and in the evening when Mr Walbridge addressed a large audience. The pole is 183 feet above ground & straight."[90] On November 4, Henry described the victory celebration as they serenaded Republican households with tin horns and bells after the local results were reported:

> Election goes off swimmingly. 250 votes poled before noon. We felt sure of 40 majority at night and though we were all tired we were anxious and could not rest. The result was beyond our most sanguine expectations[:] out of 300 votes we polled 82 republican majority. It stormed and the mud was deep but we thought music would not be inappropriate to the occasion & the sound of 40 horns was heard

above the whistle of the wind, and every republican in the village was cheered at his door. It must have shocked our honest pious citizen after it was all over to look back upon themselves with a tin horn stuck in his mouth or a bell in his hand capering about in the mud working every muscle & bone in his frame to keep the *music* up.

The jubilation of the Republicans was premature, however. The day after the election, Henry wrote: "Waiting for news. [A]ll anxious some betting."[91] On November 6, he concluded: "Good news from every county in the state & New York. Pensylvania looks dark. Buchanan will undoubtedly be elected but we beat them bad in the free states." Due to the rain, only about fifty or sixty people attended the Republican oyster supper on November 7, so Henry "had a good time & *plenty* of oysters." On November 10, Henry considered the consequences of the election: "We have given up the contest. Buchanan is no doubt elected. Kansas will probably be a slave state and in the end we shall all have to file in and become slave institutions. The rich will grow richer and the poor God help them." Henry accepted the Republicans' contention that a Buchanan victory would result in the spread of slavery at the expense of poor white workers.[92] Following party rhetoric, Henry identified the institution of slavery as the cause of a growing income inequality among white Americans that threatened his own future prosperity.

While Henry participated in party politics, Harriet took responsibility for the daily care of their daughter. Henry described a series of mishaps when Isa was eighteen months old:

> Remained at home all day in consequence of a series of accidents which commenced late in the morning when I put Isa upon her chair and went below & built a fire. When she was taken off by her mother it was ascertained that I had not removed the nightgown so that as she came off the floor & her person were some daubed. Isa next kick[ed] a little on her mother & she called for some water. I brought it & sat it down by them & Isa kicked it over & the water ran all over the floor & down through the plastering & I ran up with a dipper full of water & fell up stairs & poured all the water on my head & shoulders & so went the whole forenoon.[93]

Henry was willing to take Isa to her "chair" but was not observant or experienced enough to remove her clothing. Henry described a similar incident a few months later: "Was repairing my table this afternoon; had it upside down & was screwing on the top, Isa sat on one leaf watching me. She had

Henry and Isa Smith, daguerreotype, ca. 1857. RHC Photographs P-4660, Stanley Barney Smith Collection, A-88, Archives and Regional History Collections, Zhang Legacy Collections Center, Western Michigan University.

been so intent upon my work that she did not speak upon a subject that was of great importance at that moment, she however said [']Papa tairs['] just as she dropped a *pile* upon the table which gave her mother a dirty job."[94] Although Henry had failed to notice any signs of an impending accident, he assumed the resulting cleaning job was Harriet's responsibility. Henry often took Isa with him as he did his household chores, however, and he took delight in her company. He wrote: "Isa is now the best natured healthiest girl in Schoolcraft. She goes out with me in all kinds of weather every day to feed the chickens &c."[95] A month later, he noted: "Every time I go home I wonder at & feel a thrill of gladness at meeting our own dear, good, healthy, sprightly child. She is the picture of health & I cannot help thinking she is pretty. She is bright anyway."[96] Henry and Harriet took Isa with them when they visited other families, and by her second birthday, she accompanied them to evening gatherings with friends.[97]

After Isa's first birthday, Henry and Harriet participated more frequently in community activities. Henry continued to sing in the Baptist church choir.[98] He and Harriet attended lectures on religion and enjoyed a series of demonstrations of phrenology, where they watched an expert assess their neighbors' characteristics based on the shapes of their heads.[99] Henry occasionally escorted Harriet to larger parties to celebrate weddings and other occasions. Harriet made herself a new dress for one event, finishing it shortly before the party.[100] Henry was apprehensive when Harriet invited fifty guests to a party at their house. After the evening passed without mishap, Henry wrote: "And this I will say, as long as I live as I do now I will never call together so many persons at our home."[101] While Harriet struggled to maintain the social rituals that marked middle-class status, Henry resumed his attendance at social events, sometimes with Harriet and sometimes alone. He "dropped in at the evening performance" of a "circus and menagerie" and occasionally played euchre or whist with friends.[102] More frequently, Henry joined his neighbors in singing or playing the fiddle.[103] Henry noted that he played "for the juveniles to dance" one evening and fiddled a few sets at a ball, where he also danced two sets.[104] Harriet began to accompany Henry to parties with dancing. In November 1856, Henry described a party he attended with Harriet that included card games as well as dancing, for which he played the fiddle.[105]

Looking to the future on New Year's Day in 1857, Henry wrote: "Wonder if in case I see ten or fifteen more I shall be any better off in the worlds gear than I am now." Two weeks later, he considered whether the West would offer better opportunities: "I wish something could be done to mend my future. I feel very uneasy[,] have a western fever. Offer my west woods for $1000.00."[106] As the winter progressed, Henry became even more disheartened about his prospects in Schoolcraft as hopes for attracting a rail line faded. He concluded: "I begin to be discouraged from looking forward to and taking an active part in the speedy reformation of this town. It never will be anything and I believe if we ever get a railroad it will [be] after I am dead & gone."[107] A week later, he wrote: "I feel down in spirits now, and cannot see a clear spot in the distant prospect to set my foot upon if anything should occur by which I should leave here."[108] The following day, Henry noted that he had received a letter from Harriet's father urging them to move to the West. "Wonder if we shall ever be anything or anybody here or any where else," he worried.[109] The previous autumn, Henry's father-in-law had written: "Henrie, are you always a going to stay in Schoolcraft? Why not come out and look at the country, and see if you can't better yourself."[110] A few weeks later, he again suggested that the family move to Illinois. After describing the rapid growth and prosperity of his community, he wrote: "Henrie—why not pick up your duds, and leave that tame lifeless town, though you have been weded to it so long, and come to Illinois, where you may catch the spirit of enterprise, and go ahead as others do?"[111] Harriet also urged Henry to join her family in Illinois. Henry noted in his diary in early March:

> For a month past I have done my own boarding of mornings. [H]ave prepared my own breakfasts, and ate them while wife & babe sleep. Hattie seems to blame me very much for not going west & to Illinois & buying a house here to live in & for buying a small half hog last fall &c &c &c &c &c—When we do go west for that I am determined to do as soon as I can raise the means she may have real trouble enough to keep such superfluities out of her mind. I believe this is not the place for me to live in unless I die soon.[112]

Henry's juxtaposition of his description of cooking his own breakfast with his discussion of Harriet's resentment suggests the discord that had developed between them.

Two weeks later, Henry described a domestic quarrel:

> I did not go to bed last night until after midnight & I feel hard & cross to day and Hattie seems to follow suit with a vengeance. I have been in trouble all day and when I came home in the evening I did not know enough to keep my amiable feelings to myself but must needs get up a family muss that must never be repeated while I live. If I ever feel as I have this evening again I will put out & leave the whole [of] my relatives until I have drilled myself awhile upon the western prairies. I never closed my eyes in sleep until morning had been one or two hours old.[113]

Two days after this argument, Henry and Harriet attended a dance with Harriet's visiting brother, Joseph, and his wife, Mary. Henry wrote:

> Hattie & Mary went to Kalamazoo & I had to wait until after nine oclock for them to get back & be ready. They did not stop for their supper but started off in the mud & we came in just as the company had commenced to dance. Mary is a perfect brick in the ball room and danced harder & more times than any one in the house & quit fresh at about 2 oclock A. M. I had to play most of the time but I danced a few times with her. Hattie did not enjoy it at all. We went home very well satisfied with the party.[114]

As Henry chronicled the growing rift in his marriage, his social activities escalated. During the same month, Henry attended three more parties with dancing, once accompanied by Harriet and Isa.[115] On five evenings in March, Henry joined friends to sing and fiddle at the homes of Mr. Brown and Mr.

Allen. Harriet and Isa accompanied him on one of these occasions, and his sister joined him on another.[116]

When Henry compared himself to more affluent men, he felt ashamed of his occupation as a clerk in a store: "John Proctor left in the stage this evening. He is doing well and when I look upon him I feel ashamed that I am as I am. I feel discouraged and when I think how long it will be before I shall be able to enjoy life as I could do in an independent life subject to no controll from my fellow men and left to follow an honorable calling by myself my gizzard drops down into the seat of my pants & I just naturally *give in*."[117] Two weeks later, Henry again complained of his employment and expressed his desire to work for himself: "I wish I was in some situation that I could enjoy the peace of my own home & business & live like other men and not be bamboozled about like a tame coon kept for my owner to vent his spleen upon."[118] Henry felt trapped in a job without potential for advancement in salary or responsibility. He found the daily interactions of clerk and customer a constant reminder of his failure to meet ideals of masculinity. Rotundo argues that because merchants found negotiating with female customers to be demeaning, they hired salesmen to replace them in this activity.[119] Brian Luskey notes that clerks in dry goods stores were ridiculed in the popular press as unmanly because they sold goods to women.[120] Working in a store was appropriate as a point of entry into the workforce, but it did not provide financial security or connote attainment of middle-class status, adulthood, or manliness.

Lacking the financial capital to acquire an established farm or business in Schoolcraft, the only way Henry could see to improve his situation was the one suggested by Republican politicians: purchasing land on the western frontier. When several men left Schoolcraft for Nebraska, Henry wrote: "How I wish I were one of the crowd."[121] Three weeks later, Henry again mentioned that he longed for the West.[122] Two days later, Henry expressed his dismay that Harriet was not at home to prepare his supper: "Came home to supper, found Hattie gone & the house full of company. I at first thought to take tea with them but as more visitors came thicker & faster I gave in discouraged & went to Helens in hopes [of] find[ing] her at tea but she was alone, had been to tea about an hour, & all the supper I got was a piece of dry bread & butter."[123] The detail with which Henry elaborated this account suggests that Harriet's unexplained absence reflected the growing tension between them. Less than two months earlier, Henry had complained that he had been cooking his own breakfast for the preceding month. The day after he missed his supper, Henry anticipated that the "western fever" might carry him off. "I told Hattie to make me six shirts to use upon such an occasion," he wrote.[124] If Henry could not force Harriet to cook his meals, he could at least tell her to make shirts for him. Henry saw the West as a chance to escape from his family and his job, a route taken by more than a few husbands in the nineteenth century.[125] Unhappy at work and at home, and with hopes for a political solution to his problems dashed, within three days, Henry decided to head west with his former employer, Rush Cobb, who had sold his interest in the store.[126]

Henry's decision to relocate to the West can be traced through multiple interwoven strands of cultural influences, economic factors, political rhetoric, gender and social class expectations, interpersonal relationships, and personal inclinations. This very personal decision that was integrally related to Henry's sense of self and his most intimate relationships was also the same decision reached by many young men of his generation. It seemed to provide a solution to the insurmountable gap between middle-class cultural expectations and the actual experiences of men like Henry. Ideals of manliness presented in the popular culture of the era, reinforced by the rhetoric of political parties and articulated in sermons and lectures, suggested that any diligent man could achieve financial success. The unspoken premise of these constructs of manhood was that the generic man they represented was understood to be white. Whiteness intersected with categories of gender and social class, providing the prerequisite for citizenship, economic autonomy, and spatial mobility. Autonomy in the workplace promised a sense of personal identity as well as manhood: a real man was in control of himself at work as well as at home. His exertion in his employment made possible his daily escape from the workplace to the intimacy of his family. The West held out the promise of a home in which a man could enjoy the family life his independent labor would support. A young white man heading west could assert his independence and his masculinity at the same time; he would hope to find both domestic happiness and material success. Personal experiences of economic failure, hardship, and lack of respect in one's community could provide a push to look for a new start in life: cultural ideals of manliness, independence, and domestic tranquility represented by racialized images of the West suggested a locale in which such an ideal life could be found.

Henry's expectations of financial success, like those of many young white men, had been encouraged by earlier Whig rhetoric and then been transposed to the West by the Know-Nothings and Republicans. Henry provided a prime target for the arguments of politicians who played on the fears and hopes of young white men struggling to meet standards of masculinity and respectability. Anne C. Rose notes that many men like Henry became involved in national parties from the 1840s through the 1890s. She describes the importance of political parties in generating interest at the local level, involving citizens in parades and clubs that featured "costuming, cheering, and marching." Rose argues that while these "visible dramas of commitment offered immediate excitement" and generated a sense of participation in the political process, they led to few tangible results.[127] Such participation may have had little impact on the course of national policy, but it may have influenced the personal decisions men like Henry made as they determined the direction of their occupational and family lives. Even if Henry's political activities did not affect national policy, they provided him with a sense of personal efficacy and enabled him to perceive his own situation as dependent in part on political and economic systems rather than as the result only of his individual character and diligence. Political rhetoric also may have provided Henry with models of behavior and suggested solutions to his personal difficulties, first through his work and leisure habits and later through relocation to the West.

This cultural framework for individual decisions intersected with personal relationships. Harriet apparently joined her father in urging Henry to move west in order to better meet his responsibility to support his family. The family's relocation in Illinois would have reunited Harriet with her own parents and brother while leaving Henry's relatives behind, a factor that may have influenced both her desire to move there and Henry's reluctance. The expectations Harriet and her father held about gender and social class influenced their assumptions about Henry's obligations as a husband and father. As Harriet had feared, the disagreements over leisure activities that had haunted the couple's courtship resurfaced after their marriage. When the tension between them escalated, both domestic tasks and community entertainment became sites of conflict. Cooking, driving the wagon, hosting a party, and dancing all took on meaning as points of negotiation of gender roles, moral principles, and social status. The discord that was developing between Harriet and Henry probably made the thought of a temporary separation while Henry established a new home bearable or even desirable. When Henry saw an opportunity to head west with his employer, some of the uncertainty and loneliness were removed from the prospect, and the scales tipped in favor of relocation. In the final instance, the decision was his to make. Legal obligation, as well as social pressure, compelled Harriet to acquiesce to Henry's choice of location. Harriet and her father could advise and chastise, but Henry ultimately determined where the family would live. Dissatisfied with his life at home and at work and disillusioned about the possibility of changing society through political participation, Henry voted with his feet when he set off for "the western prairie."

Chapter Four

YANKEES AND PIONEERS

"How shall we manage without *Webster's Large Dictionary*?"[1]

When Henry's employer, Rush Cobb, made plans to purchase a farm in Missouri, he offered to help Henry buy farmland nearby with the understanding that Henry, who was eleven years younger and an experienced farmer, would help the forty-one-year-old widower establish a farm. Delamore Duncan, a fifty-two-year-old merchant with several business ventures in Michigan, and his twenty-one-year-old nephew, Lee Clark, would accompany them to Missouri to look for farmland. Although Henry was reluctant to settle in a state that allowed slavery, he was reassured by the ease of rail travel between Kalamazoo and St. Louis and by the presence of several cousins in St. Louis and Harriet's oldest brother in Palmyra. Rush and Henry traveled by rail from Kalamazoo to Chicago, where they boarded a train to Quincy, Illinois, on the banks of the Mississippi River. They crossed the Mississippi by boat, landing downstream in Hannibal, Missouri, and took the train fourteen miles northwest to Palmyra, where they spent a few days with Henry's sister-in-law while they waited for Duncan and Lee to join them.[2] Here, Henry first encountered slavery: he learned that Lizzie hired out four or five "chattels" she had inherited, earning $80 to $200 annually for a skilled young man. Henry was unimpressed with Palmyra, which he found dirty, and with unfamiliar food, including sauerkraut, rice, and brown sugar. He discovered that the construction of a rail line that would cross Missouri from Hannibal west to St. Joseph had driven up the price of land in the previous year.[3]

After they purchased a covered wagon and horses, the four men set off across the state in search of less expensive farmland. They camped in the wagon at night, and Henry supplemented the food they bought from farmers by hunting rabbits and prairie chickens to cook over an open fire. As they headed west through Shelby, Macon, and Linn counties, Henry appreciated the rich soil and abundance of mules and horses but was discouraged by the price of land at twelve dollars per acre. The men decided to head south to find more affordable farms away from the route of the railroad but discovered that land was even more expensive as they approached the Missouri River.[4] After they were ferried across to Saline County, Henry admired the beautiful "boundless prairies." He was surprised to see prosperous farms with the owner's house and "a little log cabin" for enslaved workers surrounded by thousands of acres of cultivated land, "as though every one was afraid he would have a neighbor." Old orchards on "land as wild as the plains" indicated to Henry that farmers had depleted the soil and cleared new fields, an agricultural practice that Republican politicians criticized as a wasteful consequence of slavery.[5] Henry was accustomed to the New England pattern of land use employed in Schoolcraft, where prosperous farmers lived in villages and cultivated small outlying fields, rotating crops to replenish the soil.[6] "I realize now more than ever that we are a poor pair and if we can get a quiet humble home that suits us I shall feel satisfied that I am better off than the many wealthy ones about us," he wrote Harriet.[7]

Diane Mutti Burke, Douglas Hurt, and other historians have examined the antebellum cultural practices of this agricultural region later known as Little Dixie. In the early nineteenth century, farmers from Kentucky, Tennessee, and Virginia settled in the fertile counties bordering the Missouri River. Many of these households included a few enslaved men and women who worked in the fields and houses alongside the farmer and his family. In contrast to cotton plantations of the Deep South with twenty or more slaves, these Missouri farmers raised livestock and grew produce to feed their households in addition to growing hemp or tobacco, marketable crops that required less labor than cotton.[8] Riverboats delivered manufactured products from St. Louis and northeastern states and transported hemp rope made in local ropewalks to southern plantations, where it was used to tie cotton bales for shipment to northern textile factories. Like other prosperous farmers of the Midwest, farmers in Little Dixie gradually replaced their log cabins with houses of clapboard or brick, purchased household furnishings from eastern manufacturers, and created literary and agricultural societies. They relied on kinship and neighborhood social networks for mutual assistance but valued the independence they gained by owning productive farmland, minimizing debt, and maintaining access to markets for their crops.[9] Unlike farmers in other Midwestern states, they shared with southern plantation owners an understanding that their prosperity depended on the labor of enslaved men, women, and children.[10]

Henry and his companions continued south to Benton County, where Rush and Duncan visited the General Land Office in Warsaw to examine the listings of public domain land the federal government offered for sale at $1.25 or less per acre. When they discovered that most of the land in the Warsaw District had already been sold, they headed further south to the Springfield District land office in Greene County.[11] As they traveled through Hickory and Polk counties, where slavery was less widespread, Henry observed a more familiar landscape with more "human looking settlements." Although Henry had not intended to move so far south, he pictured his family living happily in houses they passed. The land office in Springfield, like the one in Warsaw, was crowded with men rushing to purchase land with cash or land warrants. Henry noted that despite the "land excitement," a "great deal of land" was still available in the Springfield District.[12] From May through November, the Springfield Land Office sold more acreage than in any of its previous twenty years of operation.[13] As prices of existing farms increased, potential buyers considered public domain land as an affordable route to farm ownership. They competed with speculators who invested in land to sell at a profit when prices rose. Settlers who had been living on public domain land as squatters also entered claims to maintain possession of the land they were farming. Changes in the Military Bounty Land Warrant program further increased demand. In 1855, additional veterans became eligible for free land, and the lifetime limit each veteran could claim was increased from forty acres to 160 acres. Veterans or their widows could sell their warrants, which purchasers could exchange for land at any federal Land Office. Dealers purchased warrants from veterans across the country at the rate of one hundred dollars for a 160-acre warrant and sold them near busy land offices for about a dollar per acre. Purchasers then exchanged the warrants for government land, otherwise selling for $1.25 per acre.[14]

In Michigan, Henry and his companions had become familiar with federal Land Office procedures. Surveyors divided a territory into survey townships by marking east-west Township Lines at six-mile intervals, intersected at right angles by north-south Range Lines, also set at six-mile intervals, to form a grid of adjacent square townships, each thirty-six square miles in area. A Township number indicates the position of a survey township north or south of an established Base Line, and a Range number indicates its position east or west of a Prime Meridian. Every survey township was divided into six rows of six square sections numbered from one to thirty-six, starting in the township's northeast corner and ending in its southeast corner. Each section was subdivided into 160-acre quarters, which could be subdivided further. This standardized system identified every plot of land regardless of changes in landmarks, boundaries, or place names. Each General Land Office maintained updated maps of every survey township in its district showing what land was offered for sale, along with indications of the terrain, vegetation, water, and soil based on surveyors' field notes.[15] After examining the township maps in Springfield, Duncan identified a promising survey township, T34 R29, in the southeast corner of Vernon County, on Missouri's western border. Although most of Vernon County was covered by the Warsaw land office, its southern row of townships was included in the Springfield Land District in the Ozark region of southern Missouri.[16] This row of townships was the northernmost offered by the Springfield land office, and its prairie terrain resembled southwest Michigan. Heading northwest to Vernon County, the men found that the land met all their needs except that it was "150 miles from any means of getting into the world again," with no prospect of railroad construction.[17]

The four men continued northward, looking for farms for sale, until they reached the Missouri River near Lexington. Here, they took stock of their situation: after more than two weeks of searching, they had not been able to find desirable farms they could afford. Duncan decided to return to Michigan. Rush agreed that affordable land in Missouri was too isolated for profitable farming. Henry remembered the "Texicans" they had seen driving herds of mustangs and mules north through Vernon County. He knew that his father had settled on remote public domain land with partners who provided capital in return for his labor and experience as a merchant. Drawing on the persuasive techniques he had developed as a traveling salesman and his experience in calculating farm profits, Henry proposed a partnership for a stock farm on the land they had identified in Vernon County. Livestock could be driven to California or sold to settlers heading west on one of the trails that began in Independence, Missouri. The proposed westward extension of the rail line that linked Jefferson City to St. Louis would intersect a cattle trail that crossed Vernon County, providing access to eastern markets. Henry, Rush, and Lee formed a partnership with Duncan as an investor. Rush took a stagecoach to Springfield to purchase land, while Lee and Henry drove the wagon back to Vernon County, and Duncan returned to Michigan.[18]

Henry explained to Harriet that their future home was a hundred miles south of the Missouri River and about sixty miles further south than St. Louis. He didn't mention that it was located approximately thirty miles east of the border with Kansas Territory, the site of violent confrontations extensively covered in the northern press. In this region, known as the Osage plains, the foothills of the Ozark Mountains met the edge of the Prairie Peninsula that cut a diagonal swath from southwest Michigan into southwest Missouri. Grasslands interspersed with wooded creek beds formed a familiar landscape with a terrain suitable for stock farming.[19] Henry assured Harriet that the site included the natural resources needed for a successful farm: "good prairie & timber & water & stone."[20] Cattle and hogs grazed on the wild grasses of the unfenced prairie in the summer and fed on acorns in the woodlands in the winter. A prairie extended diagonally through the township from the northeast corner to the southwest corner. A network of spring-fed creeks provided water, and the surrounding woods were a source of timber for building.[21] The terrain and settlement pattern resembled those of Schoolcraft Township in Michigan. Both were tall-grass prairies interspersed with woods, including openings where sparse timber partially shaded a grassy forest floor. Numerous meandering streams and rivers intersected the prairies, but neither region included a navigable waterway. The terrains of both regions had been shaped by the agricultural practices of native tribes who had traded with French fur traders and then with missionaries from the northeast and early settlers from the upland south who also combined subsistence farming with hunting and foraging. Like Schoolcraft, the nearby village of Montevallo was located at a crossroads, creating a local hub for farmers and an intersection for travel between towns. As in western Michigan, roads were wide trails worn by the passage of horses, livestock, and wagon wheels across the prairies between villages and mills, intersecting the numerous streams at shallow crossing points.[22]

Land in the counties along Missouri's western border was offered for sale later than other regions of the state because most had been reserved for local Osage Indians or relocated eastern tribes until they were removed again, this time to Kansas. In 1841, when surveyors subdivided survey township T34 R29 into sections before offering the land for sale, they found only a few isolated settlers living in cabins in the woods, where they grew "bread" corn and enough vegetables to supplement wild game and free-range livestock. William Withers opened a store in the northern end of the township in 1850 near James Ray's blacksmith shop.[23] By the time the southern half of Bates County became Vernon County in 1855, the eastern tier of sections in survey township T34 R29 was already part of Cedar County. The five tiers of sections remaining in Vernon County formed the southeast corner of Montevallo Township.[24] When Henry arrived in 1857, the village of Montevallo included about twenty-five houses. A steam sawmill was located on a nearby stream, and an academy building was under construction. Most residents still farmed small plots of land, many with fewer than twenty acres cultivated, and hogs

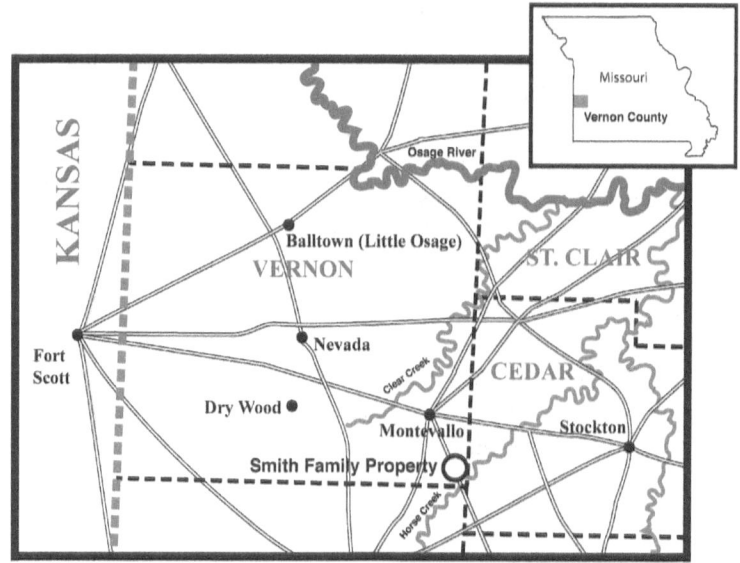

Map of Vernon County, Missouri, based on *Lloyd's Official Map of Missouri, 1861*, Library of Congress. Map drawn by Timothy Motz.

and cattle continued to roam the unfenced prairie. During the land boom of 1857, almost all the remaining land in Montevallo Township was purchased.[25]

A road ran south from the village of Montevallo through Lamar, Carthage, and Neosho into Arkansas and northeast from Montevallo through Osceola and Warsaw to the Missouri River at Boonville. Other roads from Montevallo led north to Lexington, also on the Missouri River, and east through Stockton to Bolivar in central Missouri. Another road angled southeast to Springfield and northwest to the town of Fort Scott, a few miles across the border in Kansas Territory, where a federal military base was established in 1842 to control interactions among white settlers in Missouri, native Osage Indians, and tribes removed from eastern states to Kansas Territory. Fort Scott had served as a trading post where Missouri residents could exchange farm products for cash or manufactured goods. After the fort was closed in 1853, the sutler operated the store as a commercial venture, and in 1857, construction of a surrounding town began.[26] When Vernon County was created in 1855, a centrally located county seat was established. By the summer of 1857, Nevada City included about twenty-five houses, a hotel, a tavern, a store, and the county courthouse. Merchants sold goods shipped from St. Louis on steamboats that navigated the Missouri River to Lexington or Kansas City, where the goods were transferred to wagons hauled by teams of oxen on an eight-day trek to Vernon County.[27]

Henry and his partners selected four adjoining 320-acre half-sections of land roughly forming a rectangle two miles long and one mile wide. They agreed to combine their property and share expenses and labor to create a large stock farm. They purchased 1,160 acres with warrants they bought at 1.085 dollars per acre.[28] Henry contributed his father's Military Bounty Land warrant for 120 acres and borrowed $893 from Rush to cover the rest of his share.[29] He would enter as a full partner by paying interest on the loan and working off some of his debt by building a house and clearing fields.[30] Henry wrote Harriet: "We intend building upon high rolling prairie, mean to build a good tight house . . . about 18 X 24 feet with a porch & next fall we can add another of the same size to it leaving a kitchen & porch between."[31] Ten days later, Henry painted a more detailed picture of the farm he envisioned:

> We have selected a beautiful spot for the house on a little nick of prairie surrounded on the north east and west by woods. The ground decends into the timber each way to a creek about a half mile from the building spot having the favorable ground on the north for an orchard on the east for a garden and on the northeast a barn &c. We aim at having the barn some distance from the house and in a position that will not incommode our noses at any time. The house will front south upon the prairie which is the prettiest sight in this town. We can overlook nearly all the farm and there will be few days that we shall not have a fresh cool breese from off the prairie as south & south east & west winds prevail in the summer.[32]

Henry's subscription to *Moore's Rural New Yorker*, a progressive agricultural magazine, probably influenced his plan. Illustrations of farmhouses from recently published books on rural architecture and floor plans submitted by readers supplemented practical advice on ways to apply concepts of efficiency and innovation in designing houses and farmsteads, as well as in farming practices.[33] As agricultural magazines suggested, Henry planned to situate the house near a garden and orchard, overlooking the farm but upwind from the barn.[34] His description of the setting of the house and the view of the prairie it would provide reflects the emphasis architectural guides placed on the visual impact of a farm as part of a domestic landscape.[35]

Henry felt confident in his ability to design a house and learn how to build it. He intended to integrate the traditional building techniques he would learn from his new neighbors with the design principles illustrated in *Moore's Rural New Yorker*.[36] "We shall no doubt make sad awkward work of it," Henry warned, "but we must all learn to be carpenters, stone masons and practice

Hand-drawn plat map showing section numbers for land purchased by Henry Smith's Missouri partnership. HP Smith account book, 1857, Box 3, Stanley Barney Smith Collection, A-88, Archives and Regional History Collections, Zhang Legacy Collections Center, Western Michigan University.

all the various mechanical trades besides doing our own *house work*."[37] He reassured Harriet: "We are hewing and peeling our logs and intend to make it tight and a log house can be made warmer than an ordinary frame one. Then the first thing I do will be to put grape vines around it and Michigan roses which grow wild here in abundance. We will have it covered with roses & grapes before the logs begin to look old. When we dissolve partnership we can build with brick stone or a frame as we please."[38] Peeling and hewing would remove the bark and square up the sides of the logs to create flat wall surfaces. As Henry envisioned their future home, he painted a picture of a snug log house, covered with grape vines and roses, surrounded by a garden, an orchard, and a few oak trees, and overlooking a rolling prairie bordered by woods. He wrote Harriet: "If you want a front yard large I can have it to contain 320 acres of gentle rolling grass with now & then [an] oak for shade. Imagine your self practicing in the saddle in our front yard."[39] Henry's description embodied the ideal prairie cottage Harriet would recognize from the popular literature she and Henry had read. Henry adopted the rhetorical strategy of authors who downplayed the disadvantages of a log cabin by directing the imagination of readers to the roses covering the walls and the view from the doorway.[40]

The domestic landscape Henry portrayed contrasts with the unkempt yards he had described to Harriet when he arrived in eastern Missouri. A month earlier, he had written: "I would give half a dollar to come into a sweet fresh yankee yard with its shrubbery in full bloom. Here, you will see yards full of lilacs, flowering almond and other beautiful shrubbery and instead of a clean carpet of fresh grass about them you will see bones, slops old rags dead fowls & cats and all manner of filth the fragrance of which has fairly turned my stomach."[41] Harriet had responded that she hoped it would "not be long before you can see a wholesome, yankee yard."[42] A few days later she had promised Henry that when she joined him, she would "make 'the wilderness blossom as the rose'—no dead fowls or cats in *our* yards, but clean, tidy & lovely, we'll excite the envy & surprise of our more careless neighbors."[43] Harriet and Henry understood a "yankee yard" to be sweet, fresh, wholesome, clean, tidy and lovely. In their eyes, a landscaped lawn surrounding a house reflected its owners' diligence, taste, and standards of cleanliness as it demonstrated their control of natural resources. Harriet and Henry assumed that their "careless" Missouri neighbors would recognize the superiority of a Yankee yard and the moral values it represented. They applied the term "Yankee" not only to people from northern states but also to the domestic landscapes they created. They used the word to identify a configuration of attitudes and norms of behavior that were enacted in the practices of everyday life and embodied in clothing and foods, as well as the built environment of houses and yards.

When the issue of whether Kansas would enter the Union as a slave state or a free state dominated the national press and political agenda in the late 1850s, northern journalists collaborated with religious leaders to solicit funds for the New England Emigrant Aid Society in support of anti-slavery settlers in Kansas. Preachers, politicians, newspaper editors, and traveling lecturers quoted reports from journalists and letters from Kansas settlers documenting the impact of northern immigrants on the landscape. They claimed these settlers would foster civilization and morality by building churches, schools, and houses modeled on the Puritan heritage of a traditional New England village, and with Yankee enterprise, they would promote progress and prosperity by constructing railroads and factories.[44] Historian Joanne Pope Melish examines the erasure of slavery and the free Black population from the narrative of New England history, leaving an imagined past with white villages full of white citizens.[45] Geographer Joseph S. Wood demonstrates that the fenced yards and the white frame houses, churches, and schools of an iconic New England village were not the products of a regional Puritan heritage: the style of architecture and landscaping developed when the villages became rural commercial hubs in the second quarter of the nineteenth century.[46] Historian Richard Bushman attributes this antebellum beautification to new middle-class standards of "vernacular gentility" facilitated by the industrial production of affordable objects for household use. He notes that when families in New England villages painted their houses white, purchased carpets and wallpaper, and removed beds from their parlors, they also replaced the trash heaps and tools in their front yards with porches, shrubs, and flowers to display their refinement and respectability.[47] Catherine E. Kelly concludes that a growing provincial middle class in antebellum New England idealized the communities that upper-class residents of coastal cities previously dismissed as cultural backwaters. They praised villages like the ones Harriet remembered from her childhood in northern Vermont as models to be replicated in the West.[48] Richard Stott traces the westward spread of this cultural transformation that equated neatness and decorum with ambition and morality.[49] Harriet's sister wrote Henry that their "little village" in upstate New York was "unusually thriving," with "fine buildings ... being erected—streets paved and shaded, fences built and yards ornamented, gas works set in motion and every nook and corner purified and improved," although they "had a Vigilance Committee organized, with a night police for protection" from increasing burglaries, murder and other crimes.[50] Two years later, Henry's sister described their attempts to "fit up the old homestead" in Schoolcraft: "The front yard is cleared & trimmed, & part of the back yard is in good order.... Mother has cleared & trimmed every one of her flower borders & beds & put them in perfect order. Indeed we are beginning to look quite tidely this spring compared with what we used to.... Father has worked nobly this spring, taking away rubbish, & fixing up everything so patiently. His garden is a perfect pattern of industry & neatness."[51] When Harriet and Henry corresponded about Yankee yards, this work had not yet occurred, and the Smith home fell short of the ideal.

Joseph A. Conforti links the iconic New England village to its fictional Yankee inhabitants. As Conforti suggests, nineteenth-century authors who sympathetically portrayed provincial social life used the setting of the gentrified New England village to domesticate the unruly Yankee of oral tradition and popular drama. During the Revolutionary War, British soldiers ridiculed Americans as ignorant rural Yankee Doodles. American troops embraced the designation of Yankee and used the derogatory British song "Yankee Doodle" to taunt retreating British forces. Shortly after the war, Royall Tyler's play, "The Contrast," introduced a self-proclaimed Yankee character as a confident but naïve servant, a veteran whose rustic clothes, speech, and manners revealed his rural New England upbringing to the more sophisticated but less patriotic New York City residents who followed London fashions. By the 1830s, many American stories and plays featured a provincial New England Yankee, often a peddler or village merchant, as a stock comic character who outwitted competitors and ridiculed pretentious urban society.[52] When the sons of New England farmers traveled through southern and western states selling factory-made products, they were commonly known as "Yankee peddlers." Based on a reputation for "sharp" practices, they were stereotyped as tricksters and vilified as swindlers, but businessmen recognized their ambition and enterprise as attributes of successful entrepreneurs.[53] In 1854, the renowned showman P. T. Barnum claimed all of these Yankee attributes in his popular autobiography dedicated to "The Universal Yankee Nation, of which I am proud to be one." Like his friend Horace Greeley, the *New York Tribune* editor who supported anti-slavery settlers in Kansas, Barnum promoted the superiority of Yankee culture.[54] While New England villages were rooted in a geographic location, Yankees were mobile, and the markers of Yankee culture were portable. By the 1850s, former residents of New England villages and farms populated the states bordering the Great Lakes. When they encountered settlers from the rural upland South, their regional differences in customs and attitudes outweighed the earlier distinction between rural Yankees and urban East Coast residents. Journalists and politicians referred to everyone with New England ancestry as Yankees, and many northerners proudly embraced the designation.[55] By 1857, New England and the region bordering the Great Lakes had become the Yankee North, and Harriet and Henry began to regard themselves as Yankees.[56]

When Henry traveled through Indiana in 1852 selling pumps and farm equipment, he contrasted a town inhabited by "nothing but hoosiers," where he "did not try to sell anything," to nearby Terre Haute, "one of the most driving places for business in the state," with "some few Yankees" whose orders for goods kept him busy all afternoon.[57] The stereotyped rural Missouri Puke, like his Indiana counterpart, the Hoosier, provided a convenient rhetorical foil to contrast with the northern Yankee settler.[58] By simplifying and exaggerating cultural distinctions, and by assigning moral values to styles of clothing, housing, and leisure, journalists provided concrete images that appeared to represent opposing ideologies. Henry's first impressions of Missouri reflected newspaper accounts he had read in Michigan. He was relieved not to encounter "ruffians" but disappointed by the absence of "energetic Yankees."[59] Northern journalists described rural Missouri settlers from the upland South as remnants of a more primitive stage of civilization who rejected Yankee values of cleanliness, self-improvement, and technological progress.[60] Soon after he arrived in Missouri, Henry lamented: "It is a shame that the inhabitants are not more civilized when they have everything at hand to live neatly and happily."⁶¹ Henry assured Harriet that he did not expect her to drink the "surface water which is used by these shiftless pukes all over the state" or live in one of the "log houses without windows except such as are made by large cracks between the unchinked logs."⁶² He described the clothing worn by children in Montevallo: "About all of our neighbors dress their children in a long shirt drawn about the neck like Isa['s] night gowns and nature supplies all other clothes. Some of these children wear one shirt from the time it is put on new till it drops off worn out."⁶³ Henry commented on the speech patterns he heard in southwest Missouri, joking to Harriet: "Tell my creditors that I will pay them soon 'I reckon.' That 'I allow to put in right smart of corn' a patch of wheat & a heap of potatoes. There will also be 'a smart chance' of stock for sale here next fall I reckon."⁶⁴ He advised Harriet that although there were no carriages "every lady has her horse" so she "must learn to ride a little."⁶⁵ He reassured her that he did not expect her to follow the example of local women in "milking the cows, making garden, howing potatoes and marketing," however.⁶⁶

As Henry became acquainted with his new neighbors in Montevallo, he struggled to avoid using the derogatory vocabulary of northern journalists to describe the people who befriended him. The term "pioneer" provided a more positive description of the Missouri settlers who were often labeled as "squatters" or "Pukes."⁶⁷ Henry warned Harriet that he knew of no neighbors in Montevallo "like our friends at home." They are "all pioneers though a well meaning kind people," he continued.⁶⁸ "Pioneer" had become part of a lexicon that Allan Kulikoff describes as the "contested languages of rural class."⁶⁹ During Congressional discussions of land policy in 1838, Democrats applied the positive term "pioneer" to the initial white settlers who moved into frontier territory before the government offered land for sale.⁷⁰ Henry's qualification of "pioneers" with the phrase "though a well meaning kind people" suggests that he and Harriet understood the term as a euphemism for farmers who followed traditional agricultural practices and shared their resources and labor to maintain a self-sufficient community. Henry reported that his new neighbors made no attempt to increase their wealth and were uninterested in material possessions or civic improvements such as railroads. He explained to Harriet: "They are not *sleepy*, just lazy enough to get together and whittle & gossip in the shade, or drink whiskey & jump & wrestle. All [that] ails them is that they are constitutionally afraid of work."⁷¹ According to northern rhetoric, whether these settlers were called "pioneers" or "Pukes," hard-working Yankees were destined to replace them.⁷²

Henry assured Harriet that they were in the vanguard of a wave of Yankee settlers. Not only would these new settlers be more congenial neighbors with familiar forms of food, clothing, houses, and yards; they would encourage the development of roads and railroads and promote habits of industry and standards of cleanliness. When Henry first described the site of their future home, he reassured Harriet that "every day brings new comers and allmost all from northern states." "This tier of counties," he continued, "is being settled fast by northern men and we may have a railroad here some day."[73] Two weeks later, Henry wrote that he hoped to "see *yankees* doing as we are for the *land* is worthy of better owners."[74] "Every *white* settler that has any enterprize in him drives away at least three of the old ones," Henry informed Harriet, "and I was told by our land agent in Springfield that if we wished to get rid of them *entirely*, to call a *rail road meeting* and it would scare them all away." Henry's descriptions of his neighbors focused on their backcountry customs rather than their southern origins. He assured Harriet that some local residents from southern states, like the Montevallo postmaster, William Withers, welcomed Yankees and shared their values. Withers proudly showed Henry his "new *yankee* house as he calls it." Henry wrote: "Mr Withers, the P. M., the merchant, miller, land agent and every thing in this vicinity is a very intelligent man, looks & acts like a yankee and is very anxious to get a yankee neighborhood here."[75] Henry assumed that Yankee settlers would outnumber pioneers from the backcountry upland South, as they had in Michigan, and join with like-minded southern settlers to establish infrastructures of transportation, communication, and education that would support a market-based agricultural economy.[76] He assured Harriet that this process was underway. Mail service had recently been established, citizens held weekly meetings in the village, and an academy was under construction.[77]

Harriet responded apprehensively to the news that Henry had bought property in Montevallo. "My own dearest and best husband," she wrote. "I am content to go with *you* a 'hundred & fifty miles out of the world' even, if it is for the best & I don't doubt for one moment your judgment in the selection, though I could have wished a home nearer the center of civilization & not so far *south*." Harriet's emphasis on her trust in Henry's judgment and her willingness to join him anywhere underlined the responsibility he had assumed for their future happiness. Harriet clearly implied that she would have made a different decision. After she received Henry's letter describing his plans for the farm, Harriet raised more specific concerns:

> Are you making general improvements on the land as a whole & is the site for your house liable to be given up to any of *your firm*? If that is

so you know we should not of course have any pleasure in little private improvements nor could we feel that we even had shares. How is it about the house—the other part I suppose is undivided but do you not choose your *own* building spot? I want you to please remember that when I come I shall wish to paper our cabin, & can it be roughly plastered overhead without much expense?[78]

Harriet's remarks reminded Henry that his precarious position in the partnership meant that they would not actually own the house he was building. She nonetheless insisted on the papered walls and plastered ceiling that would distinguish the house of a middle-class Yankee family from the rough log cabins of their neighbors. The modes of clothing, housing, and transportation that Henry described represented more than regional variations: they signified fundamental distinctions of social class. The rituals of genteel society to which Harriet aspired required appropriate clothing, a carriage, and a house with specialized rooms. These material goods measured and displayed economic status, knowledge of current styles, and acceptance of codes of behavior that stressed self-discipline and hid evidence of labor. Even in a modest log farmhouse, Harriet hoped to create a version of the wallpapered parlor that denoted middle-class status.[79]

The following day, Harriet added that she intended to bring their rocking chairs and other essential furniture: "Dear Henrie can we ever sit down again & read by our own fireside? You must not say that we can't move our principle articles of furniture for how can we get along without them there & we cannot afford to give away here & buy again there—if we could sell the table, give mother the chairs all but the rocking chairs, I think we might box the rest & take them for we should need them *so much*."[80] Reading together in comfortable chairs in front of the fireplace was central to Harriet's ideal of family life. The consumption of literature and the consumption of objects worked in tandem to script gendered and racialized middle-class behavior. Literature assigned meaning to objects and provided directions for their use in social situations, while household furnishings created a setting for reading.[81] Chairs played a prominent role in the performance of class and gender. Together with clothing, they facilitated and limited posture and movements. Their design and placement structured interactions among family members as well as guests.[82] Reading and rocking chairs were bound together in the creation of domestic intimacy. Harriet wanted to rebuild in Missouri the social and intellectual life she enjoyed in Michigan. She asked: "Henrie how shall we manage without Websters Large Dictionary? I expect we shall miss a great many things. I only hope to be able to live so that we shall not travel backward in customs and manners. You and I are as you say too much influenced by external circumstances, but we will try and do our duty."[83] The dictionary represented knowledge, literacy, and culture. It was the repository of authority on the standardized language usage shared by a literate public. The dictionary enabled Harriet and Henry to read books and articles with unfamiliar vocabulary and avoid errors in their own writing. Leaving the dictionary behind reminded Harriet of the difficulty of maintaining genteel "customs and manners" in their new surroundings. Echoing the rhetoric of the northern press, Harriet worried that she and Henry might slide backward on the scale of civilization to join their pioneer neighbors.[84]

Henry argued that their prospects for financial independence and a home of their own were better in Missouri than in Michigan. "I think I am doing better towards making myself and family a competence than I ever was before," he wrote Harriet. Henry assured his future brother-in-law: "With regard to my location & business here if I am not mistaken nothing short of mismanagement can produce a failure."[85] He reminded Harriet of their limited options: "And now when you are mistress of the log house you will know which is preferable a *farmers* wife with a log home or a clerks wife with no home at all or the remotest prospect of having one." A week later, he responded to Harriet's misgivings. "I think it will be much better for us 10 years hence," he explained. "Schoolcraft is a *poor place for a poor man with a family*."[86] Henry assured Harriet that in Missouri, his hard work would pay a reward: "You may thank your stars now you have made such a bad bargain and married a *poor fiddler*, that I am able to work."[87] Henry looked forward to spending more time with his family than the long hours of a clerk allowed. He realized why his new neighbors sat idle during the middle of the day. Henry and his partners rested in the wagon during the hot afternoons, reading Shakespeare and playing backgammon. He explained to Harriet: "The sun pours down in the middle of the day as it never does in Mich[igan] and we have found out that it is not judicious for us to work much after 10 oclock in the morning except in the evening. Every day we have been here however we have had the cool breeze and I often imagine how we could enjoy our home at such times. I will not be obliged to be at the store. The only trouble will be that I shall be a little too constant."[88] Annette Kolodny notes that in popular literature, the western prairie home represented a self-sufficient household untainted by industrialization, where a father could spend time with his children.[89]

Borrowing the vocabulary of authors who praised the virtues of the western prairie home, Harriet reassured Henry: "Will there not be society enough in our own household—are you not going to be with us much more—I shall not be *lonely*—there will be enough to occupy head heart & hands & what would there be left for 'society.'"[90] "Henry," she wrote in another letter, "I am thankful you will take us away from here—I feel as though among strangers & away from the children of this village we can guard our precious treasure more surely."[91] Several weeks later, Harriet again considered the advantages of removing their daughter from the influence of their neighbors and Henry's family in Schoolcraft, "I look forward with a sigh of relief to the time when I can draw our child wholly within the influence of home—our home.... With you and Isa every moment passed together is far sweeter, to me, than hours amid the gayest crowds.... Give me my husband, my child & *home* and I'll try to be contented. When shall we all gather around our own fireside?"[92] As she envisioned her future home, Harriet reverted to the theatrical style she had used earlier to imagine herself as a wife. Phrases authors employed to idealize motherhood and domesticity helped Harriet convince herself that her household responsibilities would "occupy head, heart & hands," although her ambivalent feelings emerged as she promised to "try to be contented" when Henry took her "away from here" to live "among strangers." Books and magazines warned readers that a home should protect children from harmful influences. A small cottage surrounded by a fenced yard would provide privacy and create a restful refuge for a family.[93] Harriet and Henry subscribed to *Harper's New Monthly Magazine*, which published an editorial entitled "Can We Improve Our Domestic Life?" a few weeks before Henry left for Missouri. The author advised that "married life demands, with the force of an instinct, a home for itself" with "a table, a fireside, a pleasant porch, shady walks, cheerful flowers, that you can call your own."[94] Harriet could claim a moral duty as a wife and mother to insist on a house of their own, with a landscaped yard and furniture for reading by the hearth. Shortly before Henry left Schoolcraft, he probably saw an illustrated article on the front page of the April 4 issue of *Moore's Rural New Yorker* featuring a farmhouse for "our friends on the prairies of the west." The "Cottage of One Story" from the 1856 architectural design book *Village and Farm Cottages* exemplifies the Yankee architectural preferences of the Michigan prairie community of Schoolcraft.[95] The wood-frame house is divided into several rooms, including a parlor, kitchen, and two bedrooms. Shrubs and vines surround large windows overlooking children playing under a tree on a fenced lawn.

In Missouri, Henry struggled to translate the abstract ideal of a prairie cottage into a workable house plan that met Harriet's expectations. As Henry observed, settlers in southwest Missouri preferred a log house with a traditional southern dog-trot floor plan consisting of two square or rectangular single-story one-room structures connected by a covered porch, with a kitchen in a separate structure or lean-to addition. Rooms were not

"A Cottage of One Story," illustration and floor plan, *Moore's Rural New Yorker* 8, no. 14 (April 4, 1857): 1.

differentiated by function, and a dirt yard was used for household work and socializing.[96] As he began building, Henry simplified his design and adapted it to the terrain. He used conventions of architectural drawing to convey how he would combine Yankee room divisions with the traditional building techniques and dog-trot house form popular in southwest Missouri. In early

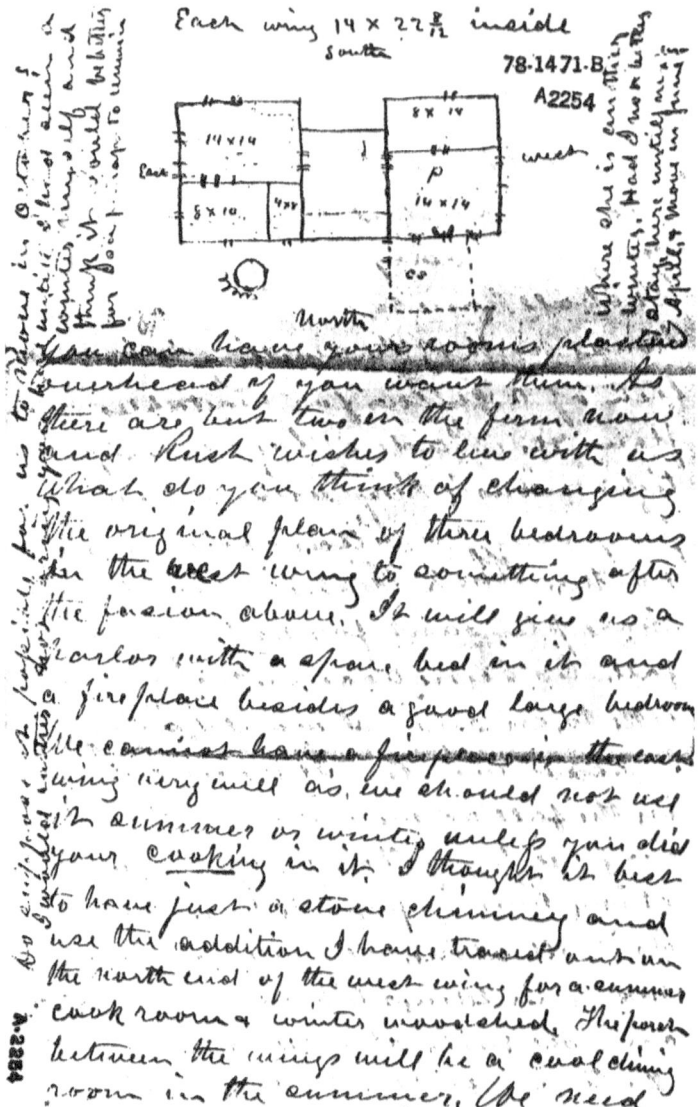

Letter from Henry Smith in Montevallo, Missouri, to Harriet Smith in Schoolcraft, Michigan, with sketch of floor plan, August 2, 1857. Stanley Barney Smith Collection, A-88, Archives and Regional History Collections, Zhang Legacy Collections Center, Western Michigan University.

July, Lee had sold his partnership shares to Rush and returned to Michigan. "As there are but two in the firm now and Rush wishes to live with us what do you think of changing the original plan of three bedrooms in the west wing to something after the fasion above," Henry wrote Harriet in August.

"It will give us a parlor with a spare bed in it and a fireplace besides a good large bedroom." Stairs would lead to "chambers" under the roof for storage and "sleeping, in emergencies." "The porch between the wings will be a cool dining room in the summer," he pointed out. A lean-to shed would serve as both "a summer cook room & winter woodshed."[97] Like a parlor, a dining room signified middle-class domesticity. It provided the setting for displaying the utensils and the table manners that would transform eating into a civilizing social ritual.[98] By labeling the open porch as a summer dining room and designating the shed as a summer kitchen, Henry tried to maintain a Yankee distinction between outside and inside while adapting to the local climate and customs. While the exterior of the house would conform to neighbors' expectations, Henry deferred to Harriet in the choice of interior decor, assuring her that the ceiling could be plastered and the floor carpeted.[99]

Henry provided a list of kitchen utensils he and Rush had on hand, including kettles, frying pans, dishes, silverware, and containers for tea, condiments, milk, butter, bread, sugar, nutmeg, and salt. "In short we have more tools, dishes &c than we have room for," he wrote. "We complain of nothing but the scarsity of eatables."[100] It would take at least a year to clear the land and raise crops and several years for the eighty-two apple trees they planted to bear fruit. Henry warned Harriet: "There is absolutely nothing here that makes our old home so pleasant to us. I have not seen a currant bush since I have been in this state and but few of the neighbors know what they are. We shall have *every thing* to bring with us. What will Isa do next summer without fruit from the garden & orchard." A few weeks later, Henry again expressed concern about how Harriet and Isa would adjust to local food: "How can you live without potatoes? What kind of a *live* would you make of it upon ham & corn bread alone? I have had nothing but bread & butter this summer except upon a few occasions. They *say* there is fruit in abundance within 60 miles of us & what we would call the necessaries of life besides, which I hope is true so that I can get potatoes & apples."[101] Henry asked Harriet to save asparagus seed "and every other choice seed Father has on the farm, even to lima beans" and suggested bringing "currant slips, strawberry vines, grape cuttings &c" to transplant in Missouri.[102]

Throughout July and August, Henry prepared logs for the house. He chopped down trees and removed branches with an axe, used horses to drag the logs to the building site, cut logs to the correct length for each wall, prepared sleepers to form the base for the log walls, and borrowed a broad axe to hew the logs, removing the bark and creating flat sides.[103] On August 22, Henry attended a log house raising, where he "learned how they do such things."[104] He explained to Harriet: "The logs were cut the right length and hauled upon the ground and we went to work to make a house out of the confused pile. One man with an axe stood upon each corner to cut the notches &c as fast as the rest of us raised up the logs.... *We* would put up two logs and then drink around until they were ready for two more." After a "sumptuous dinner" and competitions in jumping, running, and rock throwing, the event concluded with a horse race.[105] When Henry's neighbors helped him raise the walls of his house a month later, he treated them to dinner at the Montevallo public house.[106] In October, Henry had lumber sawn into boards. He raised the roof rafters, covered them with sheeting, and attached wood shingles to make the roof waterproof. On the two gable ends, he attached boards to cover the triangular space between the log sides and the roof. He borrowed a crosscut saw to cut openings for the windows and doors and remove the protruding ends of logs at the notched corners. Rush's health had declined during the summer, leaving Henry with the heavy work of clearing the land, building fences to protect crops from neighbors' livestock, and erecting a henhouse to serve as a temporary home. Henry and Rush were surprised to discover how difficult it was to hire workers. The availability of inexpensive land provided an alternative to working for wages, while the institution of slavery and the practice of hiring enslaved men for farm labor stigmatized white men who worked as farmhands.[107]

Henry entertained Harriet with sketches of colorful local residents, highlighting the ways they fit the stereotype depicted by northern journalists. He described the man living on an adjoining farm:

> Our nearest neighbor *Mr Brown* must enjoy this rain vastly as he has moved out of his house into open air without any shelter so much as a tent to cover his large family, to give room to his *race horse*. Mr B is a good honest member of the Baptist church but he has a race on hand and thinks the horse must have a stable to be fitted in though his family do live out doors for a few weeks. Mr B. has lived here 18 years and is now very poor. In a few years he will be in Texas or California with his wife & children & dogs, & horse & gun.[108]

When Henry attended a district school meeting, he discovered that he had been elected unanimously as trustee. One of three other literate men in the district applied for a teaching position, promising to "teech authografy, reading & wrighting for thre dollers per scholler or twenty dollers a month," keep good order, and teach good "morrils." Henry was faced with a dilemma: "He told me it was my duty to examine him and if he had a good moral character and I thought he could keep good order and his price was low enough to give him a certificate. The responsibility of my position came with a crushing weight upon devoted head & shoulders and for a moment made me irresolute but I *rallied* thought of my duty to my constituents, . . . told my wondering friends I would take the school laws home with me & post myself & meet my fellow officers next Tuesday." Henry wrote Harriet that he had "created a *sensation*" by reading a chapter of the document to his neighbors, one of whom asked him "to read to them a large show bill of some circus company which he had papered his house walls with."[109] Henry adopted the tone of an author entertaining a literate audience with humorous descriptions of ignorant rural residents, but Harriet probably found these accounts of her future neighbors more disconcerting than amusing.

Despite the position of superiority Henry assumed in his anecdotes, he recognized that many of his neighbors shared his ideals of literacy and self-improvement. After describing his illiterate neighbors, Henry added: "There is scarsely a man in our town of this class who is not anxious to become *somebody* and they all wish to have their children taught to read & write."[110] Henry appreciated the generosity of his neighbors and respected their resourcefulness. "I have only to ask any favor that can be granted & it is given," he wrote. "We partly subsist now upon kindness, for all the milk we use and garden [produce] (which by the way is very limited in variety) is given us by the neighbors."[111] Henry wrote:

> I have just received a call from our nearest neighbor and family Mr & Mrs Boyd and six little Boyds. She does our baking & washing &c besides attending to her own household duties hoing corn pulling flax making garden milking & etcs of the dairy included. Her husband is a kind, easy, sensible sort, perfectly honest & one of natures choice men minus the knowledge of reading & writing. They drove up in their schooner minus the covering with the children' heads sticking up between the bows, on their way to the *city* to meeting and invited me to go but I . . . had to forego the pleasure.[112]

Even the young "border ruffians" who "drink, fight, run horses" elicited Henry's admiration. He wrote Harriet: "It is a wild novel sight to see a party of ruffians mounted upon their wild haggard looking steeds, their spanish saddles & bridles & lariats, tall gaunt wild long haird men full of health & vigor, always ready to *shoot* when insulted but no match for the *pioneer yankee* at anything except to undergo privations. They are pests yet I like them an hundred times better than your *respectable* young blades that prowl about in good society." Henry realized that some of his neighbors preferred a frontier community and intended to move further west when new settlers arrived. John Brown offered to sell Henry his land and stock because he was "*afraid they will build a rail road here* & 'spile the beauty of the country.'" Henry noted that Brown, the horse-racer he described a week later as "very poor," owned "2 good cows, 25 hogs, 11 acres of the best corn I ever saw," and 120 acres of land. The arrival of a railroad that would connect the community to the network of a market economy was a signal to pioneers that it was time to sell their land and move further west, where they would again clear land to sell at a profit.[113] They "never stay in a place longer than the wild game and do not wish for any more than they have in the way of mind or goods & chattels," Henry explained.[114]

Henry expected that the northern settlers who would populate Missouri would eliminate slavery, as previous generations of voters had done in northern states.[115] He reported to his future brother-in-law: "The *only* objection I find as yet is its distance from home, & slaves yet we hope both will be obviated ere many years pass over our heads."[116] Three years later, fewer than five percent of Vernon County households included enslaved individuals, with an average of two people enslaved in each of those households. Three households in Montevallo Township each held two enslaved people. Five held one enslaved person: two of these slaveholders, an orphaned twelve-year-old girl and a Montevallo village storekeeper, lived in Henry's survey township.[117] Henry assured Harriet that many current residents opposed slavery: "My friend Withers says that if a vote could be taken tomorrow this state would declair herself *free*. Every body that I have talked with about it seems to look forward *anxiously* to the day when we shall be a free state. Is not that encouraging? This feeling gains ground & this tier of counties to Iowa is being settled by *free men* too." Henry justified his decision to settle in a state that allowed slavery by suggesting that he could help to bring emancipation as well as literacy, temperance, a work ethic, and technological improvements to Missouri. "Truly this is a great field to labor in," he wrote Harriet, using a metaphor she would recognize as the daughter of a Baptist frontier missionary. "Another thing cheers me; every barbarian of us is ready to lift the voice of freedom and anxiously await the time when it is judicious to act," Henry continued.[118]

Like many Midwesterners, however, Henry envisioned an ideal community populated only by white residents.[119] When Henry met slaveholders from Greene County looking for a missing mule and three enslaved men, he wrote Harriet that he hoped the men would escape safely to Canada, "where they will not interfere with us."[120] The dehumanizing racist sayings Henry had learned in Michigan as ways to describe hot weather and other undesirable conditions made the superiority of whiteness seem part of the natural world.[121] In Seneca Falls, Frederick Douglass and other abolitionist lecturers had challenged Henry's assumptions about race. A year later, back in Schoolcraft, Henry used a derogatory term in his diary to describe a visitor who caused "some whispering" when he "escorted" a white woman to church and sat next to her. In the next sentence, Henry explained that the guest "lectured at the Baptist church in the evening and proved to be quite a smart *color person*."[122] Henry recognized that the visiting lecturer did not fit prevailing racist stereotypes: like Douglass, he seemed to exemplify a different racial category based on demeanor and education as well as appearance. Henry's brother-in-law Joseph suggested the complicated relationship of skin color to racial designations when he assured Harriet that the woman he met and married in New Orleans was "a full blooded *Englishman*," although she was "a shade darker" than the stepmother who raised them and "her complexion resembles somewhat the *quadroons* South."[123] However flexible Henry's racial categories had become, he reverted to a familiar derogatory term to describe the enslaved people he observed as he traveled through Missouri.

When Henry spent several days in the central Missouri town of Bolivar in September, he developed a more nuanced understanding of "aristocratic" Missouri residents and their defense of slavery. Because the landlord of the local hotel recognized Henry as "a sort of a brother puke," he only charged him half price for meals, with "all the privileges of the first class customers." Henry explained to Harriet: "They treat me kindly and with respect and seem glad that I am going to bring on so many improvements from the north; yet they would be ready to tar & feather or hang an abolitionist if they knew where he was." He added that these "first class customers" were "just awaking to the realization of Blair's assertion." Frank Blair had been elected to Congress from St. Louis after several years in the Missouri legislature. He argued that Missouri would benefit if Kansas entered the Union as a free state, attracting a transcontinental railroad through Missouri and providing markets for agricultural products. Blair advocated gradual compensated emancipation in Missouri, followed by deportation of all black residents to a colony in Central or South America.[124] Henry realized that his new acquaintances' appreciation of northern technology and willingness to debate the future of slavery in Missouri did not lessen their hostility to abolitionists. While they accepted him as a northern immigrant "without being suspected of having the yankee taint," he would not be welcome if he expressed opposition to slavery.[125] In several highly publicized incidents, abolitionists had been tarred and feathered, assaulted, threatened, and driven out of the state.[126] From 1838 to 1865, forty-two men were imprisoned in Missouri for encouraging or aiding people escaping from slavery.[127]

Henry's brother-in-law, Archie, who hoped to join him in Montevallo, inquired about "the state of feeling as to northern men at this time" in response to Henry's assertion "that in the old and wealthy counties they look upon them jealously but in the new counties as quite welcome." Harriet's sister added that she worried about Henry's safety as "a Northern man" living near Kansas. She wrote that even her own brother Solomon would not "deign to notice his Antislavery friends" until "Missouri becomes a free state and the go-ahead Yankee has filled it with cities, railroads, energy, wealth and intelligence."[128] After a few weeks in Missouri, Henry had discarded the coat, cravat, collar, and pants of a clerk for the more practical denim overalls and checked shirt of a farmer. He developed a deep suntan and long hair, and his clothes became threadbare, torn, and dirty.[129] Although his appearance was indistinguishable from his neighbors, Henry maintained his Yankee identity. In Montevallo, he was "known as the yankee Smith from Michigan" to distinguish him from Massachusetts Smith.[130] In October, Henry assured Harriet that he was "daily finding congenial male friends, most of them northern men" and expected to see "many more newcomers from the north" the following spring.[131] He joked that a deer he saw near his new cabin probably "was astonished and grieved to find his home occupied by a yankee abolitionist."[132] In Michigan, Henry had grown accustomed to rowdy competition between men who identified with different political parties and to friendly banter among natives of different states. In Missouri, he had expected to find a similar tolerance for differing customs and views among citizens who shared white Michigan residents' assumptions of racial superiority and national identity. He was beginning to understand that some Missouri residents viewed all Northerners as Yankees, and many viewed all Yankees as abolitionists.[133]

Henry found a way to encourage northern immigrants. He reported to Harriet that he "wrote a puff for this new country & sent it to the *Rural*, giving them the liberty to publish it if they chose."[134] A month later, Harriet informed him that his letter had been published in the latest issue of *Moore's Rural New Yorker*.[135] Henry described his transformation from a sickly clerk to a robust farmer: "Since renewing my subscription for the Rural I have changed my residence and occupation. In a few short months I have been transformed from a dyspeptic retailer of dry goods in Michigan to a tolerably hardy pioneer in this yet wild portion of Missouri." Applying principles of progressive agriculture and Republican ideology as well as regional stereotypes, Henry contrasted his Missouri neighbors' preference for traditional methods of subsistence farming with the market-oriented practices of northern settlers who embraced the journal's motto of "Progress and

Improvement": "I find many of my neighbors, who have lived here eighteen or twenty years, now occupying the same little open log house, and cultivating the same two acre 'corn patch,' which they commenced with; and thus many of them will live until they sell out and move further toward the setting sun [making room for] a more industrious people, who are determined to *try* to do something towards improvement—others are rousing up, and show themselves in every way capable of becoming good examples to their neighbors." Henry asked readers to advise him on a plan to raise mules and promised to report the results. "As we are new beginners, we shall try some experiments that may not be uninteresting to those of your subscribers, who, like ourselves, are groping somewhat in darkness and seek light, and if agreeable you may hear from us again," he wrote.[136]

The exchange of practical information based on personal experience encouraged readers of progressive agricultural magazines to envision themselves as part of a national network of rural Yankee entrepreneurs. Henry used his letter to the editor to communicate with a virtual community of fellow "practical intelligent subscribers" whose innovative farming methods sometimes put them at odds with their neighbors.[137] When he introduced his imagined self to an imagined community of literate farmers, Henry presented his experiences in the most favorable light possible, omitting his concerns about the future and his precarious financial position. With his fellow subscribers to "the *Rural*," Henry could achieve the status he had been unable to attain among his actual neighbors in Michigan, New York, or Missouri. By the time he wrote to Harriet two weeks later, Henry had received five responses from residents of New York and Ohio asking about conditions in Missouri.[138] As Henry completed his log house in late October, he wrote Harriet that he planned to answer the letters from prospective settlers.[139] In November, another letter from Henry appeared in the magazine, providing details about the availability of building materials, the climate, soil quality, water supply, and current prices for land and livestock. Perhaps feeling responsible for the influence of his earlier "puff piece," Henry advised any potential settler to "come and see for himself before bringing his family from good homes to an untried life and climate."[140] He warned readers that a railroad was unlikely in the near future and that it was impossible to hire farm labor.

Like Henry, Harriet thought of herself as belonging to a community of readers. Her interactions with friends and family included reading aloud as well as sharing and discussing books and magazines. On a more abstract level, she shared a literary frame of reference with other Americans who read current publications. While Henry worried about how Harriet would adjust to the physical environment of Missouri, Harriet's anxiety focused on social relationships. In Montevallo, she would miss both friendships based on shared reading experiences and access to published information. Harriet worried that she would lose her place in the discourse of literate middle-class culture. She informed Henry that her brother-in-law Charlie brought home a new book "by the authoress of the 'Wide, Wide World' & we have been alternately listening and reading." In *The Hills of the Shatemuc*, by the popular author Susan Warner, a spoiled rich girl learns humility through adversity.[141] Elder Prentiss, who had moved from Maumee to Schoolcraft, loaned Harriet *Ida Norman, or Trials & their Uses*, "a very good, moral story" of a wealthy young woman who becomes a teacher after she is left motherless and poor.[142] Some of the books Harriet read addressed the institutional causes of social problems. *Hot Corn* advocated temperance and exposed the consequences of poverty in New York City.[143] Harriet wrote that "one of Cooper's latest stories, 'The Ways of an Hour'" was "intended to illustrate the evils of our social system, more particularly in administering criminal justice."[144] Charlie also selected *The Wilds of the West*, which seemed "some like Cooper's Prairie only not so good."[145] All of these books would have reinforced Harriet's acceptance of a simple rural life as preferable to either urban poverty or idle wealth. Harriet also read *Jane Eyre*. "Nice Sunday reading—but I must pass the long hours some way," she explained to Henry. "I like it very much—read it years ago but had forgotten. Mary Barney has just bought Charlotte Bronte's works complete & her life—& offers them to me to read."[146] Harriet later wrote that she was reading "Currer Bell's Professor—the last published, though the first written—I like it very well though it is not so exciting as either of the others."[147] Harriet probably read a review of Bronte's *The Professor*, published under her pseudonym, in *Harper's* August 1857 issue.[148] Like many readers, she was interested in the author's life and the relationship of her books to one another.[149] Harriet looked forward to reading with Henry in their new home. "If you could sit down & read some of these books with me I should enjoy them much better," she assured him.[150] At Henry's request, she forwarded issues of the *New York Tribune*, *New York Ledger*, *American Phrenological Journal*, and *Moore's Rural New Yorker*. Henry and Rush eagerly read these publications that addressed aspects of daily life and current events from a Yankee perspective.[151]

When Harriet informed Henry that his letter had been published in "the Rural," she reminded him that it was time to renew their subscription to *Harper's*. "Our Harper will take the place of other books & furnish an equivalent for society—I have become much attached to it—like it better than "Putnam" a great deal," she explained.[152] Without access to new books or a community of readers, Harriet would depend on magazines for information about national issues and current styles as well as for entertainment. In the absence of the social network she enjoyed in Michigan, Harriet also planned to rely on magazines for a sense of companionship and connection to a virtual community of readers who shared her values, taste, and field of reference.[153] In May 1857, the editor assured readers that *Harper's* understood that they "want a dessert" with their literary meals. "We have aimed to amuse and instruct," he wrote, "we have spied the world and chatted of its little daily incidents."[154] Like the magazine's other features, travel accounts reinforced readers' assumptions of the superiority of middle-class taste and customs. As Henry described their log house and their new neighbors, the reality of the life Harriet would lead became more concrete. An illustration in "A Winter in the South" in *Harper's New Monthly Magazine* crystallized her anxiety. Harriet described the image to Henry, indirectly expressing her fear that their new home would also seem "wild," "lonely," and "almost desolate":

> In this number there is a picture of a clean log house, nicely hewn—with a smaller one near it & a few leafless trees around—the ground lightly covered with a southern snow, some hens perched upon a roost, close by & a little child standing in the door. I looked long at it and wondered if *our* home would seem any like this new, wild & almost desolate scene, when for the first time, perhaps in mid winter—I shall look upon it. I tried to realize my feelings then—lonely as the picture seemed I thought *we* might be happy *together* there—but it would require some fortitude to live *alone*.[155]

The illustration accompanied a serialized description of travels through the Appalachian mountain region.[156] Although the author pointed out the admirable qualities of the local people, he also drew attention to their dialect, clothing, and way of life as different from northern middle-class culture. Harriet worried that her new home would resemble this Appalachian cabin rather than the picturesque prairie cottage she had imagined.

In the same letter, Harriet told Henry she had removed their curtains and carpet. Following Henry's instructions, she disassembled their bed, packed the bureau drawers with clothing and household goods, and had both items crated for shipping by rail. She warned Henry that she could not sell their furniture for cash. "'Hard times, hard times, come again no more' will be the song of the million," she predicted, quoting a popular 1854 song by Stephen Foster.[157] A week earlier, Henry's brother-in-law in upstate New York had written that banks had suspended payments and money was scarce. Two weeks later, Henry's uncle, John Parker, who had agreed to enter the

"Tom Wilson's Cabin," illustration, *Harper's New Monthly Magazine* 15, no. 90 (November 1857): 734.

partnership with Henry and Rush, wrote that grain and livestock prices were falling rapidly, and he now thought the financial crisis would be severe and prolonged. "Business matters look worse than I have seen them for the last 20 years," he warned his partners. "It is true that we can live in Missouri and improve the lands, grow stock, live cheap, get used to hog & hominy Bean & Squash Soup &c " he concluded, "and when the commercial world recovers its equilibrium we would be on paying ground with the rest of mankind but I fear before that time comes round the hairs 'of some of us at least' would look somewhat hoary."[158] The Panic of 1857, which began suddenly in August, had deepened in October, hitting Michigan and surrounding states especially hard. In Missouri and Kansas, the rush of settlers slowed drastically, railway expansion halted, and land prices fell.[159]

By this point, Henry had almost completed the exterior of the house. He hired a carpenter to build and install the doors and windows. In November, Henry dug stone to build a chimney, chinked the cracks between the logs, laid the wood floors, and installed studs for the interior walls. He realized that in order to move his family to Missouri in time for spring planting, he would need to leave for Michigan before finishing the interior of the house. Until a well could be completed, the family would carry water from a well located a mile away.[160] Henry wrote Harriet: "By the way our bedroom is a very small one and if our bedstead is more than 5 feet wide it will occupy a part of the doorway[;] otherwise it will just go in and leave a place for a stand and a nice little cloth[e]s press." Looking to the future, he added optimistically: "When the whole house is completed we shall have nothing left to do but live and enjoy the toils of making other things equal to it in point of comfort. How long it seems to look forward to the time when if we are so fortunate as to live and enjoy ordinary health we shall have the comforts and necessaries of life such as fruit and comfortable houses for all and farms made and everything ready to enjoy the life we are now going to lead." Henry associated his ability to provide a home for his family with his identity as a man. He wrote Harriet: "Never before have I felt so much like a *man* as I have since this campaign and I hope when it is over I can at least feel that I am one whether others recognize me as such or not." He continued, "I shall not be as long in *making* everything here which we need for comfort as I should have been behind the counter in Schoolcraft. I can truly say with all my hardships since I left that *glorious manly calling* I have never regretted it a minute and when we come together again I hope you will never have cause to."[161] In December, Henry returned to Michigan. As he had promised, he deeded the Schoolcraft farm back to his father.[162] On February 8, the family began the journey by train from Kalamazoo to Jefferson City, Missouri, stopping in Clinton, Illinois, to visit Harriet's parents and in St. Louis to visit Henry's cousins. They completed the trip by covered wagon, struggling along muddy roads for nine days until they arrived in Montevallo on March 3, 1858.[163]

Chapter Five

LOYALTIES AND LIES

"Harder times than we expected ever"[1]

Finally, after sheltering from an unseasonable snowstorm, the family reached their new home. Isa recalled: "The cabin of logs, chinked with prairie mud, stood in the edge of the timber. One large oak spread its branches wide in the front yard and to the south the prairie stretched like a billowy sea into the distance. On three sides the forest embraced the little home with protecting arms. The road like a ribbon wound over the prairie past the west front of the house and was lost in the woods beyond.... Within the floor of the one large room was scoured to perfect whiteness."[2] Rush Cobb greeted the family at the house they would share. Rush soon left Montevallo to visit Michigan, where he learned that John Parker intended to leave the partnership due to the continuing financial crisis.[3] Rush wrote Henry: "I see no prospect at present of changing the arrangement of affairs there to the advantage of either of us, and I think the better way will be for you (if contented) to retrench expenses as much as possible—make the place support you, if you can, and, like Mr Macawber, wait for something to turn up."[4] In *David Copperfield*, Dickens depicts Mr. Macawber and his growing family living in squalor as they wait for "something to turn up" to provide the affluent lifestyle they anticipate. Although the fictional Macawber eventually succeeds after a stint in debtors' prison, the analogy was hardly flattering to Henry. By July, Rush was engaged to a young woman in Schoolcraft and had decided to remain there.[5] Henry agreed to "take charge of the farm & stock as it is for two years and have two thirds of the proceeds."[6] Although Henry's partners had left him to farm alone, Harriet's longtime friends and colleagues from Maumee and Kalamazoo, Maurice Page and his wife Marion, joined them in Montevallo, where they purchased a neighboring farm. Two more families and four unmarried men also arrived from Kalamazoo County. Henry arranged for one of the men, William Leslie, to assist him on the farm in return for room and board.[7]

Isa later wrote that their first summer in Missouri "was spent in building a log barn, fences, making a log kitchen which stood a little apart from the house on the east, trying to finish up the house itself, putting in crops and attempting to dig a well." She explained: "After going down about 27 feet and boarding a gang of rough men for days, finding nothing but solid rock it was given up and served during our residence in Missouri as a refrigerator. Mother hung cream, butter &c in it."[8] The house was located a mile from Henry's farmland, which contained the only functioning well. Isa wrote: "Although the water after standing 24 hours became filled with animal life, we were obliged to depend entirely upon it and on one or two springs which were liable to fail during dry weather."[9] She described the difficulty of transforming the prairie into farmland with horses that "were not used to the work and the breaking sod was a slow process especially as they were pastured on the prairie and it often took half the forenoon to find them."[10] Isa recalled that the family "lived on pork, white bread when we could get the flour, but a great part of the time we had only corn bread, and sometimes a mess of wild gooseberries or strawberries. Occasionally father was able to buy grass fed beef which was very fine. He went fishing a number of times hoping to add a little to our larder but seldom caught anything."[11] Many families who settled on a prairie faced similar hardships during their first year: in unfamiliar terrain and climate, they underestimated the difficulty of breaking the sod, the uncertainty of the water supply, and the severity of the winter weather. If the fields were not ready for planting early enough in the growing season, a family might not be able to store enough food to last through the first winter.[12] In August, Henry noted that *Michigan Smith* was elected Justice of the Peace, although, as Isa later wrote, their tobacco-chewing neighbor said he "would not vote for a man who wore such good clothes and whose wife would not let him spit on the floor."[13] Following the model of his father and uncles, Henry looked to holding a local office as a way to enhance his stature in the community and potentially supplement his income.[14] Adapting to local norms, he apparently ran as a Democrat and dropped the designation of Yankee.[15]

While Henry was struggling to provide water, food, and shelter for his family and earn his neighbors' respect, he paid little attention to events occurring across the border in Kansas Territory. After Henry returned to Michigan, anti-slavery voters in Kansas had boycotted an election that would allow slavery under a proposed state constitution. Two weeks later, Kansas voters had rejected the entire constitution but had elected officials under its provisions. A predominantly anti-slavery territorial legislature in Topeka and a pro-slavery constitutional convention in Lecompton each claimed authority and accused the other of having been fraudulently elected. When the US Congress convened in January, representatives debated whether to admit Kansas as a slave state under the constitution proposed by the Lecompton Constitutional Convention. For three months, newspapers across the nation provided extensive coverage of impassioned congressional speeches. While Congress debated in Washington, anti-slavery activists led by James Lane, Charles Jennison, and James Montgomery assaulted pro-slavery settlers and skirmished with federal troops near Fort Scott, Kansas, only a few miles from Vernon County, Missouri.[16] Rush had written from Montevallo to reassure Henry: "Did not know that there was any fresh trouble in Kansas till I saw it in a Michigan paper, so that you may infer that the excitement in these parts is not very terrible. They do not get so many recruits from these parts as they did when Fort Scott was attacked before." In April, when Henry was back in Montevallo, Congress approved a compromise to return a modified constitution to Kansas for a final vote in August. Henry's brother-in-law joked that the letter he sent Henry "may be like *Lecompton laid on the table*."[17] After pro-slavery Missouri residents captured and shot anti-slavery Kansas residents in May, killing five men and injuring four, Montgomery and his allies tried to burn the Western Hotel, a gathering place for pro-slavery men in Fort Scott. The governors of Kansas Territory and Missouri cautiously cooperated to diminish conflict and protect their citizens by stationing troops on either side of the border to maintain peace. Jeremy Neely notes that some residents of the region expressed little concern over these isolated violent incidents. The border remained quiet for several months.[18]

Even before Kansas voters rejected the modified pro-slavery state constitution in August, national press coverage of the conflict diminished as a consensus emerged that anti-slavery settlers would prevail, and eventually, Kansas would enter the Union as a free state.[19] Harriet and Henry's northern friends and family assumed that Missouri would follow suit by eliminating slavery. Harriet's friend wrote from Ohio's Yankee-dominated Western Reserve that two neighbors had moved to Missouri, which "will soon be filled with northern men who will release it from its present thralldom and make it bloom as beautiful a place as man need have for his home." "There is not the shadow of a doubt of all this," he concluded confidently. A Schoolcraft resident originally from Vermont urged Harriet and Henry to "leave Old Missouri with its Slavery, its Old Pukes and other abominations, and live among a people who are not quite so barbarous." She continued: "But I trust the time is not far distant when you will gather about you a few civilized families and the curse of slavery will be removed, and you will have a beautiful country for your abiding place."[20] As the financial stress of "Hard Times" persisted, Harriet's sister, Edelia, and her husband, Archie, confirmed their intention to buy a farm near Montevallo. Henry's father and paternal uncle in Michigan, and Harriet's father and brother Joseph in Illinois, expressed interest in bringing their families to join Henry and Harriet in Missouri.[21] In October, Henry mourned the death of Mr. Withers, the man he had described a year earlier as his "general advisor" and "an out & out Southern man" who was "anxious to have this state do away with slavery & get settled up with northern men." Rush wrote Henry: "It will take a good many of those northern men such as he had collected around him to fill his place."[22] Despite the loss of his influential supporter, Henry was re-elected as school trustee in December.[23]

Henry didn't mention in his diary that James Montgomery and his antislavery followers attacked Fort Scott again in December in response to an assault on Montgomery's home or that Kansas abolitionist John Brown repeatedly crossed the border into Missouri to lead enslaved men and women to Kansas and eventually to freedom in Canada, or even that Brown's raid on a Vernon County farm on December 20 left a Missouri farmer dead.[24] In Michigan, Rush read news accounts of events on the border. He warned Henry the following February that the resurgence of violence might discourage immigration from northern states to western Missouri: "I suppose the troubles in your region with Kansas will make some difference this season though it is likely there is more noise abroad about that than at home."[25] Henry was alarmed only when he encountered "three roving blades well armed with pistol knives and rifle" while he was out on the prairie looking for a missing horse one evening. Henry put his musical and social skills to good use. "A merry time we had of it," he wrote in his diary. He "fiddled and sang songs" with the men until they all fell asleep.[26] In January, Henry had organized a petition to the governor nominating him for a vacant seat as one of three county judges. On February 27, he learned that he had been appointed to fill the vacancy. Henry was sworn in as Vernon County judge in Nevada City, the county seat, on March 7, 1859.[27] Isa and Harriet were confined at home, first by unusually cold weather and deep snow and then by Harriet's pregnancy. Isa remembered: "The first winter we suffered greatly from cold for the house was unfinished and our stove was not suitable."[28] Although Harriet felt lonely and isolated, she hoped to replicate the ideal of a prairie cottage. She wrote her friend Mary that they had named their new house "Tanglewood Cot." "You are very romantic," Mary replied, "Have you yet planted your sunflowers—to have them *creeping* all over your doors & windows?"[29] Mary's own married life had fallen short of the expectations she and Harriet had shared a few years earlier when they read novels together and discussed their hopes for the future: her response suggests that she saw Harriet's gestures as futile attempts to transform the material reality of her situation to match literary images of rural domesticity. During the cold winter months, Harriet and Henry read Sir Walter Scott's historical novel, *Quentin Durward*. Scott's tales of male bravery, loyalty, and resistance to unjust authority were popular, especially in southern states.[30]

In contrast to Henry's anxiety about Isa's birth, he first mentioned Harriet's pregnancy in his diary on June 5, 1859, when he noted that Mrs. Page and another neighbor assisted with the birth of his son: "About 11 or 12 oclock the child was born and as neither of the women present could act I tied the string & cut the cord and waited until the afterbirth came. It is a fine healthy boy. Did not close my eyes in sleep during the night. Doctor Dade came about two hours [after] the child was born." The family was suffering from malaria and lack of food. Three weeks later, Henry wrote: "Felt a little relish for food but we have nothing to eat. Crawled down to the creek & hooked up a big bull frog & though it most finished me I ate him for dinner & called him *good*."[31] By mid-July, six-week-old Walter experienced convulsions and cried frequently. Henry remained emotionally distant from the son he expected to lose. "It is very doubtful whether we ever take him to his grandfathers & mothers home," he wrote. "He may find a better."[32] A week later, Henry described a miserable household: "Hattie[']s mouth sore and she is sick of life & is obstinate as a mule & I am discouraged & as obstinate as another mule. Walter worries all day."[33] Sick and malnourished, Henry and Harriet were crowded into a one-room log house with a four-year-old child and a crying baby in the summer heat. Walter's birth coincided with the beginning of a disastrous drought that lasted for sixteen months, from June of 1859 to November of 1860. Water supplies dried up, and crops withered throughout the Osage plains, which stretched from western Missouri across Kansas.[34] Henry and his partners dissolved their partnership and divided their land holdings.[35] One by one, family members who had considered joining Henry in Missouri decided against the move. Harriet's brother-in-law, Archie, wrote that he and Edelia would remain in upstate New York. He explained that although he saw signs of change "in the spirit of St Louis & in the growing desire of your people to encourage the coming in of northern men," it might be "a long time before any general change will be affected." He concluded that he could not move to a slave state. "There is a feeling of loneliness & desolation in its very atmosphere which sends a sort of moral chill throughout my soul," he wrote. "The spirit of intolerance is so great even in your state that no one is really safe who says aught against it."[36] Henry's uncles, Foster Smith and John Parker, purchased farms in Michigan, and Parker was elected Republican state senator.[37]

In September, Henry was hired to teach at the one-room district school. He wrote: "My school teaching has but one merit as: $25, pr month cash up & no grumbling."[38] He tried to maintain order among thirty-two students of various ages: "I called the scholars together & told them I would thrash every one of them that quarreled adopted more stringent rules about whispering &c and had a very quiet time."[39] Apparently, the community supported Henry's threats of corporal punishment: he heard that he didn't whip enough.[40] While Henry was occupied at the schoolhouse one October day, Harriet watched the sky darken along the horizon. Isa remembered this traumatic day from a child's vantage point:

> All at once I caught sight of a dark cloud of smoke rising over the ridge of the prairie and called to mother to see it. She, however, had been observing it for some time, but kept quiet lest it alarm me. She took pains to speak in an unconcerned manner, and when the bright tongues of flame began to shoot into the air as it approached, she spoke of the beauty of the sight. Nothing could disguise the fact, however, that the fire was sweeping over the prairie and would soon be upon us. There were no men near and not a drop of water on the place except what was in the pail for drinking. Between the house and the approaching demon was a pasture fenced by rails and near our door yard the calves had been so often fed that the ground was tramped hard and all verdure destroyed. On the west side of the door yard, the dry, dusty road extended into the woods beyond, and east of us was the garden with a strip of dead grass running the length of the premises. It seemed almost certain that we would be swallowed up in spite of everything.[41]

Mary Boyd, the Smiths' fifteen-year-old neighbor, galloped to the school on her pony to warn Henry that his cornfield was burning. He wrote: "I dismissed my school, told the boys to go down to the fire & help, mounted before Mary and galloped to the scene of action. I went to my stacks—just in time to see a sheet of flames 20 feet high sweep across the field and wrap them in their hot embrace and reduce them to ashes." Henry hung his coat on the fencepost where William Leslie had tied Henry's team of horses and ran to help save the fence rails. He turned to see that the flames had reached the post: his horses, wagon, and coat were gone.[42] A mile away, Isa watched the approaching flames:

On came the fire, devouring the pasture fence, but it was arrested by the strip of bare ground along the south side. Once the fire caught at the rails in the corner of our yard, but mother threw them down, and wonder of wonders the flames divided and swept by us on the west, and across the dry grass in the garden on the east. The fence near one of the hay stacks caught fire, however, and mother took the last drop of water and put it out, well knowing that if the hay once took fire the home and everything would go. In the midst of this excitement the horses, with the wagon, came dashing up over the burned prairie. A barrel of water was rocking and splashing on the wagon for one of the men had gone to the farm for a supply. Without a driver and frightened they stopped at the bars, and mother succeeded in tying them so they stood quietly only casting apprehensive glances at the flames which ran up the tall trees in the near woods.[43]

Henry suddenly realized the fire was heading in the direction of his house:

When I came to the top of the hill, I thought the whole premises was in flames, and I forgot that I was tired & ran for dear life until I could see the house as yet untouched by the flames but surrounded by a circle of hungry demons that had made a mark of our devoted home. I let the pasture fence that was all in fire, burn and commenced firing round the north side of the premises to keep it out of the stacks there & I did it. We worked until midnight and went to bed poorer than ever, not to sleep a moment.[44]

If the house had been surrounded by grass and shrubbery, as Harriet had intended, the flames might have engulfed it.

With the fence gone, cattle and hogs demolished "everything about the house," including the apple trees, within a week.[45] Henry calculated that he needed 4,100 wood rails to rebuild the half-mile of fence, which would require cutting timber, splitting rails, and setting fence posts.[46] Two days later, Henry saw flames emerge around the chimney. "I ran up and as good luck had it I had a few pails of water at the house which extinguished the flames but it burned up another *oilcloth* coat for me and I burned my hands afresh in putting out the fire," he wrote. "Also burned up or nearly so 2 quilts 2 sheets & part of our feather tick."[47] Replacing the bedding would require yards of fabric and many hours of hand sewing. In the meantime, the family would face winter without the bed coverings they needed for warmth. Now they were threatened by cold as well as hunger and illness: as they watched their water, then food, and then shelter disappear, Henry and Harriet began to fear for their family's survival. While they suffered through a second winter in their log house, Henry and Harriet read *Guy Mannering*, another historical novel in Sir Walter Scott's Waverly series.[48]

The 1860 federal agricultural census reveals that in June, Henry had sixteen acres of farmland in cultivation and owned 224 additional acres of land. His farm included two horses, two milk cows, four other cattle, and two hogs. Henry owned farm equipment worth $300, including a threshing machine and a combined reaper and mower. The farm had produced six hundred bushels of corn and five gallons of molasses the previous year. Henry's farm was one of 158 farms in Montevallo Township, each with four to 150 "improved" acres under cultivation. Twenty-seven farmers, including Henry, farmed fewer than twenty improved acres, while only four owned 120 or more improved acres. White tenant farmers occupied eleven farms. Five farm households included enslaved laborers: two each with one young man, one with a young man and woman, one with a fourteen-year-old girl and a five-year-old boy, and one with a fifteen-year-old mother and newborn baby. The remaining 142 farms in the township were occupied and farmed by the white landowners and their families. Only a few households included a farm laborer or farmer with a different surname who may have been a hired farmhand. Almost every farmer in the township owned at least one horse, and most had a team of horses or oxen or both. A few also owned a mule. Almost every farm kept at least one milk cow, and several kept six to twelve. Most farms raised a few beef cattle and a larger number of hogs. Some also kept small herds of sheep for wool production. Almost all farms grew corn in varying amounts. A few also produced small crops of wheat, oats, potatoes, flax, hay, tobacco, or cotton. Most farms produced butter, and some also produced molasses or, less commonly, honey. In contrast to farms near the Missouri River, none produced hemp.[49]

While Henry's farm, with sixteen improved acres, was among the smallest twenty percent of the township farms, the acreage farmed by his "closest neighbor," John Brown, was among the largest three percent. Three years earlier, Henry had predicted that Brown, his "very poor" and illiterate neighbor from Tennessee, soon would "be in Texas or California with his wife & children & dogs, & horse & gun."[50] Now, together with his wife and his four sons and two daughters, ranging in age from ten to twenty, Brown cultivated 120 of the seven hundred acres he owned, using farm equipment worth one hundred dollars, five horses, a mule, and eight oxen. He kept four milk cows and raised thirty hogs. In the previous year, he earned ninety dollars from slaughtered livestock, and his prosperous farm produced three hundred bushels of wheat, two thousand bushels of corn, thirty-three pounds of wool, twenty bushels of potatoes, seventy gallons of molasses, and 150 pounds of butter. On a farm that bordered Brown's property as well as Henry's, Mark Boyd more tenuously supported a three-generation household of twelve on twenty improved acres with farm equipment worth thirty-five dollars, two horses, and four oxen. Boyd's family kept six milk cows and, in 1860, raised three beef cattle, eight sheep, and twenty-two hogs that foraged on their three hundred unimproved acres. The farm produced two hundred bushels of corn, fifteen pounds of wool, ten bushels each of potatoes and buckwheat, 150 pounds of butter, and twenty gallons of molasses in the previous year. Like John Brown's household, none of Boyd's family could read or write, and the children did not attend school. However, belying regional stereotypes, the Boyd family previously lived in Illinois: Boyd's mother was born in New Jersey, Boyd in Ohio, and his wife in Pennsylvania. Maurice Page, like Henry, owned 240 acres, but since he had purchased a partially improved farm, he had more acreage in production. He supported his wife and young son by farming forty acres with farm equipment worth two hundred dollars, two horses, two oxen, and the assistance of a farmhand. He kept four milk cows and raised six beef cattle and twelve hogs in 1860. The previous year, the Page farm produced six hundred bushels of corn, seventy-five bushels of oats, fifty pounds of butter, and sixteen gallons of molasses.[51] As the new Director of the Montevallo Academy, "Professor" Page would no longer be dependent solely on farming for his livelihood.[52] Jeremy Neely locates Vernon County farmers as poised at the southern edge of the Corn Belt in 1860, waiting for the extension of the railroad that would allow them to emerge from a "corn-and-hog frontier strategy" to "the commercial production of both corn and livestock."[53] Like John Brown and Maurice Page, Henry comfortably met the criteria for Corn Belt agriculture outlined by geographer John C. Hudson: producing at least 7.5 bushels of corn per improved acre and 18.5 bushels of corn per head of livestock. Boyd did not meet Hudson's criteria for Corn Belt livestock husbandry. Like many other farmers in the region, he relied on unimproved prairie and woods to feed his cattle, sheep, and hogs.[54] By July, Henry was afraid the continuing drought would destroy his corn crop.[55] On July 23, he noted that the temperature had ranged from 108 to 112 degrees for several weeks, and two local children had died from diarrhea caused by drinking muddy creek water.[56] In late July, Henry's brother-in-law offered to hire him as a bookkeeper in his store. Realizing that returning to Michigan for a year or two might enable him to pay his debt to Cobb, Henry wrote to Isaiah expressing interest in the position.[57] As the drought continued,

Boyd's hogs demolished five acres of Henry's corn.[58] By August 8, Henry had decided that he would return if Isaiah could offer an annual salary of five hundred dollars. On August 14, when Boyd's hogs ate grain stored in Henry's corncrib and a torrential storm drenched "nearly every corner " inside their house, Henry lowered his salary expectations to four hundred dollars.[59] On August 19, Henry wrote to Isaiah that he would work for nine hundred dollars for two years or $1,500 for three years. In early September, Henry noted that several more neighbors died of diarrhea.[60] Harriet suffered from a toothache and had seven teeth extracted.[61] Yet another agricultural crisis emerged. Texas longhorn cattle carried a tick-borne disease to which they were immune, but that was fatal to Missouri breeds.[62] Henry joined his neighbors in patrolling the Carthage-Boonville road to prevent Texas ranchers from driving their herds through Vernon County to reach the railroad that now extended to Sedalia. He drafted an agreement that began: "Resolved: 1st That as we the citizens of Vernon County believe all droves of Spanish or Texan cattle communicate the disease called Spanish fever to our cattle we take immediate measures to intercept the driving of Texas and Spanish cattle through our county."[63] Despite these efforts, by the middle of September, one of Henry's milk cows had died, and the other was ill. Now, the family had no milk or butter.[64] When Isaiah agreed to his salary figure, Henry accepted the position.[65] He wished he could return to Schoolcraft "with full enough hands to keep ourselves up with the rest of mankind and get a good subsistence independently of our friends and relatives" however.[66]

In the midst of these hardships, Henry began to reap the benefits of the relationships he had developed as a county judge, and reinforced by taking a degree at the Masonic Lodge in the northern Vernon County community of Balltown in July.[67] Isa remembered: "He met several men in Nevada and at court who proved most agreeable acquaintances, so while his trips left us for days very lonely, they were pleasant and profitable to him."[68] Among the "agreeable acquaintances" Henry made in Nevada City were county clerk DeWitt Clinton Hunter (known as Clint) and county sheriff Henry Taylor. Both men were active members of the Balltown lodge, as were other prominent citizens, including Dr. Albert Badger and Thomas H. Austin.[69] In addition to the courthouse, county office, and about fifty homes, Nevada City housed a cabinetmaker specializing in coffins and bedsteads, a potter, and three stores. A hotel and three saloons did brisk business, especially during court sessions.[70] When the county court was in session in Nevada City, Henry played backgammon and euchre with the judges and other men in the evenings.[71] He also took his fiddle. He played one evening "to please Dr. Badger," although he had only three strings.[72]

George Caleb Bingham, *Fiddler* (study for *The Jolly Flatboatman*), drawing, 1846. Nelson-Atkins Museum of Art, Lent by the People of Missouri; acquired through the generosity of the Louis D. Beaumont Foundation. Public domain via Wikimedia Commons.

As a county judge, Henry participated in decisions about roads, bridges, schools, elections, and other civic matters. In February of 1860, the county court approved the incorporation of the village of Montevallo, which had grown rapidly to include about fifty houses as well as three stores, three hotels, and a livery stable. In addition to a blacksmith, the village housed the shops of a ploughmaker, a cabinetmaker, and a wagonmaker. Other residents practiced trades and professions as masons, physicians, druggists, and tailors. On the outskirts were a sawmill, a gristmill, and the Montevallo Academy.[73] The village provided services to the farmers who constituted most of Montevallo Township's population, as well as farmers in adjoining Cedar County townships. Montevallo businesses also served travelers on the roads between Boonville and Carthage and between Springfield and Fort Scott, Kansas. County judges often presided at ceremonial events. On July 4, 1,200 people from Vernon County attended an Independence Day barbecue at the newly incorporated village of Montevallo. Henry read the Declaration of Independence, and the Director of the Montevallo Academy, Maurice Page, gave a speech. The celebration provided an opportunity for Harriet to expand her social circle. Decades later, Isa wrote: "Mother says it was at this Barbecue that her attention was drawn towards a young lady of fair face and noble form. She was dressed in white and was distinguished from others by the refinement of her appearance and manners. This was Nora Mayfield whose name became familiar in connection with more than one daring exploit during the early part of the war."[74] When Henry's friends in Nevada City learned that he planned to return to Michigan, they promised to help him secure an appointment as the first Probate Judge of Vernon County. The annual salary of $1,500 and the status associated with the position tempted Henry to remain in Missouri.[75]

On Election Day, Henry recorded the votes as Montevallo voters announced their choices to the clerk and onlookers. He accompanied Dr. Dade to Nevada City to deliver the poll books to Vernon County Clerk Clint Hunter and stayed in Tom Austin's home while he participated in the county vote count.[76] Abraham Lincoln was elected President with only ten percent of the Missouri vote and no votes from Vernon County. Henry had not yet been offered an appointment as Probate Judge, but Dr. Badger encouraged him to "risk it" and turn down the Michigan job. James Gatewood, a Montevallo resident newly elected to the state legislature, promised to assist Henry in obtaining the office.[77] Henry drafted a petition from Vernon County citizens requesting the legislature to establish a Probate Court and appoint him as Probate Judge.[78] Now that Henry was a county official, renewed threats of violence along the county's border with Kansas became his concern. He learned that supporters of militant Kansas abolitionist James Montgomery hanged and shot several pro-slavery residents near Fort Scott. Henry reported in his diary that Nevada City "has a panic for fear he will take and burn the town."[79] Two days later, Vernon County residents sent a petition to Missouri's governor, supported by a letter from Sheriff Henry Taylor, requesting weapons to arm the local militia.[80] Governor Robert Stewart responded by sending state militia troops to Balltown, north of Nevada City, to protect citizens from the expected invasion. Many Vernon County residents resented the arrival of these St. Louis troops.[81] In the midst of the turmoil, Henry rode to Balltown with County Clerk Clint Hunter in Hunter's buggy, accompanied by twenty Nevada men on horseback, to attend a meeting of the Masonic Lodge, where Henry took another degree on December 5, 1860.[82] Three days later, the governor recalled most of the troops, leaving a small unit in Balltown to guard the border.[83]

On January 6, 1861, Henry noted in his diary that South Carolina had seceded. He predicted that the rest of the southern states would follow. "What a hell will we represent for the next year or two if things go on in this way,"

The County Election, 1847, John Sartain, engraver (after painting by Missouri politician and artist George Caleb Bingham). Metropolitan Museum, 52.572, Elisha Whittelsey Collection, Elisha Whittelsey Fund.

he wrote.[84] Henry had collected 133 signatures on his petition for Vernon County Probate Judge. On January 12, he mailed the petition to Gatewood. By January 26, Mississippi, Florida, Alabama, Georgia, and Louisiana had seceded, and Claiborne Jackson, recently inaugurated Missouri Governor, hoped his state would join them.[85] "Perhaps we shall," Henry wrote. "God forbid. In that case I am out of this."[86] Kansas finally entered the Union as a free state on January 29. Two days later, Henry "went to town to see if there was any news about our Union." He concluded: "I believe there will be a dissolution but where Missouri will go I cannot tell. Gloomy times this."[87] Henry accompanied Mr. Page to a "union meeting" in Montevallo regarding the election of delegates to a state convention to determine whether Missouri would secede. Henry wrote: "I drew up some resolutions which were adopted after drawing out some discussion in which several debates showed as strong a hand as any *black republican* ever I saw."[88] Abolitionists, labeled "Black Republicans" by their opponents, represented a minority of the Missouri residents who wanted the state to remain in the Union. In Missouri and other border states, proslavery Unionists organized local meetings to defuse secessionist sentiment and build a coalition to preserve the Union.[89] Many citizens felt a strong loyalty to the national government. Others concluded that staying in the Union would best preserve slavery. Some wanted Missouri to remain neutral, and some hoped a compromise could be negotiated.[90] The special convention, authorized by the Missouri legislature and led by former governor Sterling Price, voted decisively against secession.[91] However, support for secession remained strong in Vernon County, especially in Montevallo and Nevada City.[92]

Isaiah wrote Henry that he had hired another man to fill the position in his Schoolcraft store since he assumed Henry would be appointed Probate Judge. Now, Henry saw no option but to remain in Montevallo, although he concluded that Representative Gatewood had not worked to gain him the appointment as he promised but instead left the decision to the County Court.[93] Henry began to understand the consequences of expressing political views. Isaiah warned him to be cautious in his correspondence: "Letters from the South are frequently opened and some of your good friends might learn something that they could use against you."[94] Henry worried that Mr. Page would come into conflict with his neighbors because he was too "far north in politics to suit them and not prudent enough to keep his abolition views to himself."[95] When Henry went into town on April 20, he found a secession flag "floating to the breese." He learned that Confederate forces had captured Fort Sumter, and Governor Jackson had refused President Lincoln's call for troops to fight them. After listening to a speech advocating secession, Henry wrote: "None of his arguments suited me at all but from this time I shall say nothing and do nothing against Missouri's joining a southern confederacy."[96] He reported that several families suspected by "some unknown individuals" of being "black Republicans," including the Underwoods from Schoolcraft, had "eloped for Kansas" after being given ten hours to leave. Henry was afraid he and his family would suffer the same fate. "I do not know how soon *I* may be ordered off in the same manner as I am a northern immigrant," he wrote in his diary. "I am gloomy at this commencement of the purging process for it cannot but be attended with trouble to many good citizens who are innocent of treason against their State."[97] Although he opposed secession, Henry apparently accepted the secessionist argument that citizens owed primary allegiance to their state rather than the federal government.[98]

Governor Jackson had called the state legislature back into session in May to organize and fund the Missouri State Guard. While the legislature was meeting in Jefferson City, federal troops took over a state militia camp near St. Louis, and civilians were killed in the melee that ensued when they marched the captured state militia through the city streets. In a midnight Extraordinary Session, irate legislators quickly approved the governor's requests. They called all able-bodied men to join local militia companies that would assemble and drill, preparing to defend the state under the leadership of the former governor, Sterling Price.[99] Representative Gatewood, a member of the legislature's Militia Committee, rushed home from Jefferson City "full of blood and thunder" to organize a company of state troops in Montevallo. Perhaps recalling the humorous anecdotes told about his father's brief service as a musician in the local militia in Schoolcraft, Henry joked in his diary: "Such another straggling ragged inferior crowd mingled with a few noble specimens never went to war as our company. I played a fife and they marched ran scrambled hopped and slouched along in my rear as we paraded the single street of the *Great Metropolis*. When the federal troops hear what we have done I reckon they'll give up St. Louis and flee for their lives without ever stopping to look back."[100] A "guard of 18 soldiers" supervised the drills and enforced a curfew after dark.[101] Two weeks later Henry listened with alarm to the "fire eating ranting" speech Gatewood made when the recruits elected him Captain. Henry explained that he did not join the troops as he had planned because, under the new militia law, they were liable to be called up at any time, and he could not leave his family alone.[102] On June 22, Henry attended ceremonies marking the departure of Captain Gatewood's company. The women of Montevallo prepared a farewell dinner and presented the soldiers with a handmade flag.[103] A year earlier, Montevallo residents were preparing to host the county's celebration of the nation's birthday; now, they gathered to send their young men into battle against federal troops. Instead of defending Montevallo or Jefferson City as they expected, the company would head south to face Union forces assembling near Springfield.[104]

While militia units were forming and training throughout Missouri, Governor Jackson and other state officials fled from Jefferson City to Boonville, where the state militia skirmished with federal troops who pursued them. The inexperienced and poorly armed militia retreated in disarray, abandoning supplies of equipment, shoes, and food.[105] Henry wrote that Governor Jackson was "dodging the U. S. Marshall," an apparent reference to Jackson's reputation as a former Border Ruffian.[106] The governor's entourage joined General Parson's 6th Division of the state militia near Tipton and continued south, gathering recruits as they passed farms and villages. They set up camp a mile east of Montevallo to rest and regroup in friendly territory while they waited for General Rains' 8th Division to join them.[107] Many of the men arrived without weapons or horses, and no system was in place to feed and equip them. On June 27, Henry wrote: "Gov Jackson arrived here just eve with the advanced guard going South. He has about 1200 men."[108] The following day at noon, two soldiers approached the Smith cabin to ask for milk. Henry "invited them to stay for dinner, which they accepted." This was not a social visit, however: "They achieved Cobbs gun and went to

Stuarts & John Browns to look for horses." Later that day, Henry discovered that a dozen soldiers had taken both of his guns "without so much as saying by your leave." "Hattie's remonstrances were no avail," he wrote. "All the satisfaction they gave her was that I could come into camp and see about it."[109] A few years later, Isa described the incident from a child's perspective:

> I was living in Missouri when the war broke out. That spring father had gone one day for gooseberries. While he was away I looked out of the door and saw a company of soldiers at the bars. We waited until they came up and in a moment the door was filled. One of them, who seemed to be the leader, came in and asked if we had any guns. Mother told him we had, but did not wish to dispose of them. The guns were hanging on the two sides of the room. He stepped up and took the shotgun and then called for the rifle but before mother could answer, he took it down and asked for the molds. Mother gave them to him and he and his company went away.[110]

Henry unsuccessfully tried to recover his guns from the state troops the next day. The man in charge of the "gun robbery department" at the military encampment offered only a receipt for much less than the value of the guns. Henry learned that "not only rifles & guns but horses, grain flour meal and men were being *pressed* into service." This intrusion into his home shocked Henry. "I am afraid we shall see harder times than we expected ever," he wrote.[111]

Henry returned to the camp on foot to avoid having his horse confiscated. He recognized several neighbors among the troops on parade. Dr. Dade informed Henry that his guns were taken because a neighbor named him a "black Republican." Dade assured Henry that after he advised the officers and the governor that Henry "was right," they agreed to return his guns.[112] Isa later explained: "A southern friend, and brother Mason, went with him to the camp exerting his influence in his behalf." On Henry's third visit to the camp, Dade introduced him to Governor Jackson. "He is a large man with rather a red face wears a wig has [a] grizzly beard a keen restless grey eye and seems to be rather rough and familiar in his general appearance among the officers," Henry wrote. He was then introduced to Colonel Clark, who was "*very* much of a gentleman," and finally to General Parsons, who agreed to return one of Henry's guns.[113] When Henry returned home, he applied bandages to make his horse appear injured. He concluded: "We are being stripped hourly of all our substance and terror seems to reign in every home circle." The next day, Henry learned that a soldier from the Nevada City

Rangers wanted his saddle. "When I found that it must be had," he wrote, "I let him take Cobbs and hid mine in the woods."[114] He was beginning to pick up the canniness he would need in order to survive. The following day, July 2, Henry wrote: "The troops departed today thank God. I took Isa up behind me to let her see them wind through the prairie and while we were looking at them from a hill a half a mile from them the picket guard sent for us. . . . We went to the Capt[ain] who let us go after being satisfied we were not *spies* and we came home."[115] Isa recalled that "the soldiers were poorly clad, and it was a very bedraggled looking army." She remembered her father walking his horse home "very slowly so he would not attract the attention of any of the weary stragglers who were on foot."[116] The militia fought past the outnumbered Union troops that tried to intercept them near Carthage, about forty miles south of Montevallo, and continued south to General Price's training camp near Missouri's border with Arkansas, which had joined the Confederacy along with Texas, Virginia, North Carolina, and Tennessee.[117] Here, the Vernon County companies became the 7th Cavalry Regiment of General Rains' 8th Division of the Missouri State Guard. Dewitt Clinton Hunter was elected Colonel, and Henry Taylor became Quartermaster.[118]

Henry reported that many residents evacuated Montevallo in fear of Kansas "Jayhawkers" who "have robbed some of the principle families in the west part of the county taking even clothing."[119] Henry and Harriet were unable to flee with their neighbors: Harriet would soon give birth to their third child. After two days of intermittent labor, assisted by Mrs. Page and Mrs. Boyd, Harriet grew so weak that Henry sent for Dr. Dade, but the baby was born before he arrived. Henry wrote: "When the newcomer first appeared into this troublesome world Wallie was on the bed and awake and as the feeble wail of the little thing stirred his ear his eyes popped wider open and he looked all around to find it." Henry, now an old hand at childbirth, remarked that Dr. Dade removed the afterbirth "but the job was really done before he came as I had got it started."[120] While Harriet was giving birth in Montevallo on July 22, the secession convention reconvened in Jefferson City. Delegates declared that the governor and the state officials and legislators who fled with him had vacated their positions. They appointed Hamilton Gamble, a slaveholding Unionist, as Provisional Governor and decided the convention would serve as Missouri's legislature until elections could be held.[121] In Vernon County, the court session scheduled for late July was canceled because the county clerk and two of the three judges were unable to attend.[122] A week after Harry's birth, Henry wrote: "In consequence of an alarm in town of Jayhawkers[,] went there[,] joined the home guards but could not go out with them as Hattie is complaining and Isa has the chills and I cannot leave them overnight and our work if we do any against these Rangers maurauders must be night work. Left my gun with Branch Ray until I join them."[123] Only a few weeks earlier, Henry had hoped that cannonballs would maim Governor Jackson, who had "committed all sorts of depradations upon good men" in Kansas before the war.[124] Now Henry was ready to defend his neighbors from raids by independent Kansas militia companies led by notorious Jayhawkers James Montgomery and Charles Jennison. Such "night work" by men who appeared to be peaceable farmers led to the accusation that most residents of western Missouri participated in guerrilla activities. As federal military leaders soon recognized, the rampant theft and terrorism committed by renegade Kansas troops drove even men who sympathized with the Union cause to take up arms to defend their homes.[125] Montevallo residents had worked together to protect their families from prairie fires, Texas cattle herds, and Kansas Jayhawkers before the war. Henry saw the troops on both sides of the conflict as outsiders threatening his community, but he especially feared the former Jayhawkers now operating as Kansas militia units.

When Harriet and Henry reread the letters they received before the conflict disrupted the precarious mail delivery system, they must have felt the great distance between their present world and the one they had left behind in Michigan.[126] Before the presidential election, Henry's sister Frank had described the participation of Henry's father and uncles in torchlight parades of the Schoolcraft Republican Wide Awake band. In a letter written in March, Frank discussed the musical performances of the Kalamazoo Quartette Club and the Schoolcraft Universalist choir. She informed Harriet and Henry that Charley had copied a drawing of "Shakespeare and his friends" from the "Art Journal." Frank noted that the family subscribed to "The Atlantic," "Tribune," "Covenant," "Gody," "Peterson's Magazine," and "Harper's." Frank assumed that Harriet and Henry found their new environment as incomprehensible as she did. She wrote: "What a strange community you are thrown among, how glad you will be to get back among congenial friends again."[127] Her sister Helen commented in the same vein: "How can you live among such a set of *cut throats*[?] I think it's *abominable* and I would leave them to their own destruction."[128] In May, Frank complained of the difficulty of sewing, making social calls, and writing letters while caring for a baby. "You know Hattie," she wrote, "how long it takes when neither self or baby have anything rigged for summer." Frank sent samples of the fabric she had purchased for two new dresses and informed Harriet of the latest styles. "Gray goods are all the go," she noted, "made goring, each breadth gored & corded with silk either to match the dress or in contrast. Also five dozen buttons covered with the same silk, are required to trim a dress." She informed Harriet that she had three vases filled with flowers and was baking a cranberry pie. Frank did not understand why the family should not express their political views in letters to Missouri. "I hardly see why there is so much danger, for we think Mo. is safe in the Union," she wrote.[129]

"Murder is an everyday affair now," Henry explained when he reported that three men were shot on their way to join the southern army.[130] About half of the militia company that the women of Montevallo had sent off with cheers, a flag, and a farewell dinner returned home on leave on August 12. The rest had been killed or injured on August 10 during the Battle of Wilson's Creek near Springfield.[131] James Ray, who had befriended and fed Henry during his first months in Montevallo, lost two sons in the battle.[132] "Cursed is the effect of war, and cursed indeed is civil war," Henry concluded.[133] In late August, he estimated 6,000 to 10,000 Missouri militia troops passed by on the road to Fort Scott.[134] At the beginning of September, Kansas troops from Fort Scott, led by James Montgomery, skirmished with Price's Missouri State Guard on Dry Wood Creek between Montevallo and the Kansas border. Price's militia continued north to Lexington with eighty-four captured mules. They forced federal troops to surrender, allowing stranded recruits to cross the Missouri River to join General Price.[135]

Kansas Senator James Lane had assumed command over regiments at Fort Scott led by Charles Jennison and James Montgomery. The three abolitionists had participated in the border conflict before the war, and they remained suspicious of all Missouri residents. Their troops carried out widespread looting as they moved through western Missouri.[136] Henry complained that "Jayhawkers" burned the house of Judge Davis, his ailing colleague on the county court.[137] While Lane's force of two thousand men torched and robbed a swath through adjacent counties, Henry noted that the clerk of the Vernon County court, Clint Hunter, now a Colonel in the Missouri State Guard, was camped near Montevallo, recruiting troops "to meet the Jayhawkers." Henry again excused his decision to remain with his family. "I can't go now any better than I could a month ago," he explained.[138] Rumors fed the natural fears of local residents. Henry wrote: "The air is full of news of the depredations of the Jayhawkers of which about one hundred p[e]r c[en]t is half true."[139] Isa remembered "several visitations from frightened refugees." She explained that Tom Austin, Henry's friend from Nevada City, "asked to bring some cattle to us for safekeeping and when he arrived there were fifty head of cattle, six horses and mules, with four white men and two negro boys, the younger one only three years old."[140] A week later, the Smiths took in Dr. Webster and his wife, along with their household goods and "chattels," and stored boxes of merchandise for Webster's father-in-law, William Scobey, a Montevallo storekeeper.[141] "I am becoming a refuge it seems," Henry observed. "God Almighty protect the innocent and confound the wicked ruthless of this mischief is my prayer," he wrote.[142] Henry learned from Dr. Webster that Lane's troops had burned Osceola, displacing over two thousand residents. Fortunately for Montevallo, the troops headed back to Kansas with their captured cattle and horses, hauling wagons loaded with furniture and clothing, as well as ammunition and food.[143] Henry's visitors returned home. Lane's troops especially targeted slaveholders, burning and looting homes and farms, as well as helping enslaved workers escape to Kansas.[144] By providing a refuge for his friends and neighbors, Henry became complicit in the institution of slavery he hoped to see eliminated. However, he did not express any hesitation in offering shelter to refugees. He could still defend his actions as protecting "the innocent" from their "wicked ruthless" pursuers.

On September 29, General Price began to move his Missouri militia south from Lexington through Montevallo to Neosho as federal troops prepared to intercept them.[145] Two days later, Henry was forced to provide supper for armed men who appeared at his door.[146] He was afraid that if he tried to take his corn to the gristmill, the troops would capture both his corn and his horses.[147] On October 12, Henry reported that soldiers arrived throughout the day asking for food. Some simply took what they wanted. "Our chickens turnips cabbage walk off without leave of absence," he complained. Henry estimated that twelve thousand of Price's soldiers were in the vicinity. "May the Lord send them in any direction," he wrote.[148] The next day, Henry ground corn in a coffee mill and baked cornbread for the men who filled the house all day. Twelve teams and forty men spent the night in his cornfield.[149] The following day, Henry visited the officers' camp to request reimbursement for the corn the soldiers had taken and protection for the rest of his crops. He secured a promise from General Price that he could keep half of his remaining corn. On his way home, Henry helped himself to almost a hundred pounds of beef discarded by the militia. He complained: "They take more than they want even here where there is not enough to winter us. Many of my neighbors are entirely stripped of their last bus[shel] of grain and all their stock. The horse and cattle stealing is done by about 500 thieves that follow the army but the corn wheat … & garden vegetables go to camp."[150] As Price's hungry soldiers moved south, federal troops under General John C. Fremont, whose Republican Presidential campaign Henry had supported five years earlier, slowly followed from staging points across the state, converging at Springfield.[151]

FEDERAL TROOPS OF FREMONT'S ARMY FORAGING IN MISSOURI.

This illustration appeared on the September 28, 1861, cover of *Frank Leslie Illustrated Newspaper* while Kansas troops known as Jennison's Jayhawkers were looting and burning homes across western Missouri. The field artist and engraver captured the distress of families deprived of eggs and dairy products by Union and Confederate troops who took their poultry and milk cows. The original caption, "'Slaughter of the Innocents,' or How the Federal Troops Did Their Foraging in Missouri," and accompanying explanation that "our hungry heroes" reimbursed the farmer trivialized the suffering of rural Missouri residents previously ridiculed by northern journalists (310). With the caption "Federal Troops of Fremont's Army Foraging in Missouri," the illustration was reprinted in Frank Leslie, *The Soldier in Our Civil War: Columbian Memorial Edition*, vol. 1 (New York, 1893), 163. Courtesy of the Missouri State Archives, MS515 Frank Wallemann Civil War Collection.

Henry's involvement escalated when Dr. Dade sent three men from Price's militia to stay with him. "I reluctantly took them in as they were gentlemen," Henry explained. Henry's description of the men as "gentlemen," a term frequently used in Masonic literature, suggests that they may have been fellow Masons.[152] Dade had helped Henry recover his gun from Price's troops on June 30 with the assistance of an officer Henry described as "*very* much of a gentleman." The Masonic oath Henry and Dade had taken required them to offer shelter or aid to worthy members in need or, if that was impossible, to refer them to another member for assistance.[153] Numerous accounts described incidents during the Civil War when men helped strangers, even enemy soldiers, who were fellow Masons.[154] Regardless of his motivation, Henry understood that housing combatants put him in danger, especially if they were scouts or spies heading north into Union-held territory. One of the men offered to mail a letter to Michigan, and Henry took advantage of the opportunity to write to his family.¹⁵⁵ The soldier mailed Henry's letter in Cass County with an anonymous message explaining to Henry's family that Kansas troops called Jayhawkers "come into the state in bands of from 30 to 100 and catch and drive out all of the stock they can get their hands on and now and then shoot some citizens." He continued:

> There is one or two such bands in this state who call themselves Southern men they rob cut up and now and then kill a man. They are condemned by the largest class of citizens here both cecession and Union. I would not allow Mr. Smith to write any political news for fear I would be taken on the road. I can tell you Mr. Smith is what we call a Southern man. He thinks the policy pursued by the Federal Gov— and especially by Kansas very unjust. I can tell you one thing Missouri is more sinned against than sinning. They have drove some 300 men from this Co. and at least as many from Bates and Vernon Counties into the Southern Army that would never have taken up arms at all. Some of them Indiannians some from Illinois and other states.¹⁵⁶

The writer's usage of the term "Southern man" to describe a political position rather than a regional identity follows a common linguistic practice that indicated a voter's advocacy of a cause or allegiance to a candidate: for example, Henry referred to supporters of the 1856 Republican Presidential candidate as "Fremont men."¹⁵⁷ Christopher Phillips notes the emergence of a "new class of dissenters," he terms "political southerners," who were motivated by "grievance, personal or collective, against the federal troops" rather than by regional identity, support of slavery, or desire to secede from the Union. Phillips argues that identifying as southern allowed border state citizens to express opposition to Union policies or military practices without advocating secession.¹⁵⁸ After estimating troop strengths of Price and Fremont in southern Missouri, the anonymous writer returned to the ongoing local conflict between Kansas and Missouri citizens: "A party of Southern Jayhawkers went over into Kansas on yesterday. Stealing some stock they were pursued within three miles of this place by 100 Kansas Jayhawkers. They drove out a good deal of stock. So it is men from Mo steal from Kansas and Kansas steal from Mo. Kansas commenced it and robbed men and these same men are now Jayhawkers themselves."¹⁵⁹ A few days after Henry's visitors departed, he wrote that Webster and Scobey, whose goods and families he had sheltered several weeks previously, left their horses and saddles "on the sly for me to keep them out of sight of soldiers." "I do not like it," Henry concluded, although it absolved him of "paying cash for some shoes I took from Scobey's goods when they were here."¹⁶⁰ Soon, Lane's Kansas troops from Fort Scott passed through Montevallo to join Fremont's forces in Springfield.¹⁶¹

A surgeon serving under Lane wrote from "Montevelo" October 28 that "neutral men are just about all of them secessionists in principle" and his commander "meant the secessionists in Missouri to *feel* the difference between being loyal and disloyal citizens and he is doing it." He explained: "We have camped where there was secession farmers on one side and Union farmers on the other, when we would leave the secession were stripped of everything like crops and fences while the others remained untouched."¹⁶² Henry noted that four thousand federal troops camped near Dr. Dade's home that night. "Two men from the southern army were sent to me to keep overnight," he wrote.¹⁶³ A day later, six "armed and mounted" Union soldiers stopped Henry on the road and questioned him.¹⁶⁴ The troops "stripped" the outspoken secessionist James Ray of all his corn and required him to take an oath of allegiance to the Union because he was accused of driving Union supporters out of town. Henry added: "But generally the citizens say the federal troops treated us like gentlemen, which I believe. I wish to God the southern soldiers knew how to treat human beings who are in their power."¹⁶⁵ While federal forces gathered at Springfield, legislators who had fled with Governor Jackson met at Neosho. Although they lacked a documented quorum, they passed an order of secession on October 28. Missouri was received into the Confederacy on November 28, 1861.¹⁶⁶ By this time, federal forces had returned north, now commanded by General Henry Halleck. They remained in control of the territory north of the Osage River, including St. Louis, Kansas City, and Jefferson City, as well as river and rail transportation, although guerrilla bands repeatedly sabotaged telegraph and rail lines and disrupted shipping. Missouri now had two governments: a Confederate government in exile near the Arkansas border and a Union government in St. Louis. Some residents of Missouri viewed the federal forces as an occupying army and the provisional state government as illegitimate, while others supported their ouster of rebellious elected officials. Many still hoped to avoid taking sides in the conflict.¹⁶⁷

After consolidating control of the executive and legislative branches of state government, Unionist politicians turned to the judicial branch, which played a central role in local government. Elected county, circuit, and probate judges regulated inheritance and debt collection, settled disputes, maintained order, kept records, and administered services. In October, the governing convention required all Missouri office-holders to file a loyalty oath within sixty days confirming allegiance to the United States and the provisional state government. Governor Gamble would appoint replacements for judges and other officials who refused. Some counties maintained or resumed local government with officials loyal to the provisional government.[168] Guerrilla bands discovered that attacks on judges and county courthouses provided both a symbolic demonstration of opposition to the provisional government and a disruption of civic operations and records. Threats of violence prevented courts from being convened in several western counties, including Vernon.[169] By the following summer, probate judges in southwest Missouri resigned or refused appointment due to intimidation and assaults.[170] These circumstances probably underlie Isa Smith's claim that Henry's petition to be named probate judge was approved by the provisional government, although Henry was not notified, and Henry's recollection that he had been appointed probate judge but was warned not to accept the appointment.[171] Henry wrote on November 28: "The clerk wants a court but I thought it would only be setting a trap to catch our soldiers in and demurred."[172] Demurring was conducive to Henry's safety as well as the security of local men returning from Price's militia. In July, Vernon County Deputy Clerk Frank Anderson, who had used a crutch since childhood, returned home on horseback after reaching Price's training camp in southern Missouri. In the absence of the county clerk, Missouri State Guard Colonel Clint Hunter, Anderson updated the county records. In October, Anderson was held for a week at Fort Scott and released after taking the oath of allegiance.[173] As deputy county clerk, he would have been responsible for scheduling court sessions and recording the new oaths required of county office-holders. In late November, Price's troops camped near Montevallo while they recruited replacements for soldiers whose six-month enlistment had ended. Assisted by unnamed Montevallo residents, Colonel Hunter removed the county records from Nevada City. Hunter locked the courthouse and county office and took the documents and keys with him when he accompanied General Price back to Springfield in December. Vernon County government operations ceased. The county court would not meet until October 1865.[174]

By December, almost all homes between Nevada City and Montevallo had been deserted, as had all but six houses in Nevada City.[175] As the weather grew colder, Henry realized his family "must have the house tight as we are so scant of clothing." He daubed the cracks between the logs to seal out drafts.[176] Harriet purchased homespun cloth for the children's clothes.[177] After several unsuccessful attempts to buy shoe leather, Henry wrapped his feet in sacking until a neighbor gave him his own extra pair of shoes.[178] When he finally obtained leather, Henry made shoes for himself and Harriet.[179] He visited "Old Man Ray" to recover the gun he had loaned to Ray's son, Branch, in July.[180] In early December, Tom Austin relayed a message from

Captain Ransom at Fort Scott that Henry's relatives had sent money "or something of that nature," and he "would not be molested" if he came to claim it.[181] Henry traveled to the federal military post in Kansas and met "the veritable Willis Ranson," who told Henry his brother-in-law, Isaiah, had written to ask whether Ransom "could get money to" Henry. Henry found letters from his sister Helen and her husband Isaiah at the Fort Scott post office, but they contained no money. He described Fort Scott: "It seems to be populated by soldiers who are well fed paid & clothed & have nothing to do but to slip over the line now & then & rob us of our horses & stock & take our men prisoners."[182] As he had expressed concern for "our soldiers" two weeks earlier, Henry identified local men imprisoned at Fort Scott as "our men" and accused the Kansas soldiers of robbing "us of our horses & stock." "The boys came in last night with 8 horses Jayhawked from Kansas. Charlie Blann had 5 horses taken from him by Kansas boys Saturday," Henry wrote in his diary on December 31, 1861. Violence was no longer a vague threat from anonymous outsiders: now, men well known to Henry were both victims and perpetrators. Henry tolerated, if not condoned, the actions of "the boys" as he had justified the rowdy behavior of his cohort of "Bohoys" in Schoolcraft ten years earlier. Stealing horses was the new normal, and accounts of the local boys' reckless adventures eased a pervasive sense of helplessness. Kansas Jayhawkers provided an identifiable target for the fear and anger Henry shared with his neighbors in Montevallo.

PART III

Montevallo, Missouri, 1862

Chapter Six

HENRY'S CIVIL WAR

"Concealing and dissimulating according to the best of my talents"[1]

As the new year began, Henry considered whether to return to Michigan: "Shall I remain and never see my old father and mother or shall I go and never own a home for my children and die a poor miserable day plodder."[2] A week later, he wrote: "I wish I could peer into the future enough to know whether it is better for me to leave every thing I have to the wolves & hyenas of war & drag myself & brood home."[3] Harry cried constantly and Wallie was sick and fussy. "How two persons like Hattie & I can live in such a turmoil & enjoy an hour of life I cannot see," Henry wrote.[4] He described "gusts of temper" in the cold and crowded house.[5] With his hopes for a happy home turning into a nightmare that surpassed even his worst fears, Henry let his thoughts wander back to the security of his childhood. He wrote: "I wish I could banish this thinking of home at the old home, it is what keeps me unsettled and the reason that I can never have a home here. I dream night & day of Father and Mother."[6] "What will become of us all between sickness war and a country full of thieves, God only knows," he concluded two days later.[7]

By the beginning of 1862, changes in Union policies had altered the context of the war in Missouri. Union General Henry Halleck, who was appointed commander of the Department of the Missouri on November 19, 1861, enforced regulations imposed by the new provisional state government, including the requirement that state and local officials swear allegiance to Missouri's provisional government and the United States.[8] In December, President Lincoln authorized the suspension of the writ of *habeus corpus*, allowing citizens to be imprisoned without trial, and the imposition of martial law in Missouri.[9] Men and women could be arrested for suspected disloyalty and tried by military commission if civil courts were not in operation.[10] Halleck ordered that anyone engaging in guerrilla activity, or providing aid, information, or encouragement to the enemy, be treated as a criminal rather than a prisoner of war. Those who failed to assist military authorities were considered Confederate sympathizers and could be required to take an oath of allegiance to prove their loyalty. If they subsequently were caught fighting against the Union, they could be punished as traitors.[11] William Blair notes that responsibility for monitoring and punishing civilian treason and disloyalty was transferred from the State Department to the Army in February of 1862.[12] General Halleck established a centralized system of Provost Marshals to gather information about the loyalty of citizens, determine who was required to take an oath of allegiance, and maintain order in the absence of local law enforcement.[13] Halleck decided to remove Kansas troops from Missouri and use new federally funded Missouri State Militia companies and units from other states to ferret out guerrilla bands and their civilian enablers.[14] After chasing Price's army into Arkansas in February, Union troops controlled the territory and transportation network of Missouri, while Unionist politicians controlled the state government. The system of local Provost Marshals, together with the state militia and federal troops, would control the civilian population. In place of troops that had swarmed through the region during previous months, residents of Montevallo now found themselves intermittently under surveillance by federal scouts and spies gathering information to locate guerrilla bands and capture Confederate recruits before they could join their units.[15]

The policies designed to control the population of Missouri depended on distinguishing loyal from disloyal citizens, guerrillas from civilians, and guerrilla bands from military units. Combatants as well as noncombatants found these distinctions difficult to determine in an environment of fluid identities and conflicting loyalties.[16] In Vernon County, there were no telegraph or rail lines to disrupt, and often no garrisoned troops to harass, but loosely organized guerrilla bands threatened and assaulted Union supporters, attacked federal scouts and stragglers, intimidated local residents, and created a climate of fear and distrust. Men who were otherwise law-abiding citizens carried out clandestine activities at night. Fugitives camped in the undergrowth surrounding Horse Creek and Clear Creek, supported by relatives and friends as well as by stealing from Union supporters.[17] Some had left Price's militia as deserters or when their terms of enlistment ended, and some had taken approved or unapproved leaves.[18] Civilians also fled to guerrilla bands for protection after they were suspected, rightly or wrongly, of misdeeds or after their homes were destroyed. Henry worked out a rationale that justified the actions of some of these men: those who had been wronged had the moral right to retaliate. He explained the distinction: "Dave Gilboney went out with Charlie Blann to get a horse but failed and got in place of it a leader put through him which is the last of poor Dave, so says Blann who escaped by running a gauntlet of balls whistling about his ears. If Dave had been robbed I should have been more sorry but the jay hawkers had not molested him & he had no business there."[19] Since Kansas Jayhawkers had stolen horses from Charlie Blann, Henry found his retaliation justifiable. Union officers recognized that attacks on innocent men were turning many loyal citizens against the Union cause.[20] These incidents gave credibility to the guerrillas' claims that they were responding to atrocities committed by invading forces.[21]

Although survey township T34 R29 extended a mile into Cedar County, its residents formed a community centered on Montevallo village. Henry knew that his neighbors held a wide range of shifting and conflicting allegiances. Markers of regional and political identity like birthplace, previous residence, slaveholding, or voting history did not reliably predict current loyalty, and commitment to an abstract cause did not always determine the actions people took in the specific situations they faced.[22] Neighbors cautiously assessed one another's loyalties, but they continued to share farm equipment, labor, and information.[23] They saw a common interest in preventing theft that diminished the community's scarce resources and protecting each other from violence. When Henry called on Mark Boyd, on an adjoining farm, and Jesse Steward, John Brim, and John Shackleford in Cedar County for pork or beef in payment for cutting their hay, they warned him about horse thieves in the area.[24] A dozen armed neighbors rode to Maurice Page's house to protect him after the men living on Horse Creek identified him as a Union supporter. Henry wrote: "This is what I am glad to see and I hope to God something may happen to put down these thieves."[25] Henry maintained cordial relations with neighbors who openly favored secession. He spent an hour or two visiting "old Mr. Ray" and an afternoon talking about "trading &c" when "Old & Young John Brown" visited him.[26] Henry also continued his friendship with anti-slavery Union supporters from Michigan. He sometimes left his family at the farm of Harriet's old friends, Mr. and Mrs. Page, on his way to the village.[27] George Upton, a former Michigan resident originally from England, spent a Sunday visiting the Smiths.[28] William Leslie, who sometimes lived with the Smiths and assisted Henry, was openly Unionist, as was his friend, George Upton's son Ed.[29]

In addition to his Montevallo neighbors, Henry participated in several intersecting social networks: his Baptist congregation, his Masonic brotherhood, and his associates in county government. Each of these groups was nested within a regional and national institutional framework with codified core values: members promised to adhere to rules governing private and public behavior. The similar tenets of these organizations reinforced one another, and their memberships often overlapped. These affiliations involved an expectation of personal loyalty that was more immediate and concrete than abstract allegiance to a national government. By 1862, all of these local groups included members arrayed along a continuum from strong Union supporters to staunch opponents. Thomas G. Dyer discovered in his study of Unionists in Civil War Atlanta that "long-standing social and economic bonds" often linked Unionists and secessionists, and "personal loyalties sometimes triumphed over political loyalties."[30] Parson Carrico described himself as a Baptist minister in the evangelical Mission branch in which Harriet was raised. In addition to Henry's closest neighbors, the Page, Boyd and Brown families, and Parson Carrico, Henry's Montevallo Baptist "church family" included the Unionist Upton boys as well as several avowed secessionists: Judge Henry, "the Mayfield boys & Company," Bob Bayles, Sam Tapp, Henry Taylor and his father-in-law George Pottorf, and Dr. Dade.[31] Maurice Page, Dr. Dade, and Henry Taylor were also Henry's Masonic brothers, as were several men Henry had met in Nevada City, including DeWitt Clinton Hunter, Albert Badger, and Thomas Austin.[32] Dyer notes that the bonds of fraternal organizations "added another layer to the complex matrix of loyalties" even in a Confederate state.[33] Mary Ann Clawson discusses the importance of pre-existing social networks, such as fraternal orders, in allowing emerging social movements to establish channels of communication and access to resources.[34] Rules forbidding discussion of politics and other controversial topics at Masonic meetings also facilitated communication and assistance that bridged political divisions.[35]

 The civic leaders Henry came to know as a Vernon County Court judge represented a complex range of fluid loyalties. County Clerk DeWitt Clinton Hunter and County Sheriff William Henry Taylor remained committed secessionists who led a series of official and unofficial military units throughout the war. Albert Badger, who had recommended Henry for Probate Judge, returned home after serving briefly in Price's Missouri State Guard. In October 1861, Badger and Thomas Austin, whose cattle Henry had kept the previous month, were picked up by the Sixth Kansas Cavalry's Captain Greeno and held several days at Fort Scott, along with Assistant County Clerk Frank Anderson. After taking the oath of allegiance, the men were released with guarantees that their property would be protected.[36] While Henry was visiting Austin in Nevada City in February 1862, Abram Redfield, a prominent early settler and an avowed Unionist, returned from Fort Scott with news that 2,000 federal troops had arrived.[37] Redfield, Austin, and Badger were slaveholders, as were many Unionists.[38] Austin was raised in Tennessee and Indiana, but Redfield grew up in New York, and Badger in Connecticut and Philadelphia. Unlike many men who took the oath, Austin and Badger apparently remained loyal to the Union, as did Anderson.[39] Like Redfield, they found this loyalty compatible with interceding on behalf of neighbors accused of disloyalty.[40] Christopher Phillips discusses the complex allegiance of slaveholding Unionists and of immigrants from free states who had to "untangle redefined political and cultural loyalties."[41] Dyer's conclusion that "loyalty was frequently imperfect, rarely unconditional, and often influenced by circumstances" aptly describes Vernon County's civic leaders, including County Judge H. P. Smith.[42]

Unionists in Nevada City assured Henry in February 1862 that the war would end before summer. Looking forward to a peaceful settlement that would leave Missouri within the Union, Henry began plans to build a house on his farmland.[43] In the meantime, he continued to store and exchange items for men who might be vulnerable to raids by federal troops. Joe Wood, who owned a livery stable in Montevallo, retrieved a harness that mill-owner Keithly or his physician son had left with Henry. A few days later, Henry bought several items at a Montevallo store and charged them to Joe Wood's account, and Henry Taylor brought a wagonload of meal to the Smith farm "for safe keeping."[44] In Montevallo, as in Schoolcraft, neighbors often visited one another, discussed people and events, and traded goods and services. Sometimes, several men were involved in a series of exchanges that passed a debt from one to another. Even the participants found it difficult to determine when these interactions took on military implications in wartime. In some cases, it was unclear which men were enlisted combatants and which groups were official military units.

A day after he reported that Captain Gatewood died from the accidental discharge of his gun while recruiting in Montevallo, Henry wrote: "Jo Wood is the leader of this independent company of Jayhawkers in Montevallo & I hope they will rob no more widows as they have done. It is a dangerous crowd to us peaceable folks. I want to go to Nevada but I am almost afraid to pass the lawless devils with old Joe and a decent saddle & bridle."[45] The term "Jayhawkers" originally referred to bands of anti-slavery Kansans who terrorized civilians and stole their horses, guns, and other possessions, but Henry and other Missouri residents began to apply the term to men on either side of the conflict who threatened, robbed, or assaulted noncombatants. Military units that employed "jayhawking" as a tactic were called "Jayhawkers," as were independent outlaw bands.[46] Henry added the following day: "I hear that the Montevallo jay hawkers are stranded & that Col Coffee will try to organize regular troops for border defense by Gen. Price's order."[47] Henry Taylor, former Vernon County sheriff, had resigned as Quartermaster of Colonel DeWitt Hunter's Missouri State Guard cavalry regiment on December 19 after a six-month enlistment. On February 17, Taylor compiled a list of Montevallo men, including John Dade, Sam Tapp, and Bob Bales, who enlisted in "Wm. H. Taylor's Company of the Missouri State Guard" to be "attached to the regiment now being organized by Colonel Jno. T. Coffee for the protection of the western boundary."[48] After completing his enlistment period in the Missouri State Guard, Colonel John Coffee, a lawyer and former leader of the Missouri state legislature, became a persuasive recruiter for troops that historian Daniel Sutherland describes as "semi-irregular" forces. Coffee addressed a receptive audience in Montevallo and established a recruiting camp nearby. General Price had recruited as far north as Osceola after federal troops pulled back from Springfield in November. He had returned to Springfield in December but was chased out on February 12 by federal troops and retreated into Arkansas.[49] Some newly organized companies that intended to join Price were waiting for orders or were constrained by the presence of Union troops. Others remained in western Missouri to defend their communities while they waited for Price to return and restore the exiled Confederate state government.[50] Apparently, the Montevallo militia company was one of these stranded units, operating independently of either Confederate or state militia discipline and chain of command.[51]

Members of this independent Montevallo unit surprised a small party of Union scouts sleeping in a house near Clear Creek, wounding several soldiers who were returning to Fort Scott after gathering information on the recruits.[52] The next day, while Henry was working in his cornfield, two soldiers stopped to ask whether he "knew that the Jayhawkers were in the county & on Clear Creek." Meanwhile, several neighbors borrowed Henry's gun and went to Montevallo to investigate. They returned to report that a hundred federal troops took several men prisoner and fatally shot "old Mr. Ray," who had offered Henry hospitality and assistance when he arrived in Montevallo.[53] Henry wrote that the seventy-six-year-old man's death could be called nothing other than a murder. He explained:

> It seems the old man went to town in the morning while Capt. Greeno's company were there not knowing anything about it and Mr Reaves motioned him back as he stood in his door but Mr. R. came on nearly to the street whereupon 3 soldiers took after him. The old man turned and ran into the woods the soldiers after him. A short

time after two shots were heard and the soldiers returned saying they had killed one damn'd old secesh and the old man lay by the road with a bullet hole through both hips near the spine. He probably dropped dead. From appearances, he was standing probably at the "halt" of the soldiers.[54]

Union General Halleck had ordered that anyone acting as a guerrilla be treated as a bandit.[55] Although official policy required that suspected guerrillas seized while engaged in peaceful activities be taken prisoner and brought to trial, many were reported as killed while trying to escape.[56] Ray was a vocal supporter of secession who had previously attracted the attention of federal authorities. Henry had written in July 1861: "The old man can hardly keep cecessionism from boiling over all the time." In October, he had commented that Ray was "nearly insane he is so mad at the 'scoundrels who ate up his corn and hay and made him take the oath of fidelity to the Union.'"[57] Henry helped transport Ray's coffin to Cedar County, near Parson Carrico's home, for burial next to two of his children.[58]

Threats of violence came from both sides. Henry learned that a band of forty "armed southern men" camped on Horse Creek "intended to rob every man that would not turn out and fight Jay Hawkers." A local Unionist who was tricked into identifying Union sympathizers had described Henry as a "doubtful case." "Wonder who's turn will come next," Henry speculated.[59] Three days later, he found four armed men on his doorstep. The man fooled by the Horse Creek guerrillas correctly labeled William Leslie, who lived with the Smith family, as a Unionist. The visitors demanded Leslie's gun and horse and, on learning that he had neither, asked about other horses on the farm. Leslie, who had traded his mare for a yoke of oxen the previous day, told the men that two horses belonged to northerner Rush Cobb. Henry protested: "After doubting & discussing the subject with me and I had explained my position and the partnership matter in full they left the horses telling me that if they were smuggled union property they would strip me to the bone." Henry added that one of the men told him: "Nothing of mine would be taken as I was all right on their books." Three-year-old Wallie "sat at the table through the whole scene with the corn bread sticking out of the corners of his mouth." "Finally he very modestly asked 'if he might speak loud,'" Henry wrote. "Poor little fellow he thought he was at school I suppose where none were allowed to speak but the *master*."[60] Although Henry joked about the incident, Wallie accurately perceived the power dynamics. When Henry pleaded with armed intruders in his own home, his inability to guarantee the security of his wife and children was painfully evident. The men left with Leslie's oxen.

W. D. Matthews, "Guerrilla Depredations: Stealing Horses," illustration, *Harpers Weekly* 8, no. 417 (December 24, 1864): 829.

Leslie found other lodging, and Henry hired Jesse Steward's son, William, whose political views would not attract the suspicion of the guerrillas.[61] In the weeks following the Union victory at the Battle of Pea Ridge in Arkansas on March 8, Henry watched soldiers from Price's militia trudge north in pairs or groups as large as forty men, some claiming to have been discharged.[62] Price was commissioned as a Confederate officer on April 8. Many Missouri State Guard soldiers enlisted in the Confederate Army and followed Price to Mississippi with the expectation that they would circle back to reclaim Missouri. Others returned peaceably to their homes or joined local guerrilla bands or new Missouri State Guard units like the Montevallo company.[63] With Price's troops out of the way, Union forces tried to consolidate their control of Missouri by capturing or driving out the remaining guerrillas. On April 7, Henry noted that a party of fifteen horsemen stopped with Harriet during a rainstorm. They "came civil & asked to feed their horses," and since some of the men "knew all about" him, Henry assumed they were guerrillas living on Horse Creek. He explained: "Where they saw the small quantity in the crib they hesitated about taking it until Hattie assured them we had more. They had been scared out by the federals."[64] During the following three weeks, men pursued by Union troops left exhausted or captured horses with Henry for safekeeping. Isa later wrote that her father knew many of the fugitives, and "quite often one of them would visit him in the field to ask for food or news."⁶⁵ "Saddle horses and saddles were secreted at our house by different parties," she recalled. "Sometimes a horse would be left or exchanged while we were away and a note of explanation found on the doorsill."⁶⁶ On April 10, Henry met "some of our wild boys with their guns & fast horses tearing through the woods." "They tell me they expect jay hawkers in soon & then they will make me a visit," he noted.⁶⁷

"Charley Blann & three other wild southern fellows came to the house fleeing from the jayhawkers that are in Montevallo. They did not stop but rode into the woods leaving a led horse with me," Henry wrote on April 11. "Shortly after Branch Ray rode up and stayed until afternoon and then concluded to go back & run the risk of being shot as his father was. Poor fellow; he has as little to fear as any man among us but I expect he dreads the name of jayhawkers."⁶⁸ Now, Henry had committed himself to keeping a captured horse left behind by escaping guerrillas. Presumably, Branch Ray's visit was not a social call but an attempt to hide from Union soldiers, even if he was innocent. Henry later learned that troops from Fort Scott had captured and imprisoned ten men near Montevallo that day. While soldiers were taking Henry Taylor captive, John Gabbert and Crawford Mayfield, known as "Crack," shot at them, hitting one in the shoulder.⁶⁹ "Two Union men (I call them) were here to dinner," Henry wrote the following day.⁷⁰ As Union scouts searched for guerrillas and their allies, it became increasingly difficult for Henry to remain a "doubtful case," precariously balanced between his ideological support for the Union and his emotional concern for his neighbors. Henry remained cautious in expressing his political views. Even in his diary, he avoided criticizing or praising either the Union or the Confederacy. The source of danger turned out to be not the "wild boys" but Henry's friends and neighbors.

On the morning of April 14, "old man Tally" arrived at the Smith farm driving a buggy that carried Dr. Dade, who had suffered a gunshot wound to his leg in a skirmish with federal troops in Montevallo. According to Henry, the local "southern jayhawkers" attacked federal soldiers sleeping in Scobey's hotel "for the sake of plundering their arms" but were "whipped or at any rate ran after killing two federals and having one of their own men killed and two wounded." "Dade was fool enough to join" these "reckless fools," Henry wrote. Jo Wood and Drake came to Henry for supper and returned for breakfast. They claimed they were not in the fight but were afraid to return home for fear of reprisals from the federal troops. Two Union soldiers had been captured at Drake's house. Henry learned that Mr. Randolph had been taken prisoner by federal troops who found two loaded guns in his house. During the assault, the Mayfield brothers fired on the soldiers from the cover of bushes near the Randolph home. Henry also heard that the troops had shot Wilson Maddox and burned his house and the grocery because they thought the attack was launched from that property.[71] According to the *History of Vernon County*, Maddox and Dade planned the attack against the advice of Jo Wood, who had become the militia company's leader after Taylor's arrest three days earlier. When Wood refused to participate, Dade and Bob Bales led the assault by twenty-five militia recruits and other local men.[72] Henry recalled that Maddox had threatened to "fire fat this summer on the union men about here," although he probably "did not expect to be killed by them also like a fattened hog." Since Randolph was "one of the best citizens in the county," Henry was confident that he would be released after a trial.[73]

On April 16, Henry wrote: "The feds searched Jo Woods house yesterday turning over the beds overhauling trunks & chests and prying into every nook and corner swearing at and abusing his poor frightened wife and swearing they would kill Jo wherever they found him. And he was a union man at heart and joined the army to be popular and save his property. I am afraid he will be killed."[74] Henry must have realized that a similar fate could be in store for his own family. Although he kept his diary hidden in a hollow log, Henry may have chosen his words carefully to avoid providing evidence that either side could use against him.[75] He wrote that he was "almost scared at the threats & maledictions against all sorts of men but rogues" that he heard at a grocery store "full of southern boys talking over the fight," including "Shackelford, Simms, Hinch and several others notorious as jayhawkers" as well as Jo Wood. Henry concluded: "House burning was not calculated to get the good will of our wild fellows. Every one they kill has his place filled by two worse ones and every house that is burned will be the signal for two heaps of ashes where stand the houses of union men."[76] In contrast to these young "wild fellows" who were "notorious as jayhawkers," like twenty-six-year-old Clay Simms, the men who came to Henry for shelter after the attack on the Montevallo hotel were otherwise responsible and law-abiding men over the age of thirty-five.[77] Untrained and inexperienced in combat and left without the leadership of Henry Taylor and James Gatewood, they saw an opportunity to steal the weapons and horses of soldiers sleeping in their midst and did not foresee the consequences.

Despite his disapproval of the attack on sleeping Union soldiers, Henry felt an obligation to help his neighbors, especially the wounded Dr. Dade, escape from the pursuing troops. He wrote that he "could [not] refuse to take the Dr. in for he was writhing with a bullet hole in his thigh." "I am sorry they came," he added.[78] Henry knew that the men could be subject to execution if captured. Later that day, two of the fugitives were captured and killed, and twenty-two were taken prisoner.[79] On March 13, General Halleck's Order Number Two had specified that guerrilla bands would not, "if captured, be treated as ordinary prisoners of war, but will be hung as robbers and murderers."[80] When Dade and Tally appeared at his door, Henry was forced to make an instant decision, and his experience would have suggested they might have been innocent victims. The distinctions between helping friends and neighbors whose lives were endangered, aiding guerrillas, and protecting one's family were ambiguous. The day Dr. Dade left the Smith home, Henry wrote: "I may be doing wrong in giving food & shelter to rebels but I must [not] turn a cold shoulder upon those that have befriended me."[81] The absence of the significant word "not" from Henry's diary entries for two days in a row could have been inadvertent omissions, a subconscious indication of conflicting loyalties, or an attempt to avoid implicating himself for harboring guerrillas. Henry regretted the circumstances, but he believed he was acting according to moral principles that transcended military authority. Henry's attitude was compatible with evangelical beliefs as well as the tradition among his southern neighbors that the unwritten code of personal honor should prevail over the dictates of the law.[82]

Bertram Wyatt-Brown discusses the extent to which southern hospitality, even in peacetime, formed part of a system of exchange. It carried an expectation of reciprocity that often was offered and accepted with ambivalence.[83] Henry's interactions with Dr. Dade were complex. Dade had helped Henry recover a rifle confiscated by the Missouri State Guard, and at Dade's request, Henry had sheltered men evading federal troops. As Masons, the men shared an obligation to assist one another, especially if one was in mortal danger.[84] In addition to his Masonic obligations, Henry relied on Dade for his family's medical care. Furthermore, he had sold Dade horses and a wagon on credit: since Dade owed him money, Henry had a financial interest in his survival.[85] Wyatt-Brown discusses the importance of personal financial debts in maintaining "long-standing social connections" in a southern community.[86] Finally, Dade was a member of Henry's Baptist "church family." These interwoven ties of affiliation and obligation led Dade to seek help from Henry, and Henry to feel obligated to provide it.

The day after he reluctantly allowed Dr. Dade to take refuge in his house, Henry described the contradiction between his responsibility for the security of his family and his reputation as an honest and honorable man:

> Those who are in an army and have but their own scalp to care for can at times be as happy as jovial society of camp life can make them but to us who have wives and children to care for there is a constant care

that makes us prematurely old. We must study our every word that we speak lest we expose ourselves to the wild wicked passions that now pervade every nook & corner of the country and then with the utmost care many are victims to the blood thirsty rapacity of the different parties of outlaws and unprincipled *loyal Christian* followers of better men. How bitterly I regret that we did not go out of this whirlpool of blood when we could have done it. I need not to have gone sneaking home like a whipt puppy but could have subsisted by my labor where labor is protected. Now I must do it as I can first earning it doubly and then keep it if I can by concealing and dissimulating according to the best of my talents.[87]

Henry concluded that his duty to protect his family and his right to guard the fruits of his labor justified lies and deceit. Like many of his neighbors, Henry came to see this behavior as morally acceptable. Michael Fellman finds the practice Henry euphemistically termed "concealing and dissimulating" to have been a common tactic used by citizens of Missouri during the Civil War. According to Fellman, civilians as well as combatants "shifted values dramatically and became, with reservations, quite hard soldiers for the duration of the war."[88] Fellman argues that "survival lying" was a necessary response to conditions of social chaos: most residents questioned by Union authorities denied their involvement or claimed that they had assisted the guerrillas only under threat of violence.[89] Guerrillas also blurred the distinction between the hospitality of their friends and the reluctant assistance they coerced by armed force.

Northern middle-class masculine ideals of honesty and diligence clearly did not mark the road to success in wartime Missouri. Henry had always been dubious about this model of manliness, and now he could draw on alternative ideals of masculine behavior that he had long found appealing. Henry's experiences in business and farming had convinced him that the economic system was inequitable and that many men in responsible positions were callous and unprincipled. Growing up in a frontier region of western Michigan had exposed Henry to financial uncertainty and male camaraderie tinged with trickery and violence. Expectations of mutual assistance and personal loyalty among companions as a defense against unpredictable hostility from those in authority made sense to Henry. By refusing to follow conventions of warfare, the guerrillas provided a model of masculine behavior compatible with antebellum working-class culture and with fraternal, reform, religious, and political organizations that challenged the ethics and masculine identity of the business elite.[90] In war, as in peacetime, Henry could choose from more than one model of manhood.

All of the participants in the conflict in Missouri drew on certain common ideals of masculinity. Combat provided opportunities to demonstrate physical strength and agility. Combatants were encouraged to act aggressively, display courage, and stifle compassion. They were expected to bear deprivation and suffering without complaint. Men confirmed their manhood by their actions in battle, often with the encouragement of wives, sisters, and mothers.[91] Combatants believed that they were protecting their honor, their families, their communities, and their nation, however they defined those terms. Like the young men who had flocked to political parties, reform organizations, fraternal orders, and informal gangs before the war, many men who joined armies or guerrilla bands were at an age when they would experience both a need for recognition as individuals and a need to affiliate with their peers. Regular and irregular military service offered opportunities to demonstrate bravery and encouraged allegiance to one's own group and hostility to outsiders.[92] Beyond these shared assumptions about manly behavior, however, both Union and Confederate troops represented a concept of manhood that differed from the masculine ideal embodied by the Missouri guerrillas.

The principles under which the regular troops of both the Union and the Confederacy operated shared many characteristics with the emerging industrial and business economy Henry had observed in Seneca Falls. Commanding officers organized troops to perform differentiated tasks which were coordinated through a chain of command, and documented in bureaucratic records. As peacetime work was separated from home and leisure, battles were clearly demarcated events, and combatants were distinguished from non-combatants. Soldiers, like businessmen and plantation owners, distanced themselves from the consequences of their actions, divorcing emotion from the business of combat. Concepts of a fair fight, waged according to rules of engagement and principles of honor, disguised the brutality of battle as they had disguised the ruthlessness of economic competition, while revenge and anger were discounted as motivating factors. Uniforms, marching in formation, hierarchy of command, and military discipline reinforced the bureaucratic and impersonal aspects of the armed forces.[93] Like successful businessmen or planters, occupying troops displayed their power by controlling people, land, and resources. Appropriation of the goods and services of enemy civilians mirrored peacetime accumulation of possessions and command of services as markers of dominance. These actions simultaneously reinforced the manhood of occupying troops and challenged the manhood of civilian men under their authority.

Guerrilla fighters rejected this model of manhood enacted by the regular military forces. They valued individual autonomy and recognized fluid leadership based on personal loyalty rather than bureaucratic rank. Many defied even the conventions of civilian masculine attire, dressing in brightly colored ruffled shirts and leaving their hair long and flowing.[94] The guerrillas' equestrian style was flamboyant and daring.[95] Instead of the drum rolls that coordinated the actions of regular troops, their movements were accompanied by deceptive silence or wild whoops. Rather than fighting distinct battles in organized formations, they engaged in spontaneous skirmishes and clandestine ambushes, often under the cover of darkness. They attacked civilians as well as military troops and often dressed in captured uniforms that obscured their identity.[96] Guerrillas denied the segregation of the military from other aspects of society, merging into the population between assaults. They did not divorce their role as combatants from their roles as sons, fathers, husbands, and neighbors. They relied on personal relationships, offering favors and expecting their return.[97] They expected women to participate actively in the conflict as they did on the family farm, providing essential food, clothing, and shelter.[98] They circulated possessions, especially horses, among themselves and exchanged them with the civilian population. They commandeered essential goods and services and sometimes destroyed property as a punishment or as a tactic to disrupt military operations, but they did not accumulate possessions or conquer land to signify dominance. Guerrillas asserted control by stalking and terrorizing their enemies and by marking the bodies of their victims.[99] Since they could not hold prisoners, guerrillas either killed their captives or stripped them of their possessions, sometimes even their clothes, and then released them in ritual humiliation. Instead of distancing themselves from emotions, guerrillas announced that they were fighting to avenge wrongs committed against themselves or their families.[100] While regular military troops ideally displayed the power of a disciplined impersonal organization, guerrilla bands represented a Romantic masculine ideal that emphasized emotion, personal loyalty, and individual honor.

As a young man, Henry realized that he would be forced to choose between furthering his financial success and helping his friends. A model of manhood that valued loyalty, mutual assistance, emotional expression, and impulsive action was compatible with Henry's experience and personality. Henry's mother, who grew to adulthood in Virginia, may have instilled ideals of manhood that proved to be congruent with those of his southern neighbors in Missouri. As the guerrilla actions began, she had encouraged Henry to remain "true to himself as a man" rather than stoop to meanness in pursuit of wealth.[101] Moving to Missouri freed Henry from markers of genteel behavior and fashion that he felt had prevented him from gaining respect and status in Schoolcraft and Seneca Falls. As one of the more literate residents of Montevallo, Henry wrote letters for some of his neighbors and read documents and newspapers to them.[102] They turned to him as a Justice of the Peace to solve disputes and elected him as a County Judge to deal with bureaucratic matters.[103] Henry explained his reluctance to leave a community where he felt valued and respected: "Here though my life may be in danger and my personal possessions as uncertain as life the place which I call home is mine and no one sneers at one for not owning more wealth. I am at least eaqual to any about me in intellect & wealth and I sometimes think there are few superior morally."[104] As a fiddler, a man eloquent with language and convivial at social gatherings, Henry was well suited to negotiating for survival when personal interactions became matters of life and death. Now, instead of calling on Henry to play the fiddle at dances, his neighbors called on him to intervene on their behalf with Union officials. He still found it impossible to refuse requests for assistance. Henry enjoyed being sought after and relied upon, and now he could see that his help was desperately needed. As long as Henry's services as an intermediary were valuable to his neighbors and possibly also to Union officers, it was in their interest to ensure his continued safety and goodwill.

Even as a young man, Henry had established friendships with men and women from a wide range of backgrounds. In wartime Missouri, he was able to bridge the gap between illiterate neighbors and literate officials or between members of a guerrilla band and military officers. In the local offices he held in Michigan and Missouri, Henry had learned rudiments of legal principles and the terminology of government documents. He could present a written or oral argument on behalf of fugitives or prisoners in language familiar to Union officials. His experiences in sales and politics prepared him to address resistant audiences and gain access to men in authority. Henry was skillful in presenting his case: he persuaded military commanders to pay for crops their soldiers had commandeered, talked guerrillas out of stealing his horses, and convinced army officers to release prisoners. Fellman notes that many Missouri residents "sought alliances with men of a wide range of loyalties as a form of contingency planning. They wanted friends and protectors in all camps."[105] Aaron Astor argues that guerrilla bands maintained prewar relationships with local leaders embedded in broader social networks.[106] Guerrillas depended on a dense family network for supplies and support.[107] However, they also needed loosely connected allies who could facilitate communication with authorities, provide safe houses, store property, and board exhausted horses without attracting attention.[108] Someone like Henry, who was cautious about expressing his political views and whose allegiances were ambiguous, was a less conspicuous ally than an outspoken partisan or a fugitive's relative. The location of Henry's farm on open prairie, by a main road and near a wooded creek bed, provided easy access and multiple escape routes. His ability to manage and care for horses and his facilities for boarding them were also useful.[109] Another asset Henry offered was the authority of a county judge to conduct marriages. Even a ceremony with only a few witnesses placed fugitives in a vulnerable situation.[110] Henry officiated at a wedding at the Mayfield home where he suspected some of the guests were "southern Jayhawkers," and he quietly married Henry Taylor to Sarah Pottorff.[111] They accepted Henry as a valid officeholder even if the provisional government did not. Perhaps most importantly, Henry's close ties with his openly Unionist neighbor, Mr. Page, his contacts with county leaders, and his northern family connections allowed him to establish channels of communication with federal officials who controlled the fate of prisoners.

Henry played on the hybridity of his regional and class background to remain in the good graces of all parties to the conflict. Isa later noted that when her mother had been uncertain of the identity of strangers asking for shelter, she parried their questions as to whether Henry was a Northerner or a Southerner by explaining that he had moved to Missouri from Michigan but was born in Virginia.[112] Isa concluded that "although father's northern sentiments were generally known or suspected, he was also known to have many friends among the southern people and his birthplace being Virginia went far to ensure their regard."[113] Harriet remarked that Union soldiers noticed Henry's books, while Southern soldiers would have commented on his spurs.[114] Although Harriet used this incident to contrast the two armies, her comment reveals Henry's ability to cross cultural boundaries. From a young age, he had shown an affinity for both books and horses, and he could converse comfortably about either. Henry had always adapted his behavior to meet the expectations of his associates and placed a higher value on personal relationships than on abstract principles. These traits enabled Henry to convince each side of the conflict that he supported its cause. He could serve as a negotiator, cautiously accepted by both sides but fully trusted by neither. The relationships he maintained with people on either side of the conflict made him a valuable asset to both groups, but it was a delicate and increasingly dangerous balance to maintain.

Over the next few weeks, Henry slipped more deeply into the turmoil as he attempted to find a path that would protect him from both Union and Confederate supporters. A few days after he sheltered the wounded Dr. Dade, Henry found that Bob Bales had reclaimed his mare but replaced it with one that had been exhausted in a twelve-mile chase by federal soldiers. The following day, Dr. Dade and his young daughter came to visit until the Kansas troops left Montevallo. Henry learned that "the feds" had taken John

Gabbert prisoner.[115] A day later, while the recuperating Dr. Dade was still his houseguest, Henry was concerned to see 120 federal soldiers approach the mill while he waited for his corn to be ground. He was relieved when they only told him the news of a Union victory, "the bloodiest one upon American soil," at Shiloh, Tennessee, near the destination of Price's Missouri troops.[116] Spreading news of Confederate casualties and defeats and displaying strength by parading through the village were tactics designed to demonstrate the power of the Union forces and convince wavering citizens to cooperate. The next day, when Henry's neighbor, John Brown, was imprisoned for "harboring jayhawkers," Henry realized that he might be subject to the same fate for sheltering Dr. Dade, who had left early that morning.[117]

Knowledge of the possible consequences did not prevent Henry from agreeing to help in "clearing poor Henry Taylor who is in irons under a charge of being a captain of a guerilla band." "I wish I knew what I believe to be true that he is innocent," Henry wrote.[118] Taylor had been captured after leading a raid on a group of federal soldiers whom he released after stripping them of their arms and horses.[119] A Kansas soldier recorded in his diary on April 27 that he traveled forty miles to see "Taylor and the forty-eight guerrillas taken with him at Montevello a few days since. Some of the party are vicious looking, others appear as harmless as men need be."[120] Taylor claimed to be acting as a recruiter for General Price rather than as a guerrilla. This was a crucial distinction since men captured as soldiers were treated as prisoners of war and might be released as part of an exchange of prisoners, while men captured as guerrillas were tried as criminals. The fact that Taylor had freed his captives was an argument in favor of his assertion that he was operating under accepted rules of combat. It would not have helped his cause that a federal soldier was shot during his capture. At the request of Thomas Austin of Nevada City, Henry agreed to travel to Fort Scott to argue on behalf of Taylor, the former county sheriff. Henry was disappointed that Mr. Page would not accompany him. It was a common practice for respected Union supporters to petition for the release of their imprisoned neighbors and vouch for their good character.[121] Like Dr. Dade, Taylor was both a member of Henry's Baptist "church family" and a Masonic brother.[122] Henry traveled from Nevada City to Fort Scott with six other men, including Judge Henry of Montevallo, Dr. Badger, and Dr. Hepler, who had treated a wounded soldier from Fort Scott in February.[123] When Henry reached Fort Scott, he learned that Taylor's trial had been postponed indefinitely. At Fort Scott, Henry saw two men he knew, Mr. Wyrick and Captain Morress, who had been arrested for stealing horses but would be released to join the Missouri militia organized by the Unionist provisional state government. Morress warned Henry

Thomas Nast, "A Group of Butternut Prisoners, Taken from Life," illustration, *Harpers Weekly* 7, no. 330 (April 25, 1863): 261.

that it would "be dangerous" to "attempt to say anything in behalf of Henry" Taylor, but Henry was determined that he would "not be scared from what I consider to be my duty." Henry again met with Major Ransom, who gave him a letter that his family in Schoolcraft had mailed in January in care of Capt Willis C. Ransom at Fort Scott.[124] Ransom later wrote that when the war began, half the residents of rural western Missouri actively supported either the Union or the Confederacy. "The remaining half were secretly hostile to the United States though professedly friends, non-combatants or neutrals," he concluded.[125] Acting as a post office allowed him to monitor the correspondence of these Missouri residents and provided leverage over citizens eager to hear from family and friends.

When Henry returned to Montevallo, he learned that the Provost Marshal expected the men who traveled to Fort Scott to report to his office. Henry saw Dr. Culvertson taken prisoner and discovered that several men he knew had given themselves up.[126] The next day, Henry learned that someone had informed the troops that he had harbored Dr. Dade. He wrote: "I cannot help it nor could not refuse to take in a sick & wounded friend. I shall expect to be taken in now. And this is freedom of conscience." Henry's next sentence was written in numeric code: "Last night Charley Blann came in."[127] Henry reported to the Union Provost Marshal in Montevallo on April 30 as ordered. He wrote: "Went to town to take an oath required of all *southern* men. Found the Provost Marshal crowded with business. My neighbors seem more willing to take the oath than they were last summer. I offered myself but Capt Chase did not think it necessary for such a *notorious* southerner as myself to take it."[128] In 1861, returning Confederate soldiers had been allowed to resume their civilian lives after taking the oath of allegiance to the Union. By the spring of 1862, the oath was used as a technique for controlling the civilian population. Anyone who took the oath and then bore arms against the Union, or aided those who did, would be subject to execution as a traitor rather than held as a prisoner of war who could be traded or released. While Confederate sympathizers could rationalize to themselves and their neighbors that the oath was not morally binding if taken under duress, federal officials were less willing to accept this excuse. Men who saw themselves as neutral and wanted to avoid being drawn into the conflict, as well as supporters of the Confederate cause, bitterly resented being forced to declare allegiance to the Union.[129] As Wyatt-Brown explains, in a society in which giving one's word represented a serious commitment, men felt that their integrity was violated when they were forced to swear to a loyalty that they did not feel.[130] Years later, Isa explained the complexity of Henry's situation. She wrote that the Mayfield brothers "brought occasionally a horse to our barn for safekeeping until it could recover from hard riding during some of their escapades." She continued: "It would have been unsafe for us to refuse aid in this way, but it is a wonder we were not brought into difficulty with the federals by so doing. The facts are, however, that when the troops were in Montevallo and forcing all the citizens in the neighborhood to take the oath of allegiance, father went with the rest desiring to be sworn but the officers said, 'Oh we know you are all right' and refused to administer the oath. This circumstance however was not made public."[131] With or without Henry's knowledge, the Provost Marshal presumably hoped to benefit from Henry's relationship with the local guerrillas. Other men reporting to the Provost Martial also may have been excused from taking the oath. "They only swore John Brown & generally let the citizens off much better than was expected, requiring bonds of but few & those only who had been identified with the Rebel army," Harriet explained in her diary.[132]

The next day, Sam Tapp, who "was in the fight" and "seemed not to like bush wacking much," approached Henry for assistance.[133] Henry offered to ask Maurice Page to help Tapp return home to his wife and nine children since, as Harriet explained in her diary, Page "is a *Union man* & Henry is a *Southern man*."[134] Page agreed to speak to the Provost Marshal only if Henry would accompany him, presumably to assure the guerrillas of his sincerity. Henry and Page ate dinner with Captain Chase, who promised that Tapp would not be punished if he agreed to take the oath and post a bond of $1,000. Henry returned home to find several federal soldiers hiding on his property: one inquired about Tapp. When eight more soldiers arrived, Henry invited them to stay for dinner. He wrote: "They seemed satisfied and chatted away as pleasantly as I could have wished until after supper when they bid us good night & departed as silently as a band of [I]ndians. They are surely well trained scouts." The hospitality offered by both Henry and Captain Chase provided a thin veneer over the threat of violence. Henry wrote: "I do not take it as a compliment from Capt Chase to send them to dog my heels after giving the confidence of myself & Tapp too & I think I will not advise him to give himself up now."[135] Tapp, however, did not return.

Henry wanted to be liked and respected by both sides or at least to ensure his family's survival by remaining useful to them. Two days later, he went to Mr. Page's home to hear a federal officers' quartet, as had been arranged when they met with Captain Chase, but the singers did not appear.[136] Henry was asked to travel to Fort Scott again to testify in Henry Taylor's rescheduled trial. Although Henry downplayed the risk, Harriet worried about his safety. She had complained in her diary after his previous trip: "Citizens here are threatened if they venture to testify in favor of any prisoner. This looks like very one sided Justice."[137] Harriet reported that a few days earlier, Frank Anderson, who asked Henry to testify, and Dr. Hepler, who had tried to testify previously, had been "fired at by a man who rode out on the prairie & took deliberate aim, chasing them & firing five or six times."[138] She heard later that "Fort Scott folks threaten to shoot Henry if he comes to the Fort again with Dr Heplar."[139] The trial was postponed again, and Henry returned home safely. With members of the Montevallo Company heading south to join Coffee, fleeing to other regions, or imprisoned at Fort Scott, and with Henry under scrutiny by Union troops, he was no longer asked to shelter horses or fugitives. His usefulness now was not providing a safe house but serving as a go-between. In mid-May, the Union troops in Montevallo suddenly departed. The quartermaster left payment for the hay they took from Henry, a tacit recognition of his loyalty, or at least usefulness, to the Union. Henry heard conflicting rumors about the location of southern troops.[140] He wrote: "I begin to think that Coffee is actually nowhere and Raines keeps him company. I am of Judge Henry's opinion that unless the southern army are strong enough to hold the state they would do better to keep out of it all together." In the anticipated battle in southern Missouri, "if the southern boys should happen to get whipped they would probably leave Missouri to her fate," Henry concluded a few days later.[141]

On May 31, Mr. Page asked Henry to carry a petition to the Provost Marshal General in St. Louis attesting to the loyalty of Mrs. Lindly's husband

and another man held in the federal military prison in Alton, Illinois.[142] Parson Carrico, who was a neighbor of both men in Cedar County, agreed to accompany Henry to the train in Sedalia. As Henry and Carrico drove their wagon through the Missouri countryside, Henry noted, "the deserted farms and heaps of ashes we pass where once were happy homes."[143] Henry described the surprise that greeted him the next day: "Arrived in Osceola about 10 oclock. But Osceola was not there. Nothing but heaps of ashes cinders and bricks where last I saw long rows of magnificent houses & in the streets were pitched tents of federal soldiers."[144] The first men Henry met in Osceola were Dr. Webster and Mr. Scobey, whose families and belongings Henry had hidden from federal troops earlier in the conflict. The Union soldiers attacked in Montevallo were sleeping in Scobey's hotel. Whichever side of the conflict they had supported at that time, Webster and Scobey now seemed to be allied with the Union. Webster introduced Henry to the station commander and the local Provost Marshal, who granted him the pass he needed to travel the rest of the way to St. Louis. Henry was calling in some of the debts he had accumulated earlier in the conflict. He and Carrico continued to Sedalia, where Henry boarded the train. He noticed that there were few travelers and that bridges and other vulnerable points were guarded.[145] In St. Louis, Henry made his way to the office of General Bernard Farrar, Provost Marshal General of the Department of the Missouri. Farrar, whom Henry described as a "Jack ass" who was "only fit to be kept in the shop window of a Taylor," refused to consider Henry's petition. Henry then employed a former Schoolcraft resident, James Knight, who was a Notary Public "acquainted with the click that have the destiny of Lindly & Brazier." This time, he was introduced to Farrar and received a guarantee that his petition and affidavit would be "attended to in a day or two." Henry left a five-dollar bill with Knight and "urged him to push it through."[146] After visiting with his cousins, one of whom was paymaster on the Union gunboat Lexington, and purchasing violin strings and other items for his neighbors and himself, Henry took the train back to Sedalia, where Carrico was waiting.[147]

As Henry and Parson Carrico made their way back to Montevallo, past charred ruins of houses and deserted farms overrun with feral livestock, Henry had time to consider the future of his own family.[148] When armies were chasing one another through Vernon County, residents had an incentive to protect each other and conserve resources that could circulate within the community. As the Union consolidated control of the state government, terrain, transportation, and population, that equation shifted. With the bureaucracy of the Provost Marshal system in place, citizens were forced to declare their allegiance or opposition to the Union. Conflicting loyalties

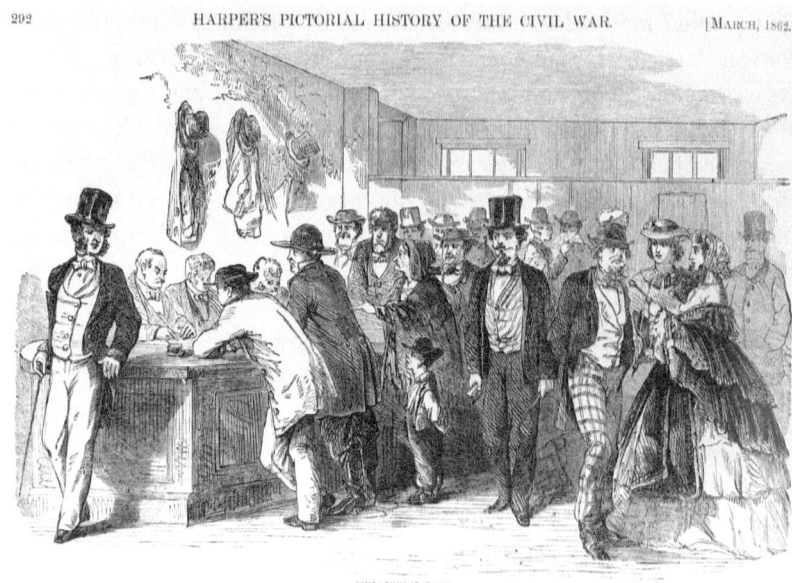

St. Louis Provost Marshal's office, March 1862. "Issuing Passes at St. Louis," illustration, *Harper's Pictorial History of the Civil War*, (Chicago [1866]), 292. Prints & Photographs Division, Library of Congress, LC-USZ62-105253.

to family, friends, neighbors, or the fictive kin of religious congregations or fraternal organizations did not excuse actions, or even speech, disloyal to the federal government or its local military or civilian agents. Henry might have to choose between providing incriminating information about his friends and neighbors or continuing to protect them from Union troops at the risk of being arrested or killed for harboring guerrillas.[149] On May 29, General Schofield warned Missouri residents: "All good citizens, who desire to live in peace, are required to give their assistance to the military authorities in detecting and bringing to punishment the outlaws who infest this State, and those who give them shelter and protection. Those who fail to do their duty in this matter will be regarded and treated as abettors of the criminals."[150] In St. Louis, Henry had opportunities to learn about Union policies from newspapers and family members. The abandoned farms and refugee women and children Henry passed between St. Louis and Montevallo demonstrated the potential for devastation that could reach his own home. The trip also revealed a way to transport his family out of the state before Price's troops returned. By the time he reached Montevallo, Henry had decided to leave Missouri.[151]

Chapter Seven

HARRIET'S CIVIL WAR

"Married life brings many realities & war reveals their *sternness*."[1]

By March of 1862, Harriet realized that the war would continue to endanger her family. Guerrillas gathered around Horse Creek, and Confederate recruiters assembled companies of local men. Federal forces intensified their efforts to control the civilian population and capture or kill Confederate guerrillas and recruits. Harriet turned to the diary that had comforted her before her marriage. On March 23, she began: "A long time has passed since I conversed with thee my journal—my old & tried friend. Eight years with their sunshine & gloom—their weal & woe—eight eventful years, have passed in noiseless succession down the 'river of Time.'" She linked her past self to her present experiences and her envisioned future self:

> Now far from old home scenes, in a wild, distracted land, have we "pitched our tent." Cares have shadowed our brows & pencilled telltale lines—a southern sun has embrowned our cheeks, labor hardened hands that once were smooth. War sits like some foul bird of prey above our pleasant prairie home. Savage scenes of violence are every day affairs—men steal & kill—women & children cower affrighted round their destitute firesides. Such is the present, but still blessed in our home—we are spared to each other—husband, wife & babes. We do not suffer for the actual necessities of life & love & hope still cheer us on. But the *romance* of the past has been sobered down, married life brings many realities & war reveals their *sternness*. I am resolved to note down the incidents of these our dark days, that they may ever keep before my mind our humble, every day life & should

the glad sunlight of *peace* break through these storm clouds may this Record of present trials teach *contentment* & a just estimate of the blessings of prosperity and plenty.

Harriet abruptly shifted her focus to describe the material reality that surrounded her as she wrote: "This has been the Sabbath, a cold, windy day, with patches of blue sky and wild, drifting clouds. The spring so far has been cold & wet—a North West wind has whistled round our cabin all day, but it is more quiet now. Henry is asleep in the big chair, Wallie & Harry in the crib while Isa is waiting for me to *rout them*—so I must stop scribbling, prepare for bed and digest the parsnip cakes I ate for supper as best I can. They are a treat though for corn bread *does* get tiresome." Even in the moments of her greatest anxiety as she contemplated marriage, Harriet never envisioned herself struggling for survival in the midst of a civil war. The brutalities of the conflict seemed to be dismantling the world she knew: her sense of self, her family, her community, her nation, her understanding of human nature and the natural environment, even her God. Without access to mail service, newspapers, or magazines, Harriet had lost contact with the world outside her local community.[2] It had been more than a year since she had heard from her family.[3] She could not safely reveal her opinions to her neighbors, even her old friends, Mr. and Mrs. Page. In this isolation, Harriet drew on the cultural resources she remembered to help her comprehend her alarming circumstances. She resumed writing in her diary to make sense of this new reality and forge a new subjectivity for the new moral order.

Drew Gilpin Faust discusses the importance many southern women placed on keeping a personal diary during the war to provide an "acknowledgement of self as individual and subject, as well as the imposition of some narrative structure of direction and purpose on the variegated events of particular lives."[4] Amy L. Wink concludes that Texan women maintained diaries "to recognize themselves even though their world changes" and to leave testimony of their wartime experiences.[5] Kimberly Harrison examines how elite white southern women also used their diaries to create a new Confederate identity.[6] Harriet shared with many of these women the fear of home invasion, the stress of living under military occupation, and the realignment of allegiances and identities. Like other diarists, Harriet juggled the roles of reporter, protagonist, and author. As a reporter, she described her experiences and observations, placing herself in the context of historic events. As the protagonist of her own story, she examined her actions and assessed her performance of social roles, linking her present self to her past and future life. As an author, Harriet used rhetorical techniques to construct a narrative that articulated her experiences with conventions of literary and oral storytelling. When she recalled her past self and envisioned better times ahead, Harriet hoped that her "Record of present trials" would remind her future self to appreciate any "blessings of prosperity and plenty." By viewing her responses to the events of war as trials that would test her faith and character, Harriet applied a familiar religious narrative template to bring order and meaning to seemingly random incidents. In the face of profound personal and social dislocation, Harriet returned to the practice of writing daily diary entries in an effort to shape the chaos she was experiencing into a comprehensible story with a moral message.[7] The detailed anecdotes she told and the vignettes she described personalized the impact of war and portrayed the effects of the breakdown of civil authority and ethical guidelines on the social fabric.

By the time Harriet resumed her diary, her youthful ideal of a family gathered around the cheerful hearth in a cozy cottage was displaced by the reality of women and children left cowering around "destitute firesides" that provided little food or warmth and offered no protection from the bands of men who might burst into their homes to "steal and kill." War hovered like a "bird of prey," ready to pounce on the most helpless victims, vulnerable even inside their own houses. Jane Schultz writes that southern women in the path of Sherman's army saw the looting of their homes as a gendered offense rather than an institutionalized policy of war.[8] Harriet similarly perceived the war in Missouri as a series of violent acts committed by men against women and children: it is men who "steal and kill," women and children who "cower affrighted."[9] War challenged the ideals of domesticity that Harriet had been raised to see as natural: she used the image of the home, frequently portrayed in popular literature, music, and art as a woman's sacred space, to highlight the impact of the conflict on the women of her community. Harriet reported: "Many wives & mothers have seen their husbands shot down before their own doors."[10] Guerrilla fighters instilled terror in the civilian population by threatening or attacking men in front of their wives and children.[11] Regular troops also intruded into the domestic realm. Many of the objects vulnerable to theft or confiscation by Union and Confederate soldiers fell within women's traditional domain.[12] Harriet described a neighbor whose house had been looted: "Mrs. Tutt, a widow, called to see about getting a place to keep house this summer. She was a strong Southern woman yet had her house stripped of every thing by some of Price's men, early last season—her bedding, dishes, cooking utensils—in short almost every thing was taken."[13] Even a widow, who might expect compassionate treatment, was forced out of her home when members of the pro-Confederate state militia confiscated the items that enabled her to live independently.

Baltimore artist Adalbert Volck envisioned the experience of civilians under federal military occupation. *Searching for Arms*, etching, 1863. National Portrait Gallery, Smithsonian Institution, NPG79.95.C.

Two weeks later, Harriet watched armed men approach her own isolated home. The openness of the terrain enabled Harriet to monitor the approach of visitors but also placed the house in a conspicuous and vulnerable position. On April 7, she wrote:

> About three o'clock when coming from the hen house I looked up & there, riding from the South, was a company of armed men. In the distance they seemed more numerous than they really were, but friend or foe they were *coming here*. My heart gave one bound as rushing into the house, I proceeded to dispose of a few articles—stuffing the money purse into my bosom—the silver ware into my dress pocket & hiding Cobb's rifle. I had just composed myself to my sewing & endeavored to calm the children who were a *little* flustered, when they came clattering up & "hallooed"—Henry was at work at the field—so I went out to play the agreeable to fourteen rough looking men, with pistols & guns. But I found *they* were the *scared* party having escaped by dint of hard riding from a company of *Feds*. They seemed to expect we were friends—said they knew Judge Smith to be "all right."[14]

Harriet enacted a bizarre travesty of the genteel woman's role as hostess, hiding the family savings in her theoretically inviolable "bosom" and reassuring the children as she assumed the studied domestic pose of tending to the family sewing. Instead of displaying her silverware for guests, Harriet hid the treasures in her pocket.[15] Harriet's socialization as a young lady who had learned to "sit just so" and give no sign of her boredom with afternoon callers would have prepared her to "play the agreeable" for her armed visitors.[16] She noted that Wallie "crawled into his crib and lay on his face while they were in the house." By describing her surprise and fear, Harriet avoided implicating herself or Henry in the punishable offense of harboring guerrillas. Despite the threatened penalties, fear of reprisals from guerrilla bands, as well as compassion for neighbors and friends pursued by federal troops, often led residents to help fugitives who appeared on their doorsteps.

Federal troops also demanded food and information from citizens. A month later, Harriet reported that eight men arrived on horseback as the family was sitting down to supper. Earlier that day, as Henry described in his diary, he had arranged for Sam Tapp to turn himself in to the Provost Marshal. Harriet explained that when Henry and his farmhand returned from the field, a soldier approached William with a drawn revolver to ask where the fugitive could be found, while two others ambushed Henry near the spring to demand the same information. Harriet described the arrival of "eight horsemen" who "dismounted and came in": "A careless look all round the room & a drink of cold water each, seemed to allay their suspicions of any 'contraband' goods in the shape of *refugees*. 'If '*it was not too much trouble,*' they would accept our invitation to wait for supper—of course it was not so we seated a table full & I prepared a second edition of same sort without corrections or revisions."[17]

By now, the children were growing accustomed to such visits. Isa later remembered that they threw a sack of precious salt into the tall grass to hide it whenever strangers approached.[18] "Wallie was seated in his high chair," Harriet wrote, "but he did not seem scared much when they gathered round him—he persisted in resolute silence, turning his back to his right hand neighbor & looking very steadily at his left—after a little he ate his supper with the rest. When they were all fed, they chatted sociably, like northern men, then mounted & withdrew in perfect order & as silently as they came."[19] Harriet, like Henry, recognized this encounter as military surveillance and implied threat thinly disguised as a social visit. A few days later two federal wagons, each drawn by six mules, "rattled into the barn yard" to collect hay Henry had promised the Quartermaster. "The men must each have a drink,

&c, &c," she wrote. "I waited upon them & began to do up my neglected housework. They wanted dinner, so I bustled around—got them some corn bread & butter, meat & milk." "My work gets along slowly with such interruptions," Harriet concluded.[20] Food became a weapon of war to be hidden or shared, stolen or traded, as the situation demanded.[21]

Harriet's role was to wait: for soldiers and guerrillas to approach the house, for Henry to return, and for troops to ebb and flow in and out of the region. Harriet described the loneliness of the days she spent without adult company: "How long the days seem before the lengthened shadows promise Henry's return from the field. Not a mark of humanity, outside our rude inclosure, do I see from morning until night, unless perchance a 'solitary horseman' breaks the monotonous line of prairie to the south, or some farmer's boy passes the house in search of a 'stray steer.'"[22] The surrounding landscape was silent and motionless. Harriet noted the occasional sounds of the wind, the creek, and the birds that broke the pervasive stillness. In this solitary environment, the movement of figures on the horizon or the rustling of bushes could alert Harriet to a potential threat. The armed local men who "came clattering up and hallooed" loudly announced their arrival. The stealthy approach of federal scouts who "withdrew in perfect order & as silently as they came" was less disruptive but even more ominous.[23] Harriet listened and watched as the social structure of her world collapsed. In April, Harriet recorded visits from neighbors most days. In May, after Henry came under surveillance by Union troops, Harriet reported only four visits, three of which occurred after the troops left Montevallo on May 17.

Harriet and Henry were conscious of being watched by their neighbors as well as by soldiers and guerrillas. Combatants on both sides encouraged and coerced citizens to inform on neighbors they suspected of disloyalty. Harriet learned to hide her opinions as well as her possessions and to distrust even her closest friends. She enjoyed occasional visits to her Unionist neighbor, Mrs. Page, sometimes taking the children with her and other times leaving seven-year-old Isa at home in charge of the younger boys.[24] Harriet worried that her long-standing friendship with Mrs. Page might be threatened by their diverging political views. She reminded herself that in wartime, it was dangerous to confide in even the most intimate friends: "Mrs. Page and I had a long talk about sundry things. Surely no shadows ought to fall between us. She is like a sister to me & God grant the feeling may always be mutual. We have been too careless in our family & I trust 'passing events' will teach a lesson! No person should be permitted to enter a family & become conversant with its private affairs—a brother even is scarcely to be trusted."[25] A few weeks later, Harriet reassured herself that despite Mr. Page's strong support for the

The landscape of a tall-grass prairie edged by wooded creek beds, preserved and restored at Prairie State Park, approximately thirty miles southwest of Montevallo, Missouri. Photograph by Koral Martin Photography.

Union, he had refused to tell federal soldiers which neighbors had corn they could commandeer. "If all were equally careful, many an honest man would escape who is now suffering persecution," Harriet observed. "Petty malice & meanness will prompt many to inform while envy & jealousy will be always powerful motives with *small* men."[26] Since people could be arrested on suspicion of disloyalty and held indefinitely without a trial, it was tempting to settle old scores by denouncing troublesome neighbors. A few days later, Harriet noted: "John Brown thinks Boyd informed against him. Every man suspects those with whom he has had any difficulty & these jealous feuds will occasion a great deal of trouble for *blood* seems to be the only thing that revenge calls for now."[27] Harriet feared that genuine Union supporters like Mr. Page, who found a threatening message on his gatepost, as well as those who claimed loyalty only to gain the protection of federal troops, would face retaliation if Confederate forces regained control of the region.[28]

Harriet described the complexity and fluidity of allegiances as the balance of power shifted with the movements of Union and Confederate troops: "Mr. Murphy was here this forenoon; were a northern man to express himself as he does how many would be down upon him as a *Union man* & consequently 'a pestilent fellow.' Well, we shall know soon, I hope, whether Mo. goes north or south, & I trust 'freedom of speech' will be permitted once more, at least *for thought*." Harriet assumed that the constraints on civilians were a temporary consequence of the struggle for control of the state. "The story now is that the 'Federals' have the state & Price is retreating southward," she added.[29] A few days later, she reported: "They say the northern part of the state in an uproar again. The Secessionists have the ground and are raising the mischief. 'Uncle Sam' will have his old quivering hands full I'm thinking before he subdues these incorrigible rebels. The young scapegraces just laugh at his venerable back the moment it is turned."[30] Harriet's metaphor fits the pattern of guerrilla movements Andrew William Fialka has identified in central Missouri, with guerrilla activity increasing after the departure of Union troops from a community.[31] When troops from Fort Scott arrived in Montevallo to investigate the attack on sleeping federal soldiers, Harriet was afraid this dynamic would play out in her community. "A Kansas company are in town & all the warlike portion are flitting fast & far as horseflesh can take them," Harriet wrote.[32] Several days later, she reported: "The Feds are scouring the country for 'Secesh' & 'Jayhawkers' but they have not come in sight of our house, though scouts are passing daily to Horse Creek. They are taking many prisoners—some quiet citizens, who have been threatened by the Secesh." "A man has little chance between the two extremes," she concluded, "yet it would seem as though Uncle Sam ought to try & not persecute his *friends*."[33] Harriet noted that Mr. Page "has been busy the past few days trying to *get out* good citizens, whom the Feds have made prisoners." She added: "I am glad yet if the tide of power should turn I am afraid his acts would only be remembered as so much evidence of his being a *Union man*."[34] A month later, the troops suddenly left. Harriet wrote: "It looks hard if the Feds *have* been scared off—for they came here & forced citizens to take the oath of allegiance and place themselves under their protection & now at the first whisper of danger we are deserted, left without arms & liable to fall victims to the revenge & animosity of men who are ruled by their worst passions."[35] The next day, she concluded: "I'm afraid bonds & oaths are of little account when there is a prospect of a return of Price's army." "The Feds were quite a gentlemanly, clever set a few days ago but now they are a parcel of rogues & cowards & the southern boys can 'whip them three to one,'" she observed.[36]

The moral clarity Harriet had valued in the past seemed elusive. She worked out a new moral code in which the climate of violence and those who had created it were evil, while its victims were innocent even if their actions were illegal. In this civilian wartime ethics, deceit and revenge were justifiable in retaliation for aggression, and the obligation to protect family and friends outweighed the duty to obey the law. Like Henry, Harriet divided the guerrillas into two categories: those who were looking for trouble, she described as outlaws, while those who were fighting to avenge attacks against their families or themselves, she viewed as victims. The moral distinction

Harriet made was not based on the principles for which the guerrillas were fighting or even the consequences of their actions but on whether they were the instigators or the targets of aggression. She criticized "the lawless desperadoes who have infested our creek bottoms & stalked unblushingly through every neighborhood, robbing honest men, insulting helpless women & terrifying children & babes."[37] In contrast, she described Charlie Blann, who was "hunted like a wild beast," as the victim of "Kansas jayhawkers": "These bloody miscreants, who under the folds of the Federal flag commit unheard of atrocities, first robbed him when a quiet peaceable citizen & now he is outlawed & persecuted for trying to get back his own. There *are* those who no doubt have done nothing but plunder for the love of it & strangers cannot be expected to discriminate such from the honest but aggravated men who have been *driven* into their company."[38] Union leaders recognized the difficulty of distinguishing between men who willingly formed outlaw bands and men driven into hiding by their resistance to the unauthorized foraging of Union troops. They realized that arresting men who acted to protect their families and homes was turning public opinion against the federal forces. Harriet wrote: "I was in hopes our country might be cleared of that dangerous class who have been so boldly committing all manner of depredations—but the *root of the evil* seems untouched—many harmless citizens have been arrested but the *rogues* are still lurking about the woods in the dark, creek bottoms, occasionally showing themselves in some obscure neighborhood but ever eluding the pursuer."[39] Harriet applied to wartime conditions the peacetime assumption that individuals could be judged by the reputations they had earned. She claimed that only the residents of a community, not strangers like the federal troops, could assess the moral character of local men. In fact, Union officials did take into account petitions from community leaders who certified the good character of civilians held in federal prisons.[40]

The experiences of civil war challenged Harriet's assumption that the dictates of personal conscience aligned with loyalty to God, country, community, friends, and family. Acts of compassion that would be applauded in peacetime could be defined as morally wrong in wartime. Harriet justified the assistance she and Henry provided to fugitives by denying that the men they aided were aggressors. "Circumstances have compelled us to open our doors in a manner that may be construed by these over zealous Federalists as 'harboring jayhawkers,'" she wrote. "Dr. Dade is not a Jayhawker—nor is Henry Taylor yet his life is at stake for that very offense."[41] Harriet could have claimed that she and Henry had been forced to harbor Dr. Dade and his companions when the armed men arrived at their isolated home after attacking sleeping Union soldiers in Montevallo, but she made no mention of feeling threatened.[42] She viewed her interactions with the fugitives as she would have approached her social duties in peacetime: it was her obligation to provide assistance and hospitality to her friends and neighbors. "What would the Feds not give to know all we do just now," Harriet explained ten days later, "but God cannot be offended with the motive which prompts our silence & I am not ashamed of my husband for the humanity that is willing to aid the wretched victims of mistimed policy."[43] The following day, she added: "Everything quiet though Mr. Page called to let Henry know that there is some talk in camp about his *harboring Dr. Dade*. Well, were it to be done over he would do the same & I would encourage him in it. Must a man stifle every emotion prompted by common humanity?"[44] Harriet's perspective makes sense in the framework of her moralist system of ethics. In addition to relying on her knowledge of Dr. Dade's character and reputation, she assumed he described his circumstances honestly. Harriet had been raised to follow her conscience and trust her understanding of the universal principles of "common humanity." She could call on the higher authority of God to justify her actions.

The day the wounded Dr. Dade arrived at Harriet's house, she wrote: "Nora Mayfield went into town today & gleaned the few particulars we have heard." In 1888, the *History of Vernon County* described the Mayfield sisters as Confederate "scouts, spies, guides, and couriers as the occasion demanded."[45] Harriet's mobility was limited by her responsibility for three young children, including a nursing baby, but she followed the progress of the war through a network of local women who continued to visit and assist one another regardless of their allegiance.[46] Harriet and Mrs. Page left messages for one another in a hollow tree located between the two farms and sometimes arranged to meet at the spring that provided water for both families. After the war, Mrs. Page rediscovered a note from Harriet that William Steward, the Smith's farmhand, had delivered to her "at the time when we were all anxious to get news from the seat of war."[47] In spite of her lack of mobility, Harriet was well-informed about battles and troop movements, and she astutely assessed the validity of the rumors she reported. Harriet summarized accounts of alleged atrocities committed by soldiers. In her early diary entries, Harriet assumed that the most appalling rumors must have been exaggerated. At the end of March, she noted that Union troops at Humansville in neighboring Polk County were "reported to have killed & mutilated the wounded." She continued: "Such barbarity does not seem possible. They have taken several quiet citizens prisoners in Cedar. I know nothing of the cause, and we can never depend upon what we do *not* see ourselves."[48] Over the following weeks, Harriet came to accept the horrifying reality underlying such accounts.

In April, Harriet told of southern troops who set fire to a house, inadvertently killing women and children when the roof collapsed. She explained:

> One would think the 'Father of Lies' would be put to his wits end after a while for at the rate people go on his resources will give out. The wildest & most extravagant stories are afloat—you never can hear a version of any affair hardly, but what the next person you meet will give an entirely different statement. Men seem to vie with each other in spreading the most glaring inconsistencies. Yet improbable as most of the stories are, in barbarous details, they fall short of the 'stern reality.' The *truth* is fearful—too fearful to be told in this enlightened age.[49]

Harriet realized that regardless of the accuracy of their "barbarous details," the accounts presented a graphic picture of the horrors of war. They were figuratively, if not literally, true. Two days later, Harriet wrote: "All sorts of improbable stories are going the rounds but no one seems sufficiently authentic to be believed."[50] In May, she described "a story of blood that seems almost too cruel to be true," although the federal soldier who told it claimed to have heard the account from the daughters of an elderly prisoner murdered by "rebel" soldiers.[51] By June, Harriet had come to believe that no report of violence could be discounted regardless of how unbelievable it might seem. She wrote: "Mr. Boyd tells some hard stories of wayside shooting. He says the prisoners when let loose are waylaid & shot down on their return home—cruel—cruel! I think there is more of the spirit of hell in Fort Scott than in any place I know of this side."[52] Federal records confirm the plausibility of Boyd's account. Troops sometimes responded to the guerrilla practice of killing their captives by executing their own prisoners and reporting that they had been killed while attempting to escape.[53] Mrs. Boyd told Harriet "a dreadful story" about two federal soldiers who were hanged in Kansas. Harriet concluded: "Such wickedness as they practiced seems almost incredible."[54] As the level of violence escalated, it became difficult to determine which tales of atrocities were too terrible to be believed. Michael E. Woods discusses how antebellum narratives crystallized sectional identities by using language intended to elicit a heightened emotional response.[55] In a society that valued eloquence in storytelling, the credibility and skill of the narrator and the local setting of the accounts enhanced the impact of narratives of wartime atrocities that graphically illustrated the inhumanity of the enemy. These accounts enabled men and women to convey information, influence opinions, generate intense feelings, and sometimes instigate revenge while maintaining the option of denying those intentions.

When the truth was "too fearful to be told," one type of story that could be repeated in detail described a seemingly powerless victim who turned the tables on his or her attacker. In contrast to her terse reports of atrocities committed against helpless civilians or captured combatants, Harriet retold these anecdotes about local individuals in dramatic fashion, including quotations of dialogue and descriptions of settings. She usually concluded by pointing out the moral of the story, following the narrative convention of traditional trickster tales in which a less powerful character outwits a stronger adversary. While rumors of atrocities reported incidents when evil prevailed, often unpunished, these tales described the triumph of good over evil, like the moralist fables Harriet read as a young woman. The narratives created a sense of distance from the events they described, even as they made the horrors of war concrete. In early April, after expressing her fear that guerrillas would target her family because they were northerners, Harriet told the story of a boy who outwitted the men who tried to rob his family. Harriet noted that "Mr Boyd told a funny story almost too good to be true" about a local man named Wily Wright. With this introduction, Harriet alerts the reader that Boyd's account was so similar to a trickster tale that she doubted its accuracy. Harriet wrote:

> Wily Wright, a notorious horse thief, & some of his chums, went to a man's house to strip him, taking what they wished in doors & then ordering him to get his horses from a pasture, which, he, instead of doing, turned out into the timber. They then mounted his boy upon one of their own & sent him for them, but the youngster was too smart for them. He went for aid & came back with armed force enough to take the men & make them return what they had before stolen. So Wily has once met his match. He has been in the habit of going round to Union men & passing himself off as a Ft Scott man, gaining all the information he could & then plundering the poor foolish victims of his ruse.[56]

Harriet's explanation that "Wily has once met his match" points out the moral of the story with a formulaic phrase describing a trickster who was fooled by his intended victim. Harriet made sense of seemingly random acts of violence by placing them in an oral tradition in which cleverness and courage could overcome superior force.[57] These narratives allowed Harriet to imagine a more active role in the war than that of a helpless victim and suggested a context in which her own acts of resistance and deceit could be given meaning.

Whether civilians intentionally or inadvertently misled soldiers was left ambiguous in some accounts. After Harriet cooked dinner for Union troops who commandeered two wagonloads of grain, she imagined what might have happened if they had tried to rob the henhouse as Ida feared. She wrote that "they would have been served as a soldier was last summer" when he "filled his pockets with a nest full" of eggs while Mrs. Wood cooked dinner for Price's troops. "They were well seated at the table when by some accident one went off. Pop—pop went the rest in rapid succession. The men staid but soon with hands over their noses left the room—no one could eat *there*. The enterprising soldier was ever after known throughout the camp by the pleasant title of '*Rotten Eggs*.'"[58] This humorous anecdote not only turned the tables on the thief but also illustrated the difficulty of telling good from bad by appearance alone. The most innocent facade could hide a rotten interior. Although mistaken identity often led to fatal consequences for innocent civilians, sometimes the local population could manipulate the codes of language as well as clothing to help neighbors elude the surveillance of federal troops. Harriet described how soldiers arrested a doctor whom they confused with the fugitive Dr. Dade. By the time they realized their error, their real target had escaped.

> At the time Dr. Dade left he had a very narrow escape on Horse Creek. He passed Parson Caricoe's in the morning & the Feds were after him at ten o'clock searching the Parson's house & premises. He went to a Mr Williams, rested and ate & left just as Dr Culbertson came up to see Mrs. W. who was sick. Dr. C. was scarcely in when up rode the Feds in hot chase—nabbed their 'little Dr.' & made off—but lo & behold there are *two* 'little Drs' in the settlement, & they have been nicely 'taken in' themselves, while *the* Dr is taking himself off as fast as the old blind horse can go.[59]

Harriet noted the double meaning of the phrase "taken in": misleading the soldiers trying to take Dade into custody, which allowed him to take off instead.

Harriet began to express a hesitant admiration for the colorful guerrillas she had despised and feared only a few weeks earlier. By telling of incidents in which Union troops were outsmarted, Confederate supporters confirmed the viability of guerrilla tactics. Harriet heard that after the raid on sleeping soldiers in Montevallo, a local man whose horse fell during a pursuit by federal troops pretended to be dead, so the soldiers would not shoot him as he lay on the ground. "As they passed him one called out 'there lies a d—d Secesh' but when they returned 'Secesh,' horse & all, had vanished," Harriet wrote.⁶⁰ Several of Harriet's narratives portrayed members of local militia groups and guerrilla bands as tricksters who outwitted superior federal forces through their cunning, daring, and audacity. Harriet described how Henry Taylor came to be held in a federal guardhouse awaiting trial: "It seems Taylor was simply a recruiting officer, with no authority at the time to do any fighting yet, with a few 'southern boys,' he surprised the picket guard of a Federal force of several thousand, drove them into a house & obliged them to surrender their arms horses & accoutriments to about half their number of men. The poor crest fallen guard had to foot it back to camp, some of them minus their fine Federal hats, with slouched Mo. hats instead." Harriet noted that after her husband and Mr. Low, a Vernon County man with a letter of introduction from President Lincoln, attested to Taylor's good character, Colonel Doubleday at Fort Scott told them privately that he "could not but express his admiration of the chivalrous feat which, though unauthorized, & enough to keep him a close prisoner, he termed a 'brilliant little affair.'"⁶¹ After Taylor's trial was postponed several times, federal officials transferred him to Fort Leavenworth as a prisoner of war. Taylor was released on parole after six weeks and later included in a prisoner exchange.⁶²

By applying traditional moral values to wartime incidents or using narratives to exemplify changing circumstances, Harriet imposed order on the turmoil that surrounded her. However, this ethical speculation undermined the concepts of absolute moral values and timeless social roles. Margaret Higonnet has noted that civil wars, in particular, cause women to question the moral order of their society.⁶³ Harriet's accounts depicted the war as a threat to domestic, civic, and religious values as well as to the physical survival of her own family. She described the dissolution of widely accepted norms of behavior: concern for one's neighbors, generosity to those in distress, male protection of women and children, the sanctity of the home, and personal honesty. The moralism that had guided Harriet as a young woman relied on the premise that diligence, self-control, and moral responsibility constituted the route to material success as well as spiritual salvation.⁶⁴ With the collapse of the legal system that settled disputes and enforced laws, the benefits of accumulating possessions were outweighed by the difficulty of protecting them. Harriet reported that Federal troops investigating the Montevallo hotel shooting imprisoned her neighbor, John Brown, and took his gun, coat, and other items, although "he has done nothing, not even as much as we." She concluded: "There is nothing to encourage labor for we have no certainty of possessing what we work for. Our bread, clothing & stock are not secure—even household furniture is liable to be taken—yet there is nothing to do but to learn well the lesson of patience & perseverance and,

With a heart for any fate,
Still achieving, still pursuing,
Learn to labor and to wait."[65]

Harriet looked for a literary precedent to guide her behavior in these unfamiliar circumstances. Henry Wadsworth Longfellow's popular poem, "A Psalm of Life," expresses Yankee ideals of initiative, work, and perseverance in the face of hardship. Although she recognized the futility of her efforts, Harriet saw no alternative but to continue to labor and wait.

As the region degenerated into chaos, Harriet abandoned her faith in a just society that operated in accordance with predictable natural laws. Planning and working for the future seemed pointless when one was unlikely to keep the fruits of one's labor. The responsibility to protect one's family often conflicted with the duty to obey the law or the obligation to assist one's friends. A reputation for good character in peacetime no longer predicted a person's behavior in wartime: to save themselves and their families from imminent death, men and women sometimes betrayed their neighbors. Combatants on both sides of the conflict seemed to disregard basic ethical principles, and distinctions among civilians, soldiers, and outlaws were unclear even to the participants. Harriet recalled two proverbs that suggested appropriate responses to her new circumstances. She found "discretion the better part of valor" and warned: "All signs fail in dry weather."[66] When soldiers, guerrillas, and civilians frequently resorted to lies and disguises, the wisest responses in any interaction were caution and distrust.[67] Conventional signs of friendly intent were no longer reliable indicators of trustworthiness. Times of war, like conditions of drought, called for new tactics for survival in an altered climate.

Wartime conditions challenged Harriet's assumption that a woman's appearance indicated her respectability and gentility. Even basic standards of hygiene and clothing became impossible to maintain. "How many things *necessity* will teach one," she wrote. "I wish among other things she would invent something for underclothes—we are all destitute & no one can 'guess' or 'reckon' where a supply will come from. Here within the domains of 'King Cotton' the article cannot be had 'for love or money.'"[68] She was delighted when Henry's cousins in St. Louis provided her with soap, a comb, and handkerchiefs.[69] Harriet was forced to dress her children in the naturally dyed homespun cloth that gave rise to the derogatory designation of rural Missouri residents as "Butternuts," and she wore shoes that Henry had made.[70] Harriet described the family's "simple fare, one day of which is a fair sample of the whole." "We have meat, cornbread & milk for breakfast," she wrote, "cornbread, butter & water for dinner, and corn cake & milk for supper with occasionally some stewed peaches—and a chicken now and then."[71] When William Steward's sister gave Wallie and Isa "*each a biscuit*," Harriet wrote: "The best confectionary would not be welcomed with much more joy & I am sure it could not do them any more good. They are heartily tired of corn bread & so am I."[72] Reliance on cornbread for subsistence took a toll on Harriet's appearance as well as her health. She wrote: "How fast are we 'growing old.' I am startled almost at the sunken eyed, wrinkled visage that looks out from the glass every time I go to it. Our friends would *never feel proud of our good looks*."[73] Malnourished and unable to protect her skin from sunlight and household labor, Harriet described herself as "a toothless, embrowned old woman" at the age of thirty.[74]

In Missouri, Harriet was freed from the social expectations of gentility and the dictates of fashion she had found burdensome. However, she came to realize that those ideals of femininity represented privilege as well as constraint. She was disconcerted that seven-year-old Isa was learning neither academic subjects nor genteel feminine demeanor: "With Isa's help was able to sew some to-day—she takes very good care of the baby. How I wish she had any desire to read—the days pass into weeks & the weeks into months, which are lost in the fast receding years & yet she makes no advancement—except in stature & untutored rudeness. What would our friends think to see us in our primitive habits. I am afraid our children can never receive any mental culture in Missouri."[75] On the other hand, Harriet commented that most girls Isa's age could not be trusted with the care of an infant and a toddler for three hours.[76] When she was forced to abandon the cultural markers of class and gender that she once had found essential, Harriet came to see class distinctions and the gender roles that accompanied them as artificial and superficial.[77] Although Harriet could imagine the consternation of her Michigan friends at her family's appearance and living conditions, she felt a sense of pride in her own resilience and Isa's maturity and sense of responsibility. Isa later remembered that her father taught her to ride horseback before her fourth birthday despite the disapproval of his sister in Michigan.[78] She soon drove the double team and led the horses. Even before the war, rural women in southwestern Missouri had followed standards of appearance and behavior that differed from those Harriet had known in Ohio and Michigan, joining men in farm labor and horseback riding.[79] Bertram Wyatt-Brown claims that southern women were expected to demonstrate toughness, courage, and honor in the face of crisis. He notes that many antebellum southern girls were taught to use guns, ride horses, and fish.[80] Harriet mentioned that some of her neighbors would have benefited from the knowledge of the manners of genteel society, but she admired the women's endurance, bravery, and survival skills.[81]

Harriet came to appreciate the version of womanhood she found in Missouri as an effective response to civil disorder as well as economic hardship. LeeAnn Whites argues that even southern white women raised in a genteel tradition remained within the boundaries of acceptable feminine behavior when they actively supported the war effort and struggled to ensure the survival of their families.[82] Harriet expressed empathy for women whose male relatives were caught up in the conflict. While Henry traveled to Fort Scott to testify on behalf of Henry Taylor, she wrote: "I am doomed to long days of anxiety & loneliness but what are my troubles to those who have husbands & brothers there to be tried for their lives."[83] When Mrs. Dade thanked Harriet for sheltering her wounded husband as he escaped from federal troops, Harriet commented: "How anxious & pale she looked. I could not keep back the tears when she thanked me for 'our kindness' to her husband—she wept & looked so sad. How should I feel to be in her place."[84] She wrote that Mrs. Dade, "with her baby on horse back, has gone to take him some clothing, a distance of only about a hundred miles." "She is a little heroine," Harriet added.[85] Without leaving her home, Harriet became part of the "household war" described by Lisa Tendrich Frank and LeeAnn Whites.[86] Her conversations with neighbors, as well as with the soldiers and guerrillas who arrived at her doorstep, helped maintain Henry's reputation and preserve the family's property.[87] While Henry was gone, Harriet advised Charlie Blann about the presence of Union troops, tried to convince Union soldiers not to arrest William Steward, and gave saddlebags and scrip to Mr. Keithly's son and "a bay horse & dark filly" to a stranger who asked for them.[88]

In the course of the war, many women redefined their domestic obligations to include protecting their family and property, caring for their fugitive husbands, and even participating in activities of guerrilla bands. The assistance they provided their male relatives, the hospitality they offered to neighbors, and the information they passed on to one another all brought women into the range of partisan activity.[89] Harriet described a woman who "interposed herself between her husband & the guns of Kansas jayhawkers" and took the rifle from the startled attacker.[90] The Mayfield sisters joined their brothers and husbands in guerrilla activities, for which they eventually were arrested and imprisoned.[91] Harriet described how the sisters helped a wounded man escape after the shoot-out in which Dr. Dade was injured: "The Feds would be sure to get him if he was not removed & only woman's wit & daring saved him. Nora Mayfield & her sister had him dressed in women's clothes & took him right among the Feds in a buggy, without exciting suspicion & so he escaped."[92] Harriet clearly admired the women's "wit and daring," traits usually attributed only to men. Like Henry, Harriet found alternative models for gendered behavior that were appropriate to the circumstances of wartime. The principles that guided her female neighbors in Missouri were not totally alien to Harriet. Even before her marriage, Harriet had rejected the frivolous behavior of women who emphasized fashion and personal appearance or who flirted and pretended to be helpless. She had preferred simple clothing and sincere conversation, and she had felt a moral obligation to make herself useful to society. Although Baptist organizations in northern and southern states had split over slavery and theological issues before the war, common tenets of simplicity and sincerity provided a bridge between Harriet's past and present religious communities. Once she reset her moral compass to align with her neighbors, she adjusted her image of appropriate feminine behavior and even began to envision her own freedom from the restrictions of polite society.[93]

On her thirtieth birthday in early May, Harriet contemplated her experiences as a wife and mother and her adjustment to the hardships of wartime domestic life:

> This is my birth day & I am *thirty years old*. I cannot realize it although I feel twice that age. The life we have led for a few years tells upon one's looks & feelings. Sometimes I look back upon the past & wonder if I ever was young & girlish like the vision memory calls up & then I turn to the present & *know* that in all those youthful days my heart was never filled with the *rich* joys of the present. I never knew a husband's love or the blessed pleasure of folding my own little ones to my bosom with the fond affection that only mothers can know. May God spare all these priceless treasures, that in no far distant *future* we may sit beneath 'our own vine & fig tree' in *peaceful content*.[94]

Despite her precarious circumstances, Harriet expressed satisfaction with marriage and motherhood. On the milestone of her thirtieth birthday, she struggled to connect her current self with her memories of the past and visions of the future, reframing her naïve youth as a prelude to her current maturity.

Harriet tried to comprehend the war by applying concepts she had learned in more peaceful times. Drawing on the rhetoric of antebellum reform movements, Harriet depicted war as an evil entity, "like some foul bird of prey."[95] Reform literature often personified alcohol and gambling as evil forces that enabled a few ruthless individuals to profit at the expense of numerous victims. Those caught in the snares of these bad habits could reform their behavior to become morally upright citizens. Similarly, she concluded that the local men who engaged in acts of violence had been led astray but could be redeemed. It seemed to Harriet that the men and women who had unleashed the forces of war bore responsibility for the results. Although she had attended at least one meeting of the Anti-Slavery Society in Schoolcraft and had objected to moving to a state that allowed slavery, Harriet directed her anger at northern abolitionists who were safe from the violence as well as at southern secessionist politicians:

> May the worst evils of it fall upon the heads of those who raised the hue & cry which has severed this once "glorious Union".... They who have helped to bring this evil down are now plotting in ignominious security—while honest hearts are pouring out their red offering upon their country's altar they believe. Alas! That brother against brother should each believe he is the champion of a holy cause. Alas! That the good & true must be the victims while the selfish, unprincipled fomentors of this terrible disunion exalt in peace & quiet. Would that every black hearted abolitionist, every fire eating, office seeking disunionist North or South, might stand in the front ranks of these armies which are now arrayed against each other, & receive the fatal charge destined to "lay low" so many better men.[96]

Harriet realized that her family and friends in northern states held radically different views from those she now shared with many of her neighbors in Missouri. In February 1861, her father asked Henry whether he sympathized with the "mad revolutionizing *treasonable* spirit of South Carolina." Like many northern Protestant clergy, Harriet's father viewed secession and the ensuing war as part of a divine plan to end slavery. He was confident that "those who battle for the *right* will triumph" and used a biblical analogy to express his belief that God would aid the Union forces: "He has seen the affliction of his oppressed people in the South, he has heard their cry, and will send deliverance; yes, and this deliverance may and probably *will* come, through the rash, indiscrete, and unreasonable course of the seceding states: as the emancipation of Israel from Egyptian bondage was attended with the destruction of their oppressors, so it may be in breaking the bands of slavery in the South."[97] In her criticism of abolitionists, Harriet repudiated her father's religious and moral convictions as well as his political position.

Harriet wished that she could feel the certainty of belief that her father demonstrated: "We know not what is in reserve for us & if I could feel the same faith & trust that sustain my dear father amid all life's ills, there would be little to fear here or hereafter."[98] The moral guidelines that had seemed natural in peacetime did not seem to fit the circumstances of war. There was no longer a community consensus to which to conform, and the dictates of conscience no longer corresponded to the dictates of law. Harriet came to see the actions of each individual in her community as a response to unique and complicated circumstances. She was shifting from a sense of moral certainty to one of moral relativism. Harriet disagreed with those on either side of the conflict who believed their opponents to be evil and themselves to be righteous.[99] In her experience, Union troops were "bloody miscreants, who under the folds of the Federal Flag commit unheard of atrocities," while guerrillas were "lawless desperadoes."[100] Militia fighting for the Union, as well as guerrillas supporting the Confederacy, had become caught up in the escalating cycle of bloodshed and revenge.[101] With family and friends in the North as well as secessionist neighbors in Missouri, Harriet found it difficult to demonize either party to the conflict, but she found much to criticize in the conduct of the war by leaders and combatants on both sides. She anticipated disastrous consequences for her generation. "If the war ever ends there may be brighter days—but *we* can never see the same prosperity & plenty there was before this ill fated year—our children *may* but our country can not recover this fearful blow in our day," she concluded.[102]

Harriet once had been certain that God and universal moral principles supported her point of view and that it was her duty to convince others of the truth.[103] In her experience, freedom to express one's convictions was inherent in the practice of politics, religion, education, and cultural activities, and laws protected citizens' rights to free speech. Her father had used his persuasive abilities as a preacher to inspire religious conversion. The political system was based on the principle that people were free to express their opinions. Newspapers, lyceums, and political campaigns provided platforms for debate. Men and women formed organizations based on the assumption that they could influence changes in laws and behavior. Public schools taught rhetorical techniques for presenting logical arguments in speech and writing. But what would be the outcome when conflicting views of moral truth were irreconcilable and neither side could be converted to the other's point of view? Harriet observed that the Civil War marked the conspicuous failure of the American experiment with a republican form of government based on the acceptance of dissent. She concluded: "Never more can we be the beacon light of all the oppressed in other lands—the noble experiment of a perfect Republic has been tried, and failed. Our government can never be rebuilt upon the old liberal foundation—the rebel States may all perhaps be subjugated, but the bond of Union must be tightened & the iron bands must be firmly rivetted, & held by a strong hand."[104] A few days later, during one of Henry's trips to Fort Scott to testify for Henry Taylor, Union soldiers arrested William Steward, the Smith's farmhand, despite Harriet's pleas and protests. He was released from the Fort Scott guardhouse, along with his father and uncle, the following day after taking the loyalty oath. Harriet wrote: "People *must not talk secession*—women *as well as men*. I wonder if some way cannot be invented to take a person up for his *thoughts* in this 'glorious republic.'"[105] The ideal of a civil society, with citizens joining together to govern themselves for the public good, seemed to have given way to the power of the state to silence dissent.

Harriet began to doubt not only her assumptions about the social order but also her understanding of the natural world. The landscape whose beauty she had enjoyed came to seem malevolent. Like many Americans, Harriet associated woods with danger and open prairie with safety.[106] In April, Harriet wrote that she dreaded the coming of spring when leaves on the thickets surrounding the creek beds would provide cover for guerrillas returning from their winter quarters in Texas.[107] A week later, Harriet welcomed the emergence of prairie flowers but realized that this peaceful scene could be disturbed at any moment by the intrusion of mounted soldiers:

> It seems impossible, when I look from my window upon the widespread landscape, clothed in Nature's loveliest garb, that the evil passions of man can prompt to deeds of violence & blood. It seems as though the calm purity of these fresh spring days & scenes would elevate every human soul above all that is brutal or debasing. I cannot begin to realize here in our quiet nook the dangers that are lurking near, & only when the sudden jingle of spurs & clatter of iron shod hoofs announce the presence of soldiers am I for the instant startled out of my dream of security—then the horrors that enthrall our beloved land—our homes & all that is dear—rise in vivid colors before my fancy.[108]

Sometimes, Harriet saw the natural environment as a metaphor for the turmoil in human society. "Vegetation is rank & green—the woods look dark & shadowy enough for secret deeds of blood & violence—the sun shines fitfully from among the scudding clouds & the big shadows flee over the waving prairie as if chased by some winged demon. *Pursuit* & *flight* are the order among the spirits of earth & I know no reason why they should not be among those of the air," she wrote.[109]

Creek bed in Montevallo Township, Vernon County, Missouri, 2015. Photograph by Timothy Motz.

Isa recalled that the "woods and prairie were a vast flower garden in the Spring and Summer."[110] She and Harriet turned to wildflowers for reassurance of the orderliness and beauty of nature. Harriet pressed and dried the flowers they picked, a small gesture of control in a chaotic environment.[111] The traditionally feminine activity of collecting wildflowers was intellectually challenging and aesthetically satisfying in an environment that offered little opportunity for either. The botanical classification of flowers represented both the complex order of nature and the ability of humans to comprehend it. Left alone with her children while Henry traveled to St. Louis to petition for the release of their neighbors from federal military prison, Harriet put "a few flowers on paper." "When I get too lonesome & blue to work," she explained, "I go to my flowers & they are a pleasant diversion. The study of Botany is, like all other Natural Sciences—peculiarly bewitching—& it occupies all my leisure thoughts & moments."[112] In the presence of so much death, flowers served as symbols of life, reminders that the natural world would continue even in the face of human carnage.[113]

By June, the confidence Harriet had felt only a few weeks earlier in her ability to cope with the hazards of war had eroded. Like many women raising children alone in wartime, she felt so overwhelmed, and perhaps so deadened to the presence of violence, that she used force to discipline her toddler.[114] On Wallie's third birthday, a few days after Henry left for St. Louis, Harriet wrote: "Wallie is three years old to-day & even now is almost too much for me to manage. To-night he took a very dirty gourd & put it into the barrel of drinking water, spoiling the whole & that just as supper was ready. I had a time with him—he was tired & sorry & spunky & *would* cry until I had faithfully tried the virtues of a good stick—tying him up & bandaging his mouth."[115] A few days later, Harriet wrote that Wallie refused to get undressed at bedtime: "Wallie is most sick, yet I had to punish him severely before putting him to bed—he was determined not to 'be undressed until papa comes,' & I humored him till he went to sleep upon the floor & then when I attempted to take off his clothes he fought like a Trojan—whipping did no good, but when I sent William for a pail of water & told him I should *put his head in if he did not stop screaming & kicking*, he quieted down instantly & went to bed very pleasantly."[116] Harriet struggled to maintain control of her children as well as her own temper in the close quarters of her log house. Ideals of motherhood, like those of femininity and domesticity, fell victim to the "many realities" of marriage and the "sternness" of war.[117]

During Henry's absence, Harriet marked their eighth wedding anniversary. She wrote:

> This is the anniversary of my wedding—have been married just eight years. Time has left deep footprints in his path & I feel that they are indelible. No one would have made me believe a picture of the *present real*, had one been placed before my mind's eye, on that bright morning, as I stood by the side of him my heart had chosen & promised those vows which made our hopes & interests *one* through life. We could not have dreamed that our home would have been so far from all the loved of earlier years—that our country with all its 'boasted liberty' would become a reproach among nations—that *we* should live to see 'the stars and stripes' scoffed at & defiled—that men of the same fatherland would burn with deadly hate & slay each other with brutal ferocity. God only knows whether we are to see the end of these dreadful conflicts or whether we are to pass through life amid stories & trials that grieve the soul of every good man. May Heaven preserve my own dear husband that *together* we may battle the tempests on this rough sea.[118]

As Henry's absence lengthened, Harriet realized that she, like many other women, might be left to face these trials alone. She was beginning to adjust to the possibility that the turmoil of war might be the condition in which she would spend the rest of her life. The changes Harriet had experienced now seemed "indelible," and she recognized the extent to which her "present real" existence had become divorced from the peacetime world that only a short time earlier had seemed natural.

Chapter Eight

REFUGEES

"Look out for a 'prairie skooner' of rags, dirt and babies"[1]

"Never was a surprise more welcome," Harriet wrote, than "the joyful cry of 'Papa has come'" that announced Henry's return from St. Louis. In a letter Boyd brought from Fort Scott, Henry's anxious parents promised to deed him their farm and urged him to move back to Michigan. Midwestern farmers enjoyed prosperity as prices of farm products rose, but wartime labor shortages and rising wages threatened profits.[2] The family's need for Henry's assistance alleviated the shame of returning as homeless refugees dependent on the charity of family and friends. Henry decided the time had come to leave Missouri, at least temporarily. He moved quickly to convert his meager assets into cattle he could drive to Sedalia to sell.[3] He traded a hog and twenty chickens to Ed Upton for a yearling and convinced Mrs. Dade to give him a cow and calf in partial payment for the wagon he had sold Dr. Dade on credit. Henry exchanged most of his farm equipment and household goods for seven head of cattle. He organized several local men, including Union and Confederate supporters, to band together to drive their cattle north to Sedalia, where the cattle trail met the railroad. Henry would return to Montevallo with cash from the sale of his cattle, and Harriet and the children would join him on the journey back to Michigan.[4] Reluctantly, Harriet sold her stove, milk pans, plates, and jars, as well as Henry's plow, and traded their "bureau, crib, safe & lounge" for more portable goods. Wallie sobbed when a neighbor removed their furniture, and Harriet almost cried when he took away the family dog.[5] Furniture and cooking utensils had become more than functional objects: they represented the security and comfort of home. Selling their possessions stripped the belongings of their sentimental meaning and returned them to the status of goods to be traded at market value. Even the pet dog was transformed into a commodity.

In spite of all the hardships Harriet had experienced in Missouri, she was reluctant to abandon the natural beauty and personal freedom she found on the prairie. She wrote: "It was almost impossible to give up the glorious panorama spread out upon all sides & cramping ourselves up in a small village our vision bounded by a narrow street & a few old tumbledown tenements."[6] Although Harriet referred to the landscape, she also dreaded returning to the confining social space she would occupy in Michigan with a new awareness of the constraints of gender and social class that once had seemed natural. Ironically, the dissolution of the world she had known seems to have led Harriet to a stronger sense of herself.[7] The flourishes of sentimentality and angst that had characterized her diary a decade earlier were replaced by confidence in her ability to survive and protect her family even in the midst of a civil war. Harriet had learned to center herself through her diary, her attention to her children, her enjoyment of nature, and her concern for the welfare of her neighbors. Alternating with the "psychic numbing" to violence that Michael Fellman found to be a common defensive mechanism for many civilians caught in the guerrilla war, Harriet responded with heightened emotions and empathy. She wrote: "What a strange mixture of feelings arise at the thought—if we could be assured of *peace* I would not wish to leave here for more than a visit; & as it is I dread going from Mrs. Page."[8] After a visit from the Page family, she commented: "My heart aches when I think of them. I cannot look forward to meeting our friends with any confidence because of the strong desire to remain. I feel almost like a 'galley slave,' scourged to perform some unwelcome task."[9] Harriet had lived in Montevallo longer than any other community, and she had come to see it as her home. However, she soon became resigned to Henry's decision. "I could not but feel sad at the thoughts of leaving our old home forever, yet there is a strange sort of apathy about it after all," she wrote.[10]

While Harriet and Henry prepared to leave Missouri, several people asked Henry to help family members in Union prisons. Harriet noted that he wrote a petition for Henry Taylor's release, which had been promised if certain men would sign on his behalf, and passed it on to Mr. Page.[11] A stranger from northern Vernon County explained to Harriet that she wanted Henry to petition for her father's release because she had heard that he "went sometimes to 'help Southern men & never failed to get them out.'"[12] John Anderson asked Henry to determine whether his fifteen-year-old son was held in the Union prison in Alton, Illinois.[13] Harriet worried that Henry's interactions with Provost Marshals would generate suspicion. She was relieved when

Riley Lindley was released from prison and returned home, vindicating Henry.[14] "Poor man he finds no rest & all his efforts seem to accomplish nothing more than to excite the vile tongue of slander in those who would fain make him a spy & informer," Harriet wrote.[15] As the provisional state government appointed replacements for elected officials who refused to take the loyalty oath, guerrilla bands found judges to be easily identifiable targets for threats, kidnapping, and murder. After the neighboring Cedar County court met under the protection of Missouri State Militia troops, Harriet heard that Judge Lindsay had been shot. "I cannot but feel worried about Henry," she noted.[16] Jesse Steward warned Henry that guerrillas planned to jayhawk Boyd and Carrico, and possibly Henry. He also advised Henry that Confederate troops approaching Montevallo might confiscate their cattle on the road to Sedalia. Henry learned that Federal troops had returned and chased Bob Bales, who sometimes left exhausted horses with Henry. "Feel a little uneasy but not scared," Henry reassured himself.[17]

The day after Henry received Steward's warning, four armed men on horseback approached the Smith home. Harriet and Henry recognized Bob Bales, Clay Simms and the Mayfield brothers, Brice and Crawford. Henry described the encounter:

> They were cordial, rode into the yard dismounted except Clay who remained on his horse as a lookout & his black eyes looked into every bush & caught every object in sight all at once while we lay upon the grass and talked over the times, the murders [and] robberies of the time and Brice recounted some of his dare devil exploits & narrow escapes since last we met. I then told them that I was *threatened* [and] asked them if they knew anything about it. They said no one would harm any of us, that we could take our cattle and no one would interfere with us.[18]

The Mayfield brothers reassured Harriet that Henry "had nothing to fear from their gang" since "his good offices for Southern men were too well known."[19] As Isa later noted, Henry had southern friends but was known to have northern sentiments. Despite his Virginia birthplace, he felt no affinity with southern culture or heritage, disapproved of slavery, and opposed secession. Henry had been a trustworthy ally and advocate for his friends and neighbors, but he was not bound by kinship or motivated by a desire for revenge that would guarantee his continued support under Union occupation.[20] Assuring the family's safe passage out of the region with their livestock would lessen the risk posed by Henry's vulnerability to the increasing pressure from Union authorities. After eating dinner, the men "disappeared as quietly as they came." "I will always praise the bridge that keeps me dry and right and if we get out of this safely we may thank these very outlaws," Henry concluded.[21] He understood the implicit reciprocal obligations involved in the exchange of his assistance to "southern men" for the guerrilla band's protection.[22]

Harriet also described the visit, distancing herself from a frightening experience by depicting it as a picturesque scene: "We saw four horsemen coming towards the house—their glistening arms showing them to be different from our other visitors. My heart went 'pit a pat,' for I knew not what or who they could be besides Militia men, coming to take Henry off as they did Mr Wood yesterday—or Southern jayhawkers bent on making a protest against our Northern trip." She was relieved to see Henry "'hail fellow, well met' with the whole quartette." Although she was wary of Simms, Harriet welcomed Bales and the Mayfield brothers, who were members of her Baptist congregation: "The Feds who were in town yesterday would have admired the picture *hugely* I'm sure & certainly I did for they were a picturesque group. Brice Mayfield is a regular guerrilla—his long beard & hair flowing over his shoulders & breast—his wild, singular style of dress would mark him in *any* crowd." "They are a daring, wild set of men, but I believe will be true to those they profess friendship for," she concluded.[23] While Henry approached the encounter as a calculated transaction, Harriet assessed the sincerity of the men's promises of protection. The guerrillas represented the antithesis of Harriet's pre-war moral values, but they resembled the heroes of popular fiction. Like Henry, Harriet could draw on more than one model of gendered behavior. She could understand the guerrillas in familiar terms of religious devotionalism and cultural Romanticism. The guerrillas claimed to follow the dictates of conscience in defiance of Federal troops. Their emphasis on personal loyalty, friendship, and secrecy replicated the antebellum Romantic nurturing of a private self reserved for an intimate circle of companions. The guerrillas reveled in the intensity of their experiences and the unbridled expression of their feelings. Even their reliance on the cover of natural vegetation and their rejection of traditional attire could be interpreted as a Romantic repudiation of civilization. Using the language of Romantic literature, Harriet wrote that "she admired the picture" the "picturesque group" of young men presented as they "rested under the old oak" in her yard.[24]

Harriet expressed her changing moral standards and loyalties by describing how the Mayfield brothers and other guerrillas planned to ambush their Union counterparts:

Down south at a place called Golden Grove, there are some men who, for some time past, have been robbing southern men as they passed. Our *guerillas* aim to take them in by a simple ruse—two of them will lay aside their arms & ride on from the south & just as they have been robbed & dismounted the rest, backed by a band of reckless Horsecreekers, will rush in & take the whole *they say* to march into camp. It is a good plan & if well executed may rid us of some of Uncle Sam's rogues. 'Tit for tat,' I say & such certainly seems to be the order of the times.[25]

Harriet referred to the men Henry called outlaws as "our guerrillas." She used the underlined phrase "*they say*" to qualify the claim that the prisoners would be marched into camp. A common practice of guerrillas was to kill their captives: this deviation from the rules of war was one of the criteria that, in principle, distinguished guerrilla fighters from regular troops.[26] Harriet recognized the incompatibility of the ambush with her previous moral standards. Using a common colloquial phrase, "tit for tat," to justify retaliation, she endorsed a plan likely to result in the death of the victims. Michael Fellman concludes that guerrilla fighting in Missouri led many civilians to harden themselves to the destruction around them.[27] Fellman describes this temporary abandonment of moral principles as a doubling of the self to create a "wartime alter-self."[28] A decade earlier, Harriet had refused to whip her students and had identified herself as a Yankee. Now, accepting the "order of the times," she applauded potentially deadly violence against "Uncle Sam's rogues." "'Tit for tat,'" she advocated.

A few days later, Henry wrote, "the cavalcade finally took up its march" to Sedalia: "It consisted of 2 waggons loaded with bedding chairs pots kettles churns babies and women."[29] Mark Boyd and Stephen Williams drove waggons loaded with their families and possessions. Charlie Robinson, Henry, and three "southern boys who were trying to get home and dodge the feds as cow drivers" drove the cattle herd, "or at least rode behind them," Henry explained.[30] On reaching Sedalia, Henry found that he could not sell his cattle for as much as he had paid for them in Montevallo. He sold five for forty-five dollars and vowed to "keep the rest till they die before I will sell at such rates."[31] While Henry sold his neighbors' cattle and purchased the goods they ordered, Boyd headed back to Montevallo. He would return with the rest of his family, along with Mr. Morris and his cattle. Another group led by Parson Carrico had already returned home, Harriet noted.[32] Henry left his remaining herd with Stephen Williams. He and Charlie Robinson rode back to Montevallo with the goods they had purchased for their neighbors loaded in John Brown's wagon, driven by fourteen-year-old George Brown, who had traveled to Sedalia with his father and brother.[33] Coordinating their travel and intermingling their livestock and the men most vulnerable to assault or arrest, all the men returned safely home.

During Henry's absence, Harriet and the children moved in with the Page family while Harriet prepared for the trip. She did her best to ensure that the family would maintain minimal standards of cleanliness and respectability. "I hope I can, at least, take back a clean feather bed," she wrote.[34] She traded a table and washtub for fourteen pounds of feathers and exchanged a comb for woolen stockings for Harry. She attached hoops inside her skirt and sewed pants and shirts for Henry and Wallie, a sunbonnet and apron for herself, and two dresses for Isa.[35] Harriet worried that Isa would not meet the expectations of femininity she would encounter in Michigan. When Mrs. Dade and her daughter visited, Harriet wrote: "Lulu looked like a doll, & made me ashamed of Isa, who, poor child, could not help her looks. For years she will be a source of mortification to others & herself because of her rude awkward manners. I hope she may wear off a few of the rough edges from the friction caused by more frequent intercourse with children of her own sex."[36] Harriet poetically summed up her situation one day: "Rain, mud & dirt, sickness & work."[37] She walked back to take a final look at the empty house. "Every thing looked natural but the deserted house—the white pussy lay upon the doorsill sunning herself & the hens went clucking about with the same maternal care, but desolation had already begun its sadenning rule," she wrote.[38] The cat sunning herself in the doorway and the chickens clucking in the yard should have signified domesticity: now they almost seemed to parody the domestic ideal. When Henry returned, he felt "more like crying than laughing" at the thought of leaving the birthplace of his boys and abandoning the cabin he had built and the land on which "every log and rail and shrub bears the mark of my hand."[39] He realized that his farm would soon become a deserted ruin like those he had passed on the road to Sedalia. When Henry traded his reaper for a yoke of oxen, he finally gave up hope of becoming one of the modern farmers described by agricultural journals.

Henry put these discouraging thoughts out of his mind as he turned his attention to packing the family's few remaining belongings. He obtained a mare of "uncertain" title to ride beside the wagon.[40] Neighbors who came to say goodbye brought precious food so Harriet could cook chicken, biscuits, and cookies for their journey.[41] Despite a false rumor that the notorious guerrilla Quantrill had sacked Fort Scott, Harriet again expressed her reluctance to leave Missouri. "How little I realize the truth that we are so soon to part with our dear friends," she wrote. "By this time our friends North begin to lay plans with reference to our return. They little imagine how hard for me to leave this beautiful country." Harriet added a final specimen to her collection of dried and pressed local flowers.[42] Two days later, Henry "bid a reluctant farewell to poor Mrs. Page and launched upon the broad prairie" with two yokes of oxen hauling the wagon carrying Harriet, their children, and all their remaining possessions. "I may regret it but I think it is for the best," Henry wrote.[43] William Steward would escort the family as far as the Osage River, and Ed Robinson would remain with them to Sedalia. Unionist William Leslie would join the family north of the Osage River and accompany them across Missouri and into Illinois. "How my heart aches for Mrs Page," Harriet recorded in her diary. "Her pale, sad face haunts me continually & all through the pleasant afternoon's drive of ten miles, I could scarcely enjoy the beautiful country."[44] Henry, Harriet, Isa, Wallie, and Harry joined the growing stream of civilians fleeing from the fighting that had become truly a "civil" war.[45]

The oxen plodded slowly north, carrying the family's diaries and letters among the few cherished belongings that could be crammed into the covered wagon. On the second day of the journey, Harriet wrote: "We are resting at a deserted house this side of Clintonville. Some family driven or scared out probably, for every thing denotes a sudden 'skedaddling.'" That evening she added: "We are camped at another deserted house, whose fallen fences, broken doors & filthy houses tell a sad tale. I am very tired & camp life is not quite as agreeable, yet I must not be discouraged so soon. We have the prospect of a storm to night, but we will stick to the old 'prairie skooner' for the sheep have rendered the buildings perfectly unendurable."[46] As in Harriet's own home, the domestic animals that could not be transported by the fleeing family remained at the deserted farm. Here, the sheep had taken over the house itself, and the countryside was reverting to its natural state. The next day, Harriet described another such scene:

> This noon we stopped a long time at the Speed place. It is a sorrowful sight to see such a fine house & pleasant grounds deserted & left to ruin. The yard is laid out quite handsomely with shrubbery & shade trees. The weeping willow, poplar, locust, catalpa and many others. I saw the first sweet briar since we left Michigan & breathed the fragrance of home, but alas the beauties of this spot are desecrated—a happy home laid waste & all that taste & wealth had done is now being fast destroyed by browsing cattle & idle mischief doers. The chambers of the house were strewn with old letters, papers & the many evidences of a hasty removal—stoves, bedsteads &c were left still standing. Oh! the wretched cruel curse of war![47]

Alfred R. Waud, [Ruined dwelling, town in distance], drawing, 1860-1865. Morgan Collection of Civil War Drawings, Prints & Photographs Division, Library of Congress, LC-DIG-ppmsca-20989.

The former residents apparently made a frantic search for their most precious possessions before they fled. In their absence, the sacred space of the home had been "desecrated": the family's private letters and papers lay strewn about for all to see, and the symbols of "taste and wealth" in which they once had taken pride were left vulnerable to marauding cattle and human looters. The Eastern trees and shrubs, recalling to Harriet and probably to their former owners the scents of a childhood home, were destined to overrun the house or perish from lack of care. Plants that had once been cultivated and animals that had once been domesticated were completing the demolition of the deserted farms and houses. Mile after mile, Harriet looked around her, stunned at the devastation. She wrote in her diary: "Have passed some fine farms lying in ruins—one where nothing remained of the house but a pile of ashes & the chimney." Abandoned houses reinforced Harriet's awareness of the dissolution of social order and the defeat of domesticity.[48]

Harriet used the language of literary Romanticism to contrast the wildness of the natural surroundings with the cultivating influence of humanity.[49] The first night on the road, she envisioned their encampment as a pastoral landscape scene: "Our chicken & biscuit relished vastly & it was not a bad picture—our white covered wagons—oxen & horses with the group seated upon the grass eating their supper in true primitive style."[50] Two days later, Harriet described a wilder scene: "We crossed the Osage this morning & passed through some wild, & romantic scenery. Upon the banks of the river Henry picked me some of the trumpet vine blossoms—they looked magnificently, suspended in rich crimson clusters from the topmost branches of gigantic old trees."[51] Harriet quickly lost enthusiasm for primitive conditions

Henri Lovie, "Refugees from Southern Missouri Driven from Their Homes By the Confederate Troops Under General Van Dorn," illustration, Frank Leslie, *The Soldier in Our Civil War: Columbian Memorial Edition*, vol. 1 (New York, 1893), 250; originally in *Frank Leslie Illustrated Newspaper* 13, no. 323 (February 1, 1862): 172. Courtesy of the Missouri State Archives, MS515 Frank Wallemann Civil War Collection.

and romantic scenery. On the third day of the journey, she described her attempt to cook over a campfire: "Henry got some sweet milk & buttermilk about half a mile back & I made my first attempt at breadmaking by an open fire—had very fair biscuit, but was driven into the wagon by the rain before they were cooked."[52] The following day Harriet noted with satisfaction: "I cooked some good biscuit which went very well with butter. I am getting a little more accustomed to cooking by camp fires." "How I begin to long for a quiet meal in a house once more," she added.[53] Harriet continued to struggle with outdoor cooking the next day. "Bought eggs & butter, but in my awkward efforts at cooking by the fire I lost a large portion of the eggs & was cheated out of my share of the supper," she wrote.[54]

The following day, as they approached Boonville, Harriet realized that they had entered a region of "fine aristocratic residences" where "the 'lords of the soil' live in luxurious ease." "Tonight we are camped in the sheep pasture of one of these sovereigns," she wrote. "The poor cattle get no feed & we are glad to take cold fare & make ready for bed," she added.[55] She complained that the "old patrician sovereigns of the soil" charged travelers to camp on their land.[56] As the family traveled through this more affluent and relatively secure region, Harriet grew painfully aware that she had become part of a large refugee population, although she didn't use the term until they left the state. The war abruptly deprived people of all social classes of even the most basic necessities of life. As long as they could remain in their own communities, families could cling to the reputations they had earned in more prosperous times. Men and women who were accustomed to being treated with respect lost all markers of status as they fled to regions in which they were strangers.[57] Although she had accepted without complaint the necessity of making do with makeshift clothing in Montevallo, Harriet had gone to great lengths to clothe her family for the journey. Perhaps recalling her own criticism of women she had viewed as shabbily dressed, Harriet especially regretted the disreputable appearance she and Isa presented. In this region where "everything denoted wealth to which we south west Missourians are little accustomed," a woman invited Isa to play with a girl who was visiting her. "Isa had a good time, but I could not help contrasting her rude, awkward manners with the self possessed little Miss of seven from Boonville," Harriet explained.[58] As they approached the place where they would join the Boyd family and the men who had driven their cattle from Montevallo, Harriet realized that her family had become indistinguishable from the rural Missouri residents whose appearance and customs had amused Henry when he arrived in the state. "Altogether I have not been more downhearted since we left," she confided in her diary. "How I dread meeting the lowlived crowd who have our cattle."[59] Two days later, Harriet wrote, they found the "scurvy looking set":

> We came upon the whole cavalcade, huddled together in a hot, narrow, dusty lane, before a house whose inmates must have had a heap of benevolence not to consider the whole affair anything *but* a public nuisance. After a great amount of talking & sparring & confusion, the disgraceful Sunday turmoil was at last quieted & we moved off—the Williams & Morris crew taking one course & we, with Boyd's family[,] another. We had a wild cow tied behind our wagon, which plunged & tore & wound herself around the wheel until she was thrown a number of times, breaking the rope in several places.[60]

Two days of rain turned the hilly dirt roads into treacherous muddy slopes. Harriet complained: "The roads are terrible & every hill threatened to tip us over. The poor cattle slipped & the wagon would slide down the siddling hills until I closed my eyes in horror feeling sure that our hour had come." A few days later, Harriet noted that they were "a dirty, muddy company of 'poor white folks' this morning" after a night of heavy rain.[61]

Illness compounded the discomfort of the journey. A week after the trek began, Harry had developed diarrhea. Now Wallie also fell ill, spending feverish days lying in the wagon, bouncing over the rough road under the hot sun. Unable to eat, he quickly grew thin and weak. Every evening, Harriet washed the clothes of the sick children in streams or knocked on the doors of nearby houses to ask for water for her laundry.[62] Harriet began to question the wisdom of the decision to return to Michigan: "Wallie rather worse—has fever & his bowels no better—Harry is bad too. I sometimes fear this was a wild venture for us to make at this season with our little ones." She continued to worry the next day: "Passed through Williamsburgh & bought some brandy & loaf sugar for Wallie. He is worse & still feverish. Between him & Harry I am kept washing at every stopping place."[63] Henry shared Harriet's anxiety. He wrote in his diary: "Poor little Wallie is getting too weak to walk alone. I am getting alarmed about him." The next day, Henry noted: "Wallie grows worse. Isa and Harry are not well and this is a hard road to travel sure." The following day, he complained: "Mud rain and sick children."[64] Three days later, Wallie remained weak and unable to eat. "All the weary day he will lie upon the bed while the cattle pull us slowly over the long, long road," Harriet wrote.[65]

Henry described another source of anxiety: "This country seems to be full of southern men who are flocking to the standards of the different bush whacking leaders. They intend to resist the order of Gov Gambles to enroll themselves in the Union ranks."[66] A week earlier, Harriet had learned that "the Feds have issued an order for all men fit for service to come up & enroll themselves as state militia." In response to General Orders Nineteen, issued July 22, requiring service in the new Enrolled Missouri Militia, many men left their homes to join the guerrilla bands the militia was intended to fight. The Confederate army had begun to authorize these guerrilla bands as loosely affiliated Partisan Rangers and had stepped up its recruitment in Missouri for military units that combined cavalry and guerrilla tactics within the regular army under leaders like Coffee.[67] Harriet reported: "Rumors of the battle, a few miles ahead, were whispered to us—every one looked askance—deserted houses & neglected farms spoke of flight & trouble."[68] The next day, near Moore's Mill, a local woman told Harriet "some of the horrid particulars respecting the battle ground" and reported that many of the wounded lay dying nearby for lack of medical care.[69] A few days later, Harriet noted: "Just before stopping we met several armed men who were after a horse thief. Porter's guerrillas are reported to be camped not far from here though every story is a new one." Harriet transformed a potentially threatening encounter with Federal troops that day into a picturesque image:

> Big Creek ran just below here—it is a beautiful pebbly bottomed stream with a covered bridge & good ford. Our cattle had a nice

drink from its clear waters & as we came up the opposite bank a party of Federals were standing one side for us to pass. We were for a moment almost startled by their sudden appearance, for their approach had been so silent as to give no warning. The scene was wild & romantic—our covered wagons toiling slowly up the ascent—the cattle & horses standing in the rocky bed of the stream—the group of soldiers—motionless, upon their horses—their arms glistening in the few slanting sun beams which found their way into this shady recess while the blue & gold of their uniforms were brought out in striking contrast with the dark green background—all made a picture, though seen but once, never to be forgotten.[70]

Surrounded by federal troops and guerrilla bands, with Wallie lying dangerously ill in the wagon, Harriet stepped back from the reality of her circumstances to view the scene as a "wild and romantic" picture like the landscapes depicted in books and paintings.[71]

Harriet noted the gap between artistic and literary depictions of a romantic scene and the experience of those who encounter it in real life. She wrote: "Before we came to camp we crossed a beautiful stream, which in this country is so rare[:] a running "branch" with pure water & a clear, pebbly bottom. We drew our wagon under a mammoth mulberry tree & Mr Boyds folks under a huge sycamore—the scene was romantic enough but the *dew* was drenching & breakfast was a tiresome & damp affair."[72] A week later, the family "stopped in the edge of the Mississippi prairie under the shade of some huge elm trees." Harriet again described a picturesque scene: "Beyond stretches the virgin prairie with its few groves of elm while way on to the eastward rise the bold Mississippi bluffs looking like the massive fortifications of a vast city. The sun is sinking to rest & the shadows lie thick upon the prairies—the far Illinois shore looks dim while the moon smiles lovingly upon the quiet landscape."[73] However, the next day, she wrote: "What a night we did have—in spite of the delusive beauty of the scene we could get no rest—the mosquitoes kept up their horrid serenade & fed upon our defenseless bodies through all the long hours." "It does look discouraging to turn our eye to the west where we can see the point of last night's camp," she added, "but then we can look forward to those bluffs which rear their hoary heads so proudly, & know that they form the Illinois bank of the *great river*."[74] The end of the journey was literally in sight.

Finally, after more than three weeks on the road, the Smiths reached the Mississippi River. The ferry made three crossings to transport the refugees and their livestock. When they reached Jersey Landing on the Illinois bank,

Harriet learned that "an order had been made forbidding any strangers crossing."[75] Henry noted on August 10 that he was threatened with arrest for "talking secesh over the river," but he convinced the authorities to release him.[76] Decades later, Isa recalled their relief at escaping the contested terrain of Missouri: "Dixie was behind us and we were again under the Stars and Stripes."[77] Harriet's relief was mingled with the humiliation of having her private domestic tasks become a spectacle for public amusement. She wrote: "We seem to be a sort of nine days wonder among these rock bound Jerseyites, but I have no great pleasure in being on exhibition & only long for rest & quiet. Henry bought some fine river fish, which I cooked for our sunday supper. We are near a beautiful, cool spring in a nice *public* place, where the good citizens may be treated to the sight gratis, a liberty they do not seem slow in availing themselves of." Harriet was eager to reach the home of her older brother, Solomon, but she dreaded "presenting him with such a rough looking company of 'poor relations.'"[78] The following evening, she wrote:

> Our road to brothers was through the timber & it was dark long before we reached his home, but the barking dogs brought him out & he stood with cold dignity awaiting the object of such an untimely intrusion. To Henry's request for lodging &c he returned a stiff refusal on the plea of his wife's absence, inconvenience &c. Henry turned to the wagon with a forlorn sigh & a "Well Hattie, we shall have to go on then" I asked if he [could] not direct us to some place of shelter for the night. Solomon stood bewildered, passing his hand through his hair a moment, then exclaimed, "That voice! Hattie! What does it mean? Hattie who?" "Hattie Smith" was Henry's quiet reply. "And who are you?" "Henry Smith." All dignity had vanished[;] he was at the wagon & my own dear brother clasped his brown, travel worn sister, with as warm a welcome as ever her heart could desire.[79]

It must have reinforced Harriet's sense of shame to be turned aside, even temporarily, by her own brother. When Solomon's wife returned home a few days later, he continued the charade. Harriet noted that he "passed us off as Mo. refugees, calling me Mrs. Brown. Lizzie did not suspect the hoax—she thought bro had become quite familiar with Mrs. Brown however—& I thought looked a little askance at our plain persons so comfortably installed in her own room—at any rate she gave sister Hatty a warmer welcome than the unfortunate Brown recieved."[80] Harriet certainly understood the irony of this introduction: she was, in fact, a "Missouri refugee" dependent on the charity of her relatives.

H[enry] L[ouis] S[tevens], "Union Refugees from Western Missouri Coming Into St. Louis," illustration, *Harper's Weekly* 5, no. 261 (December 28, 1861): cover.

The following day, when her sister-in-law received visitors, Harriet realized that she did not have appropriate clothing for greeting callers. "I was ashamed for my obsolete wardrobe was scarcely presentable," she wrote, "but with the aid of Lizzie's collar she declared herself satisfied & I was duly presented to Mr. Curtis, wife & daughter." Harriet felt humiliated by the need to borrow clothes to make herself "presentable" enough to be introduced to Lizzie's friends. She was further disconcerted to hear their political views: "Mrs. Curtis talks *Unionism* I suppose it is called. To me it seems fanaticism of the most rabid stamp. My blood boils to hear women laugh at the wrongs of good Southern men & talk about '*crushing* out this unholy rebellion with the *iron heel*.' I am afraid our northern friends will have little relish for our *rebel sympathies*—but '*right* is *right*'—North or South—& I detest these abolition ranters, who can see but one side."[81] Only a few years earlier, Harriet had shared the certainty that came from seeing only one side. As distressing as conditions in Missouri had been, it was a shock to return to a world in which she once had felt at home but now found herself a stranger. Harriet's surviving diary ends abruptly a week later, but Henry's diary describes subsequent events. The Smiths remained with Harriet's brother for more than two months while Wallie gained strength, and Henry sold most of his cattle and helped Solomon harvest crops.

At the beginning of October, Henry worried that Wallie still was not healthy enough to travel, but he realized that it was "now or not this fall if we go in a waggon."[82] Harriet wrote Henry's family to warn of their arrival:

> You will find your house more than full with my three children & I know you will be disappointed in us all except Henry. I am so old looking that strangers take me to be older than my brother, who is nine years my senior. I am toothless, brown, wrinkled & grey. Isa is large, lazy & clumsy[;] her nose grows flat & short every year—her teeth large & uneven. Wally is the best looking & he is a perfect "border ruffian" with his home made clothes. Harry never can be called pretty—his eyes are the color of skim milk—the lids are always a little red from a tendency to cry—his hair thin & like sun burnt flax, in short we are a rough looking family & have I do not doubt brought the blush to brother's cheek many times since our visit, but fortunately his heavy beard prevented my discovering it. I am woefully behind the times in every thing & Henry is terribly out at the elbows. Since we have been here the children have been so constantly sick that I could not make what materials we have on hand even—so look out for a "prairie skooner" of rags, dirt & babies.[83]

By October 10, Wallie had developed a serious infection, with "erysippelas" spreading on his leg and ear. Henry wrote in his diary: "Hattie & I hung over our pet all night to catch his every look & word to remember when he should be taken from us."[84] After three days, Wallie began to recover, although he remained so weak he could barely raise his hand. As Wallie's health improved, Henry expressed the resentment he and Harriet felt:

> If there is anything I want now more than another after the recovery of my boy and the welfare of the others it is to get into a haven of my own where we are not a nuisance to those upon whose charity we subsist. And this is the last visit like this I ever make. This is one degree lower in degredation than I ever expected to feel. We are becoming more than a dead weight upon Lizzie and it is with the utmost difficulty that Hattie controls herself enough to keep from replying to the numerous hints and taunts dropped by our fair sister.[85]

The arrival of Harriet's father spared Henry and Harriet the difficult decision of whether to risk the arduous wagon trip with a sick child. He offered to accompany Harriet and the children on the train to Chicago, where he would help them board another train to Kalamazoo.

Isa later recorded her memories of the last portion of the journey. When the train arrived in Kalamazoo, Harriet carried Harry into the station and then returned to carry Wallie, who was still too weak to walk. A group of men watched without offering assistance. If Harriet had felt self-conscious under the stares of strangers in Missouri and Illinois, she must have felt humiliated by the treatment she received as a refugee arriving in the familiar town of Kalamazoo. By the time Harriet managed to move her baggage and children into the depot, the hacks that had come to meet the train had left the station. Harriet left Isa in charge of the boys and their belongings while she set off on foot to look for Henry's uncle. Peering into the window of a bank, she finally recognized a man from Schoolcraft who was able to summon Uncle John Parker to take the family home.[86] Henry set off from Illinois in the wagon, now pulled by five horses, on the two-week journey to Michigan. On November 15, Henry at last approached his hometown, uncertain of the reception that awaited him:

> I hurry on scarse looking a man I meet in the face for fear he will recognize the refugee. The old prairie is the same that I wandered about when a boy only everything looks smaller. I meet several of my old friends grown but little older in 6 years and but two or three know me. As I drew near the village I could pick out the same old houses and the good old souls that occupy them yet. And when I at last turn down towards *my home* I seemed only to have *slept* a few hours. It certainly does not seem as though I had been away more than a few months.[87]

Henry was reassured of his welcome when he "shook a great many hands" the following day. "I surely have more friends than I was aware of," he wrote.[88]

The instinct or information that had led Henry to flee Missouri proved sound. By early August, as the Smith family made their way eastward across the state, troops allied with the Confederacy converged near Montevallo to gather recruits.[89] Coffee camped on Horse Creek, nearly doubling his force of two hundred men. On August 7, several local men attempting to join him were killed or captured when they skirmished with federal troops outside Montevallo.[90] Henry and Harriet learned the details in a letter from Mr. Page:

You left at exactly the right time. In less than a month after your departure Quantrell (alias Jones) from the north, Coffee, Hunter (Clint), Jackman and others from the South came pouring in upon Horse & Clear Creeks enraged enraging & outraging everybody. Our corn-cribs, oat-stacks, meat tubs & pork barrels suffered. Coffee & Quantrell camped near the old meeting house ... and I very much doubt whether *regions* of *darkness* could have furnished from its sulpher seethed populace a more fiendish crew.

My feelings may be imagined but never described: while some were pulling to peices this others were sticking their noses into that and still others using the most insulting language, demanding food at all times of day & night. Then to finish up two well armed men came to me while plowing & demanded my team saddle & bridles[,] took colts & all & away they went.

Page found an indirect way to express his anger: "One morning while Coffee was camped below here a large number of men called for breakfast. After breakfast I asked them to stop for prayers, most went away [but] one old man took his chair & sat out under the locust trees south of [the] house[.] [I] read the 8th chapt. of Isaiah. [I]t was a little to sharp for the old fellow[:] he caught his hat & ran before I finished reading."[91] In the Old Testament passage Page selected, the prophet Isaiah predicts divine punishment of nations that form alliances to protect their interests instead of trusting in God. The King James Version warns that those who "refuseth the waters of Shiloah" and join in "a confederacy" will "stumble, and fall, and be broken, and be snared, and be taken."[92] Page wrote that federal troops captured several local men, including "Jo Wood, Sims[,] Gabbart & others who were going to the camp" to enlist with Coffee. "Right north of our house, on the prairie," Page continued, "shots were exchanged," and several men were killed. "All was hushed as the grave for a few days," he wrote. "The Feds pursued & drove Coffee & co. back in a few days, they then went on to Clear creek & thence to Lone Jack, Bates Co. where the Ka. boys took up the viol & played out the tune." Page informed Henry that his former farmhand, William Steward, was among the men who joined Coffee's forces.[93]

On August 11, the day the Smiths arrived at the home of Harriet's brother in Illinois, Quantrill and his men captured the western Missouri town of Independence. The next day, all available Union troops gathered at Fort Scott for a sweep into Missouri. They skirmished with troops led by Coffee, Clint Hunter, and others at Lone Jack on August 16. In the following months, conditions in Montevallo disintegrated even further. Many of the Smiths' former neighbors fell victim to robbery, murder, and arson committed by regular and irregular troops on both sides and sometimes even by members of their own community.⁹⁴ Page reported an accurate rumor that the Mayfield boys had been killed. He continued the saga of events after the Lone Jack fight:

> Then came another calm. The organization of the militia went on slowly but surely. A large number of Brush wackers as they were called began to gather into bands & rob houses. Mr Upton's house was robbed 5 times in one week . . . S. W. Mo. has been since you left a *boiling cauldron*. The Feds & Militia scour the country frequently. Captain Morton's Co. with which the Upton boys are connected took 4 fellows but a few days since found they had forged passes & stolen horses[:] they administered *blue pill* & left them where they found them.⁹⁵

Several weeks later, Page provided more details about neighbors shot by Union troops. The previous fall or early winter, about sixty men led by Raily and Jo Allen robbed Greenfield in Dade County. A captured man named other participants, including John Brown's sons. Page continued:

> A quantity of goods were found at Allens & John Brown was accused of harboring his boys & keeping them out of the way of troops who were seeking them. Warick [Wyrick] also told Brown he had better leave the country. Brown started south but could not get through, on his way back stopped at Mrs Capehearts [Gabbert] to warm & the Feds came in sight[:] he mounted his horse & ran, the Feds after him & shot him. Before he was found the hogs had eaten his face badly. Brown called upon Carrico a day or two before he left & asked his advice[:] he said he knew his boys "had done *monstrous* bad" but he could not help it & if children of his came to him for protection he could not turn them out doors. Wood Tapp Clendennon & Amos were shot by a body of men calling at their houses in the night. Amos was unable to go out & was shot in bed. Clendennon was called out to the fence. Tapp was taken prisoner & shot within a few rods of his house. Wood was taken prisoner & they said they were going to take him to Ft Scott[;] when but a few rods from the house he was shot[,] cut with the sabre & then shot again.

Page informed Henry that several men had gone north or moved to Kansas, but Parson Carrico still remained "at his old post." He had heard that Jo Allen and Charlie Robinson were in the Union prison at Springfield.⁹⁶

Mrs. Page maintained friendships with secessionist as well as Unionist women. She wrote Harriet that she liked Mrs. Dade: they exchanged visits and made preserves together. While Judge Henry spent the winter in the south, his lonely wife had sent for Mrs. Page, who made a "grand good visit" of three days duration. Two Tapp girls in succession had stayed with Mrs. Page to help with her work. When Sarah Tapp left, Matilda Upton took her place. She was afraid to live at home because her Unionist father's life had been threatened.[97] Two months later, Mrs. Page informed Harriet that Mrs. Dade was living with her father-in-law in Springfield, and Mr. Tapp's family had left Montevallo and planned to return to Kentucky. She reported that John Brown's widow "took her baby and nearly all the money her husband left and went back to her friends, leaving Lucy with the little boys to get along as best they could." The widow's fifteen-year-old stepdaughter, Lucinda, remained in Montevallo with her four younger brothers. "Old Mrs Raie says she and Branch were always Union and now she is 'most a *melutiaman*,'" Mrs. Page commented. She wanted to tell Harriet in person "many things which have transpired here which it will not do to write." She informed Harriet that someone had removed the lilacs, some of the rosebushes, and most of the currents from the Smiths' deserted home. Only one "quite wild" old hen remained.[98]

Mr. Page described the fires that had devastated the area. Cobb's field had been burned, but Henry's was saved, although most of the fence surrounding the house and orchard had been lost. Page's pasture had been burned, but Mrs. Page saved most of the fences. After his horses were stolen, Mr. Page resorted to hitching his steers to the plow.[99] He reported that twenty-one horses had been stolen from the region in only two weeks.[100] In May, Mr. Page narrowly missed suffering the fate of his neighbors who were taken from their beds and shot. After several friends warned him that Alek Railey's guerrilla band planned to kill him, he left Montevallo suddenly one night and arrived at Fort Scott the next morning. That night, the men came looking for Page but found that he had escaped. Mrs. Jones and Mrs. Randolph helped Mrs. Page pack the family's belongings in a wagon and drive their livestock toward Kansas, where she and her two young children joined Mr. Page. Even after leaving Montevallo, Mrs. Page maintained her friendship with women who supported the Confederacy. Mattie Henry came to visit her in Fort Scott. After selling their livestock and furniture, the Page family took the train back to Maumee, Ohio.[101]

Mr. Page returned to Kansas, arriving in Lawrence on the afternoon of August 21 to discover that Quantrill's band had ransacked the city that morning, burning homes and killing men and boys. Page described to Henry the horrors he found:

I arrived at this town (or what was left of it) about 4 p.m. on the memorable 21st of Aug. A. D. 1863. *That day Quantrell burned Lawrence.* Such a view as we approached the town from the North! May it never appear to me again. The black smoke moved in one dense mass away to the N. E. Crumbling wall of 4 & 6 story buildings came thundering to the earth. Yet what was all this destruction of property to the nearly 200 *murders* committed & in such barbarous manner.

The *Fiends* (for I can call them by no better names) came rushing in to the town about daylight. Many of the people were still in bed. As soon as any person appeared in sight 8 or 10 shots were fired at him. Many were aroused and driven from the dwellings by the flames without being able even to procure a single rag of clothing except their night clothes. Many were wounded & burned in their houses. The inhuman *Devils* even refused to let wives & daughters remove the wounded bodies of husbands & fathers.[102]

Mrs. Page's cousin, Circuit Court Judge S. O. Thatcher, had escaped by swimming across the river and hiding on an island. Mr. Page joined the judge and his wife in helping the wounded. As they walked down the streets of Lawrence, they heard the groans of dying men and the anguished calls of women searching for their husbands and sons.

Mr. Page read law in Lawrence and established a law practice in Garnett, Kansas, where Mrs. Page and their children joined him. She wrote to Harriet: "I care but little where we go if we can only have peace and he be safe. O: Hattie I have suffered so much before we came out of Missouri that I now think I could be happy almost anywhere if Mr. Page's life was not in danger." She reported that Mr. Leslie had finally joined the Union army, and the Upton family had moved to Lawrence, Kansas.[103] Even after she left Missouri, Mrs. Page did not dare to write the reason Ed Upton fled.[104] Mr. Page advised Henry that only two houses remained in Montevallo and claimed that Henry's former farmhand, William Steward, had set fire to the home of the Unionist Upton family.[105] Mrs. Page informed Harriet: "Our place in Missouri has all been burned over[;] it is now perfectly desolate." She remained haunted by the traumatic events. "If I could only see you and tell what I cannot write it would be such a comfort to me," she concluded.[106] Residents of northern Vernon County had been forcibly removed under the infamous Order 11. Although Montevallo and Nevada City were not included, most residents were driven out by violence and arson. In 1865, Mrs. Page wrote to Harriet that William Leslie was seriously ill in a Lexington hospital. She informed Harriet that Parson Carrico was in Audrain County, Missouri,

Mr. Randolph was living with his family at Fort Scott and had joined the militia, and Mr. Upton, a stonemason, was working in Kansas. She noted that Mr. and Mrs. Jones had named their baby after "Honest Abe."[107] As the war ended, Mrs. Page reported that Dr. Badger had gone to St. Louis, Tom Austin remained in Nevada City, and Henry Taylor, whom she called "one of the worst of guerrillas," surrendered and moved to Illinois. She wrote Harriet: "We shall never try Missouri any more."[108] Mr. Page had become District Deputy Prosecuting Attorney and purchased a 280-acre farm outside Garnett, Kansas.[109] The man who bought the Page's Missouri farm when the war ended reported that almost all the buildings had been burned, along with the fences and most of the peach trees. He found the area deserted: only Judge Henry's family had returned.[110] About a dozen houses stood in Nevada City. The village of Montevallo had been burned to the ground.[111]

Harriet learned that two of her brothers, Volney and Joseph, served in the Union army. In June 1861, Volney joined the Nineteenth Illinois Infantry as a Sergeant, serving in southeastern Missouri until his company was sent to Kentucky in September. After fighting in Tennessee and Alabama in 1862, Volney was promoted to Second Lieutenant. The brigade's harsh treatment of civilians, especially their looting in Athens, Alabama, resulted in Colonel John Turchin's court-martial and reinstatement. Volney was captured on December 31. He was paroled at Richmond, sent to Annapolis, and made his way home to Illinois to wait for a prisoner exchange. He rejoined his unit and accompanied them to Georgia, where he missed the Battle of Chickamauga due to illness. Volney mustered out with his regiment as a First Lieutenant in 1864. In September 1862, while Harriet was at her brother Solomon's farm in Illinois, Joseph enlisted in the 112th Illinois Infantry as a Hospital Steward. He served in Kentucky until June 1863, when he was captured in Tennessee while participating in Sanders Raid. Joseph was paroled from Libby Prison in Richmond and housed in the Union's Benton Barracks near St Louis until he was exchanged and returned to his unit.[112] Joseph accompanied Sherman to Atlanta, returned to fight in Tennessee, and rejoined Sherman in North Carolina, where he contracted typhoid fever. He recovered a few months before the war ended. Joseph disowned his brother Solomon, whom he viewed as a traitor because he was a "Peace Democrat" who opposed the war. Soon after the war ended, the three brothers were reunited in Alton, Illinois, where Joseph resumed his occupation as a druggist and Volney worked as a store clerk.[113]

On the flyleaf of his 1865 diary, Henry noted the address of his friend Hurley from Schoolcraft: "Col O. H. Moore / Commanding 2nd Brigade / 2nd Division 23 Army Corps / Nat'l Hotel Washington." After enlisting in

1856, Second Lieutenant Orlando Hurley Moore served at Fort Leavenworth in Kansas Territory. In 1861, he protected the federal armory at Benecia, California, from General Johnston and other officers who joined the Confederacy. While Henry and Harriet were returning from Missouri, Moore was appointed Colonel in command of the Twenty-fifth Michigan Infantry. The regiment was sent to Kentucky, and Colonel Moore was appointed Provost Marshal of Louisville in April 1863. He discovered that people freed by President Lincoln's Emancipation Proclamation in Confederate states were captured while traveling north through Kentucky, where slavery remained legal, and sold at auction in Louisville. When Moore refused a command to revoke his order forbidding the practice, the commanding General removed him as Provost Marshal and sent him to defend a position in the path of Confederate cavalry led by General John Hunt Morgan, who was heading north after chasing Sanders' raiders in Tennessee. On the Fourth of July, with fewer than three hundred men facing two to three thousand soldiers supported by an artillery unit, Moore refused to surrender. The former portrait painter and fiddler directed his bugle calls and his men's movements, sounds and silences in the acoustics of the rocky terrain to create the illusion of a larger force with approaching reinforcements. Morgan retreated after suffering significant casualties. He abandoned any plans to raid the federal arsenal in Louisville. Later, as a brigade commander, Colonel Moore played an important role in the Battle of Franklin in the Tennessee campaign and the capture of Fort Anderson in the Carolinas campaign. When the war ended, Hurley Moore returned to the rank of Captain in the US Army.[114]

Henry and Harriet faced financial hardship and emotional stress as they reintegrated into life in Schoolcraft, where their family and friends strongly supported the Union. Henry registered for the military draft instituted in 1863: as a married man over thirty-five years old, he was listed as Class II.[115] After losing an election for township treasurer, Henry complained on his thirty-seventh birthday that he "never was so poor."[116] Henry remained discouraged a year later: "Thirty eight years today I have sojourned on earth and I feel truuly that I am [an] old man. My children a ragged group gather about & join their mother in wishing for more of the comforts of this world and I have nothing but my two hands to satisfy their wants with. We are indeed homeless and in a strange land and God knows when we will be otherwise." He expressed guilt over his role in the war. "If I had taken a part in pushing this rebel hord to their final resting place I should feel better about it," he added.[117] Henry joined his neighbors in raising funds to support Union troops, playing Squire Shallow in a fund-raising tableau for the Soldier's Aid Society.[118] Henry considered moving back to Missouri, but Mr.

Page warned him that it was not safe to return to Montevallo: "You speak of taking sheep to Mo. I tell you H it wont do for you or me to go back there at present sheep or no sheep. You have no idea of the state of the country."[119] During the fall and winter of 1864, Henry suffered from illness. His friends and neighbors contributed food and wood. Fellow Masons donated clothing, and the lodge remitted his annual dues.[120] As the war drew to a close, Henry assessed his situation with resignation: "I [am] nearly 39 years of age and have not laid up anything for old age[;] have been sick all winter and feel as though I was doomed to be a poor man the remainder of my days. I am too old to go back to Missouri to make over the farm the rebels have destroyed for me and think a little snug home here with my *friends* would be my best situation after all. I shall be a better man not to get rich[;] I am sure of it for I see it illustrated every day."[121] On April 15, 1865, Henry wrote in his diary: "Last night while we were singing a new song of victory an assassin shot our president while he was at the theater. He died this morning at about 7 oclock 20 minutes. Thus falls the greatest & best man that ever stood at the head of our nation to direct her course through the most critical savage relentless prodigious rebellion the world ever knew. Yesterday we were all joy & today we are mourning."[122] Like the Union army veterans in Missouri who became, in Aaron Astor's terms, "belated Confederates" after the war, Henry reclaimed his identity as a Yankee and a Republican.[123]

CONCLUSION

Henry set aside his ambition of creating a profitable stock farm in Missouri and resigned himself to the more modest goal of making a living on the family farm in Michigan. Henry and his family continued to live with his parents, and Henry worked alongside his father on the farm. In 1866, the railroad finally reached Schoolcraft. A year later, Harriet complained that she and Henry were "not much ahead yet," but the purchase of a sewing machine helped her make the family's clothing, including pants, shirts, and socks.[1] Henry took charge of farming operations after his father suffered a stroke in 1868.[2] He and Harriet gradually became more active in the community. Harriet participated in a Reading Circle organized by her friend and neighbor, Mary Barney.[3] Henry served as Justice of the Peace beginning in 1864 and Township Supervisor beginning in 1866. He was elected Schoolcraft Village Assessor in 1867 and Trustee in 1870.[4] Henry learned to play a bass drum and joined a brass band that performed at holiday celebrations and political rallies.[5] In 1869, he helped write the constitution and by-laws of the Schoolcraft Musical Association, which was created "to promote and encourage the healthful moral and pleasing art of vocal music." Henry also continued to play the fiddle. His two handwritten dance call books contain contradances accompanied by traditional jigs and reels as well as quadrilles, including his original arrangements and those from his copy of Elias' Howe's *American Dancing Master*.[6]

In Missouri, landowners were assessed retroactive property taxes for war years, and many Vernon County farms were auctioned for delinquent taxes.[7] Henry decided to pay the taxes on his Missouri land and sell it when land prices recovered.[8] By 1878, Henry had sold his Missouri property to several purchasers, including his former neighbor, young John Brown, who returned to Montevallo with his brother George.[9] New residents purchased most of the surrounding farms, and a new village was built.[10] Rush Cobb sold the rest of the original Missouri partnership property: by 1887, it had become a successful stock farm.[11] Riley Lindley, John Brazier, and Joseph

"Chicken Polka Quadrille" and "Waltz Lanciers by H.P.S.," H.P. Smith, Call Book, 1869. Box 6B, Stanley Barney Smith Collection, A-88, Archives and Regional History Collections, Zhang Legacy Collections Center, Western Michigan University.

Carrico resumed farming in Cedar County. Carrico returned as pastor of the Montevallo Baptist church that had disbanded in 1862. Nora Mayfield and her sister-in-law, Eliza Gabbert, both remarried. They remained in Vernon County, as did Henry's friend, Tom Austin. George Upton built his family a stone house in Nevada City.[12] Vernon County government gradually reopened, and lawlessness and violence eventually subsided. In the first county election after the war, when only former Unionists could vote or run for office, Branch Ray was elected Assessor, and Frank Anderson was elected Treasurer. Anderson became a successful merchant and railroad contractor. Dr. Badger was the first Vernon County Probate Judge. After restrictions on former Confederates were lifted, Henry Taylor was elected County Sheriff and eventually appointed as postmaster of Montevallo. Clint Hunter returned to practice law but did not hold public office.[13]

In Schoolcraft, Henry inherited the family farm when his father died in 1876. His mother continued to live in the family home with Henry, Harriet, and their children until her death in 1888. Henry's widowed sister, Frank, ran a boarding house next door, and his sister Helen, also a widow, lived nearby.[14] Henry built his Schoolcraft farm into a quintessential Yankee endeavor: a hundred-acre dairy farm. Harry became Henry's partner in

Harriet Smith (Leonard F. Woodward, photographer), Schoolcraft, Michigan, 1884–1885. RHC Photographs P-4507, Stanley Barney Smith Collection, A-88, Archives and Regional History Collections, Zhang Legacy Collections Center, Western Michigan University.

the dairy business.[15] Neither he nor Isa married, and both remained in the family home in Schoolcraft. Isa gave music lessons and tuned pianos.[16] She was an active member of the Schoolcraft Ladies Library Association, where she presented papers on literary and historical topics. Harriet sometimes attended but did not join or give presentations.[17] Walter learned to play the cornet, joined his father in the Smith and Bonfoy dance band, and played with Hull and Arnold's Quadrille Band, which Henry directed from 1884 to 1888.[18] In 1885, John Philip Sousa hired Walter as a cornet soloist in the United States Marine Band. Walter conducted the band in Sousa's absence. When Sousa left to form Sousa's New Marine Band in 1892, Walter followed.[19]

In 1892, Henry sold insurance as well as farming and serving as Trustee of Schoolcraft Village.[20] At the age of sixty-six, Henry still occasionally played the fiddle at dances.[21] "I do not feel as ambitious as I used to ... but I do not forget every thing yet," he wrote.[22] Henry lived to see the marriage of his son Walter and the Smith's next-door neighbor, Agnes Barney, in 1894 and the birth of his only grandchild a year later. Walter reenlisted in the US Marine Band in 1898 and was appointed Second Leader.[23] Henry had become one of the oldest original settlers of Schoolcraft, respected as a long-time resident, traditional fiddler, successful dairy farmer, and civic leader. He remained an

Schoolcraft Dairy delivery wagon. RHC Photographs P-4693, Stanley Barney Smith Collection, A-88, Archives and Regional History Collections, Zhang Legacy Collections Center, Western Michigan University.

active Mason, Republican, and temperance advocate. In April 1898, Isa read Henry's "Reminiscences of a Young Pioneer" at the Pioneer Day Exercises of the Schoolcraft Ladies' Library Association. Two months later, Henry died at the age of seventy-two.[24] Harriet managed the dairy business after Henry's death.[25] Harry continued to make daily milk deliveries. Harriet lived with Harry and Isa for another twenty-six years until she died in 1924 at the age of ninety-one.

In Harriet and Henry's later decades, their four years in Missouri remained an isolated but important episode in their memories of their long lives. Among the few possessions they brought back from Missouri in their covered wagon were their diaries and the letters they received. In 1890, Henry rediscovered the "journals and letters lately resurrected from old trunks and boxes, stowed away in the garret" and created an abridged version of his 1856-1865 diaries for his children.[26] After Henry's death, Isa drew on his diaries, Harriet's diaries and recollections, and her own childhood memories to write her "Reminiscences of Missouri" in 1904. Harriet turned back to the diary entries she had written decades earlier, remembering her younger self, and made a revised copy. Fortunately, Harriet and Henry, and their children and grandson, kept the original diaries and letters that trace the trajectories of their lives during a decade when their growth into mature adulthood

Isa Smith (Richard D. Bayley, photographer), Schoolcraft, Michigan, 1904–1914. RHC Photographs P-4505, Stanley Barney Smith Collection, A-88, Archives and Regional History Collections, Zhang Legacy Collections Center, Western Michigan University.

coincided with dramatic changes in American society. These daily records document their integration of cultural influences, personal relationships, and lived experiences. They provide insight into the elusive moments of crisis when certainty became uncertainty, and Henry and Harriet recalibrated their understanding of society, moral principles, and their own identities.

In 1853, when Harriet and Henry discussed their choice of occupation, decision to marry, reputation in the community, and definition of moral behavior, they saw their actions as shaping their future lives. Although they were aware of cultural debates and conflicts as well as technological and economic changes, their world was essentially a stable one in which moral certainty was possible. They assumed that they would live the rest of their lives in such a world. Harriet and Henry scanned outward in their early diaries, depicting nested layers of society with compatible values and customs: their immediate and extended family, their neighbors and friends, their community, their region, their nation, and the Anglo-American Victorian culture that marked the limits of their known world. When the Smiths moved to Missouri a few years later, the rhetoric of politicians and journalists crystallized their awareness of themselves as Yankees: progressive, hard-working, literate northerners whose taste and customs, as well as their goals and ideals, distinguished them from their Missouri neighbors. Henry and Harriet saw themselves as the bearers of civilization and morality, and they had no doubt that their culture of modernity would prevail.

War shattered assumptions of stability, progress, cultural superiority, and moral certainty. Faced with the collapse of local civic and cultural institutions and cut off from communication with their northern family and friends and from the publications that promoted northern middle-class values, the Smiths were forced to rely on their own assessment of events, their memories of past experiences, and their personal relationships with their neighbors in Missouri. It was no longer possible to follow shared standards of morality since the community was divided in allegiance, with each faction claiming the moral high ground. As the community had shattered, so had the nation. The commonality of interest among neighborhood, region, and nation no longer existed, and even the definitions of those imagined communities were contested. Circumstances forced men and women to decide whether they owed loyalty to their family, their friends and neighbors, their state, their region, or their nation. Harriet and Henry used their diaries to work out new moral principles for these unprecedented circumstances. The use of disguises and deceit by both soldiers and guerrilla bands challenged the stability of personal identity. The destruction of material markers of gentility, such as houses, food, and clothing, further unraveled the cultural fabric. Moral certainty and the ability to determine one's own destiny no longer appeared possible. Despite the uncertainty and danger of living in the midst of war, both Harriet and Henry dreaded returning as impoverished refugees to the constraints of a northern town. As Harriet warned Henry's relatives, they arrived at Schoolcraft, a "rough looking family" of "rags, dirt and babies," stripped of the possessions that signified respectability and transformed from the couple who had left only four years earlier.[27] More than a year later, Henry still felt "homeless and in a strange land" in his hometown.[28] The Smiths' trajectory was unique, but the disruption in their sense of who they were and where they fit in the world was replicated across the country. Like many families, they struggled to rebuild their interrupted lives and heal the physical, emotional, and moral wounds they had suffered.

When they looked back on their lives three decades later, Harriet and Henry saw the outcomes of the choices they had made and the changes they had experienced. In the biographical information Henry submitted for publication in 1892, he fit his years in Missouri into a narrative of lifelong community service that confirmed his identity as a Republican Yankee.[29] Playing the bass drum in the Schoolcraft band on national holidays muffled memories of living under military occupation. The *History of Vernon County, Missouri*, published in 1888, describes a local population that supported the

Harriet Smith at home, Schoolcraft, Michigan. RHC Photographs P-4533, Stanley Barney Smith Collection, A-88, Archives and Regional History Collections, Zhang Legacy Collections Center, Western Michigan University.

Confederacy, with the exception of a few slaveholding Unionists. The author assumed that Virginia-born County Judge H. P. Smith was among the men who joined the state militia to fight invading Union troops. According to the county history, most Unionists living in Montevallo, including Professor Page, left when the war began, and the few who remained repaid the harsh treatment they suffered by reporting their neighbors to Union officials.[30] Later generations relied on these local histories and the oral accounts passed down in the families of long-term residents to shape the historical identities of their communities.[31] A century later, residents of Schoolcraft, Michigan, preserved the house of Dr. Nathan Thomas to affirm their town's role in the Underground Railroad, and residents of Nevada, Missouri, created the Bushwhacker Museum to commemorate their town's Confederate heritage. Ambiguities of loyalty and complexities of identity were smoothed over as twentieth-century communities told their stories of the nineteenth-century war. As more information has become available in the twenty-first century, understandings of regional heritage have become more complicated and nuanced. The lives of Henry and Harriet Smith do not fit neatly into narratives of North versus South. The documents they left behind provide an opportunity to explore the experiences and perspectives of a family who struggled to understand and survive the turmoil of a community torn apart by civil war and come to terms with the choices they made and the people they had become.

NOTES

Introduction

1. "Henry P. Smith," in *Portrait and Biographical Record of Kalamazoo, Allegan and Van Buren Counties, Michigan* (Chicago, 1892), 567.

2. *History of Vernon County, Missouri* (St. Louis, 1887), 203.

3. Aaron Astor, *Rebels on the Border: Civil War, Emancipation, and the Reconstruction of Kentucky and Missouri* (Baton Rouge: Louisiana State University Press, 2012); Christopher Phillips, *The Rivers Ran Backwards: The Civil War and the Remaking of the American Middle Border* (New York: Oxford University Press, 2016); Jennifer L. Weber, *Copperheads: The Rise and Fall of Lincoln's Opponents in the North* (New York: Oxford University Press, 2006); Jarret Ruminski, *The Limits of Loyalty: Ordinary People in Civil War Mississippi* (Jackson: University Press of Mississippi, 2017); John C. Inscoe and Robert Kenzer, ed., *Enemies of the Country: New Perspectives on Unionists in the Civil War South* (Athens: University of Georgia Press, 2001); Daniel E. Sutherland, ed., *Guerrillas, Unionists, and Violence on the Confederate Home Front* (Fayetteville: University of Arkansas Press, 1999).

4. Christopher Phillips, *Making of a Southerner; William Barclay Napton's Private Civil War* (Columbia: University of Missouri Press, 2008); Jeremy Neely, "'A Pure Son of Missouri': Freeman Barrows at the Crossroads of the Slaveholding Frontier," *Missouri Historical Review* 109, no. 4 (July 2015), 215-33; Judkin Browning, *Shifting Loyalties: The Union Occupation of Eastern North Carolina* (Chapel Hill: University of North Carolina Press, 2011); Thomas G. Dyer, *Secret Yankees: The Union Circle in Confederate Atlanta* (Baltimore: Johns Hopkins University Press, 1999); Robert Tracy McKenzie, *Lincolnites and Rebels: A Divided Town in the American Civil War* (New York: Oxford University Press, 2006); Jonathan Dean Sarris, *A Separate Civil War: Communities in Conflict in the Mountain South* (Charlottesville: University of Virginia Press, 2006).

5. Stanley Barney Smith, "Notes on the Village of Schoolcraft in the 1850's," *Michigan History* 40, no. 2 (June 1956): 129, n. 1. The Stanley Barney Smith Collection in Western Michigan University's Zhang Legacy Collections Center in Kalamazoo includes more than fifty document boxes containing cataloged personal papers of Smith's extended family, plus fifteen boxes of books and glass negatives.

6. Michel de Certeau, *The Practice of Everyday Life*, trans. Steven Rendall (LA: University of California Press, 1984), 20, xiv–xv.

7. Michel de Certeau, Luce Giard and Pierre Mayol, *The Practice of Everyday Life, Volume 2: Living and Cooking*, revised edition, ed. Luce Giard, trans. Timothy Tomasik (Minneapolis: University of Minnesota Press, 1998), 39–46, 163–64.

8. Richard Johnson, "What is Cultural Studies Anyway?" in *What is Cultural Studies: A Reader*, ed. John Storey (New York: Arnold, 1996), 103–4; Chris Weedon, *Feminist Practice and Poststructuralist Theory* (Oxford: Blackwell, 1987), 21, 33.

9. See Joan Scott, "Experience," in *Feminists Theorize the Political*, ed. Judith Butler and Joan W. Scott (New York: Routledge, 1992), 22–40.

10. On the social context of letters and diaries, see Ronald J. Zboray and Mary Saracino Zboray, *Everyday Ideas: Socioliterary Experience among Antebellum New Englanders* (Knoxville: University of Tennessee Press, 2006), 3–25.

11. Amy L. Wink, *She Left Nothing in Particular: The Autobiographical Legacy of Nineteenth-Century Women's Diaries* (Knoxville: University of Tennessee Press, 2001); Jennifer Sinor, *The Extraordinary Work of Ordinary Writing: Annie Ray's Diary* (Iowa City: University of Iowa Press, 2002); Jane Hunter, "Inscribing the Self in the Heart of the Family: Diaries and Girlhood in Late-Victorian America," *American Quarterly* 44, no. 1 (March 1992): 51–81; Suzanne L. Bunkers, "'Faithful Friend': Nineteenth-Century Midwestern American Women's Unpublished Diaries," *Women's Studies International Forum* 10, no. 1 (1987): 7–17; Thomas Augst, *The Clerk's Tale: Young Men and Moral Life in Nineteenth-Century America* (Chicago: University of Chicago Press, 2003), 19–61.

12. See Michael Denning, *Mechanic Accents: Dime Novels and Working-Class Culture in America*, revised edition (New York: Verso, 1998); Karen Halttunen, "Cultural History and the Challenge of Narrativity," in *Beyond the Cultural Turn: New Directions in the Study of Society and Culture*, ed. Victoria E. Bonnell and Lynn Avery Hunt (Berkeley: University of California Press, 1999), 165–81; Cathy N. Davidson, *Revolution and the Word: The Rise of the Novel in America* (New York: Oxford University Press, 1986); Bruce Burgett, *Sentimental Bodies: Sex, Gender, and Citizenship in the Early Republic* (Princeton, NJ: Princeton University Press, 1998).

13. Sinor, *Extraordinary Work*, 48–49. See also Felicity Nussbaum, "Toward Conceptualizing Diary," in *Studies in Autobiography*, ed. James Olney (New York: Oxford University Press, 1988), 128–40, and Dan Doll, "British Diary Canon Formation," in *The Diary: The Epic of Everyday Life*, ed. Batsheva Ben-Amos and Dan Ben-Amos (Bloomington: Indiana University Press, 2020), 75–87.

14. Beth Barton Schweiger explores the skills required for writing and the levels of literacy they provide. *A Literate South: Reading Before Emancipation* (New Haven: Yale University Press, 2019), 39–122.

15. Katherine G. Morrissey, *Mental Territories: Mapping the Inland Empire* (Ithaca, NY: Cornell University Press, 1997), 12–19, 32–35.

16. Wilson Waters, *History of Chelmsford, Massachusetts* (Lowell, 1917), 10–13, 59–60, 134–35, 615–17, 754–55.

17. Michael Fellman, *Inside War: The Guerrilla Conflict in Missouri During the American Civil War* (New York: Oxford University Press, 1989); T. J. Stiles, *Jesse James: Last Rebel of the Civil War* (New York: Vintage, 2002); Mark W. Geiger, *Financial Fraud and Guerrilla Violence in Missouri's Civil War, 1861–1865* (New Haven: Yale University Press, 2010).

18. Joseph Beilein, *Bushwhackers: Guerrilla Warfare, Manhood and the Household in Civil War Missouri* (Kent, Ohio: Kent State University Press, 2016); LeeAnn Whites, "Forty Shirts and a Wagonload of Wheat: Women, the Domestic Supply Line, and the Civil War on the Western Border," *The Journal of the Civil War Era* 1, no. 1 (March 2011), 56–78; Andrew Fialko, "A Spatial Approach to Civil War Missouri's Domestic Supply Line," in *The Guerrilla Hunters: Irregular Conflicts during the Civil War*, ed. Brian D. McKnight and Barton A. Myers (Baton Rouge: Louisiana State University Press, 2017).

19. Jeremy Neely, *The Border Between Them: Violence and Reconciliation on the Kansas-Missouri Line* (Columbia: University of Missouri Press, 2007); Matthew Stith, *Extreme Civil War: Guerrilla Warfare, Environment, and Race on the Trans-Mississippi Frontier* (Baton Rouge: Louisiana State University Press, 2016).

20. Daniel Sutherland, *American Civil War Guerrillas: Changing the Rules of Warfare* (Santa Barbara: Praeger, 2013), 29–30.

Chapter One. Love and Work

1. Henry Smith, diary, July 10, 1853. Unless otherwise cited, all diary entries are in the Henry Parker Smith Papers, Bentley Historical Library, University of Michigan (hereafter BHL). Original spelling and punctuation from handwritten diaries and letters have been retained. Periods have been added only where spacing and capitalization clearly indicate sentence breaks. Brackets are used sparingly, only when a missing word or punctuation mark is essential for basic readability.

2. Smith, diary, June 19, 1853.

3. Harriet Johnson, diary, June 19, 1853, Henry Parker Smith Papers, BHL.

4. Johnson, diary, June 20, 1853.

5. Edelia to Hattie, December 22, 1850; W. G. Johnson to H. A. Johnson, February 24, 1851. Stanley Barney Smith Collection, A-88, Archives and Regional History Collections, Zhang Legacy Collections Center, Western Michigan University (hereafter SBSC).

6. W. G. Johnson to Hattie, June 13, 1853, SBSC.

7. Bill J. Leonard, *Baptists in America* (New York: Columbia University Press, 2005), 231–32; Hadley Kruczek-Aaron, *Everyday Religion: An Archaeology of Protestant Belief and Practice in the Nineteenth Century* (Gainesville: University Press of Florida, 2015), 25–28, 173.

8. March 21 [1836], Wakeman G. Johnson journal, Box 5, SBSC. See Mary P. Ryan, *Cradle of the Middle Class: The Family in Oneida County, New York 1790–1865* (New York: Cambridge University Press, 1981), 98–101, 158–61, and *The Empire of the Mother: American Writing About Domesticity, 1830–1860* (New York: Haworth Press, 1982), 49–54. Richard Brodhead discusses "disciplinary intimacy" in *Cultures of Letters: Scenes of Reading and Writing in Nineteenth-Century America* (Chicago: University of Chicago Press, 1993), 19–22.

9. Johnson, diary, June 22, 1853. See Leonard, 82–83.

10. Johnson, diary, June 25, 1853. On fishing as courtship, see Ronald J. Zboray and Mary Saracino Zboray, "The Romance of Fisherwomen in Antebellum New England," *American Studies* 39, no. 1 (1998): 6–12.

11. Johnson, diary, June 25, 1853. See Karen Lystra, *Searching the Heart: Women, Men and Romantic Love in Nineteenth-Century America* (New York: Oxford University Press, 1989), 28–55, and Ellen K. Rothman, *Hands and Hearts: A History of Courtship in America* (Cambridge: Harvard University Press, 1987), 102–7.

12. Johnson, diary, April 19, 1853.

13. Johnson, diary, June 26, 1853.

14. Johnson, diary, June 28, 1853.

15. Charles Sellers, *The Market Revolution: Jacksonian America, 1815–1846* (New York: Oxford University Press, 1991), 30–31, 158–59.

16. Johnson, diary, April 12, June 21 & 29–30, July 5–6, 1853; Frances B. Cogan, *All American Girl: The Ideal of Real Womanhood in Mid-Nineteenth-Century America* (Athens: University of Georgia Press, 1989), 240.

17. Johnson, diary, June 29, 1853.

18. Harriet A. Johnson, "The Departed Year 1850," Composition No. 5, November 27, 1850, SBSC.

19. Johnson, diary, June 21, 1853.

20. Johnson, diary, June 29, 1853; Cogan, 88–91; Ryan, *Empire*, 39–40.

21. Johnson, diary, July 1, 1853. On the dichotomy between ambition and domesticity, see Rothman, 154–56.

22. Johnson, diary, July 2, 1853. Nancy Cott found similar anxiety about marriage in earlier generations. *The Bonds of Womanhood: "Woman's Sphere" in New England, 1780–1835* (New Haven: Yale University Press, 1977), 80. See also Steven Seidman, *Romantic Longings: Love in America, 1830–1980* (New York: Routledge, 1991), 55–57.

23. Martha Tomhave Blauvelt notes that dashes and exclamation points in sentimental fiction and young women's diaries indicated emotional intensity. *The Work of the Heart: Young Women and Emotion 1780–1830* (Charlottesville: University of Virginia Press, 2007), 31–32.

24. Johnson, diary, July 2, 1853. On religious language in courtship, see Lystra, 242–50, and Catherine E. Kelly, *In the New England Fashion: Reshaping Women's Lives in the Nineteenth Century* (Ithaca: Cornell University Press, 1999), 144–45.

25. Smith, diary, June 26, 1853. See also Smith, diary, August 4, 6, 9, and 14, 1853.

26. Johnson, diary, July 4, 1853.

27. Marilyn Ferris Motz, "Sharing Secrets in Nineteenth-Century America," in *The Diary: The Epic of Everyday Life*, ed. Batsheva Ben-Amos and Dan Ben-Amos (Bloomington: Indiana University Press, 2020), 265–66; Thomas Augst, *The Clerk's Tale: Young Men and Moral Life in Nineteenth-Century America* (Chicago: University of Chicago Press, 2003), 105–6. For an earlier example, see Lucia McMahon, "'While Our Souls Together Blend': Narrating a Romantic Readership in the Early Republic," in *An Emotional History of the United States*, ed. Peter Stearns and Jan Lewis (New York: New York University Press, 1998), 66–90.

28. Smith, diary, July 3, 1853.

29. Johnson, diary, July 3, 1853. Lystra, 21–42; Rothman, 108–14; Cogan, 177–91. On similar attitudes in the early nineteenth century, see Blauvelt, 92–108. On the importance of sincerity, see Karen Halttunen, *Confidence Men and Painted Women: A Study of Middle-Class Culture in America, 1830–1870* (New Haven: Yale University Press, 1982), 33–55.

30. Unattributed quotation, HP Smith account book, 1846, Box 3, SBSC.

31. Johnson, diary, July 3, 1853.

32. Susan E. Gray, *The Yankee West: Community Life on the Michigan Frontier* (Chapel Hill: University of North Carolina Press, 1996), 1–15; John C. Hudson, "Yankeeland in the Middle West," *Journal of Geography* 85 (September-October 1986): 195–200. See also Sellers, 364–69.

33. Kenneth Lewis, *West to Far Michigan: Settling the Lower Peninsula, 1815–1860* (East Lansing: Michigan State University Press, 2002), 134; Gregory S. Rose, "American and European Immigrant Groups in the Midwest by the Mid-Nineteenth Century," in *Finding a New Midwestern History*, ed. Jon K Lauck, Gleaves Whitney, and Joseph Hogan (Lincoln: University of Nebraska Press, 2018), 77. Gray's *The Yankee West* examines the influence of New England culture on three Kalamazoo County townships.

34. *Vital Records of Sudbury, Massachusetts to the Year 1850* (Boston: New-England Historic Geneological Society, 1903), 133–35; Duane Hamilton Hurd, *History of Middlesex County, Massachusetts*, vol. 1 (Philadelphia, 1890), 254; Joseph Alfred Harwood, *Records of Littleton, Massachusetts* (Concord: Patriot Press, 1900), 39; Wilson Waters, *History of Chelmsford, Massachusetts* (Lowell: Courier-Citizen, 1917), 7–9; Edwin R. Hodgman, *History of the Town of Westford in the County of Middlesex, Massachusetts, 1659–1883* (Lowell, 1883), 463–64; Henry S. Nourse, *History of the Town of Harvard, Massachusetts, 1732–1893* (Harvard, 1894), 28, 76, 85–86; Massachusetts towns' vital records: https://www.mass.gov/doc/list-of-vital-records-to-1850/download.

35. "Henry P. Smith," in *Portrait and Biographical Record of Kalamazoo, Allegan and Van Buren Counties, Michigan* (Chicago, 1892), 566–67; A. D. P. Van Buren "Address at Kalamazoo County Reunion," in *Michigan Historical Collections* (hereafter MHC) 14 (Lansing, 1890), 524–25; Samuel W. Durant, *History of Kalamazoo County, Michigan* (Philadelphia, 1880), 517.

36. Gray, *Yankee West*, 15.

37. Lewis, 134; E. Lakin Brown, "The Beginning of Schoolcraft," in *Pioneer Day Exercises* (Schoolcraft, Michigan, 1898), unpaginated, BHL; Durant, 516–21.

38. "Rev. Wakeman G. Johnson," *Minutes of the Thirty-Third Annual Meeting of the Illinois Baptist Pastoral Union* (Aurora, 1878): 8.

39. Johnson, diary, February 1, 1854. Cynthia Ainsworth to Harriet Johnson, December 4, 1846, and March 9, 1849; Aksah Barton to Harriet Johnson, December 14, 1848, SBSC. William J. Lamson, *Descendants of William Lamson of Ipswich, Mass., 1634–1917* (New York: Tobias A. Wright, 1917); vital records for Lorraine, New York; Randolph, Vermont; Brookfield, Massachusetts.

40. Harriet asked her father to send her the names, birthdates, birthplaces and occupations of his ancestors because she knew "so little outside of our own immediate family." Hattie to father and mother, February 15, 1869, SBSC.

41. Henry Smith, diary, November 19, 1852. Durant, 528; James M. Thomas, *Kalamazoo County Directory: With a History of the County from its Earliest Settlement* (Kalamazoo, 1869), 86.

42. Theodore S. Gold, *Historical Records of the Town of Cornwall, Litchfield County, Connecticut* (Hartford, 1877), 183, 253–54; Edward C. Starr, *A History of Cornwall*,

Connecticut: A Typical New England Town (New Haven: Tuttle, Morehouse & Taylor, 1926), 195, 324, 478–79; Michael R. Gannett, "Hanky-Panky in the Hollow," *Cornwall Chronicle* 7, no. 4 (May 1997): 2–3 (https://cornwallchronicle.org/archives/); "Amy Johnson (1713–1796)," *Women's Rights: Cornwall's Radicals, Rebels and Reformers* (online exhibition), Cornwall Historical Society: https://cornwallhistoricalsociety.org/amy-johnson-1.

43. One uncle was imprisoned for preaching without a license. Two cousins were expelled from Yale for opposing the established church. H. D. Paine, ed., *Paine Family Records*, vol. 2 (New York, 1883), 156–63, 259; Newton Reed, *Early History of Amenia* (Amenia, 1875), 30–32; Mary Hewitt Mitchell, *The Great Awakening and Other Revivals in the Religious Life of Connecticut* (New Haven: Yale University Press, 1934), 15–18; Starr, 478–79, 495; Cornwall, Connecticut vital records (Barbour Collection); Cornwall Congregational Church Marriage Records: https://newhorizonsgenealogicalservices.com/connecticut-genealogy/litchfield/cornwall_connecticut_congregational_church_marriage_records_1800.htm.

44. Mrs. L. M. Hammond, *History of Madison County, State of New York* (Syracuse, 1872), 417–18, 430–33, 444–45; James H. Smith, *History of Chenango and Madison Counties* (Syracuse, 1880), 545–73; B. F. Bronson et al., ed., *The First Half Century of Madison University* (New York, 1872), 35.

45. Franklin B. Hough, *History of Jefferson County in the State of New York* (Albany, 1854), 199, 393; Maria Perciaccante, *Calling Down Fire: Charles Grandison Finney and Revivalism in Jefferson County, New York, 1800–1840* (Albany: State University of New York Press, 2003), 67; John Peck and John Lawton, *An Historical Sketch of the Baptist Missionary Convention of the State of New York* (Utica, 1837), 60.

46. Hough, 199; Bronson, 203.

47. Bronson, 37–44, 203–4, 428; "A Catalog of the Students and Alumni of the Baptist Literary and Theological Seminar in Hamilton, New York" (1827), Baptist Educational Society of the State of New York records, A1010, Special Collections and Archives, Colgate University; Rebecca Downing, "Before Payne's Farm," Colgate University: https://200.colgate.edu/index.php/looking-back/places/paynes-farm.

48. Bronson, 432. Solomon Johnson to Cynthia Ainsworth, November 7, 1848 and W. G. Johnson to Harriet and Solomon Johnson, June 4, 1851, SBSC. Harriet's sister also married a Baptist preacher. Cynthia Ainsworth to Harriet Johnson, February 2, 1850 and Amasa Heath to Wakeman Johnson, August 1, 1851, SBSC.

49. W. G. Johnson to Harriet, June 17, 1850, SBSC; Harriet Johnson, diary, Nov. 2–4, 1853; Leonard, 9–21, 88; Nathan Hatch, *The Democratization of American Christianity* (New Haven: Yale University Press, 1989), 95, 139, 205; Peck and Lawton, 30–177; Mark A. Noll, *America's God: From Jonathan Edwards to Abraham Lincoln* (New York: Oxford University Press, 2002), 182–83, 197.

50. George C. Rable, *God's Almost Chosen Peoples: A Religious History of the American Civil War* (Chapel Hill: University of North Carolina, 2010), 24; Leonard, 29; Jon Butler, Grant Wacker, and Randall Ballmer, *Religion in American Life: A Short History*, updated edition (New York, Oxford University Press, 2008), 180–81.

51. Lystra, 128. See also Rothman, 97–98; Cogan, 3–23; Joan Wallach Scott, *Gender and the Politics of History* (New York: Columbia University Press, 1988), 28–32; J. A. Mangan

and James Walvin, "Introduction," and E. Anthony Rotundo, "Learning About Manhood: Gender Ideals and the Middle-Class Family in Nineteenth Century America," in *Manliness and Morality: Middle-Class Masculinity in Britain and America, 1800–1940*, ed. J. A. Mangan and James Walvin (New York: St. Martins Press, 1987), 2–3, 35–36.

52. Rothman 91.

53. E. Anthony Rotundo, *American Manhood: Transformations in Masculinity from the Revolution to the Modern Era* (New York: Basic Books, 1993), 113, 134–35, 169; Seidman, 55–57; Rothman, 94–95, 163; Ryan, *Cradle*, 180.

54. Rotundo, *American*, 114, 132–33; Rothman, 150–51; Lystra, 129–36; Ryan, *Cradle*, 179; Kelly, 131–32.

55. In *The Politics of Domesticity: Women, Evangelism and Temperance in Nineteenth-Century America* (Middletown, Conn.: Wesleyan University Press, 1987), Barbara Epstein argues that in the "new culture of commercial capitalism" the sons of farmers had little chance to advance from wage earners to property owners (72).

56. Gray, 107–9, 117; Stephen M. Frank, *Life with Father: Parenthood and Masculinity in the Nineteenth-Century North* (Baltimore: Johns Hopkins University Press, 1998), 143–46.

57. Durant, 515.

58. Smith, diary, October 5, 1849.

59. Gray, 43–56, 79–83.

60. US Census (Population), 1850, Schoolcraft Township, Kalamazoo County, Michigan.

61. Quit-claim deed, November 16, 1850, Box 3, SBSC. See also George V. N. Lothrop to Thaddeus Smith, January 6, 1844, SBSC.

62. Durant, 169–70, 186, 521; Lewis, 204–7, 283–91; David S. Harley, *Map of Kalamazoo Co., Michigan* (Philadelphia, 1861), Library of Congress (hereafter LC): https://www.loc.gov/item/2012593151.

63. US Census (Industry), 1850, Seneca Falls, New York; William T. Gibson, *Topographical Map of Seneca County, New York* (Albany, 1850), LC: https://www.loc.gov/item/2013593233/. See also Henry Stowell, "History of Seneca Falls," *Brigham's Geneva, Seneca Falls and Waterloo Directory* (Geneva, NY, 1862), 22–28.

64. Sandra S. Weber, *Special History Study: Women's Rights National Historical Park, Seneca Falls, New York* (US Department of the Interior, National Park Service, 1985), https://www.nps.gov/parkhistory/online_books/wori/shs1.htm.

65. Smith, diary, May 3, 1851.

66. Ryan, *Cradle*, 108 and 181.

67. Stuart Blumin, *The Emergence of the Middle Class: Social Experience in the American City, 1760–1900* (New York: Cambridge University Press, 1989), 76–77, 130–33; Scott A. Sandage, *Born Losers: A History of Failure in America* (Cambridge: Harvard University Press, 2005), 88–92.

68. Rotundo, *American*, 19, 20. On attitudes toward business failure, see Sandage, 1–58, and Rotundo, *American*, 178–85.

69. Rotundo, *American*, 170.

70. Smith, diary, January 9, 1851.

71. Smith, diary, March 4, 1851.

72. Sandage, 81–94.

73. Smith, diary, May 12, 1851.

74. Mother to Henry, February 15, 1852, SBSC; H. P. Smith to Mother, March 1852, SBSC.

75. Smith, diary, November 20, 1851; May 13, 1852. See also January 20, February 24, and April 7, 1852.

76. Smith, diary, April 30, June 2, 1852.

77. Downs and Co. to Henry P. Smith, June 17 and September 23, 1852, February 3, 1853, SBSC. See David Jaffee, "Peddlers of Progress and the Transformation of the Rural North, 1760–1860," *Journal of American History* 78, no. 2 (Sept. 1991): 511–35.

78. Smith, diary, June 7–November 6, 1852.

79. Smith, diary, September 7, 1852.

80. Smith, diary, October 8, 1852.

81. Smith, diary, February 18, March 2, 1853; Downs & Co. to H. P. Smith, February 3, 1853, SBSC.

82. Smith, diary, November 19, 1852.

83. Smith, diary, December 19, 1852.

84. Smith, diary, February 27, 1853.

85. Smith, diary, March 2, 1853.

86. Smith, diary, April 27, May 9–10, 1853; S. S. Gould to H. P. Smith, May 20, 1853, SBSC.

87. Smith, diary, May 6, 1853.

88. Johnson, diary, May 5, 1853.

89. Smith, diary, May 18–23, 1853.

90. Smith, diary, June 27, 1853.

91. C. L. Ainsworth to Harriet, June 28 [1853]. Cynthia and Harriet alternately called one another "cousin" and "sister." Cynthia was nineteen years older than Harriet. Harriet's mother raised Cynthia, her deceased sister's daughter. Cynthia remained in the Johnson household as an "assistant" after Harriet's mother died and Harriet's father remarried. Leonard and Cynthia Ainsworth to George Lamson, August 12, 1815; Olivia Reed to Cynthia Ainsworth, July 1, 1834; C. L. Ainsworth to Sister (Hatty A. Jonson), March 9, 1849; all SBSC.

92. Richard Rabinowitz, *The Spiritual Self in Everyday Life: The Transformation of Personal Religious Experience in Nineteenth-Century New England* (Boston: Northeastern University Press, 1989), 108–23; Kruczek-Aaron, 14–15, 173; Noll, 205, Leonard, 231–32.

93. Johnson, diary, June 19, 1853.

94. Barbara Myerhoff, "Rites of Passage: Process and Paradox," in *Celebration, Studies in Festivity and Ritual*, ed. Victor Turner (Washington, DC: Smithsonian Institution Press, 1982), 111.

95. Rabinowitz, 160–63, 205–11, 236–37.

96. Lystra, 30.

97. Rabinowitz, 174–75, 210–11; Lystra, 30–55; Kelly, 128–29, 139–50.

98. Rothman, 102–8; Lystra, 185–86.

99. Smith, diary, July 4, 1853.

100. Johnson, diary, July 5, 1853.

101. Johnson, diary, July 5, 1853.

102. Nicholas E. Tawa, *High-Minded and Low-Down: Music in the Lives of Americans, 1800–1861* (Boston: Northeastern University Press, 2000), 36; Leonard, 231–32; Paul M.

Gifford, "Fiddling and Instrumental Folk Music in Michigan," in *Michigan Folklife Reader*, ed. C. Kurt Dewhurst and Yvonne R. Lockwood (Lansing: Michigan State University Press, 1987), 192–93.

103. On views of Protestant clergy on leisure activities, see Cindy S. Aron, *Working at Play: A History of Vacations in the United States* (New York: Oxford University Press, 1999), 34–44.

104. Father to Hatty, November 2, 1848, SBSC. See Halttunen, 4–5, and Rabinowitz, 117.

105. Sandage, 99–188; Richard Stott, *Jolly Fellows: Male Milieus in Nineteenth-Century America* (Baltimore: Johns Hopkins University Press, 2009), 65–73, 90–92; Halttunen, 46–50.

106. Bruce Dorsey, *Reforming Men and Women: Gender in the Antebellum City* (Ithaca: Cornell University Press, 2002), 125–29; Cogan, 108, 137–41; Stott, 86–87.

107. Rothman, 107–8; Cogan, 163–68.

108. Smith, diary, January 8, February 11, July 1, 1853.

109. Gifford, 188–91.

110. Smith, diary, December 19–21, 1851.

111. Smith, diary, July 5, 1853.

112. Johnson, diary, July 7, 1853.

113. Johnson, diary, October 16, 1853. See also Henry Smith, diary, August 18, 1853.

114. Smith, diary, July 8, 1853.

115. Smith, diary, July 10, 1853.

116. Johnson, diary, July 10, 1853.

117. See Cogan, 177–96.

118. Johnson, diary, July 7, 1853. On testing a fiancé's commitment, see Lystra, 157–91.

119. Smith, diary, August 23, 1853.

120. Ira S. Drake, *Mitchell's new traveller's guide through the United States, showing the rail roads, canals, stage roads &c. with distances from place to place* (Philadelphia, 1853), 50, LC: https://www.loc.gov/item/gm70005367/.

121. John A. Smith, *The History of Maumee, 1748–1926* (Toledo: Henry Schmit, 1926), 119.

122. Johnson, diary, August 23, 1853.

123. Charles Sumner Van Tassell, *Story of the Maumee Valley, Toledo, and the Sandusky Region*, vol. 2 (Chicago: S. J. Clark Publishing Company, 1929), 1681.

124. Smith, *History*, 26-31, 50, 119, 181–97.

125. Johnson, diary, September 5–6, 1853.

126. Johnson, diary, September 22–23, 1853.

127. Johnson, diary, September 8, 1853.

128. Johnson, diary, September 27, 1853.

129. Brodhead argues that schools' replacement of corporal punishment with "disciplinary intimacy" reinforced emerging northern middle-class values and child-rearing practices (13–27). On opposition to corporal punishment, see also Louise Stevenson, *The Victorian Homefront: American Thought and Culture, 1860–1880* (New York: Twayne, 1991), 12–13.

130. On teaching as an occupation, see Cogan, 238–41.

131. Johnson, diary, November 11, 1853.

132. D. F. DeWolf, "Toledo: A Brief History of Educational Efforts in Toledo, with a Summary of Such History in the Neighboring Towns of the Maumee Valley, as Connected with Efforts in Toledo" (Toledo: 1876), 1–2.

133. Johnson, diary, November 9, 1853.
134. Johnson, diary, November 22–23, 1853.
135. Johnson, diary, November 22, 1853.
136. Johnson, diary, January 3, 1854; February 3, 1854.
137. Johnson, diary, February 7–8, 1854.
138. Johnson, diary, February 9, 1854.
139. Johnson, diary, February 10, 13, 16–17, 20, and 22, March 10, 1854.
140. Johnson, diary, February 16, 1854.
141. Johnson, diary, March 10, 1854.
142. Johnson, diary, March 27, 1854.
143. Johnson, diary, November 15 and 28, 1853; February 25–27, 1854. See also Smith, diary, August 18, 1853.
144. Smith, diary, July 22, 1853.
145. Smith, diary, December 14–15, and 18, 1852; March 4, 1854; Gray, 60–63, 180–82.
146. Smith, diary, September 26, October 1, 4, 5, and 13, November 16, 1853.
147. Smith, diary, October 5, 1853.
148. Smith, diary, October 7, 1853.
149. Daniel Vickers, "Competency and Competitive Economic Culture in Early America," *William and Mary Quarterly* 47, no. 1 (January 1990): 3–29. On competency and farming, see Kim M. Gruenwald, *River of Enterprise: The Commercial Origins of Regional Identity in the Ohio Valley, 1790–1850* (Bloomington: Indiana University Press, 2002), xv, 4, 12, 19, 105–6, 133, 156. See also Bruce Laurie, *Artisans into Workers: Labor in Nineteenth-Century America* (New York: Noonday Press, 1989), 44, 47, 57; Kelly, 93; Rothman, 150–51; Sandage, 81.
150. Smith, diary, May 14, June 27, 1853. Warrant number 59,683 (Scrip Warrant Act of 1850), SE quarter of SW quarter, Section 15, Prairie Ronde Township, Kalamazoo County, Michigan. General Land Office Records, US Bureau of Land Management (https://glorecords.blm.gov).
151. Smith, diary, November 25, 1853.
152. Smith, diary, April 3–4, 1854; Durant, 514. On local status and family ties of officeholders, see Gray, 150, 156–57.
153. Smith, diary, May 15, 1854.

Chapter Two. Leisure and Literacy

1. Harriet Johnson, diary, July 4, 1853, Henry Parker Smith Papers, BHL.
2. Johnson, diary, October 1, 1853. On engagement, see Ellen K. Rothman, *Hands and Hearts: A History of Courtship in America* (Cambridge, Mass.: Harvard University Press, 1987), 162–64.
3. Johnson, diary, September 15, 21, and 27, November 12, December 29–31, 1853; January 10, 28, and 31, February 27, March 11 and 23, 1854. On similar visits in antebellum New England villages, see Karen V. Hansen, *A Very Social Time: Crafting Community in Antebellum New England* (Berkeley: University of California Press, 1994), 79–93, 107–9, and Catherine E. Kelly, "'Well Bred Country People': Sociability, Social Networks, and

the Creation of a Provincial Middle Class, 1820–1860," in *Cultural Change and the Market Revolution in America, 1780–1860*, ed. Scott C. Martin (New York: Rowman & Littlefield, 2005), 112–15, 118.

    4. Johnson, diary, November 2–3, 18, and 24, December 12 and 26, 1853; January 31, 1854.

    5. George Reynolds, a mill-owner, previously worked for Solomon Johnson's brother in Jefferson County. Reynold's father-in-law, Dr. Amos Page, married Abigail Johnson's widowed sister. Reynold's brother-in-law, Maurice Page, had known Harriet's family since childhood. He attended Madison College with Harriet's oldest brother. Johnson, diary, October 3, 1853; John A. Smith, *The History of Maumee, 1748–1926* (Toledo: Henry Schmit, 1926), 192–93; George W. Reynolds to Alfred D. Lowe, April 18, 1893, in Frederick H. Kimball, "Reynolds Corners Was First Settled in 1815," Depauville Scrapbook No. 1, Part 4, http://jefferson.nygenweb.net/tid23.htm; Abigail Johnson to Harriet, February 23, 1850, SBSC; M. M. Page to Hattie, December 15, 1863, SBSC; New York State Census, 1855, Champion, Jefferson County; Amos B. Page Will, Jefferson County Will Index, http://jefferson.nygenweb.net/wills/amospagewill.htm; B. F. Bronson et al., ed., *The First Half Century of Madison University* (New York, 1872), 432 and 446.

    6. Kelly, "Well," 111–19, and *In the New England Fashion: Reshaping Women's Lives in the Nineteenth Century* (Ithaca: Cornell University Press, 1999), 162–68, 212–13.

    7. US Census (Population), 1850, Waynesville, Lucas County, Ohio.

    8. Johnson, diary, September 7, 1853.

    9. See Susan Williams, *Savory Suppers and Fashionable Feasts: Dining in Victorian America* (Knoxville: University of Tennessee Press, 1996), 76–90, 126–28, 185–87; Jane C. Nylander, *Our Own Snug Fireside: Images of the New England Home 1760–1860* (New York: Alfred A. Knopf, 1993), 240–45; Anne C. Rose, *Victorian America and the Civil War* (New York: Cambridge University Press, 1992), 127–28.

    10. Johnson, diary, October 24, 1853.

    11. Johnson, diary, March 28, 1854.

    12. Johnson, diary, December 31, 1853.

    13. Katherine Grier, *Culture and Comfort: Parlor Making and Middle-Class Identity, 1850–1930* (Washington, DC: Smithsonian Books, 1997) [orig. Rochester, New York: Strong Museum, 1988], 1–3, 76–77, 122–27; Karen Halttunen, *Confidence Men and Painted Women: A Study in Middle-Class Culture in America, 1830–1870* (New Haven: Yale University Press, 1982), 102–5.

    14. Johnson, diary, November 19, 1853.

    15. John F. Kasson, *Rudeness and Civility: Manners in Nineteenth-Century Urban America* (New York: Noonday Press, 1990), 147–81. On contradictions between sincerity and etiquette, see Grier, 100–103, and Halttunen, 98–101.

    16. Johnson, diary, November 8, 1853. On emotion work, see Martha Tomhave Blauvelt, *The Work of the Heart: Young Women and Emotion 1780–1830* (Charlottesville: University of Virginia Press, 2007), 1–14, 184–201.

    17. Johnson, diary, December 1, 1853.

    18. Johnson, diary, December 10, 1853.

    19. See Grier, 100–103; Halttunen, 80–83, 96–101; Kelly, "Well," 126, 131; Kelly, *In*, 165–66, 174–75.

20. Johnson, diary, January 12, 1854.

21. Johnson, diary, January 11, 1854. On increasing formality of weddings, see Rothman, 168–72.

22. Hadley Kruczek-Aaron, *Everyday Religion: An Archaeology of Protestant Belief and Practice in the Nineteenth Century* (Gainesville: University Press of Florida, 2015), 7–18, 35–39; Louise Stevenson, *The Victorian Homefront: American Thought and Culture, 1860–1880* (New York: Twayne, 1991), 36; Halttunen, 56–91; Richard Sellers, *The Market Revolution: Jacksonian America, 1815–1846* (New York: Oxford University Press, 1994) [1991], 158–59; Kelly, *In*, 214–26.

23. Johnson, diary, October 17, 1853.

24. Stuart Blumin, *The Emergence of the Middle Class: Social Experience in the American City, 1760–1900* (New York: Cambridge University Press, 1989), 185–86; Barbara Epstein, *The Politics of Domesticity: Women, Evangelism and Temperance in Nineteenth-Century America* (Middletown, CT: Wesleyan University Press, 1987), 71–72; Stevenson, xxii; Kelly, *In*, 222–25.

25. Johnson, diary, October 23, 1853.

26. Johnson, diary, October 13, 1853.

27. Kelly argues that an ideal of New England village social life based on simplicity, sincerity, and informality obscured the influence of elite urban customs that enhanced class distinctions in northern communities. "Well," 130–2; *In*, 10.

28. Cynthia Ainsworth to Harriet, February 2, 1850, and Father to Hattie, June 4, 1851, Stanley Barney Smith Collection (SBSC), A-88, Archives and Regional History Collections, Zhang Legacy Collections Center, Western Michigan University. On refinement, see Grier, 154–58. On female teachers' social status, see Stevenson, xxiv.

29. Johnson, diary, October 25, 1853.

30. See Sellers, 237; Halttunen, 95; Stevenson, xxii; Epstein, 69–72; Kelly, *In*, 10.

31. Richard Rabinowitz, *The Spiritual Self in Everyday Life: The Transformation of Personal Religious Experience in Nineteenth-Century New England* (Boston: Northeastern University Press, 1989), 127–28, 140, and 210; John S. Gilkeson, Jr., *Middle-Class Providence, 1820–1940* (Princeton: Princeton University Press, 1986), 55–70; Richard Stott, *Jolly Fellows: Male Milieus in Nineteenth-Century America* (Baltimore: Johns Hopkins University Press, 2009), 72–73; Kelly, *In*, 212–13, 231–41.

32. See Sellers, 158–59; Stott, 77; Kruczek-Aaron, 14–18 and 173; Mark A. Noll, *America's God: From Jonathan Edwards to Abraham Lincoln* (New York: Oxford University Press, 2002), 205; Bill J. Leonard, *Baptists in America* (New York: Columbia University Press, 2005), 231–32.

33. On teachers' vulnerability to gossip, see Hansen, 127–32.

34. Johnson, diary, October 1, November 15, December 9, 1853.

35. Johnson, diary, October 1, 1853.

36. Gilkeson, 55–94.

37. Lori Merish, "'The Hand of Refined Taste' in the Frontier Landscape: Caroline Kirkland's *A New Home, Who'll Follow?* And the Feminization of American Consumerism," *American Quarterly* 45, no. 4 (December 1993): 485–523; Sellers, 364–65; Kelly, "Well," 131–32; Kelly, *In*, 249.

38. Rabinowitz, 127–30.

39. Johnson, diary, July 4, 1853. Gilkeson, 61–62; Stott, 89; Nicholas E. Tawa, *High-Minded and Low-Down: Music in the Lives of Americans 1800–1861* (Boston: Northeastern University Press, 2000), 203–5.

40. Johnson, diary, January 17, 1854.

41. Johnson, diary, December 22, 1853. See Halttunen, 17–20; Stott, 77; Leonard, 231–32.

42. Grier, 78-9; Rose, 124–25; Halttunen, 174–86.

43. Johnson, diary, January 30, 1854; December 7, 15, 29, 1853.

44. Johnson, diary, December 12, 1853; September 15, 1853. Harriet mentioned *Lily Dale* and *Lament of the Irish Emigrant*. She also enjoyed *The Blind Boy* and Stephen Foster's *Oh Boys, Carry Me Long, a Plantation Melody* (October 24, 1853), and *The Sister's Call* (January 30, 1854). On evoking memories, see Daniel Cavicchi, *Listening and Longing: Music Lovers in the Age of Barnum* (Middletown, CT: Wesleyan University Press, 2011), 145.

45. Johnson, diary, September 15, 1853.

46. Johnson, diary, December 12, 1853. See Tawa, *High-Minded*, 64–67.

47. Tawa, *High-Minded*, 55–56 and 62–63; Nicholas E. Tawa, *Sweet Songs for Gentle Americans: The Parlor Song in America, 1790–1860* (Bowling Green, Ohio: Bowling Green University Popular Press, 1980), 32–35 and 123–48.

48. Johnson, diary, August 31, 1853.

49. Johnson, diary, September 2, 1853. Metta Victoria Fuller, *The Senator's Son, or, the Maine Law; a Last Refuge; A Story Dedicated to the Lawmakers* (Cleveland, 1853). Metta Fuller later married Orville Victor, chief editor at the Beadle publishing firm that produced inexpensive paper-covered books. She wrote over a hundred dime novels. Robert W. Rydell and Rob Kroes, *Buffalo Bill in Bologna: The Americanization of the World, 1869–1922* (Chicago: University of Chicago Press, 2005), 34; Nina Baym, *Woman's Fiction: A Guide to Novels by and about Women in America, 1820–1870* (Ithaca: Cornell University Press, 1978), 267–68.

50. Johnson, diary, September 14, 1853.

51. Johnson, diary, October 20, 1853.

52. Johnson, diary, November 8, 1853.

53. Johnson, diary, June 20, 1853.

54. Frances B. Cogan, *All-American Girl: The Ideals of Real Womanhood in Mid-Nineteenth-Century America* (Athens: University of Georgia Press, 1989), 108, 137–41.

55. Johnson, diary, September 10, 1853.

56. Smith, diary, March 1, 1850.

57. Smith, diary, July 4, August 13, 1849; May 13, 1853; May 13, 16, and 22, July 1, 1851.

58. Johnson, diary, August 24, 1853. Elizabeth Stuart Phelps [H. Trusta], *The Last Leaf from Sunny Side* (New York, 1860) [orig. 1853].

59. Smith, diary, September 2, 1853. T. S. Arthur, *The Two Wives; or, Lost and Won* (Philadelphia, 1858) [orig. 1851]. Hymen was the Greek god of marriage.

60. See Judith Pascoe, "Tales for Young Housekeepers: T. S. Arthur and the American Girl," in *The Girl's Own: Cultural Histories of the Anglo-American Girl, 1830–1915* (Athens: University of Georgia Press, 1994), 34–51.

61. Nina Baym, *Novels, Readers, and Reviewers: Responses to Fiction in Antebellum America* (Ithaca, New York: Cornell University Press, 1984), 214–15. On moral fables, see Baym, *Woman's*, 33–34.

62. November 19, 1853. See also October 13 and 17, December 10, 1853; January 12, 1854.

63. See Kelly, "Well," 125.

64. Michael Denning, *Mechanic Accents: Dime Novels and Working-Class Culture in America*, revised edition (New York: Verso, 1987), 78.

65. T. S. Arthur, *The Lady at Home; or Happiness in the Household* (Philadelphia, 1853).

66. In a book Harriet borrowed from Mrs. Page, a sister inspires reform. December 13, 1853. Mrs. L. C. [Louisa Caroline] Tuthill, *Onward! Right Onward!* (Boston, 1845).

67. On working and living conditions of urban seamstresses and servants see Christine Stansell, *City of Women: Sex and Class in New York, 1789–1860* (Urbana: University of Illinois Press, 1987), 105–19, 154–68.

68. Pascoe notes Arthur's positive depictions of servants (40).

69. Johnson, diary, December 14, 1853.

70. See David Paul Nord, "Religious Reading and Readers in Antebellum America," *Journal of the Early Republic* 15, no. 2 (Summer 1995): 261, 269; Barbara Sicherman, "Reading and Middle-Class Identity in Victorian America," in *Reading Acts: U.S. Readers' Interactions with Literature, 1800–1950*, ed. Barbara Ryan and Amy M. Thomas (Knoxville: University of Tennessee Press, 2002), 144–45, 150–51. On books in educated New England families, see Ronald J. Zboray and Mary Saracino Zboray, "Books, Reading, and the World of Goods in Antebellum New England," *American Quarterly* 48, no. 4 (December 1996): 587–622, and "'Have You Read...?': Real Readers and Their Responses in Antebellum Boston and Its Region," *Nineteenth-Century Literature* 52, no. 2 (September 1997): 165–70. On Baptist schisms, see Leonard, 21–22, 29.

71. Johnson, diary, July 9, October 7, 1853. MA Page to Miss Hattie, January 24, 1853, SBSC.

72. Johnson, diary, December 13 and 24, 1853; January 30–31, March 1, 1854.

73. Johnson, diary, September 7, October 7, 12, and 17–20, November 17–18, 1853; February 4, March 1, 1854. C. A. Bloss, *Heroines of the Crusades* (Muscatine, Iowa, 1852); Horace Mann, *A Few Thoughts on the Powers and Duties of Woman* (Syracuse, 1853). On reading aloud, see Rose, 123, and Zboray and Zboray, "Books," 600–602, and "Reading and Everyday Life in Antebellum Boston: The Diary of Daniel F. and Mary D. Child," *Libraries & Culture* 32, no. 3 (July 1997): 285–322. Harriet complained that her uncle selected books she had read (October 20, 1853). On silently reading new books rather than rereading and reading aloud, see Denning, 71–72. Isabel Lehuu discusses antebellum criticism of this reading practice. *Carnival on the Page: Popular Print Media in Antebellum America* (Chapel Hill: University of North Carolina Press, 2000), 127–41.

74. Nord, 241–72; Mark S. Schantz, "Religious Tracts, Evangelical Reform, and the Market Revolution in Antebellum America," *Journal of the Early Republic* 17, no. 3 (Fall 1997): 425–66; Lehuu, 16–35; Nathan Hatch, *The Democratization of American Christianity* (New Haven: Yale University Press, 1989), 139–46; Ronald Zboray, *A Fictive People: Antebellum Economic Development and the American Reading Public* (New York: Oxford University Press, 1993), 3–68, and "Antebellum Reading and the Ironies of Technological Innovation," in *Reading in America: Literature & Social History*, ed. Cathy N. Davidson (Baltimore: Johns Hopkins University Press, 1989), 180–200; Sicherman, 139–41, 147–49; Richard D. Brown, *Knowledge is Power: The Diffusion of Information in Early America, 1700–1865* (New York: Oxford University Press, 1989), 12–15.

75. Johnson, diary, January 31, February 4, 1854. Hannah More, "Two Wealthy Farmers," in *The Works of Hannah More* (New York, 1835), 24–104. See Schantz, 432–36, 440–42.

76. Zboray and Zboray, "Have," 162–63; Baym, *Novels*, 146, 152, 173–95; Sicherman, 142–43.

77. Johnson, diary, March 1, 1854. Possibly Grace Aguilar's *Home Influence: A Tale for Mothers and Daughters* (New York, 1848).

78. Critics singled out French novels as condoning immoral behavior. Baym, *Novels*, 57, 178–80, 184–86; Nord, 248–50.

79. A Pastor's Wife [Martha Hubble Stone], *The Shady Side; or, Life in a Country Parsonage* (Cleveland, 1853), 63. When Harriet's uncle read the book aloud, Harriet remembered reading it with her friend Mary in Schoolcraft (October 7, 1853).

80. Phelps [Trusta], 261.

81. Johnson, diary, August 27, 1853. N. Parker Willis, *People I Have Met: or Pictures of Society and People of Mark, Drawn Under a Thin Veil of Fiction* (New York, 1850).

82. Emerson Bennett, *Leni-Leoti; or Adventures in the Far West* (Cincinnati, 1849).

83. Johnson, diary, January 14, 1854.

84. Johnson, diary, January 29, 1854. On destroying objectionable books, see Nord, 268–9, and Sicherman, 158 (n. 46).

85. Lehuu, 126–41; Nord, 248–55; Baym, *Novels*, 56–57.

86. Edelia to Harriet, September 7, 1846, SBSC.

87. Ada [Edelia] to Harriet, April 20, 1851, SBSC. In the 1840s, eight-page weekly story papers featured tales of adventure and romance accessible to readers of varying ages and reading ability. Denning, 10; Richard Brodhead, *Cultures of Letters: Scenes of Reading and Writing in Nineteenth-Century America* (Chicago: University of Chicago Press, 1993), 76–84; Dawn Fiske Thomsen, "'It is a Pity it is no Better': The Story Paper and Its Critics in Nineteenth-Century America," in *Scorned Literature: Essays on the History and Criticism of Popular Mass-Produced Fiction in America*, ed. Lydia Cushman Schurman and Deidre Johnson (Westport, CN: Greenwood, 2002), 83–95.

88. Blauvelt, 24–26; Kelly, *In*, 6–7.

89. Johnson, diary, December 3, 1853.

90. Baym, *Woman's*, 21–29, 35–38; Cogan, 103–33. On the influence of sentimental fiction on young women's diaries and courtships in an earlier generation, see Blauvelt, 15–49, 82–115.

91. Edelia to "parents," April 26, 1842, SBSC.

92. W. G. Johnson to Hattie, June 13, 1853, SBSC.

93. Leonard, 21–22; Hatch, 205; Roger Finke and Rodney Stark, *The Churching of America, 1776–1850: Winners and Losers in Our Religious Economy* (New Brunswick: Rutgers University Press, 1992), 76–86.

94. Johnson, diary, October 2, 1853.

95. Johnson, diary, July 6, 1853.

96. Kelly discusses literacy as a marker of gentility for antebellum New England women (*In*, 6–7).

97. David Mead, *Yankee Eloquence in the Middle West: The Ohio Lyceum 1850–1870* (East Lansing: Michigan State College Press, 1951), 179.

98. Johnson, diary, January 4–6 and 13, 1854. See Ronald J. Zboray and Mary Saracino Zboray, *Everyday Ideas: Socioliterary Experience Among Antebellum New Englanders*

(Knoxville, University of Tennessee Press, 2006), 60, and Richard D. Brown, *The Strength of a People: The Idea of an Informed Citizenry in America, 1650–1870* (Chapel Hill: University of North Carolina Press, 1996), 110, 127–28. Kelly found that provincial New England women participated more often as audience members than as writers and speakers (*In*, 196–99).

99. Hattie to Hattie [Johnson], April 18, 1852, SBSC. On constraints on women's public speech, see Nancy Isenberg, *Sex and Citizenship in Antebellum America* (Chapel Hill: University of North Carolina Press, 1998), 55–59.

100. Johnson, diary, November 5, 1853.

101. Johnson, diary, March 17, 1854.

102. Susan Coultrap-McQuin, *Doing Literary Business: American Women Writers in the Nineteenth Century* (Chapel Hill: University of North Carolina, 1990), 2; Baym, *Woman's*, 30–32; Brodhead, 74–77; Cogan, 248–50.

103. Mary A. Bigelow to Harriet, March 25, 1850, SBSC. Frank Leslie worked for a weekly family-oriented paper and other publications before he launched *Frank Leslie's Illustrated Newspaper* in 1855. Joshua Brown, *Beyond the Lines: Pictorial Reporting, Everyday Life, and the Crisis of Gilded Age America* (Berkeley: University of California Press, 2002), 18–22.

104. Jane L. Boynton to Harriet, April 6, 1849, SBSC.

105. V. C. Johnson to Hattie, February 20, 1853, SBSC.

106. Johnson, diary, December 20, 1853. David Donald and Frederick A. Palmer, "Toward a Western Literature, 1820–60," *Lincoln Reconsidered: Essays on the Civil War* Era, ed. David Donald, (New York: Vintage, 1956), 174–75. Cincinnati had been a regional publishing center for two decades (Mead, 8–12).

107. Johnson, diary, September 7, November 7, December 3, 1853. Marilyn Ferris Motz, "Sharing Secrets in Nineteenth-Century America," in *The Diary: The Epic of Everyday Life*, ed. Batsheva Ben-Amos and Dan Ben-Amos (Bloomington: Indiana University Press, 2020), 264.

108. Johnson, diary, November 7, 1853.

109. Johnson, diary, October 2, 1853.

110. Johnson, diary, October 9, 1853.

111. Brodhead argues that reading (particularly fiction) was central to mid-nineteenth-century northern middle-class family relationships and child-rearing practices (43–47).

112. See Brown, *Knowledge*, 193–94.

113. Smith, diary, April 28, 1848. Sue wrote a series of stories illustrating the cardinal sins.

114. Baym, *Novels*, 57, 178–80, 184–86; Nord, 248; Lehuu, 135; Sicherman, 148.

115. Smith, diary, October 20, 1850. Edward Bulwer Lytton, *Earnest Maltravers* (New York, 1837); Baym, *Novels*, 174, 177–78; Lehuu, 135.

116. Smith, diary, November 6, 1849. Maria Edgeworth, *Helen* (Philadelphia, 1834).

117. Baym, *Novels*, 146, 173–78; Thomas Augst, *The Clerk's Tale: Young Men and Moral Life in Nineteenth-Century America* (Chicago: University of Chicago Press, 2003), 88–90.

118. Smith, diary, February 11, 1851. On the importance of conversation in the "literary leisure" of young businessmen, see Augst, 93–104. Brown examines how middle-class cultural activities provided information to northern white men (*Knowledge*, 218–44). On the role of reading in establishing middle-class identity, see Augst, 12–16, 65–66, 81–82, and Sicherman.

119. Smith, diary, March 10, 21, and 27, April 5, 17, and 27, May 4 and 7, June 8 and 24, 1851; January 4, 1852. James Fenimore Cooper, *The Last of the Mohicans; a Narrative of 1757* (Philadelphia, 1826); Frederika Bremer, *The Neighbors: A Story of Every-Day Life*, trans. Mary Howitt (Boston, 1843); Philip J. Bailey, *Festus: A Poem,* Third American Edition (Boston, 1846); Bayard Taylor, *Eldorado; or, Adventures in the Path of Empire: Comprising a Voyage to California, via Panama; Life in San Francisco and Monterey; Pictures of the Gold Region, and Experiences of Mexican Travel*, 2 volumes (New York, 1850).

120. Smith, diary, March 27, 1851. Charles Dickens, *Barnaby Rudge: A Tale of the Riots of '80* (Philadelphia, [1841]); Baym, *Novels*, 152–72.

121. Smith, diary, March 10, 1851. Charles Dickens, *David Copperfield* (Philadelphia, [1850]).

122. Smith, diary, March 21, 1851. Henry also read Charles Dickens, *Martin Chuzzlewit* (Philadelphia, [1844]).

123. Captain [Frederick] Marryat, *Jacob Faithful; or the Adventures of a Waterman*, vol. 2 (Meredith Bridge, NH, 1848) [orig. 1834], 235; Captain Frederick Marryat, *Mr. Midshipman Easy* (Philadelphia, 1836). Henry also read Captain [Frederick] Marryat, *The King's Own* (Meredith Bridge, NH, 1843) [orig. 1830].

124. Smith, diary, November 11, 1852. Donald Grant Mitchell [Ik Marvel], *Reveries of a Bachelor; or, A Book of the Heart*, Ninth Edition (New York, 1851).

125. Samuel W. Durant, *History of Kalamazoo County, Michigan* (Philadelphia, 1880), 435, 516–19.

126. H. P. Smith, "Reminiscences of the Life of a Young Pioneer," *Pioneer Day Exercises* (Schoolcraft, MI, 1898), unpaginated, BHL (hereafter "Young Pioneer"); A. H. Scott, "Indians in Kalamazoo County," *MHC* 10 (1887): 166. See also A. D. P. Van Buren, "Address at Kalamazoo County Reunion, 1889," *MHC* 14 (1890): 524. On "exchange networks" of women, see Susan Sleeper-Smith, "Silent Tongues, Black Robes: Potawatomi, Europeans, and Settlers in the Southern Great Lakes, 1640–1850" (PhD dissertation, University of Michigan, 1994), 143. On Eliza Smith's role in trading, see Durant, 517.

127. "Young Pioneer"; William M. Cremin, David de Fant, and Conrad Kaufman, "The Indian and the Prairie: Prehistoric and Early Historic Utilization of Native Grassland Environments in Kalamazoo County, Michigan, with Emphasis on Gourd-Neck Prairie in Schoolcraft Township, Project No. S85-212" *Archaeological Reports* 16 (1986): 11–14 (https://scholarworks.wmich.edu/archaeological_reports); Kenneth Lewis, *West to Far Michigan: Settling the Lower Peninsula, 1815–1860* (East Lansing: Michigan State University Press, 2002), 87–88, 154–56; Susan E. Gray, "Limits and Possibilities: White-Indian Relations in Western Michigan in the Era of Removal" *Michigan Historical Review* 20, no. 2 (Fall 1994): 80–89; Scott, 165; Helen Hornbeck Tanner, ed., *Atlas of Great Lakes Indian History* (Norman: University of Oklahoma Press, 1987), 19, 134–35. On alliances, exchange, and gifts in Potawatomi culture, see Sleeper-Smith, 37–38, 52–54.

128. "Young Pioneer"; Durant, 435; Cremin, 11–14, 16–17; Sleeper-Smith, 119–45, 157, 180–87; "Summary under the Criteria and Evidence for Proposed Finding: Huron Potawatomi, Inc.," Office of Federal Acknowledgment, Bureau of Indian Affairs, US Department of the Interior (1995), 259–76 (https://www.bia.gov/sites/default/files/dup/assets/as-ia/ofa/petition/009_hurpot_MI/009_pf.pdf). For other descriptions of

Potawatomi as neighbors, see A. D. P. Van Buren, "Kalamazoo County," *MHC* 10 (1887): 156–57; Durant, 89; Gray, "Limits," 87–9; Susan E. Gray, *The Yankee West: Community Life on the Michigan Frontier* (Chapel Hill: University of North Carolina Press, 1996), 78–79.

129. E. Lakin Brown, *Autobiographical Notes*, rev. ed., A. Ada Brown, ed. (Schoolcraft, MI, 1906) [rpt. vol. 30, *Pioneer and Historical Collections*], 36.

130. Durant, 509. See also *Kalamazoo County Directory: With a History of the County from its Earliest Settlement* (Kalamazoo, 1869), 81.

131. "Young Pioneer." See also Durant, 511–13.

132. "Young Pioneer"; Lewis, 88; *Summary*, 266–82; R. David Edmunds, *The Potawatomis: Keepers of the Fire* (Norman: University of Oklahoma Press, 1978), 270–74; Sleeper-Smith, 244–45; Tanner, 166, 178.

133. Smith, diary, November 30, 1848; April 4, 1849.

134. Smith, diary, October 16, 1848; December 18, 1849.

135. Smith, diary, October 10–12, 1848.

136. Lewis, 170–72, 193–98, 204. See Scott C. Martin, *Killing Time: Leisure and Culture in Southwestern Pennsylvania, 1800–1850* (Pittsburgh: University of Pittsburgh Press, 1995), 46–49.

137. Smith, diary, September 10, 1848.

138. Smith, diary, August 28, 1848.

139. Smith, diary, March 2 and 10, 1849.

140. Smith, diary, June 11, 1848. Grocery stores served as gathering spots for men, who often engaged in rowdy behavior (Stott, 10–11).

141. Stansell, 90–91; Stott, 103–9, 146–47. See also Elliott J. Gorn, "'Good-Bye Boys, I Die a True American': Homicide, Nativism, and Working-Class Culture in Antebellum New York City," *Journal of American History* 74, no. 2 (September 1987), 403–10.

142. Gorn, 407. See Howard P. Chudacoff, *The Age of the Bachelor: Creating an American Subculture* (Princeton: Princeton University Press, 1999), 29–35, on urban bachelor subcultures.

143. Smith, diary, April 18–19, 1850.

144. Smith, diary, May 23, June 8, and 14, 1850. Prairie Ronde House dance invitation (1850), Miscellaneous Social Programs Folder, Box 4, SBSC. See Tawa, *High-Minded*, 180–81, 187–90.

145. Paul M. Gifford, "Fiddling and Instrumental Folk Music in Michigan," *Michigan Folklife Reader*, ed. C. Kurt Dewhurst and Yvonne R. Lockwood (East Lansing: Michigan State University Press, 1987), 190–91.

146. Smith, diary, December 24–25, 27, and 31, 1849; January 18, 1850. Gifford, 190–91.

147. Smith, diary, July 4, 1849; January 1, February 14, July 4, 1850.

148. Gifford, 190–91.

149. Smith, diary, December 25, 1848.

150. Smith, diary, July 4, 1850.

151. Smith, diary, January 1, 1850. Gifford, 191–92.

152. Smith, diary, February 11, 1851.

153. Smith, diary, December 19, 20, and 21, 1851.

154. Smith, diary, June 4 and 15, July 12, October 23, 1851; February 21, May 6–8 and 31, June 1, August 8, 1852. On church choirs and musical societies, see Cavicchi, 66–71.

155. Tawa, *Sweet*, 28; Tawa, *High-Minded*, 246–51.
156. Smith, diary, June 28, 1851.
157. Smith, diary, February 5, 1852.
158. Smith, diary, November 12, 1851.
159. Cavicchi, 3–5, 24–30, 75–87.
160. See Bruce A. McConachie, "Pacifying American Theatrical Audiences, 1820–1900," in *For Fun and Profit: The Transformation of Leisure into Consumption*, ed. Richard Butsch (Philadelphia: Temple University Press, 1990), 53–58; Martin, 47–48; Cavicchi, 25.
161. Smith, diary, January 4, June 1, November 17, 1851.
162. Smith, diary, June 10, July 18, 1851. Cavicchi, 14–19, 33–9.
163. Smith, diary, February 26, March 29, 1852.
164. McConachie; Cavicchi, 31, 200 (n. 43).
165. Smith, diary, July 16, 1851.
166. Smith, diary, July 8, August 15, September 4, 1851. See Rydell and Kroes, 26.
167. Smith, diary, September 9, 1851.
168. See Eric Fretz, "P. T. Barnum's Theatrical Selfhood and the Nineteenth-Century Culture of Exhibition" in *Freakery: Cultural Spectacles of the Extraordinary Body*, ed. Rosemarie Garland Thomson (New York: New York University Press, 1996), 97–107. See also Rydell and Kroes, 27–28, and Patricia C. Click, *The Spirit of the Times* (University Press of Virginia, 1989), 25–31.
169. See Brett Mizelle, "'I Have Brought My Pig to a Fine Market': Animals, Their Exhibitors, and Market Culture in the Early Republic," in *Cultural Change and the Market Revolution in America, 1789–1860*, ed. Scott C. Martin (New York: Rowman & Littlefield, 2005), 181–216; Jennifer L. Mosier, "The Big Attraction: The Circus Elephant and American Culture," *Journal of American Culture* 22, no. 2 (June 1999), 7–18; Janet M. Davis, *The Circus Age: Culture and Society Under the American Big Top* (Chapel Hill: University of North Carolina Press, 2002).
170. Smith, diary, July 4, 1851.
171. Anne C. Coon, "Introduction," *Hear Me Patiently: The Reform Speeches of Amelia Jenks Bloomer*, ed. Anne C. Coon (Westport, CT: Greenwood, 1994), 5–12; Isenberg, 48–53.
172. Smith, diary, March 4, 1851.
173. On Potawatomi women's leggings, see A. B. Copley, "The Pottawattomies," and Edwin S. Smith, "Pioneer Days in Kalamazoo and Van Buren," *MHC* 14 (1890), 264, 273. On elegant Potawatomi clothing, including leggings, see Sleeper-Smith, 161–70, 237.
174. For example, Stanton described Amelia Bloomer's women's lounge at the post office as "a neat little room." *Eighty Year and More* (New York: Schoken, 1971), p. 200 (cited in Sandra S. Weber, *Women's Rights National Historical Park* (Seneca Falls: National Park Service, 1985), Ch. 4, n. 32 (https://www.nps.gov/parkhistory/online_books/wori/shs4.htm).
175. Coon, 10–12; Isenberg, 48–53.
176. Smith, diary, November 25, 1851.
177. On October 25, 1852, a few days after the birth of Stanton's first daughter, Mrs. Gould wrote Henry: "Mrs. Stanton has a daughter. She considers it a great wonderment that the scale has turned with her, as her children are all Sons." Amelia Gould wrote Henry on March 29, 1854, about attending Mrs. Stanton's masquerade party: "She gave out over

200 invitations but you know that there [are] a great many that are too conscientious to go to such a place." SBSC.

178. Smith, diary, March 9, 1851. Kelly organized Thompson's lecture tour and substituted for him in Seneca Falls. She often faced hostile audiences who objected to a woman lecturing in public. Dorothy Sterling, *Ahead of Her Time: Abby Kelly and the Politics of Antislavery* (New York: W. W. Norton, 1991), 269–71; Isenberg, 61–64.

179. Smith, diary, May 21, 1851.

180. Smith, diary, June 6, 1852.

181. Kristin Hoganson, "Garrisonian Abolitionists and the Rhetoric of Gender, 1850–1860," *American Quarterly* 45, no. 4 (December 1993), 556–95; Bruce Dorsey, *Reforming Men and Women: Gender in the Antebellum City* (Ithaca: Cornell University Press, 2002), 193–94.

182. Smith, diary, August 21, 1852.

183. Smith, diary, April 16, 1853.

184. Smith, diary, June 10, 1853.

185. Smith, diary, August 13, 1853.

186. Stott, 19–20.

187. Smith, diary, January 6, 1853. See Tawa, *High-Minded*, 70–74, 155–63.

188. August 29, September 7, November 25, December 26, 1852; January 23 and 30, February 20, March 6 and 20, April 24, May 1, 1853. See Tawa, *High-Minded*, 93–98; Kelly, *In*, 195–96; Cavicchi, 66; Hansen, 81.

189. Smith, diary, December 17, 1852. See Cavicchi, 70–72.

190. Smith, diary, August 23–24 and 26, November 26, December 17, 22–23, and 30, 1852; January 19, 22, and 24, February 12 and 16–17, March 2, July 12, 1853.

191. Smith, diary, December 17 and 22, 1852; February 9 and 26, March 18, May 9, 1853. Henry to Mother, March 7, 1852, SBSC.

192. Smith, diary, August 22 and 28, September 1 and 11, October 11 and 23, November 5–6 and 27, December 4, 1853; January 4, 7, 17, and 29, February 2 and 5, April 10, May 7, 1854.

193. Smith, diary, September 16, November 19–20, 1853; April 23, 1854.

194. Smith, diary, December 21, 1853.

195. Smith, diary, February 17, 1854.

196. Smith, diary, April 3, 1854.

Chapter Three. Family and Nation

1. Henry Smith, diary, June 6, 1854, Henry Parker Smith Papers, BHL.

2. Smith, diary, May 25, 1854.

3. Smith, diary, June 2, 1854.

4. Smith, diary, June 6, 1854.

5. Smith, diary, June 6, 1854. Stanley Barney Smith, "Notes on the Village of Schoolcraft in the 1850's," *Michigan History* 40, no. 2 (June 1956), 134.

6. Smith, diary, June 6, 1854.

7. Hattie to "My Own Dear Husband," August 21–27, 1854, Stanley Barney Smith Collection (SBSC), A-88, Archives and Regional History Collections, Zhang Legacy Collections Center, Western Michigan University.

8. Smith, diary, July 19, 1853.

9. Henrie to Hattie, August 10–13 and 14–20, 1854, SBSC; Smith, "Notes," 151 n. 158.

10. Harriet to Henry, July 16, 1854, SBSC.

11. Harriet to Henry, August 2–6, 1854, SBSC.

12. Smith, diary, August 7, 1854. On the stress of pregnancy soon after marriage and anxiety about childbirth, see Sylvia D. Hoffert, *Private Matters: American Attitudes toward Childbearing and Infant Nurture in the Urban North, 1800–1860* (Urbana: University of Illinois Press, 1989), 37–41.

13. Smith, diary, March 11, 1853. Richard W. and Dorothy C. Wertz, *Lying-In: A History of Childbirth in America* (New York: Free Press, 1977), 119–26; Hoffert, 108–12.

14. Carl N. Degler, *At Odds: Women and the Family in America from the Revolution to the Present* (New York: Oxford University Press, 1980), 213–14. See also Harvey Green, *The Light of the Home: An Intimate View of the Lives of Women in Victorian America* (New York: Pantheon, 1983), 32–33; John D'Emilio and Estelle B. Freedman, *Intimate Matters: A History of Sexuality in America*, second edition (Chicago: University of Chicago Press, 1997), 61; Janet Farrell Brodie, *Contraception and Abortion in Nineteenth-Century America* (Ithaca: Cornell University Press, 1974), 28–30, 79–85.

15. Hoffert, 16. D'Emilio and Freedman note that the drop in fertility was especially prominent among northern native-born white urban women (58). See also Brodie, 2–3; Mary P. Ryan, *Cradle of the Middle Class: The Family in Oneida County, New York 1790–1865* (New York: Cambridge University Press, 1981), 155–56; Charles Sellers, *The Market Revolution: Jacksonian America, 1815–1846* (New York: Oxford University Press, 1991), 240. On a decline in the northern rural birthrate, see Alan Kulikoff, *The Agrarian Origins of American Capitalism* (Charlottesville: The University Press of Virginia, 1992), 48–51.

16. Hoffert, 15–20. See also Karen Lystra, *Searching the Heart: Women, Men and Romantic Love in Nineteenth-Century America* (New York: Oxford University Press, 1989), 82–84. On availability of contraceptive devices, see D'Emilia and Freedman, 59–61; Brodie, 207–10; Ryan, 155–57; Degler, 215–20.

17. Henry to Harriet, August 6 and 14–20, 1854, SBSC.

18. Degler, 227–41. See also D'Emilio and Freedman, 63–65; Ryan, 156; Brodie, 33, 224–27, 254; Sellers, 241.

19. Harriet to Henry, August 7–13, 1854, SBSC.

20. Henry to Harriet, August 10–13, 1854, SBSC.

21. Henrie to "My own true hearted wife," August 14–20, 1854, SBSC.

22. Hattie to "My Own Dearest Husband," August 21–25, 1854, SBSC.

23. Susan E. Gray, *The Yankee West: Community Life on the Michigan Frontier* (Chapel Hill: University of North Carolina Press, 1996), 79–81.

24. H. P. Smith to Brother [Joseph Johnson], November 19, 1854, SBSC.

25. Smith, diary, January 26, 1855.

26. Barbara Epstein notes that borrowing money was essential to financial success but caused resentment against affluent people by those dependent on them for access to credit. *The Politics of Domesticity: Women, Evangelism and Temperance in Nineteenth-Century America* (Middletown, CT: Wesleyan University Press, 1987), 71–72.

27. Smith, "Notes," 147.

28. William E. Gienapp, *The Origins of the Republican Party, 1852–1856* (New York: Oxford University Press, 1987), 104–5. See also Michael Holt, "Making and Mobilizing the Republican

Party, 1854–1860," in *The Birth of the Grand Old Party: The Republicans' First Generation*, ed. Robert F. Engs and Randall M. Miller (Philadelphia: University of Pennsylvania Press, 2002), 29–30; Michael F. Holt, *The Fate of Their Country: Politicians, Slavery Extension, and the Coming of the Civil War* (New York: Hill and Wang, 2004), 111–12. E. Lakin Brown, Henry's mother's cousin, was elected to the Michigan Senate as a Republican.

29. Smith, diary, April 3, June 11, November 7, 1848; April 18, 1850; May 27, November 4, 1851; September 29, 1854.

30. Gienapp, *Origins*, 105.

31. Tyler Anbinder, *Nativism and Slavery: The Northern Know Nothings and the Politics of the 1850s* (New York: Oxford University Press, 1992), 22–24, 43.

32. Thomas Brown, *Politics and Statesmanship: Essays on the American Whig Party* (New York: Columbia University Press, 1985), 39–46; Michael F. Holt, *The Political Crisis of the 1850s* (New York: John Wiley & Sons, 1978), 136.

33. Anbinder, 103–6.

34. Smith, diary, March 7, 1855.

35. Smith, diary, March 19, 1855.

36. Hoffert, 63, 74–76. On the presence of husbands during childbirth, see Wertz, 75–76, and Stephen M. Frank, *Life with Father: Parenthood and Masculinity in the Nineteenth-Century American North* (Baltimore: Johns Hopkins University Press, 1998), 84, 96–101. Frank uses Henry Smith as an example (101–5).

37. Smith, diary, March 25, 1855.

38. Smith, diary, April 24, 1855.

39. Hoffert, 122–32; Frank, 107–8.

40. Hoffert, 116–19.

41. Smith, diary, April 25, 1855.

42. Smith, diary, July 2, 1855. See Smith, "Notes," 136.

43. Charly [Wheeler] to Cousin [Henry], June 2, 1855, SBSC. See Degler, 217–20; D'Emilio and Freedman, 60; Brodie, 207–10.

44. Ryan, 157.

45. Smith, diary, June 14, 1855.

46. Smith, diary, July 19, 1855. See Smith, "Notes," 139–40.

47. On baby bottles with rubber nipples, see Green, 38, and Hoffert, 148.

48. Smith, diary, July 22, 1855.

49. Smith, diary, July 23, 1855; July 24, 1855. See Smith, "Notes," 136.

50. Smith, diary, July 26, 1855.

51. W. G. Johnson to Henrie and Hattie, August 6, 1855, SBSC.

52. Smith, diary, August 10, 1855.

53. Smith, diary, September 29, 1855; October 1, 1855. Fathers often nursed seriously ill children (Frank, 76–78). On high rates of infant mortality and parental anxiety, see Hoffert, 157–60, and Frank, 77.

54. Smith, diary, October 16, 1855.

55. Smith, diary, October 18, 1855.

56. Anne C. Rose, *Victorian America and the Civil War* (New York: Cambridge University Press, 1992), 90.

57. Gray, 10–15.

58. On Know-Nothing membership as a stage in voters' transition from Whig or Democrat to Republican, see Gienapp, *Origins*, 444–46; Holt, *Political*, 172–76; William E. Gienapp, "'Politics Seem to Enter into Everything': Political Culture in the North, 1840–1860," *Essays on American Antebellum Politics, 1840–1860*, ed. Stephen E. Maizlish and John J. Kushman (College Station: Texas A & M University Press, 1982), 58.

59. Anbinder, 206–19; Holt, "Making," 39–41; Gienapp, *Origins*, 259–62, 418–22, 445–46; Holt, *Political*, 171.

60. Eric Foner, *Politics and Ideology in the Age of the Civil War* (New York: Oxford University Press, 1980), 73–74; Holt, "Making," 42–49; Gienapp, *Origins*, 348–65.

61. Holt, Fate, 114-7.

62. Craig Miner, *Seeding Civil War: Kansas in the National News, 1854–1858* (Lawrence: University Press of Kansas, 2008).

63. Gienapp, *Origins*, 435–38.

64. Foner, 48–49, 73–74.

65. Smith, diary, April 2, 1856.

66. Smith, diary, April 5, 1856.

67. For examples of the term "fanatic" to describe abolitionists, see Miner, 65, 83, 88, 127, 144, 185, and George C. Rable, *Damn Yankees! Demonization & Defiance in the Confederate South* (Baton Rouge: Louisiana State University Press, 2015), 19–22. Gray discusses partisan identification in Kalamazoo County local elections (150–53).

68. Smith, diary, July 18, 1856.

69. Smith, diary, July 29, 1856.

70. Smith, diary, July 30, 1856.

71. Smith, diary, August 4, 1856.

72. Smith, diary, September 1, 1854. See also Harriet Johnson, diary, December 13, 1853, Henry Parker Smith Papers, BHL.

73. Smith, diary, July 19, 1856.

74. E. Anthony Rotundo argues that masculine rituals of parades and pole-raisings "exalted the shared manhood" of participants. *American Manhood: Transformations in Masculinity from the Revolution to the Modern Era* (New York: Basic Books, 1993), 218. On liberty poles, see Simon P. Newman, *Parades and the Politics of the Street: Festive Culture in the Early American Republic* (Philadelphia: University of Pennsylvania Press, 1997), 24–26.

75. Charles True Goodsell and Willis Frederick Dunbar, *Centennial History of Kalamazoo College* (Kalamazoo: Kalamazoo College, 1933), 204, 208.

76. Michael D. Pierson, *Free Hearts and Free Homes: Gender and American Antislavery Politics* (Chapel Hill: University of North Carolina Press, 2003), 140–6. See also Gienapp, "Politics," 16–17; Gienapp, *Origins*, 375.

77. Smith, diary, August 27, 1856. See Smith, "Notes," 148–51.

78. Abraham Lincoln, *Lincoln's Kalamazoo Address Against Extending Slavery*, annotated by Thomas I. Starr (Detroit: Fine Book Circle, 1941), 33–46.

79. Foner, 73–74.

80. Gienapp, "Politics," 53–59.

81. Smith, diary, September 5, 1856.

82. Smith, diary, September 6, 1856.

83. Smith, diary, September 11, 1856.

84. Gienapp notes that volunteer party workers could expect the reward of a job or contract after a successful election ("Politics," 43, 51–52).

85. Smith, diary, September 15, 1856. On the connection of party affiliation, office-holding, and local status in Kalamazoo County, see Gray, 139–68.

86. Smith, diary, September 24, 1856; September 27, 1856.

87. Smith, diary, October 17, 1856.

88. Smith, diary, November 2, 1856. See Gienapp, "Politics," 52.

89. Gienapp, "Politics," 32–35.

90. Smith, diary, November 3, 1856. On music in political campaigns, see Nicholas E. Tawa, *High-Minded and Low-Down: Music in the Lives of Americans 1800–1861* (Boston: Northeastern University Press, 2000), 198–203.

91. Smith, diary, November 5, 1856.

92. Holt, *Political*, 189–97; Holt, "Making," 42–44; Gienapp, *Origins*, 355–65.

93. Smith, diary, September 21, 1856.

94. Smith, diary, December 3, 1856. Robert Griswold finds that fathers seldom took responsibility for routine care of children. *Fatherhood in America: A History* (New York: Basic Books, 1993), 19.

95. Smith, diary, November 26, 1856.

96. Smith, diary, December 31, 1856.

97. Smith, diary, April 8, August 1, 1856; March 4 and 23, 1857.

98. Smith, diary, June 29, November 9 and 16, 1856; February 8, 1857.

99. Smith, diary, February 22–24, 1856; January 31–February 4, 1857.

100. Smith, diary, September 20, 1855; January 18, March 27, December 24, 1856; March 27, 1857.

101. Smith, diary, January 21, 1857.

102. Smith, diary, June 10, 1856; February 15, 1856; January 7, 1857.

103. Smith, diary, March 2 and 11, July 20, December 12, 1856.

104. Smith, diary, December 9, 1856; January 28, 1857.

105. Smith, diary, November 28, 1856.

106. Smith, diary, January 15, 1857.

107. Smith, diary, February 24, 1857.

108. Smith, diary, March 2, 1857.

109. Smith, diary, March 3, 1857.

110. W. G. Johnson to "children," September 6, 1856, SBSC.

111. W. G. Johnson to Henrie and Hattie, October 24, 1856, SBSC.

112. Smith, diary, March 4, 1857.

113. Smith, diary, March 16, 1857.

114. Smith, diary, March 18, 1857.

115. Smith, diary, March 5, 23, and 30, 1857.

116. Smith, diary, March 1, 4, 21–22, and 31, 1857.

117. Smith, diary, March 20, 1857.

118. Smith, diary, April 7, 1857.

119. Rotundo, 210–11.

120. Brian P. Luskey, *On the Make: Clerks and the Quest for Capital in Nineteenth-Century America* (New York: New York University Press, 2010), 83–118.

121. Smith, diary, April 1, 1857.

122. Smith, diary, April 21, 1857.

123. Smith, diary, April 23, 1857.

124. Smith, diary, April 24, 1857.

125. See Linda Peavy and Ursula Smith, *Women in Waiting in the Westward Movement: Life on the Home Frontier* (Norman: University of Oklahoma Press, 1994), 3–17.

126. Smith, diary, April 27, 1857.

127. Rose, 194, 223.

Chapter Four. Yankees and Pioneers

1. Hattie to Henrie, August 16, 1857, Stanley Barney Smith Collection (SBSC), A-88, Archives and Regional History Collections, Zhang Legacy Collections Center, Western Michigan University.

2. Henrie to Hattie, May 21, June 9–12, 1857; HP Smith to Charley [Wheeler], August 16, 1857; Solomon to Mother, November 20, 1856; C. F. Wheeler to Cousin Henry, April 2, 1855; all SBSC. On ties between St. Louis and the Northeast, see Louis S. Gerteis, *Civil War St. Louis* (Lawrence: University Press of Kansas, 2001), 37–44, and Christopher Phillips, *The Rivers Ran Backward: The Civil War and the Remaking of the American Middle Border* (New York: Oxford University Press, 2016), 57–58.

3. Henrie to Hattie, May 23, 1857, SBSC. On the prevalence of slave hiring in Missouri, see Diane Mutti Burke, *On Slavery's Border: Missouri's Small Slaveholding Households, 1815–1865* (Athens: University of Georgia Press, 2010), 10, 29, 90, 107–18; Douglas Hurt, *Agriculture and Slavery in Missouri's Little Dixie* (Columbia: University of Missouri Press, 1992), 238–43; Kristen Epps, *Slavery on the Periphery: The Kansas-Missouri Border in the Antebellum and Civil War Eras* (Athens: University of Georgia Press, 2016), 63, 105–6.

4. Henrie to Hattie, May 26–27, 1857, SBSC. On rising land prices, see Phillips, 53 and 81.

5. Henrie to Hattie and Isa, June 1, 1857, SBSC. Adam Wesley Dean, *An Agrarian Republic: Farming, Antislavery Politics and Nature Parks in the Civil War Era* (Chapel Hill: University of North Carolina Press, 2015), 3, 26–35, 40.

6. Sally McMurry, *Families and Farmhouses in Nineteenth-Century America: Vernacular Design and Social Change* (Knoxville: University of Tennessee Press, 1997), rpt. 1988, 62–63.

7. Henrie to Hattie and Isa, June 1, 1857, SBSC.

8. Burke, *On*, 5–12, 25–26, 56–57, 99–100; Hurt, 80–124, 221–23.

9. Burke, *On*, 57–58, 71–74, 100–102; Hurt, 165–69, 187–88, 206; Phillips, 49–55.

10. Burke, *On*, 28–29, 236, 263–65; Hurt, 220–23.

11. Henrie to Hattie and Isa, June 1, 1857, SBSC. Gary W. Beahan, "Missouri's Public Domain: United States Land Sales, 1818–1922," *Missouri State Archives Information Bulletin* 2, no. 3 (July 1980): 18, 27.

12. Henrie to Hattie, June 3, 1857, SBSC.

13. *History of Greene County, Missouri* (St. Louis, 1883), 245.

14. Phillips, 53 and 81; *History of Vernon County, Missouri* (St. Louis, 1887), 171, 187–88, 194, 202 (hereafter *HVC*); Beahan, 12–14; Dean, 44.

15. Walter A. Schroeder, *Presettlement Prairie of Missouri*, 2nd ed. (Jefferson City: Missouri Department of Conservation, 1982), 4–5, 8.

16. *HVC*, 194.

17. Henrie to Hattie, June 9–11, 1857, SBSC.

18. Henrie to Hattie, June 9–11, 1857, SBSC; Jeremy Neely, *The Border Between Them: Violence and Reconciliation on the Kansas-Missouri Line* (Columbia: University of Missouri Press, 2007), 30–31, 34–35, 208, 218–19.

19. Henrie to Hattie, June 9–11, 1857, SBSC; Neely, 28.

20. Henrie to Hattie, June 18, 1857, SBSC.

21. *HVC*, 851–53.

22. Neely, 7–30; Kenneth Lewis, *West to Far Michigan: Settling the Lower Peninsula, 1815–1860* (East Lansing: Michigan State University Press, 2002), 2–10, 56–58, 87–204, 235–52, 262–63; Schroeder, 6–7, 11–12, 18–20, 35.

23. *HVC*, 586, 851–54.

24. The four survey townships that comprised the original civic township of Montevallo were separated later into Badger, Virgil, Dover, and Montevallo Townships. *HVC*, 194, 199, 438, 854.

25. Henrie to Hattie, June 18, 28, 1857, SBSC; *HVC*, 187–88, 851.

26. Neely, 20–22; *HVC*, 174–76; Kristen K. Epps, "Before the Border War: Slavery and the Settlement of the Western Frontier, 1825–1845," in *Bleeding Kansas, Bleeding Missouri: The Long Civil War on the Border*, ed. Jonathan Earle and Diane Mutti Burke (Lawrence: University Press of Kansas, 2013), 43–44.

27. *HVC*, 596–98.

28. Henrie to Hattie, June 28, 1857, SBSC.

29. Henrie to Hattie and Isa, June 30–July 5, 1857, SBSC. General Land Office Warrant No. 13,538 entered in Springfield, Missouri to Thaddeus Smith, assigned to Henry P. Smith. As a Black Hawk War veteran (Michigan militia musician), Henry's father became eligible for 120 additional acres of military bounty land in 1855. General Land Office Records, US Bureau of Land Management: https://glorecords.blm.gov/default.aspx.

30. Henrie to Hattie, June 9–11, 1857, SBSC.

31. Henrie to Hattie, June 18, 1857, SBSC. A typical prairie cabin measured sixteen by eighteen feet. Glenda Riley, *The Female Frontier: A Comparative View of Women on the Prairie and the Plains* (Lawrence: University Press of Kansas, 1988), 55.

32. Henrie to Hattie, June 28, 1857, SBSC.

33. McMurry, 25–86. See also David Blanke, *Sowing the American Dream: How Consumer Culture Took Root in the Rural Midwest* (Athens: Ohio University Press, 2000), 33–38.

34. McMurry, 62–66; James E. Davis, "How Nature and Culture Shaped Early Settlement in the Midwest," in *Finding a New Midwestern History*, ed. Jon K. Lauck, Gleaves Whitney, and Joseph Hogan (Lincoln: University of Nebraska Press, 2018), 25–38.

35. Richard L. Bushman, *The Refinement of America: Persons, Houses, Cities* (New York: Alfred A. Knopf, 1992), 245–50.

36. See McMurry, 30-3, 47-49.

37. Henrie to Hattie, June 18, 1857, SBSC.

38. Henrie to Hattie and Isa, June 30–July 5, 1857, SBSC. On the stigma of living in a log cabin, see Bushman, 425–31.

39. Henrie to Hattie, June 28, 1857, SBSC.

40. Annette Kolodny, *The Land Before Her: Fantasy and Experience of the American Frontiers, 1630-1860* (Chapel Hill: University of North Carolina Press, 1984), 8–9, 145–48, and 164–77. Mary P. Ryan also found that flowers, vines and shrubbery surrounding a house were important "emblems of domestic warmth." *The Empire of the Mother: American Writing about Domesticity, 1830–1860* (New York: Haworth, 1982), 110–11.

41. Henrie to Hattie, May 23, 1857, SBSC.

42. Hattie to Henrie, May 26, 1857, SBSC.

43. Hattie to "My Own Dearest Husband," May 31, 1857, SBSC.

44. Craig Miner, *Seeding Civil War: Kansas in the National News, 1854–1858* (Lawrence: University Press of Kansas, 2008), 48–49, 73–82, 109–30, 195; Susan-Mary Grant, *North Over South: Northern Nationalism and American Identity in the Antebellum Era* (Lawrence: University Press of Kansas, 2000), 54–58, 130–47; Neely, 39–40; Michael Fellman, *Inside War: The Guerrilla Conflict in Missouri During the American Civil War* (New York: Oxford University Press, 1989), 11–18.

45. Joanne Pope Melish, *Disowning Slavery: Gradual Emancipation and "Race" in New England, 1789–1860* (Ithaca: Cornell University Press, 1998), 210–37.

46. Joseph S. Wood, *The New England Village* (Baltimore: Johns Hopkins University Press, 1997).

47. Bushman, 250–65.

48. Catherine E. Kelly, *In the New England Fashion: Reshaping Women's Lives in the Nineteenth Century* (Ithaca: Cornell University Press, 1999), 181–87, 240–49. See also Stephen Nissenbaum, "New England as Region and Nation," in *All Over the Map: Rethinking American Regions*, ed. Edward L. Ayers, Patricia Nelson Limerick, Stephen Nissenbaum, and Peter S. Onuf (Baltimore: Johns Hopkins University Press, 1996), 38–61.

49. Richard Stott, *Jolly Fellows: Male Milieus in Nineteenth-Century America* (Baltimore: Johns Hopkins University Press, 2009), 65-73.

50. Archibald and Edelia [Servoss] to Brother, September 18, 1857, SBSC.

51. Frank to Brother and Sister, April 30, 1859, SBSC.

52. Joseph A. Conforti, *Imagining New England: Explorations of Regional Identity from the Pilgrims to the Mid-Twentieth Century* (Chapel Hill: University of North Carolina Press, 2001), 123–202. See also Alexander Saxon, *The Rise and Fall of the White Republic: Class Politics and Mass Culture in Nineteenth-Century America* (New York: Verso, 1990), 110–23. For earlier discussions, see Constance Rourke, *American Humor: A Study of the American Character* (Tallahassee: University Presses of Florida, 1986) [1931], 16–30, and William R. Taylor, *Cavalier and Yankee: The Old South and American National Character* (Garden City: Doubleday Anchor, 1963) [1957], 72–119.

53. Joseph T. Rainer, "The 'Sharper' Image: Yankee Peddlers, Southern Consumers, and the Market Revolution," in *Cultural Change and the Market Revolution in America, 1780-1860*, ed. Scott C. Martin (New York: Rowman & Littlefield, 2005), 89–110; David Jaffee,

"Peddlers of Progress and the Transformation of the Rural North, 1760–1860," *Journal of American History* 78, no. 2 (September 1991), 511–35; Richard Sellers, *The Market Revolution: Jacksonian America, 1815–1846* (New York: Oxford University Press, 1994) [1991], 18–19, 162; Nicole Etcheson, *The Emerging Midwest: Upland Southerners and the Political Culture of the Old Northwest, 1787–1861* (Bloomington: Indiana University Press, 1996), 7–8, 109, 118–19; John C. Hudson, *Making the Corn Belt: A Geographic History of Middle-Western Agriculture* (Bloomington: Indiana University Press, 1994), 62–63, 93–95; Conforti, 156–58; Matthew E. Stanley, *The Loyal West: Civil War and Reunion in Middle America* (Urbana: University of Illinois Press, 2017), 25; Susan E. Gray, *The Yankee West: Community Life on the Michigan Frontier* (Chapel Hill: University of North Carolina Press, 1996), 3, 13–14. See also Scott A. Sandage, *Born Losers: A History of Failure in America* (Cambridge, MA: Harvard University Press, 2005), 83–94.

54. Karen Halttunen, *Confidence Men and Painted Women: A Study in Middle-Class Culture in America, 1830–1870* (New Haven: Yale University Press, 1982), 30–1; Neil Harris, *Humbug: The Art of P. T. Barnum* (Chicago: University of Chicago Press, 1973), 207–16. On Greeley, see Miner, 80–81. On earlier European descriptions of Americans as the "universal Yankee nation," see George C. Rable, *Damn Yankees! Demonization & Defiance in the Confederate South* (Baton Rouge: Louisiana State University Press, 2015), 8.

55. Gray, 2–14; Conforti, 150–51; Sellers, 364–65, 392–94; Allan Kulikoff, *The Agrarian Origins of American Capitalism* (Charlottesville: University Press of Virginia, 1992), 91–93, 216–21; Stanley, 12–35; Blanke, 16–17; Etcheson, *Emerging*, 2–8, 95–119. Kim Gruenwald, *Rivers of Enterprise: The Commercial Origins of Regional Identity in the Ohio Valley, 1790–1850* (Bloomington: Indiana University Press, 2002), 140–46.

56. See Michael E. Woods, *Emotional and Sectional Conflict in the Antebellum US* (New York: Cambridge University Press, 2014), 106–67; Grant; Miner; Peter S. Onuf, "Federalism, Republicanism and the Origins of American Sectionalism," in *All Over the Map: Rethinking American Regions*, ed. Edward L Ayers, Patricia Nelson Limerick, Stephen Nissenbaum, and Peter S. Onuf (Baltimore: Johns Hopkins University Press, 1996), 29–30; Melish, 235–36.

57. Henry Smith, diary, October 19–22, 1852, Henry Parker Smith Papers, BHL. On nineteenth-century Hoosier culture, see John Lauritz Larson, "Pigs in Space; or, What Shapes America's Regional Cultures," in *The American Midwest: Essays in Regional History*, ed. Andrew L. Cayton and Susan E. Gray (Bloomington: Indiana University Press, 2001), 69–77.

58. In the 1850s, northern anti-slavery journalists adopted an existing derogatory term, "Puke," to stereotype poor Missouri farmers from southern states. Fellman, 11–16, 271 note 21; Kulikoff, 93. See also Stanley, 24–6. On "Hoosier," see Gruenwald, 146.

59. Henrie to Hattie, May 26–27, 1857, SBSC. See Gray, 4; Fellman, 12–14.

60. Fellman, 11–16. See also Bushman, 383–98.

61. Henrie to Hattie, May 23, 1857, SBSC.

62. Henrie to Hattie, June 28, 1857, SBSC; Henrie to Hattie and Isa, June 30–July 5, 1857, SBSC.

63. Henrie to Hattie and Isa, June 30–July 5, 1857, SBSC.

64. Henrie to Hattie, June 28, 1857, SBSC.

65. Henrie to Hattie, June 1 and 28, 1857, SBSC.

66. Henrie to "My Wife & Darling," July 12, 1857, SBSC. On Yankee men milking cows, see Etcheson, *Emerging*, 4, and Hudson, 62.

67. Kulikoff, 60–64, 93–95.

68. Henrie to Hattie, June 28, 1857, SBSC.

69. Kulikoff, 63.

70. Kulikoff, 80–86.

71. Henrie to Hattie, July 26, 1857 [misdated 1858], SBSC.

72. Fellman, 11–18.

73. Henrie to Hattie, June 28, 1857, SBSC. Jeremy Neely calculates that northern-born residents of Vernon County and the two counties to its north increased from fifteen percent of the population in 1850 to twenty-one percent in 1860. However, most were born in Ohio, Illinois, and Indiana (including children of southern-born parents). Fewer than two percent of residents were born in New England, New York, Michigan, or Wisconsin (253-6). See also Phillips, 54, 78.

74. Henrie to Hattie, July 12–19, 1857, SBSC.

75. Henrie to Hattie, July 26, 1857 [misdated 1858], SBSC.

76. Gray, 3, 10–12, 175. In 1850, sixty-four percent of immigrants to Michigan were born in New York or New England. Only one percent were born in southern states. Gregory S. Rose, "American and European Immigrant Groups in the Midwest by the Mid-Nineteenth Century," in Lauck, Whitney, and Hogan, 77.

77. Henrie to Hattie, June 18 and 28, 1857, SBSC.

78. Hattie to Henrie, June 22–28, July 11, 1857, SBSC. Riley notes that men often went west alone to select and purchase land, leaving their wives with little voice in selecting a location (47).

79. On the importance of parlors to middle-class identity, see Katherine Grier, *Culture and Comfort: People, Parlors, and Upholstery, 1850–1930*. Washington, DC: Smithsonian Books, 2010 [orig. Rochester, New York: Strong Museum, 1988]; Stuart Blumin, *The Emergence of the Middle Class: Social Experience in the American City, 1760–1900* (New York: Cambridge University Press, 1989), 239; Louise Stevenson, *The Victorian Homefront: American Thought and Culture, 1860–1880* (New York: Twayne, 1991), 1–29. Riley describes women's efforts to decorate and furnish prairie cabins according to ideals of domesticity (54–56).

80. Hattie to Henry, July 12, 1857, SBSC.

81. Robin Bernstein, *Racial Innocence: Performing American Childhood from Slavery to Civil Rights* (New York: New York University Press, 2011). See also: Elaine Freedgood, *The Ideas in Things: Fugitive Meanings in the Victorian Novel* (Chicago: University of Chicago Press, 2006); Bridget T. Heneghan, *Whitewashing America: Material Culture and Race in the Antebellum Imagination* (Jackson: University Press of Mississippi, 2003); Grier, 1–9.

82. Kenneth Ames, *Death in the Dining Room and Other Tales of Victorian Culture* (Philadelphia: Temple University Press, 1992), 185–232; Grier, 117–42; Bushman, 271–72.

83. Hattie to Henrie, August 16, 1857, SBSC.

84. Fellman, 12–14.

85. Henrie to Hattie and Isa, June 30–July 5, 1857, SBSC; HP Smith to Charley [Wheeler], August 16, 1857, SBSC.

86. Henrie to "My Dear Wife," August 16, 1857, SBSC; Henrie to Hattie, August 23-28, 1857, SBSC.

87. Henrie to "my own dear wife," September 26, 1857, SBSC. On settlers' descriptions of western land as good "poor man's country," see Katherine G. Morrissey, *Mental Territories: Mapping the Inland Empire* (Ithaca, NY: Cornell University Press, 1997), 32-35.

88. Henrie to Hattie, June 28, 1857, SBSC. On Shakespeare's widespread popularity, see Lawrence Levine, *Highbrow/Lowbrow: The Emergence of Cultural Hierarchy in America* (Cambridge, MA: Harvard University Press, 1988), 13-81.

89. Kolodny, 160-77.

90. Hattie to Henrie, July 11, 1857, SBSC.

91. Hattie to Henry, July 5, 1857, SBSC.

92. Hattie to Henrie, August 23, 1857, SBSC.

93. Ryan, *Empire*, 108-10.

94. "Editor's Table: Can We Improve Our Domestic Life?" *Harper's New Monthly Magazine* (March 1857): 558.

95. "A Cottage of One Story," *Moore's Rural New-Yorker* 8, no. 14 (April 4, 1857): 109; Marshall McLennen, "Vernacular Architecture: Common House Types in Southern Michigan" in *Michigan Folklife Reader*, ed. C. Kurt Dewhurst and Yvonne Lockwood (East Lansing: Michigan State University Press, 1987), 15-45.

96. Jean Sizemore, *Ozark Vernacular Houses: A Study of Rural Homeplaces in the Arkansas Ozarks, 1830-1930* (Fayetteville: University of Arkansas Press, 1994); William J. Macintire, *The Pioneer Log House in Kentucky* (Frankfort: Kentucky Heritage Council, 1998), https://heritage.ky.gov/Documents/PioneerLogHouse.pdf; Burke, *On*, 71-72; Hurt, 187.

97. Henrie to Hattie, July 11, August 2, 1857, SBSC.

98. McMurry, 112-6; Clifford E. Clark, Jr., "The Vision of the Dining Room: Plan Book Dreams and Middle-Class Realities," *Dining in America, 1850-1900*, ed. Kathryn Grover (Amherst: University of Massachusetts Press and Margaret Woodbury Strong Museum, 1987), 142-72.

99. Henrie to Hattie, August 2, 1857, SBSC.

100. Henrie to Hattie, August 9, 1857, SBSC.

101. H. P. Smith, account book, 1857, Box 3, SBSC; Henrie to Hattie, July 26, 1857 [misdated 1858], SBSC; Henrie to "My Dear Wife," August 16, 1857, SBSC.

102. Henrie to Hattie, August 2 and 9, 1857, SBSC.

103. Henrie to Hattie, August 9, 1857, SBSC; Henrie to "My Dear Wife," August 16, 1857, SBSC.

104. Henry Smith, diary, August 22, 1857, Henry Parker Smith Papers, BHL.

105. Henrie to Hattie, August 23-28, 1857, SBSC. Henry assured Harriet he only pretended to drink.

106. Henrie to "My own dear wife," September 28, 1857, SBSC.

107. Henrie to "dear wife," October 2, 1857; Henrie to Hattie, July 26, October 9-11, 1857; Henrie to "My own dear deserted wife," October 18, 1857; Hattie to Henrie, November 1-2, 1857; all SBSC. See Neely, 27; Burke, *On*, 103-4; Hurt, 239-40; Phillips, 38.

108. Henrie to Hattie, August 9, 1857, SBSC.

109. Henrie to Hattie, August 30, 1857, SBSC.

110. Henrie to Hattie, August 30, 1857, SBSC.

111. Henrie to Hattie, June 28, 1857, SBSC. Grain crop failures in 1856 and damage to fruit and corn in 1857 caused food shortages through the summer of 1857. The influx of new residents further strained the food supply. *History of Greene County*, 245, 248; *HVC*, 188.

112. Henrie to "My Wife & Darling," July 12, 1857, SBSC. A "prairie schooner" is a wagon topped by hoops, called "bows," supporting a cloth cover.

113. Henrie to Hattie, August 2, 1857, SBSC; Kulikoff, 216.

114. Henrie to Hattie, August 23, 1857, SBSC.

115. Phillips, 36; Melish.

116. H. P. Smith to Charley [Wheeler], August 16, 1857, SBSC.

117. Neely, 89; Burke, *On*, 97; US Census (Slave Inhabitants), 1860, Montevallo Township, Vernon County, Missouri (https://s1.sos.mo.gov/records/archives/census/pages/slave).

118. Henrie to Hattie, August 2 and 30, 1857, SBSC.

119. On exclusionary Black Laws and assumptions of white supremacy in Midwestern states, see Phillips, 10, 27–43, 49, 63–77; Stanley Harrold, *Border War: Fighting over Slavery before the Civil War* (Chapel Hill: University of North Carolina Press, 2010), 19–20, 55–69; Gruenwald, 141–44; Etcheson, *Emerging*, 67–71; Stanley, 20–23, 38–40; Hudson, 112–16, 123–29.

120. Smith, diary, September 10, 1857.

121. For example, see Henry Smith, diary, May 28 and October 18, 1848.

122. Smith, diary, February 5, 1854.

123. J. C. Johnson to "Sister & friends," May 22, 1856, SBSC.

124. Henrie to Hattie, September 12–21, 1857, SBSC. Adam Arenson, *The Great Heart of the Republic: St. Louis and the Cultural Civil* War (Cambridge, MA: Harvard University Press, 2011), 59–60, 78–81, 90–100; William W. Freehling, *The South vs. The South: How Anti-Confederate Southerners Shaped the Course of the Civil War* (New York: Oxford University Press, 2001), 23–32; Michael D. Robinson, *A Union Indivisible: Secession and the Politics of Slavery in the Border South* (Chapel Hill: University of North Carolina Press, 2017), 26–28; Gerteis, 58–60.

125. See Burke, *On*, 58, 100–101, 264–66; Hurt, 165-9; Phillips, 62–80; Rable, 8–20. It is unclear whether Henry knew that Dr. Nathan Thomas and his wife Pamela, who was Henry's mother's cousin, had fed and housed over a thousand people escaping slavery. For twenty years, their Schoolcraft home had been part of an Underground Railroad route from Missouri to Canada. Pamela Thomas, "History of Anti-Slavery" in Ella Thomas, "History of the Underground Railroad," 24–30, unpublished manuscript, Box 1, Nathan M. Thomas Papers: 1818–1889, BHL (https://quod.lib.umich.edu/t/thomas/browse.html#series2).

126. Miner, 134; Michael E. Woods, *Bleeding Kansas: Slavery, Sectionalism, and Civil War on the Missouri-Kansas Border* (New York: Routledge, 2017), 34–35; Kristen Tegtmeier Oertel, *Bleeding Borders: Race, Gender, and Violence in Pre-Civil War Kansas* (Baton Rouge: Louisiana State University Press, 2009), 45, 127-30; Epps, 142–47; Burke, *On*, 264–66; Diane Mutti Burke, "Scattered People: The Long History of Forced Eviction in the Kansas-Missouri Borderlands," in *Civil War Wests: Testing the Limits of the United States*, ed. Adam Arenson and Andrew R. Graybill (Oakland: University of California Press, 2015), 74.

127. Harriet C. Frazier, *Runaway and Freed Missouri Slaves and Those Who Helped Them, 1763–1865* (Jefferson, NC: McFarland, 2004), 124–40, 152–62, 183–84.

128. Archibald and Edelia [Servoss] to Brother, September 18, 1857, SBSC.

129. Henrie to Hattie, June 3 and 9–12, November 7 and 14, 1857, SBSC; Henrie to "My dear wife," October 24, 1857, SBSC. Henry's father also wore checked shirts (Frank to Henry and Hattie, July 5, 1859, SBSC). Henry's sister later wrote that she was making her father-in-law, a merchant, a blue checked shirt to wear when he worked in their garden: "now that he has 'gone to farming,' he dresses accordingly." Frank to Brother and Sister, April 30, 1859, SBSC.

130. Henrie to Hattie, July 26, 1857, SBSC.

131. Henrie to "My dear wife," October 24, 1857, SBSC.

132. Henrie to Hattie, November 1, 1857, SBSC.

133. Nicole Etcheson, *Bleeding Kansas: Contested Liberty in the Civil War Era* (Lawrence: University of Kansas, 2004), 45; Rable, 8–9.

134. Henrie to Hattie, August 30, 1857, SBSC.

135. Hattie to "My own dearest husband," October 4, 1857, SBSC.

136. H. P. Smith, "Letter from Missouri," *Moore's Rural New-Yorker* 8, no. 39 (September 26, 1857): 310. On raising mules: HP Smith to Charley, August 16, 1857, SBSC; Henrie to "dear wife," August 16, 1857, SBSC; Henrie to Hattie, August 23, 1857, SBSC; Hurt, 144–50.

137. H. P. Smith, "Letter;" McMurry, 3–6.

138. Henrie to "My own dear deserted wife, "October 18, 1857, SBSC. See also Henrie to Hattie, November 1 and 7, 1857, SBSC.

139. Henrie to "My dear wife," October 24, 1857, SBSC.

140. H. P. Smith, "Western Missouri," *Moore's Rural New-Yorker* 8, no. 48 (November 28, 1857): 382.

141. Hattie to Henrie, May 26–27, 1857, SBSC. S[usan] Warner, *The Hills of the Shatemuc* (New York, 1856). Nina Baym, *Woman's Fiction: A Guide to Novels by and about Women in America, 1820–1870* (Ithaca: Cornell University Press, 1978), 140–43, 156–57.

142. Hattie to Henrie, May 21, 1854, June 22, 1857, SBSC. Mrs. Lincoln [Almira Hart] Phelps, *Ida Norman; or, Trials and their Uses* (Baltimore, 1848). Reprinted with additional volume (New York: Sheldon, 1855). Baym, *Woman's*, 82–83.

143. Hattie to Henrie, June 1–8, 1857, SBSC. Solon Robinson, *Hot Corn: Life Scenes in New York Illustrated* (New York, 1854).

144. Hattie to Henry, July 12, 1857, SBSC. J[ames] Fenimore Cooper, *The Ways of the Hour* (New York, 1850).

145. Hattie to Henrie, August 16, 1857, SBSC.

146. Hattie to "My own dearest husband," October 4, 1857, SBSC. Currer Bell [Charlotte Bronte], *Jane Eyre* (London, 1847). Elizabeth Gaskell, *The Life of Charlotte Bronte* (London, 1857). See Nina Baym, *Novels, Readers, and Reviewers: Responses to Fiction in Antebellum America* (Ithaca: Cornell University Press, 1984), 269.

147. Hattie to Henrie, November 1–2, 1857, SBSC. Currer Bell [Charlotte Bronte] *The Professor* (London, 1857).

148. *Harper's New Monthly Magazine* 15, no. 87 (August 1857): 404.

149. Baym, *Novels*, 249–51, 266–69.

150. Hattie to Henrie, November 1–2, 1857, SBSC.

151. Henrie to Hattie, June 9–12, August 2 and 23–28, 1857, SBSC; Hattie to Henrie, July 11, 1857, SBSC; Miner, 21–22, 80–81, 122–24.

152. Hattie to "My own dearest husband," October 4, 1857, SBSC. "Society" refers to a social network of friends and neighbors (Kelly, 191).

153. On fiction replacing local community, see Ronald J. Zboray, *A Fictive People: Antebellum Economic Development and the American Reading Public* (New York: Oxford University Press, 1993), 118–21.

154. "Editor's Easy Chair," *Harper's New Monthly Magazine* 14, no. 84 (May 1857): 847–88.

155. Hattie to "My Own Dear Husband," October 26-28, 1857, SBSC.

156. "Tom Wilson's Cabin," illustration, *Harper's New Monthly Magazine* 15, no. 90 (November 1857): 734.

157. Hattie to "My Own Dear Husband," October 26-28, 1857, SBSC; Henrie to "My own dear wife," September 28, 1857, SBSC; Henrie to Hattie, October 9-11, 1857, SBSC.

158. Archibald [Servoss] to Brother, October 19, 1857, SBSC; J. Parker to Cobb and Smith, October 31, 1857, SBSC; Henrie to Hattie, September 12-21, 1857, SBSC.

159. Charles W. Calomiris and Larry Schweikart, "The Panic of 1857: Origins, Transmission, and Containment," *The Journal of Economic History* 51, no. 4 (December 1991): 807–34; Huston, James L., *The Panic of 1857 and the Coming of the Civil War* (Baton Rouge: Louisiana State University Press, 1987).

160. Henrie to "My dear wife," October 24, 1857, SBSC. See Burke, *On*, 34.

161. Henrie to Hattie, November 7, 1857, SBSC. On stereotypes of dry goods clerks as unmanly, see Brian P. Luskey, *On the Make: Clerks and the Quest for Capital in Nineteenth-Century America* (New York: New York University Press, 2010), 83–118.

162. Henrie to Hattie, August 9, 1857, SBSC; Quit claim deed, Henry and Harriet Smith to Thaddeus Smith, February 2, 1858, Box 2, SBSC.

163. W. G. Johnson to Henrie and Hattie, January 25, 1858, SBSC; E. S. Johnson to H and H, May 23, 1858, SBSC; Henry Smith, diary, February 8–March 1, 1858; Isa H. Smith, "Reminiscences of Missouri," unpublished manuscript (October 18, 1904), 1–4, Box 5, SBSC (hereafter "Reminiscences").

Chapter Five. Loyalties and Lies

1. Henry Smith diary, June 28, 1861, Henry Parker Smith Papers, BHL.

2. "Reminiscences," 1.

3. Jack P[arker] to Henry, April 11, 1858; M. R. Cobb to H. P. Smith, April 21, 1858. Stanley Barney Smith Collection (SBSC), A-88, Archives and Regional History Collections, Zhang Legacy Collections Center, Western Michigan University.

4. M. R. Cobb to H. P. Smith, May 29, 1858, SBSC.

5. Helen to Brother and Sister, May 11, 1858, and Frank and Charley to Henry and Hattie, June 13-28, 1858, SBSC.

6. Smith, diary, July 11, 1858.

7. M. R. Cobb to H. P. Smith, May 3, 1858, and Helen, Frank and Charley to Brother, April 11, 1858, SBSC; "Reminiscences," 3, 10–12. Settlers on the prairie often joined family and friends. Glenda Riley, *The Female Frontier: A Comparative View of Women on the Prairie and the Plains* (Lawrence: University Press of Kansas, 1988), 47; Jeremy Neely, *The*

Border Between Them: Violence and Reconciliation on the Kansas-Missouri Line (Columbia: University of Missouri Press, 2007), 26.

8. "Reminiscences," 4–5. Prairie settlers usually cooked in the central room or outside until they added a kitchen (Riley, 56).

9. "Reminiscences," 7.

10. "Reminiscences," 5.

11. "Reminiscences," 5–6.

12. Riley, 42–3; Joanna L. Stratton, *Pioneer Women: Voices from the Kansas Frontier* (New York: Touchstone, 1981), 58–61, 91–98.

13. Smith, diary, August 2 and 5, 1858; "Reminiscences," 8.

14. Samuel W. Durant, *History of Kalamazoo County, Michigan* (Philadelphia, 1880), 514; J. Parker to Nephew, February 6, 1859. Susan E. Gray examines the interconnections of family ties, office-holding, and social status in Kalamazoo County, Michigan. *The Yankee West: Community Life on the Michigan Frontier* (Chapel Hill: University of North Carolina Press, 1996), 142–62.

15. M. R. Cobb to H. P. Smith, September 20, 1858, SBSC.

16. Nicole Etcheson, *Bleeding Kansas: Contested Liberty in the Civil War Era* (Lawrence: University Press of Kansas, 2004), 191–92; Craig Miner, *Seeding Civil War: Kansas in the National News, 1854-1858* (Lawrence: University Press of Kansas, 2008), 210–39.

17. M. R. Cobb to Smith, January 18, 1858, and Helen, Frank and Charley to Brother, April 10, 1858, SBSC.

18. Etcheson, 192–96; Neely, 68–74.

19. Etcheson, 190; Neely, 65–66; Miner, 239–41.

20. Charlie [Gould] to Hattie, October 20, 1858, and S. T. Allen to My Dear Friends, May 8, 1859, SBSC. See Stanley Harrold, *Border War: Fighting over Slavery before the Civil War* (Chapel Hill: University of North Carolina, 2010), 121.

21. Archie [Servoss] to Br and Sister, May 12, 1858; Archibald [Servoss] to Brother, June 7, 1858; W. G. J. to "My dear children," September 15, 1858; Thad Smith to Son, September 19, 1858; Wakeman Gold Johnson to "children," December 1, 1858; Uncle Foster [Smith] to "My Dear Nephew & Niece," January 9, 1859, all SBSC.

22. Smith, diary, October 15, 1858; undated loose sheet in diary [1857]; M. R. Cobb to Dear Sir, November 22, 1858, SBSC.

23. Smith, diary, December 5, 1858.

24. Neely, 74–76; Etcheson, 197–203.

25. M. R. Cobb to Friend Smith, February 10, 1859, SBSC.

26. Smith, diary, February 17, 1859.

27. Smith, diary, January 22, February 27, March 7, 1859; "Reminiscences," 12–13.

28. "Reminiscences," 11.

29. Mary [Palmer] to Hattie, January 27, 1859, SBSC. On February 8, 1857, Mary had written from the Kentucky girls' school her husband directed: "Life in a slave state, & in a boarding-school, is to me like being buried alive, only worse." SBSC.

30. Smith, diary, January 9 and 16, 1859. Hattie Hubbell to Harriet, May 29, 1859, SBSC. Emily B. Todd, "Walter Scott and the Nineteenth-Century American Literary Marketplace: Antebellum Richmond Readers and the Collected Editions of the Waverly Novels." *Papers*

of the Bibliographical Society of America 93, no. 4 (December 1999): 495; James Cobb, *Away Down South: A History of Southern Identity* (New York: Oxford University Press, 2005), 45.

31. Smith, diary, June 27, 1859.
32. Smith, diary, July 15, 1859.
33. Smith, diary, July 23, 1859. Persistent fussy crying was called "worrying."
34. Stratton, 97–101; Neely, 78–79; Etcheson, 220.
35. M. R. Cobb to Smith, March 23, 1859, and J. Parker to "Judge," June 20, 1859, SBSC.
36. Archibald to Brother and Sister, July 25, 1859, SBSC.
37. Frank to Brother and Sister, November 17, 1859, and J. Parker to Nephew, February 6, 1859, SBSC.
38. Smith, diary, September 22, 1859.
39. Smith, diary, October 10, 1859; "Reminiscences," 14.
40. Smith, diary, December 26, 1859.
41. "Reminiscences," 14–15.
42. Smith, diary, October 26, 1859.
43. "Reminiscences," 15–16.
44. Smith, diary, October 26, 1859. On the danger of prairie fires and strategies of clearing vegetation around a house and setting backfires to divert the flames, see Riley, 43, and Stratton, 81–85.
45. Smith, diary, November 1, 1859.
46. Smith, diary, February 4, 1860.
47. Smith, diary, October 28, 1859.
48. Smith, diary, December 25, 1859.
49. US Census (Agriculture) and US Census (Slave Inhabitants), 1860, Montevallo Township, Vernon County, Missouri. M. R. Cobb to H. P. Smith, May 29, 1858, SBSC; H. P. Smith deed for threshing machine (July 1859 correspondence), SBSC.
50. Henrie to Hattie, August 9, 1857, SBSC.
51. US Census (Agriculture), 1860, Montevallo Township, Vernon County, Missouri. Mr. Page's first name is recorded as "Morris," as it was pronounced. On farm locations, see M. R. Cobb to Friend Smith, December 29, 1858, SBSC.
52. "Reminiscences," 23.
53. Neely, 213.
54. Neely, 213–14. See John C. Hudson, *Making the Corn Belt: A Geographical History of Middle-Western Agriculture* (Bloomington: Indiana University Press, 1994).
55. Smith, diary, July 8–9, 1860; *HVC*, 186–87.
56. Smith, diary, July 23, 1860.
57. Smith, diary, July 22, 1860; Isaiah W. Pursel to Brother Henry, July 11, 1860, and I. W. Pursel to Henry, August 3, 1860, SBSC.
58. Smith, diary, July 31, 1860.
59. Smith, diary, August 8 and 14, 1860. See Stratton, 101.
60. Smith, diary, August 19, September 1 and 9, 1860.
61. Smith, diary, September 25, 1860.
62. Neely, 218–19; Hudson, 141–43; R. Douglas Hurt, *Agriculture and Slavery in Missouri's Little Dixie* (Columbia: University of Missouri Press, 1992), 144.

63. Draft resolution (undated), Henry Smith Papers 1854-1889, Box 1, SBSC.

64. Smith, diary, September 17, 1860.

65. Smith, diary, September 15, 1860; Frank to Henry and Hattie, September 2, 1860; I. W. Pursel to H. P. Smith, September 2, 1860; Frank to Henry and Hattie, October 14, 1860; all SBSC.

66. Smith, diary, October 26, 1860.

67. Smith, diary, July 21, 1860.

68. "Reminiscences," 13.

69. *HVC*, 609-10; J. B. Johnson, ed., *History of Vernon County Missouri Past and Present*, vol. 1 (Chicago: C. F. Cooper, 1911), 490-91, 687-89. As in early nineteenth-century lodges, many local office-holders and lawyers were active members. Stephen C. Bullock, *Revolutionary Brotherhood: Freemasonry and the Transformation of the American Social Order, 1730-1840* (Chapel Hill: University of North Carolina, 1996), 207.

70. *HVC*, 598-99; US Census (Industry), 1860, Center Township, Vernon County, Missouri.

71. Smith, diary, September 7, 1860; March 4, 1861.

72. Smith, diary, September 7, 1860.

73. *HVC*, 358-59; US Census (Population) and US Census (Industry), 1860, Montevallo Township, Vernon County, Missouri.

74. "Reminiscences," 22-23. See Mary A. Barney to Hattie, August 5, 1860, SBSC.

75. Smith, diary, September 2 and 28, 1860. Thaddeus Smith to son and Mother to Henry, October 31, 1860, and I. W. Pursel to Br. Henry, November 27, 1860, SBSC.

76. Smith, diary, November 6 and 7, 1860.

77. Smith, diary, November 12, 1860.

78. Draft petition to Missouri General Assembly for Vernon County Probate Judge, Henry Smith Papers 1854-1889, Box 1, SBSC.

79. Smith, diary, November 19, 1860. See Neely, 89-94; *HCV*, 244-49, 269-70.

80. "Documents in Relation to Border Difficulties Accompanying the Governor's Message," *Journal of the House*, 21st General Assembly, 1861 (hereafter 21st GA), 1st Regular Session, Appendix, 3-4, MSA (MDH: https://cdm16795.contentdm.oclc.org/digital/collection/housej/id/4862/rec/2); *HVC*, 249-50; Neely, 76-77.

81. "Message from the Governor," 21st GA, 1st Regular Session, 26-7, MSA (MDH: https://cdm16795.contentdm.oclc.org/digital/collection/housej/id/5705/rec/3); Neely, 94-95; Daniel Sutherland, *A Savage Conflict: The Decisive Role of Guerrillas in the American Civil War* (Chapel Hill: University of North Carolina Press, 2009), 11; *HVC*, 255-63; Harrold, 193; Phillip T. Tucker, "'Ho, For Kansas': The Southwest Expedition of 1860," *Missouri Historical Review* 86, no. 1 (October 1991): 22-36.

82. Smith, diary, December 5, 1860.

83. Neely, 95; Tucker, 33-35.

84. Smith, diary, January 6, 1861.

85. Phillips, 136; Louis S. Gerteis, *Civil War St. Louis* (Lawrence: University Press of Kansas, 2001), 80; Neely, 100; T. J. Stiles, *Jesse James: Last Rebel of the Civil War* (New York: Vintage, 2002), 67.

86. Smith, diary, January 26, 1861.

87. Smith, diary, January 31, 1861.

88. Smith, diary, February 9, 1861. "Black Republicans" was a pejorative term for supporters of Abraham Lincoln and the Republican Party (Stiles, 66). On "Black Republicans" in rhetoric surrounding slavery in Kansas, see Kristen Tegtmeier Oertel, *Bleeding Borders: Race, Gender, and Violence in Pre-Civil War Kansas* (Baton Rouge: Louisiana State University Press, 2009), 46, 127–28.

89. Michael D. Robinson, *A Union Indivisible: Secession and the Politics of Slavery in the Border South* (Chapel Hill: University of North Carolina Press, 2017), 92–99; Matthew E. Stanley, *The Loyal West: Civil War and Reunion in Middle America* (Urbana: University of Illinois, 2017), 45; Christopher Phillips, *The Rivers Ran Backward: The Civil War and the Remaking of the American Middle Border* (New York: Oxford University Press, 2016), 107–8. For a detailed examination focused on Virginia, Tennessee and North Carolina, see Daniel W. Crofts, *Reluctant Confederates: Upper South Unionists in the Secession Crisis* (Chapel Hill: University of North Carolina Press, 1989).

90. Phillips, 120–26, 134–36; Robinson, 80–83, 96–98, 117–18, 136; Harrold, 196–97; Neely, 100.

91. Michael Fellman *Inside War: The Guerrilla Conflict in Missouri During the American Civil War* (New York: Oxford University Press, 1989), 5; Neely, 101; Phillips, 123–24; Thomas W. Cutrer, *Theater of a Separate War: The Civil War West of the Mississippi River, 1861–1865* (Chapel Hill: University of North Carolina Press, 2017), 27; Robinson, 140–44; Stiles, 68.

92. Neely, 88–91, 100–101; *HVC*, 269–72, 599, 855.

93. Smith, diary, April 6, 1861. Henry later realized that he had misunderstood the situation. In February, Gatewood successfully introduced a bill that created the position of Probate Judge for Vernon County. Although the governor appointed county judges to vacant positions between elections, county courts selected probate judges to fill vacancies. Johnson, 383; 21st GA, 1st Regular Session, 288, MSA (MDH: https://mdh.contentdm.oclc.org/digital/collection/housej/id/5967).

94. I. W. P. and Helen to Henry, February 28, 1861, SBSC.

95. Smith, diary, April 14, 1861.

96. Smith, diary, April 20, 1861. Neely, 101; Cutrer, 28–29; Stiles, 68; Dennis K. Boman, *Lincoln and Citizens' Rights in Civil War Missouri* (Baton Rouge: University of Louisiana Press, 2011), 28–29.

97. Smith, diary, May 9, 1861. See Phillips, 140; Neely, 99–100; Boman, 26–27. William A. Blair discusses popular definitions of treason in *With Malice Toward Some: Treason and Loyalty in the Civil War Era* (Chapel Hill: University of North Carolina Press, 2014), esp. 65.

98. "Governor's Message," 21st GA, Called Session, 13–16, MSA (MDH: https://cdm16795.contentdm.oclc.org/digital/collection/housej/id/17757/rec/1); William C. Harris, *Lincoln and the Border States: Preserving the Union* (Lawrence: University Press of Kansas, 2011), 137; Gerteis, 134; Blair, 76.

99. Neely, 101–2; Sutherland, 12–13; Mark W. Geiger, *Financial Fraud and Guerrilla Violence in Missouri's Civil War, 1861–1865* (New Haven: Yale University Press, 2010), 16–18; Phillips, 137–41; Gerteis, 95–117; Harris, 134–37; Robinson, 173–75; 21st GA, Called (Extraordinary) Session, 54–85, MSA (MDH: https://cdm16795.contentdm.oclc.org/digital/collection/housej/id/17798/rec/1).

100. Smith, diary, May 18, 1861. "Committee on Militia Report," 21st GA, Called (Extraordinary) Session, 56, MSA (MDH: https://cdm16795.contentdm.oclc.org/digital/collection/housej/id/17800/rec/1); Samuel W. Durant, *History of Kalamazoo County, Michigan* (Philadelphia, 1880), 509, 532.

101. Smith, diary, May 15, 1861.

102. Smith, diary, June 1, 1861. Strong advocates of secession were known as "fire eaters." Robinson, 11, 85–111.

103. Smith, diary, June 22, 1861. Similar ceremonies occurred in the Confederate states. Drew Gilpin Faust, *Mothers of Invention: Women of the Slaveholding South in the American Civil War* (Chapel Hill: University of North Carolina Press, 1996), 15; George Rable, *Civil Wars: Women and the Crisis of Southern Nationalism* (Urbana: University of Illinois Press, 1989), 47.

104. Smith, diary, June 24, 1861.

105. Sutherland, 13–14; Gerteis, 123–24; Jay Monaghan, *Civil War on the Western Border, 1854–1865* (Lincoln: University of Nebraska Press, 1955), 134–41; Cutrer, 35–36; Phillips, 140–41; Robinson, 176–77.

106. Smith, diary, June 24, 1861; *HVC*, 214–15

107. Johnson, 128–29.

108. Smith, diary, June 27, 1861; Cutrer, 36–39.

109. Smith, diary, June 28, 1861.

110. Isa Smith, "A Scene in Missouri," unpublished manuscript, 1864–1865, Box 4, SBSC.

111. Smith, diary, June 28, 1861.

112. Smith, diary, June 30, 1861.

113. "Reminiscences," 29. Smith, diary, June 30, 1861. On Masonic networks, see Michael A. Halleran, *Better Angels of Our Nature: Freemasonry in the American Civil War* (Tuscaloosa: University of Alabama Press, 2010).

114. Smith, diary, June 30, 1861; July 1, 1861.

115. Smith, diary, July 2, 1861.

116. "Reminiscences," 31.

117. Monaghan, 149–57; Cutrer, 39; Harrold, 196-7; Johnson, 129.

118. Johnson, 275–6.

119. Smith, diary, July 8, 1861; Neely, 103.

120. Smith, diary, July 22, 1861.

121. Phillips, 141; Neely, 102; Boman, 31–35; Harris, 138; Geiger, 20; Robinson, 188.

122. *HVC*, 203. The county history incorrectly states that Judge H. P. Smith was with Price's troops.

123. Smith, diary, July 31, 1861.

124. Smith, diary, July 5, 1861.

125. Sutherland, 15–16; Richard Brownlee, *Gray Ghosts of the Confederacy: Guerrilla Warfare in the West, 1861–1865* (Baton Rouge: Louisiana State University Press, 1958), 40–50; Fellman, 35–37; Neely, 103–8; General Orders No. 8, Headquarters, Department of the Missouri, November 26, 1861 in *The War of the Rebellion: A Compilation of the Official Records of the Union and Confederate Armies*, Series 1, vol. 8 (Washington DC, 1883), 380–81 (hereafter *OR*, vol. 8).

126. Brownlee, 69–70.

127. Frank to Henry and Hattie, September 2–3, October 14, 1860, March 27–April 1, 1861, SBSC.

128. Helen to Hattie, April 8, 1861, SBSC.

129. Frank to Henry and Hattie, May 26, 1861, SBSC.

130. Smith, diary, August 8, 1861.

131. *HVC*, 855.

132. Smith, diary, August 12, 1861; Johnson, 276; Cutrer, 50.

133. Smith, diary, August 14, 1861.

134. Smith, diary, August 30, 1861. *HVC*, 855.

135. Neely, 104–5; Boman, 57–58; Harris, 142; Gerteis, 145–46: Johnson, 270–78.

136. Johnson, 278–82; Monaghan, 182; Brownlee, 38–49; Neely, 103–8; Phillips, 148–51; Sutherland, 16; Mark A. Lause, *Race and Radicalism in the Union Army* (Urbana: University of Illinois, 2009), 50–51; Fellman, 35, 155–58.

137. Smith, diary, August 31, 1861; "Reminiscences," 45.

138. Smith, diary, September 14, 1861; Neely, 105.

139. Smith, diary, September 17, 1861.

140. "Reminiscences," 33; Smith, diary, September 9–13, 1861. Faust notes that in the Carolinas in 1861, "refugee" was a pejorative term for aristocrats who removed their livestock and enslaved workers from the path of Union troops (40). The term had "connotations of privilege and self-interest" (41).

141. Smith, diary, September 22, 1861; "Reminiscences," 32.

142. Smith, diary, September 22, 1861.

143. Smith, diary, September 24, 1861; Monaghan, 195–7; Neely, 105; Lause, 51.

144. Neely, 105–6; Sutherland, 15–16; Boman, 106–8.

145. Monaghan, 198; Sutherland, 57; Stiles, 74.

146. Smith, diary, October 1, 1861.

147. "Reminiscences," 33.

148. Smith, diary, October 12, 1861.

149. Smith, diary, October 13, 1861.

150. Smith, diary, October 14, 1861.

151. Boman, 58; Monaghan, 199–204; Gerteis, 157–58.

152. Smith, diary, October 20, 1861. A Missouri guerrilla recalled that his captor recognized him as "a gentleman" when he gave the Masonic call of distress. The soldier then cared for him with all the "tenderness of a brother." Lindsay T. Baker, ed., *Confederate Guerrilla: The Civil War Memoir of Joseph M. Bailey* (Fayetteville: University of Arkansas Press, 2007), 37–38. An early Masonic song associates the brotherhood with polite behavior that defines a gentleman: "We make it plainly to appear, / By our Behavior every where, / That where you meet a Mason, there / You meet a Gentleman." Bullock, 34–35.

153. Halleran, 160–61.

154. Masons sometimes saved wounded enemy Masons (Halleran, 78–97) and homes containing Masonic regalia (Halleran, 61–67, 74–77). Elissa R. Hencken discusses two twentieth-century oral narratives about General Sherman's troops sparing the houses of fellow Masons in Georgia. "Taming the Enemy: Georgian Narratives About the Civil

War," *Journal of Folklore Research* 40, no. 3 (2003), 296–98. For accounts of enemy Masons providing funerals, assisting prisoners, and protecting Masonic lodges, see Thomas G. Dyer, *Secret Yankees: The Union Circle in Confederate Atlanta* (Baltimore: Johns Hopkins University Press, 1999), 195–96, 258–59, and Mark Tabbert, *American Freemasons: Three Centuries of Building* Communities (New York: New York University Press, 2005), 82. A Missouri guerrilla's memoir describes sparing the life of a captured Mason. O. S. Barton, *Three Years With Quantrill: a True Story Told by his Scout John McCorkle* (Norman: University of Oklahoma Press, 1992) [1914], 96–98. Frank Anderson confirmed Henry Taylor's account that federal troops who burned most of Nevada released him when they saw his Masonic documents. *HVC*, 317; Johnson, 133.

155. "Reminiscences," 35. On sending mail with travelers, see Amy M. Taylor, *The Divided Family in Civil War America* (Chapel Hill: University of North Carolina Press, 2005), 112.

156. "Yours in Friendship" to Mr. Smith, October 31, 1861, SBSC.

157. Smith, diary, September 6, 1856.

158. Phillips, 157, 159.

159. "Yours in Friendship" to Mr. Smith, October 31, 1861, SBSC.

160. Smith, diary, October 24, 1861. Henry charged the men $8.75 for "keeping 2 horses 3½ weeks." He applied the credit to buy Hattie a sidesaddle from Scobey's store (November 17 and 20, 1861).

161. *HVC*, 292; Monaghan, 204; *OR*, vol. 3: 554.

162. Joseph H. Trego to his wife, October 28, 1861, quoted in Fellman, 52, and Neely, 105–6.

163. Smith, diary, October 29, 1861.

164. Smith, diary, October 30, 1861.

165. Smith, diary, October 31, 1861.

166. Phillips, 143–44; Robinson, 193–94; Stiles, 78; Geiger, 20.

167. Stiles, 76–79; Fellman, 51–52; Neely, 96–108; Sutherland, 19–25; Lause, 47–49.

168. Stiles, 76–77; Blair, 173; Boman, 65, 139. See correspondence regarding loyalty oaths: Hamilton Rowan Gamble, 1861–1864, Office of Governor, Record Group 3.16, MSA (MDH: https://mdh.contentdm.oclc.org/digital/collection/msa/search/searchterm/loyalty%20oath%201862/page/1).

169. Brownlee, 147; Geiger, 94–95.

170. Nelson McDowell to Hamilton Rowan Gamble, August 3, 1862, and D. H. Connaway to Hamilton Rowan Gamble, July 1, 1862, Hamilton Rowan Gamble, 1861–1864, Office of Governor, Record Group 3.16, MSA (MDH: https://mdh.contentdm.oclc.org/digital/collection/msa/id/5094/rec/1 and https://mdh.contentdm.oclc.org/digital/collection/msa/id/4930/rec/1).

171. Decades later, Isa wrote: "A petition to the Legislature was sent in and already favorably acted upon, when Jackson, the Governor of Missouri decamped with his sesesh Legislators and although the Federal officials who took their places were reported to have ratified the appointment it was never received." "Reminiscences," 24. "Henry P. Smith," *Portrait and Biographical Record of Kalamazoo, Allegan and Van Buren Counties, Michigan* (Chicago, 1892), 567.

172. Smith, diary, November 28, 1861.

173. Johnson, 129–30.

174. *HVC*, 203, 293. Hunter later transported the records to Arkansas. They were captured by federal troops and returned after the war. *HVC*, 294.

175. Smith, diary, December 11, 1861.

176. Smith, diary, November 16, 1861.

177. "Reminiscences," 35. On the stigma of wearing homespun, see Faust, 221–22.

178. Smith, diary, November 20 and 27, December 24 and 28, 1861. On the shortage of shoes in the Confederacy, see Rable, 95, and Faust, 222.

179. "Reminiscences," 35.

180. Smith, diary, November 20, 1861.

181. Smith, diary, December 11, 1861.

182. Smith, diary, December 12, 1861. See Neely, 115.

Chapter Six. Henry's Civil War

1. Henry Smith diary, April 15, 1862, Henry Parker Smith Papers, BHL.

2. Smith, diary, January 15, 1862.

3. Smith, diary, January 25, 1862.

4. Smith, diary, January 26, 1862.

5. Smith, diary, February 1, 1862.

6. Smith, diary, February 3, 1862.

7. Smith, diary, February 5, 1862.

8. Dennis K. Boman, *Lincoln and Citizens' Rights in Civil War Missouri: Balancing Freedom and Security* (Baton Rouge: Louisiana State University Press, 2011), 63–65, 93; William A. Blair, *With Malice Toward Some: Treason and Loyalty in the Civil War Era* (Chapel Hill: University of North Carolina Press, 2014), 173; Richard Brownlee, *Gray Ghosts of the Confederacy: Guerrilla Warfare in the West, 1861–1865* (Baton Rouge: Louisiana State University Press, 1958), 157; T. J. Stiles, *Jesse James: Last Rebel of the Civil War* (New York: Vintage Books, 2002), 76–79; Mark Grimsley, *The Hard Hand of War: Union Military Policy Toward Southern Civilians, 1861–1865* (New York: Cambridge University Press, 1995), 48–51.

9. Abraham Lincoln to Major General H. W. Halleck, December 2, 1861, *OR*, vol. 8: 401; Brownlee, 146; Daniel E. Sutherland, *A Savage Conflict: The Decisive Role of Guerrillas in the American Civil War* (Chapel Hill: University of North Carolina Press, 2009), 24–25; Louis S. Gerteis, *Civil War St. Louis* (Lawrence: University Press of Kansas, 2001), 172–74; Boman, 44–47, 70–71.

10. Michael Fellman, *Inside War: The Guerrilla Conflict in Missouri During the American Civil War* (New York: Oxford University Press, 1989), 61; Brownlee, 149-50; Boman, 97–102; Christopher Phillips, *The Rivers Ran Backward: The Civil War and the Making of the American Middle Border* (New York: Oxford University Press, 2016), 185; Blair, 55–58.

11. General Orders No. 13, December 4, 1861, and General Orders No. 1, January 1, 1862, Headquarters, Department of the Missouri, *OR*, vol. 8: 405–7, 476–78; Brownlee, 157–58; Phillips, *Rivers*, 153, 182–91; Boman, 71, 87–89, 116.

12. Blair, 54.

13. Phillips, *Rivers*, 184–85; Brownlee, 151, 173–74; Stiles, 75–76; Boman, 97–102, 115–20; Blair, 100–107.

14. Stiles, 76–78; Boman, 60–62, 87–90; Blair, 173; Sutherland, *Savage*, 60; Jeremy Neely, *The Border Between Them: Violence and Reconciliation on the Kansas-Missouri Line* (Columbia: University of Missouri Press, 2007), 115.

15. David T. Holstead, "Guerrilla War in 'Little Dixie': Understanding Conflict Escalation in Missouri During the American Civil War" (Fort Leavenworth, Kansas: US Army Command and General Staff College, 2014), 24, 41–42; Sutherland, *Savage*, 124; Boman, 98–99; Phillips, *Rivers*, 186.

16. Phillips, *Rivers*, 98, 134–36, 183–84, 229; Neely, 113.

17. On women providing guerrillas with food, clothing, shelter, and information, see the introduction to *Occupied Women: Gender, Military Occupation, and the American Civil War*, ed. LeeAnn Whites and Alecia P. Long (Baton Rouge: Louisiana State University Press, 2009), 7, and LeeAnn Whites, "Forty Shirts and a Wagonload of Wheat: Women, the Domestic Supply Line, and the Civil War on the Western Border," *Journal of the Civil War Era* 1, no. 1 (March 2011), 56–78.

18. Sutherland, *Savage*, 57.

19. Smith, diary, February 12, 1862. Gilboney's wife, Sallie, later escaped from a Union prison with her sister, Jennie Mayfield. *HVC*, 337–42.

20. Fellman, 89–90; Brownlee, 47–50; Phillips, *Rivers*, 155–57.

21. Fellman, 155–58, 166–68, 184–85; Brownlee, 38–39, 42–43, 47–52.

22. Phillips, *Rivers*, 98, 120–36, 159–60, 229; Boman, 106–8.

23. Smith, diary, December 28 and 30, 1861; January 11 and 20, February 22 and 28, March 10–16, April 2, 9, and 17, 1862.

24. Smith, diary, January 18, 19, 20, and 27, 1862.

25. Smith, diary, March 18, 1862. See Fellman, 39–40.

26. Smith, diary, January 26, February 6, 1862.

27. Smith, diary, January 26, February 25, March 12 and 18, April 18, 1862.

28. Smith, diary, February 23, 1862.

29. Smith, diary, September 1, 1861; March 14, 1862.

30. Thomas G. Dyer, *Secret Yankees: The Union Circle in Confederate Atlanta* (Baltimore: Johns Hopkins University Press, 1999), 268.

31. US Census (Population), 1860, Joseph Carrico, Cedar County, Missouri; loose sheet in Henry Smith diary, 1858.

32. Johnson, 490–91; "Reminiscences," 29; M. A. Page to H. P. Smith and Lady, April 10, 1865, Stanley Barney Smith Collection (SBSC), A-88, Archives and Regional History Collections, Zhang Legacy Collections Center, Western Michigan University.

33. Dyer, 258–59.

34. Mary Ann Clawson, *Constructing Brotherhood: Class, Gender, and Fraternalism* (Princeton: Princeton University Press, 1989), 7–8. Geiger identifies Masonic lodges as communications networks for Missouri slaveholders. Mark W. Geiger, *Financial Fraud and Guerrilla Violence in Missouri's Civil War, 1861–1865* (New Haven: Yale University Press, 2010), 80.

35. Steven C. Bullock, *Revolutionary Brotherhood: Freemasonry and the Transformation of the American Social Order, 1730–1840* (Chapel Hill: University of North Carolina, 1996), 31–33.

36. Johnson, 129–32, 296, 688–89.

37. Smith, diary, February 13–17, 1862; Johnson, 265, 272.

38. In 1860, Redfield held an enslaved thirty-two-year-old woman and four children ages one to fourteen. Austin held an enslaved twelve-year-old boy and Badger a fourteen-year-old girl and five-year-old boy. US Census (Slave Inhabitants), 1860, Vernon County, Missouri; Boman, 106–8.

39. Johnson, 265, 299, 345–46, 688. Badger, age forty-one in 1862, served in the US Navy later in the war. Forty-five-year-old Austin's properties were spared when Union troops burned Nevada City in 1863 as were Anderson's. Redfield was elected to the state legislature in 1862 but died of natural causes before serving. *HVC*, 316–17, 347–48, 390–91, 440–41, 520–21, 613–14, 665.

40. Johnson, 277, 562–63.

41. Phillips, *Rivers*, 135.

42. Dyer, 267.

43. Smith, diary, February 13, 17, and 27, 1862. On Union expectations of victory in 1862, see Grimsley, 47, 93–94, and Blair, 54.

44. Smith, diary, February 22 and 27, 1862.

45. Smith, diary, February 10, 1862.

46. Sutherland, *Savage*, xi, 58–59, 97.

47. Smith, diary, February 11, 1862. See Boman, 129.

48. R. F. Bales, John Dade, S. P. Tapp, W. H. Taylor, Roll 0178, Roll 0181, Roll 0190, Compiled Service Records of Confederate Soldiers Who Served in Organizations from the State of Missouri, Publication M322, NARA 586957, Carded Records, Record Group 109 (fold3.com).

49. Sutherland, *Savage*, 133; *HVC*, 300. Geiger defines Coffee as a guerrilla commander (104–5), as does Brownlee (79).

50. On recruiting for a planned insurrection, see Boman, 129.

51. *HVC*, 299–300. See Stiles, 77.

52. *HVC*, 296–98.

53. Smith, diary, February 28, 1862. The neighbors included Cedar County residents Allen, Robinson, and Steward.

54. Smith, diary, March 1, 1862. See also *HVC*, 856.

55. General Orders 1, Headquarters, Department of the Missouri, January 1, 1862, *OR*, vol. 8: 476–78; Fellman, 87–88.

56. Fellman, 118–26.

57. Smith, diary, July 16, 1861; October 31, 1861.

58. Smith, diary, March 1–2, 1862.

59. Smith, diary, March 14, 1862.

60. Smith, diary, March 17, 1862.

61. Smith, diary, March 8, March 19–24, 1862.

62. Smith, diary, March 29, April 5, 1862.

63. Brownlee, 28–30; Stiles, 79; Neely, 108.

64. Smith, diary, April 7, 1862.

65. "Reminiscences," 41–42.

66. "Reminiscences," 34.

67. Smith, diary, April 10, 1862.

68. Smith, diary, April 11, 1862.

69. Smith, diary, April 14, 1862. Gabbert was married to Mayfield's sister, Nora. His father, William, led a guerrilla band affiliated with the Mayfield family (*HVC*, 335–42; Neely, 109; Sutherland, *Savage*, 201).

70. Smith, diary, April 12, 1862.

71. Smith, diary, April 14–15, 1862. Twenty-eight men from the 1st Iowa Cavalry stationed in Osceola stayed overnight in Montevallo as part of a larger force sent to disrupt the Horse Creek guerrilla camp. *HVC*, 300; *OR*, vol. 13: 53–57.

72. *HVC*, 300–303; Smith, diary, April 15, 1862.

73. Smith, diary, April 15, 1862. Maddox survived his wounds (*HVC*, 304). A September 1860 flier advertising the Montevallo Male and Female Academy, directed by Prof. Page, lists W. B. Randolph as a trustee (1860 Correspondence Folder, SBSC)

74. Smith, diary, April 16, 1862. Harriet reported that Unionist Ed Upton escorted Jo Wood's wife and children to join him after he escaped (April 28, May 6, 1862).

75. "Reminiscences," 34.

76. Smith, diary, April 17, 1862.

77. In 1862, John Dade was thirty-seven years old and Berry Tally was fifty-one. US Census (Population), 1860, Montevallo Township, Vernon County, Missouri. On the "respectable, middle-class status" of many guerrillas, see Daniel E. Sutherland, *American Civil War Guerrillas: Changing the Rules of Warfare* (Santa Barbara: Praeger, 2013), 7.

78. Smith, diary, April 14, 1862.

79. *HVC*, 302–3, 437–38; *OR*, vol. 13: 54–57.

80. Brownlee, 64–65; Fellman, 87–88. See Sutherland, *Savage*, 59–61.

81. Smith, diary, April 15, 1862.

82. Bertram Wyatt-Brown, *Southern Honor: Ethics and Behavior in the Old South* (New York: Oxford University Press, 1982), 71; Richard Carwardine, *Evangelicals and Politics in Antebellum America* (New Haven: Yale University Press, 1993), 291. On the intersection of Baptist faith, manliness, and honor, see David T. Moon, Jr., "Southern Baptists and Southern Men: Evangelical Perceptions of Manhood in Nineteenth-Century Georgia," *Journal of Southern History* 81, no. 3 (August 2015), 563–606.

83. Wyatt-Brown, 335–39.

84. Michael A. Halleran, *Better Angels of Our Nature: Freemasonry in the American Civil War* (Tuscaloosa: University of Alabama Press, 2010), 160–61.

85. Smith, diary, July 24, 1861; January 26, 1862.

86. Wyatt-Brown, 345. See also Geiger, 95.

87. Smith, diary, April 15, 1862.

88. Fellman, 151–52.

89. Fellman, 48–50, 94.

90. See Elliott J. Gorn, "'Good-Bye Boys, I Die a True American': Homicide, Nativism, and Working-Class Culture in Antebellum New York City," *Journal of American History* 74, no. 2 (September 1987), 403–10, and Clyde Griffen, "Reconstructing Masculinity From the Evangelical Revival to the Waning of Progressivism: A Speculative Synthesis" in *Meanings for Manhood: Constructions of Masculinity in Victorian America*, ed. Mark C. Carnes and Clyde Griffen (Chicago: University of Chicago Press, 1990), 183–204.

91. LeeAnn Whites, *The Civil War as a Crisis in Gender: Augusta, Georgia, 1860–1890* (Athens: The University of Georgia Press, 1995), 38-40; Drew Gilpin Faust, "Altars of Sacrifice: Confederate Women and the Narratives of War," *Journal of American History* 76, no. 4 (March 1990), 1209–11; Drew Gilpin Faust, *Mothers of Invention: Women of the Slaveholding South in the American Civil War* (Chapel Hill: University of North Carolina Press, 1996), 12–19; Lyde Cullen Sizer, *The Political Work of Northern Women Writers and the Civil War, 1850–1872* (Chapel Hill: University of North Carolina Press, 2000), 84–89; Stephen Berry: *All That Makes a Man: Love and Ambition in the Civil War South* (New York: Oxford University Press, 2003), 166–73.

92. Fellman, 142. See also Gorn, 406–9.

93. Fellman, 97–107, 112–18; Sutherland, *Savage*, 99–100; Sutherland, *American*, 17–18; Reid Mitchell. "Soldiering, Manhood, and Coming of Age: A Northern Volunteer," in *Divided Houses: Gender and the Civil War*, ed. Catherine Clinton and Nina Silber (New York: Oxford University Press, 1992), 43–54; Nina Silber, "Intemperate Men, Spiteful Women, and Jefferson Davis," in Clinton and Silber, 285–89; Lorien Foote, *The Gentlemen and the Roughs: Manhood, Honor, and Violence in the Union Army* (New York: NYU Press, 2010).

94. Stephen V. Ash, *When the Yankees Came: Conflict and Chaos in the Occupied South, 1861–1865* (Chapel Hill: University of North Carolina Press, 1995), 47–49; Brownlee, 104; Sutherland, *American*, 9, 25–26; Joseph M. Beilein Jr., *Bushwackers: Guerrilla Warfare, Manhood, and the Household in Civil War Missouri* (Kent, Ohio: Kent State University Press, 2016), 101–9, 116–17, 121–22.

95. Beilein, 130–34.

96. Fellman, 23–29; Beilein, 111–15.

97. Ash, 49; Beilein, 47–48. See Wyatt-Brown, 33–34, 336–37.

98. Whites, "Forty Shirts"; Whites and Long, 7; Beilein, 46–48.

99. Fellman, 176–89; Beilein, 118–21.

100. Fellman, 132–48; Sutherland, *American*, 34; Beilein, 187–88. On a southern code of honor, see Wyatt-Brown, 34–36, 42–43, 53–59, 71–74, 366–69.

101. Helen, Frank, and mother to Henry and Hattie, December 21, 1861–January 8, 1862, SBSC.

102. Smith, diary, February 28, 1860; March 16, 1862.

103. Smith, diary, April 27, 1858; September 6, 1861.

104. Smith, diary, February 9, 1862.

105. Fellman, 174.

106. Aaron Astor, "Who is 'Tinker Dave' Beaty? Hunting Guerrilla Social Networks," in *The Guerrilla Hunters: Irregular Conflicts During the Civil War*, ed. Brian D. McKnight and Barton A. Myers (Baton Rouge: Louisiana State University Press, 2017), 166–68.

107. Beilein; Whites, "Forty."
108. Sutherland, *American*, 29–30.
109. See Beilein, 134–35.
110. Beilein, 37–38.
111. Smith, diary, March 17–18, 1862; "Reminiscences," 46. See also Harriet Smith diary, April 14, 1862.
112. "Reminiscences," 38–39.
113. "Reminiscences," 44.
114. Harriet Smith, diary, May 7, 1862.
115. Smith, diary, April 18–20, 1862.
116. Smith, diary, April 21, 1862.
117. Smith, diary, April 22, 1862. See also Harriet Smith diary, April 21–22, 1862.
118. Smith, diary, April 22, 1862.
119. *HVC*, 309, 330–1.
120. Fellman, 165.
121. Smith, diary, April 22–23, 1862. See Fellman, 48.
122. *HVC*, 317, 331, 610, 874; Halleran, 160–61.
123. Smith, diary, April 23, 1862. See also *HVC*, 298; Johnson, 130, 284, 689.
124. Smith, diary, April 24, 1862. Wyrick and Morris, independent Unionist Jayhawkers, were charged at Fort Scott on April 15, 1862, with stealing horses from Vernon County citizens, including Albert Badger. Item 1034, Reel F1584 (NARA Roll 5), Union Provost Marshals' File of Papers Related to Two or More Civilians, Microcopy 416, National Archives Microfilm Publications, MSA (MDH: https://www.sos.mo.gov/archives/provost/provostPDF) (hereafter PM); Johnson, 265, 271, 277.
125. W. C. Ransom to Thomas Ewing, Jr., May 30, 1871, quoted in Christopher Phillips, "'A Question of Power Not One of Law': Federal Occupation and the Politics of Loyalty in the Western Border Slave States during the American Civil War," in *Bleeding Kansas, Bleeding Missouri: The Long Civil War on the Border*, ed. Jonathan Earle and Diane Mutti Burke (Lawrence: University Press of Kansas, 2013), 135–36.
126. Smith, diary, April 25, 1862.
127. Smith, diary, April 26, 1862. Harriet's diary indicates that Mr. Page warned Henry that someone had reported him for helping Dr. Dade (April 26, 1862).
128. Smith, diary, April 30, 1862.
129. See Fellman, 93–94; Boman, 42–43, 116; Brownlee, 157–59.
130. Wyatt-Brown, 55–59.
131. "Reminiscences," 45–46.
132. Harriet Smith, diary, April 30, 1862.
133. Smith, diary, May 1, 1862.
134. Harriet Smith, diary, May 1, 1862. Christopher Phillips discusses the evolution of the term "southerner" from a slaveholder in the early nineteenth century to a supporter of the institution of slavery in the antebellum era to an opponent of Union forces during the Civil War (*Rivers*, 97, 110–11, 159).
135. Smith, diary, May 2, 1862. On scouts, see Sutherland, *Savage*, 124–25.
136. Smith, diary, May 4, 1862.

137. Harriet Smith, diary, April 25, 1862.
138. Harriet Smith, diary, May 14, 1862.
139. Harriet Smith, diary, June 7, 1862.
140. Smith, diary, May 13, 18–21, and 25, 1862. On removal of federal troops from Missouri, see Boman, 118–19.
141. Smith, diary, May 24, 1862; May 29, 1862.
142. Smith, diary, May 31, 1862. See also Harriet Smith diary, May 4, 1862. Vernon, Dade, and Cedar County citizens submitted a petition dated May 9, 1862, for Riley Lindley's release as a law-abiding citizen who refused to fight against the Union. Reel F1481, Union Provost Marshals' File of Papers Relating to Individual Citizens, Microcopy 345, National Archives Microfilm Publications, MSA (MDH: https://s1.sos.mo.gov/records/archives/archivesdb/provost/Default.aspx). The local Provost Marshal certified that the petitioners included some of "the best citizens of this county" (fold3.com). On May 25, 1862, Cedar County residents J. R. Lindly and John Brasher requested to take the loyalty oath and post bond for release from Alton military prison. The unarmed men were captured March 7 on the road from Fayetteville, Arkansas, to Springfield, Missouri, a few miles from the Pea Ridge battleground. Item 1164, Frame 0320, Reel F1585 (NARA Roll 6), PM.
143. Smith, diary, June 3, 1862. See Fellman, 76–77, on deserted towns and countryside.
144. Smith, diary, June 4, 1862.
145. Smith, diary, June 7, 1862.
146. Smith, diary, June 9, 1862; "Reminiscences," 48. Henry P. Smith of Vernon County submitted an affidavit on June 9, 1862, attesting that J. R. Lindly was a loyal citizen who had been a mule dealer since before the war and had never joined the military. He attested that John Brazier left the military after three months and was not involved in guerrilla activity or recruiting. Item 1085, Frame 0049, Reel F1585 (NARA Roll 6), PM.
147. "Seneca Falls" pocket notebook, Account Books of HP Smith 1847–1853, Box 3, SBSC.
148. Smith, diary, June 9–15, 1862.
149. On hazards to Unionists of Union occupation, see Ash, 111–30.
150. General Orders 18, Headquarters, Missouri State Militia, May 29, 1862, *OR*, vol. 13: 402–3. Schofield assumed command of the Military District of Missouri. Major-General Halleck, General Orders 30, Headquarters, Department of the Mississippi, June 1, 1862, *OR*, vol. 13: 409.
151. "Reminiscences," 48.

Chapter Seven. Harriet's Civil War

1. Harriet Smith diary, March 23, 1862, Henry Parker Smith Papers, BHL.
2. Richard S. Brownlee, *Gray Ghosts of the Confederacy: Guerrilla Warfare in the West, 1861–1865* (Baton Rouge: Louisiana State University Press, 1958), 68–71; Michael Fellman, *Inside War: The Guerrilla Conflict in Missouri During the American Civil War* (New York: Oxford University Press, 1989), 53.
3. Smith, diary, April 1, 1862.
4. Drew Gilpin Faust, *Mothers of Invention: Women of the Slaveholding South in the American Civil War* (Chapel Hill: University of North Carolina Press, 1996), 162.

5. Amy L. Wink, *She Left Nothing in Particular: The Autobiographical Legacy of Nineteenth-Century Women's Diaries* (Knoxville: University of Tennessee Press, 2001), 126–27.

6. Kimberly Harrison, "The American Civil War: Confederate Women's Diaries," in *The Diary: The Epic of Everyday Life*, ed. Batsheva Ben-Amos and Dan Ben-Amos (Bloomington: Indiana University Press, 2020), 299–316.

7. In "On Holocaust Diaries," Batsheva Ben-Amos discusses diaries written under Nazi occupation as simultaneously testimonials of collective experiences and personal coping mechanisms (Ben-Amos and Ben-Amos, ed., 364–82).

8. Jane E. Schultz, "Mute Fury: Southern Women's Diaries of Sherman's March to the Sea, 1864–1865" in *Arms and the Woman: War, Gender and Literary Representation*, ed. Helen M. Cooper, Adrienne Auslander Mainich, Susan Merrill Squier (Chapel Hill: University of North Carolina Press, 1989), 59–79. See also George Rable, *Civil Wars: Women and the Crisis of Southern Nationalism* (Urbana: University of Illinois Press, 1989), 158–59, 172–73.

9. Smith, diary, March 23, 1862.

10. Smith, diary, March 24, 1862.

11. Fellman, 205–7.

12. Megan Kate Nelson, *Ruin Nation: Destruction and the American Civil War* (Athens: University of Georgia Press, 2012), 72–87; William A. Blair, *With Malice Toward Some: Treason and Loyalty in the Civil War Era* (Chapel Hill: University of North Carolina Press, 2014), 151.

13. Smith, diary, March 26, 1862.

14. Smith, diary, April 7, 1862.

15. Faust notes that white women on plantations hid valuables in their clothing with the expectation that they would not be searched (199).

16. Johnson, diary, November 19, 1853.

17. Smith, diary, May 2, 1862.

18. "Reminiscences," 34. On salt shortages, see Matthew Stith, *Extreme Civil War: Guerrilla Warfare, Environment and Race on the Trans-Mississippi Frontier* (Baton Rouge: Louisiana State University Press, 2016), 106.

19. Smith, diary, May 2, 1862.

20. Smith, diary, May 7, 1862.

21. See Fellman, 26–27, 48, 126; Joan E. Cashin, *War Stuff: The Struggle for Human and Environmental Resources in the American Civil War* (Cambridge: Cambridge University Press, 2018), 54–68.

22. Smith, diary, May 23, 1862.

23. Smith, diary, April 7, 1862; May 2, 1862. On wartime sounds, see Mark M. Smith, *The Smell of Battle, The Taste of Siege: A Sensory History of the Civil War* (New York: Oxford University Press, 2015), 30–38, and "Of Bells, Booms, Sounds, and Silences: Listening to the Civil War South," in *The War Was You and Me: Civilians in the American Civil War*, ed. Joan Cashin (Princeton, NJ: Princeton University Press, 2002), 9–34.

24. Smith, diary, March 25, May 4 and 21, June 10 and 22, 1862. Mrs. Page visited Harriet April 25, June 6, and June 25, 1862.

25. Smith, diary, March 25, 1862.

26. Smith, diary, April 22, 1862.

27. Smith, diary, April 29, 1862.

28. Smith, diary, April 25 and 30, May 19–20, 1862.

29. Smith, diary, March 24, 1862.

30. Smith, diary, March 28, 1862.

31. Andrew William Fialka, "Controlled Chaos: Spatiotemporal Patterns within Missouri's Irregular Civil War," in *The Civil War Guerrilla: Unfolding the Black Flag in History, Memory, and Myth*, ed. Joseph M. Beilein, Jr., Matthew C. Hulbert, Christopher Phillips, and Victoria E. Bynum (Lexington: University Press of Kentucky, 2015), 43–69.

32. Smith, diary, April 19, 1862.

33. Smith, diary, April 24, 1862.

34. Smith, diary, April 25, 1862.

35. Smith, diary, May 19, 1862. On similar concerns in occupied Confederate states, see Stephen V. Ash, *When the Yankees Came: Conflict and Chaos in the Occupied South, 1861–1865* (Chapel Hill: University of North Carolina Press, 1995), 111–12.

36. Smith, diary, May 20, 1862.

37. Smith, diary, April 14, 1862.

38. Smith, diary, April 25, 1862.

39. Smith, diary, April 29, 1862.

40. Fellman, 48.

41. Smith, diary, April 22, 1862. *HVC*, 299–304, 309, 330–31.

42. See Fellman, 49–51, on Missouri residents' claims that they aided guerrillas only because their lives were threatened.

43. Smith, diary, April 25, 1862.

44. Smith, diary, April 26, 1862.

45. Smith, diary, April 14, 1862; *HVC*, 338.

46. Harriet exchanged food with the Wood, Boyd, and Page families (March 31, April 2 and 9, June 10, 1862). Mrs. Dade and other women who supported the Confederacy visited Mrs. Page, a Unionist. The following year, Mrs. Page wrote Harriet that she admired and liked Mrs. Dade (January 25, 1863), Stanley Barney Smith Collection (SBSC), A-88, Archives and Regional History Collections, Zhang Legacy Collections Center, Western Michigan University.

47. Smith, diary, June 5–6, 1862; M. M. Page to Hattie, December 23, 1866, SBSC.

48. Smith, diary, March 30, 1862. On March 26, 1862, Henry Taylor's Missouri State Guard company unsuccessfully raided the federally funded Missouri State Militia at Humansville (*HVC*, 331).

49. Smith, diary, April 16, 1862.

50. Smith, diary, April 18, 1862.

51. Smith, diary, May 7, 1862.

52. Smith, diary, June 9, 1862.

53. Fellman, 86, 123–24.

54. Smith, diary, June 13, 1862.

55. Michael E. Woods, *Emotional and Sectional Conflict in the Antebellum US* (New York: Cambridge University Press, 2014), 2–3, 9–15, 21–31, 74. On how rumors validate

beliefs and intensify emotions during social unrest and censorship, see Gary Alan Fine and Ralph L. Rosnow, *Rumor and Gossip: The Social Psychology of Hearsay* (Elsevier, New York: Scientific Publishing Company, 1976), 30–62.

56. Smith, diary, April 1, 1862.

57. On traditional oral narratives about outlaw heroes, including western Missouri guerrilla Jesse James, see Richard Meyer, "The Outlaw: A Distinctive American Folktype," *Journal of the Folklore Institute* 17, nos. 2–3 (May–December 1980): 94–124.

58. Smith, diary, May 7, 1862.

59. Smith, diary, May 19, 1862.

60. Smith, diary, April 17, 1862. During the spring of 1862, Union commanders endorsed the previously unofficial practice of killing guerrilla fighters rather than taking them captive (Fellman, 123).

61. Smith, diary, May 17, 1862.

62. *HVC*, 330–31.

63. Margaret R. Higonnet, "Civil Wars and Sexual Territories," in Cooper, Mainich, and Squier, 80–96.

64. Rabinowitz, 131–37, 227–33.

65. Smith, diary, April 26, 1862. Henry Wadsworth Longfellow, *Voices of the Night* (Cambridge, MA: 1839), 7.

66. Smith, diary, May 11 and 14, 1862.

67. Fellman, 28–32, 48–51; Ash, 59–60, 70–72.

68. Smith, diary, April 3, 1862. See Faust (221) and, on decreased cotton production in 1862, Richard H. Sewell, *A House Divided: Sectionalism and Civil War, 1848–1865* (Baltimore: Johns Hopkins University Press, 1988), 95–96, 116.

69. Smith, diary, June 14, 1862. On soap, see Rable, *Civil*, 95.

70. "Reminiscences," 35; Fellman, 159. On similar shortages of cloth, dye, and shoe leather in the Confederacy, see Faust, 45–51, 220–22; Sewell, 116; Rable, *Civil*, 92–95.

71. Smith, diary, May 24, 1862. See also March 23, June 11, 1862.

72. Smith, diary, June 11, 1862.

73. Smith, diary, April 6, 1862.

74. Smith, diary, May 15, 1862.

75. Smith, diary, May 22, 1862.

76. Smith, diary, June 10, 1862.

77. Faust concludes that wartime clothing shortages led white women on southern plantations to begin to understand gender as performance and gender categories as fluid and arbitrary (220–21).

78. "Reminiscences," 9–10; Helen Purcell to Henry and Hattie, February 16, 1859, SBSC.

79. See Glenda Riley, *The Female Frontier: A Comparative View of Women on the Prairie and the Plains* (Lawrence, Kansas: University Press of Kansas, 1988), 52–53.

80. Bertram Wyatt-Brown, *Southern Honor: Ethics and Behavior in the Old South* (New York: Oxford University Press, 1982), 231–36.

81. Smith, diary, April 2, May 10, 1862.

82. Whites argues that violations of norms of domesticity and gentility were culturally appropriate responses to the endangerment of the more important patriarchal institution

of the autonomous household. *The Civil War as a Crisis in Gender: Augusta, Georgia, 1860–1890* (Athens: The University of Georgia Press, 1995), 18, 40. See also Wink, 83–121.

83. Smith, diary, May 12, 1862.

84. Smith, diary, May 2, 1862.

85. Smith, diary, May 19, 1862.

86. Lisa Tendrich Frank and LeeAnn Whites, eds., *Household War: How Americans Lived and Fought the Civil War* (Athens: University of Georgia Press, 2019).

87. Kimberly Harrison examines the rhetorical strategies privileged southern white women employed with occupying troops and within their own communities. *The Rhetoric of Rebel Women: Civil War Diaries and Confederate Persuasion* (Carbondale: Southern Illinois University Press, 2013), 1–117.

88. Smith, diary, April 12, May 12, June 2, June 3, 1862.

89. Blair, 129. Rebekah Weber Bowen finds that white women in Saline County, Missouri, protected family property and male family members, reversing traditional gender roles. "The Changing Role of Protection on the Border: Gender and the Civil War in Saline County," *Women in Missouri History: In Search of Power and Influence*, ed. LeeAnn Whites, Mary C. Neth, and Gary R. Kremer (Columbia: University of Missouri Press, 2004), 119–33. LeeAnn Whites argues that Missouri women's provision of food, clothing, shelter, and information created an essential domestic supply line for guerrillas. "Forty Shirts and a Wagonload of Wheat: Women, the Domestic Supply Line, and the Civil War on the Western Border," *The Journal of the Civil War Era* 1, no. 1 (March 2011), 56–78. See also LeeAnn Whites and Alecia P. Long, eds., *Occupied Women: Gender, Military Occupation, and the American Civil War* (Baton Rouge: Louisiana State University Press, 2012), 7. Kristen L. Streater examines Kentucky women's similar support for Confederate soldiers in another Union border state. "'She Rebels' in the Supply Line," in Whites and Long, 88–102, and "'Not much a friend to traiters no matter how beautiful': The Union Military and Confederate Women in Civil War Kentucky," in *Sister States Enemy States: The Civil War in Kentucky and Tennessee*, ed. Kent T. Dollar, Larry H. Whiteaker, and W. Calvin Dickinson (Lexington: University Press of Kentucky, 2009), 245–64. On southern white women's growing awareness of the intrusion of political issues into the private domestic domain, see Faust, 12. Faust finds that women in border regions of Confederate states were more likely to be held accountable for their actions and defined as participants in the conflict (200). Elissa R. Hencken examines oral narratives about women who saved their homes or communities from destruction by General Sherman's federal troops in 1864. "Taming the Enemy: Georgian Narratives About the Civil War," *Journal of Folklore Research* 40, no. 3 (Sep.–Dec. 2003), 289–307.

90. Smith, diary, April 25, 1862.

91. *HVC*, 337–42; Daniel Sutherland, *A Savage Conflict: The Decisive Role of Guerrillas in the American Civil War* (Chapel Hill: University of North Carolina Press, 2009), 201.

92. Smith, diary, June 26, 1862. See Faust on southern women helping men escape in women's clothing (228–29) and on female Confederate spies (214–19). Two years earlier, Harriet had noticed Nora Mayfield's refined appearance and manners. "Reminiscences," 22–23.

93. Lyde Cullen Sizer finds that northern women discovered an enhanced "personal and cultural vision of possibility" in wartime: *The Political Work of Northern Women Writers*

and the Civil War, 1850–1872 (Chapel Hill: University of North Carolina Press, 2000), 4, 84. Faust notes that southern white women in slaveholding families also questioned categories of race, class, and gender during the war (4).

94. Smith, diary, May 5, 1862.

95. Smith, diary, March 23, 1862. See Bruce Dorsey, *Reforming Men and Women: Gender in the Antebellum City* (Ithaca: Cornell University Press, 2002), 113–35.

96. Smith, diary, April 2, 1862. See Blair, 61. Secessionist politicians were called "fire eaters." Michael D. Robinson, *A Union Indivisible: Secession and the Politics of Slavery in the Border South* (Chapel Hill: University of North Carolina Press, 2017), 11, 85–111. Randall Jimerson, *The Private Civil War: Popular Thought during the Sectional Conflict* (Baton Rouge: Louisiana State University Press, 1988), 39–44, discusses the bitterness many northerners felt toward abolitionists whom they blamed for instigating the war.

97. W. C. Johnson to "My dear children," February 19, 1861, SBSC. George C. Rable, *God's Almost Chosen Peoples: A Religious History of the American Civil War* (Chapel Hill: University of North Carolina Press, 2010), 84–85, 153–57.

98. Smith, diary, May 25, 1862.

99. Sizer discusses northern women writers who saw the war as carrying out God's will and as morally preferable to compromise on slavery (100–2). Faust describes southern women's confidence that God favored the Confederacy (180–81). Rable notes an increase in dehumanizing and demonizing of the enemy as the war progressed (*God's*, 163–64).

100. Smith, diary, April 25, 1862; April 14, 1862.

101. Fellman, 56, 89–93, 101, 113, 120–21; General Orders No. 8, Department of the Missouri, November 26, 1861, and General Orders No. 2, North Missouri R. R., January 1, 1862, in *OR*, vol. 8: 380–81, 478.

102. Smith, diary, April 2, 1862.

103. On northern women's "prewar insistence upon the power of moral suasion," see Sizer, 5.

104. Smith, diary, May 8, 1862.

105. Smith, diary, May 13, 1862. Harriet noted that Jesse Steward and Charlie Robinson were required to post bond of $2,000 and $1,000, respectively.

106. On mid-nineteenth-century female authors' preference for prairie over woods, see Annette Kolodny, *The Land Before Her: Fantasy and Experience of the American Frontiers, 1630–1860* (Chapel Hill: University of North Carolina Press, 1984), 175.

107. Smith, diary, April 30, 1862. See Fellman, 98, 106.

108. Smith, diary, May 8, 1862.

109. Smith, diary, May 18, 1862.

110. "Reminiscences," 4.

111. Smith, diary, April 17, May 8, June 3, 7, and 9, 1862.

112. Smith, diary, June 9, 1862. See Kolodny, 48–49.

113. Smith, diary, May 4, 1862. See Wink, 18–22, 43–44.

114. As a teacher, Harriet had opposed corporal punishment (September 8 and 27, 1853). She avoided physical punishment of Isa at a similar age (Hattie to Henrie, September 13, 1857, SBSC) and criticized another mother for hitting a crying child (Hattie to Henrie, November 1, 1857, SBSC). Wakeman Johnson's journal (March 21, 1836) describes how he

disciplined three-year-old Harriet without using physical force (Box 5, SBSC). Faust notes that some southern white women on plantations inflicted impulsive or abusive punishment on their children, especially sons, during the wartime absence of their husbands (132–34).

115. Smith, diary, June 5, 1862.
116. Smith, diary, June 11, 1862.
117. Smith, diary, March 23, 1862.
118. Smith, diary, June 6, 1862.

Chapter Eight. Refugees

1. Hattie and Henrie to Father and Mother, October 5, 1862, Stanley Barney Smith Collection (SBSC), Archives and Regional History Collections, Zhang Legacy Collections Center, Western Michigan University.

2. Harriet Smith diary, June 14, 1862, Henry Parker Smith Papers, Bentley Historical Library (BHL); R. Douglas Hurt, "The Agricultural Power of the Midwest During the Civil War," in *Union Heartland: The Midwestern Homefront During the Civil War*, ed. Ginette Aley and J. L. Anderson (Carbondale: Southern Illinois University Press, 2013), 73–82. One Michigan resident wrote in 1862: "The farmers around here were never as well off . . . as they are at present." Richard H. Sewell, *A House Divided: Sectionalism and Civil War, 1848–1865* (Baltimore: Johns Hopkins University Press, 1988), 105.

3. "Reminiscences," 48–49.
4. Smith, diary, June 18, 19, 21–24, and 29, July 7, 1862, Henry Parker Smith Papers, BHL.
5. Smith, diary, June 23–24, 1862.
6. Smith, diary, June 22, 1862.
7. Drew Gilpin Faust notes a similar sense of self among southern white women in slaveholding families who suffered hardship during the war. *Mothers of Invention: Women of the Slaveholding South in the American Civil War* (Chapel Hill: University of North Carolina Press, 1996), 234–35.
8. Smith, diary, June 15, 1862.
9. Smith, diary, June 25, 1862.
10. Smith, diary, June 28, 1862.
11. Smith, diary, June 24, 1862.
12. Smith, diary, July 3, 1862. In Henry's absence, Mr. Page wrote the petition.
13. "Seneca Falls" pocket notebook, Account Books of HP Smith 1847–1853, Box 3, SBSC.
14. Smith, diary, June 18, 1862.
15. Smith, diary, July 7, 1862.
16. Smith, diary, July 4, 1862. D. H. Connaway to Hamilton Rowan Gamble, July 1, 1862 (Cedar County) in Hamilton Rowan Gamble, 1861–1864, Office of Governor, Record Group 3.16, MSA (MDH: https://mdh.contentdm.oclc.org/digital/collection/msa/id/4930/rec/1).
17. Smith, diary, June 24, 1862.
18. Smith, diary, June 25, 1862.
19. Smith, diary, June 25, 1862.
20. "Reminiscences," 44. On kinship and revenge binding guerrilla networks, see Aaron Astor, "Who is 'Tinker Dave' Beaty? Hunting Guerrilla Social Networks," in *The Guerrilla*

Hunters: Irregular Conflicts During the Civil War, ed. Brian D. McKnight and Barton A. Myers (Baton Rouge: Louisiana State University Press, 2017).

21. Smith, diary, June 25, 1862.

22. Joseph M. Beilein, Jr., *Bushwhackers: Guerrilla Warfare, Manhood, and the Household in Civil War Missouri* (Kent, Ohio: Kent State University Press, 2016), 47–48.

23. Smith, diary, June 25, 1862. See *HVC*, 335–36.

24. Smith, diary, June 25, 1862. Richard Rabinowitz, *The Spiritual Self in Everyday Life: The Transformation of Personal Religious Experience in Nineteenth-Century New England* (Boston: Northeastern University Press, 1989), xxix–xxx, 237.

25. Smith, diary, June 26, 1862.

26. Michael Fellman, *Inside War: The Guerrilla Conflict in Missouri During the American Civil War* (New York: Oxford University Press, 1989), 107. Regular troops were also reported as killing captured soldiers and civilians (Fellman, 117–26, 185).

27. Fellman, 58–59.

28. Fellman, 49.

29. Smith, diary, June 29, 1862.

30. Smith, diary, June 28, 1862; June 29, 1862.

31. Smith, diary, July 6, 1862.

32. Smith, diary, July 5, 9, 1862.

33. Smith, diary, June 27 and July 7, 1862.

34. Smith, diary, June 24, 1862.

35. Smith, diary, June 16, 27, July 2–4, 9–12, 16, 1862.

36. Smith, diary, July 10, 1862.

37. Smith, diary, July 15, 1862.

38. Smith, diary, July 1, 1862.

39. Smith, diary, July 15, 1862.

40. Smith, diary, July 17–18, 1862.

41. Smith, diary, July 16–17, 1862.

42. Smith, diary, July 16, 1862.

43. Smith, diary, July 18, 1862.

44. Smith, diary, July 18, 1862.

45. By the end of the war, hundreds of thousands of Missouri residents had become refugees. Fellman, 73.

46. Smith, diary, July 19, 1862.

47. Smith, diary, July 20, 1862.

48. Smith, diary, July 21, 1862. Troops set fire to houses as military strategy or retribution. Megan Kate Nelson, *Ruin Nation: Destruction and the American Civil War* (Athens: University of Georgia Press, 2012), 62–72. Nelson discusses ruins as a trope in landscape paintings, book and magazine illustrations, and travel narratives (5). Soldiers also described abandoned homes and farms in Missouri (Fellman, 76–77).

49. On pioneer women's use of the terminology of romanticism to place themselves in the natural environment and make an alien landscape seem familiar, see Amy L. Wink, *She Left Nothing in Particular: The Autobiographical Legacy of Nineteenth-Century Women's Diaries* (Knoxville: University of Tennessee Press, 2001), 6–30.

50. Smith, diary, July 18, 1862.

51. Smith, diary, July 20, 1862.
52. Smith, diary, July 21, 1862.
53. Smith, diary, July 22, 1862.
54. Smith, diary, July 23, 1862.
55. Smith, diary, July 24, 1862.
56. Smith, diary, July 25, 1862.
57. Fellman describes the destitute condition of Missouri refugees forced to abandon their property (74–80). On refugees in southern states, see George Rable, *Civil Wars: Women and the Crisis of Southern Nationalism* (Urbana: University of Illinois Press, 1989), 182–88. On refugees and class consciousness, see Thavolia Glymph, *The Women's Fight: The Civil War's Battles for Home, Freedom and Nation* (Chapel Hill: University of North Carolina Press, 2020), 60–76. Wink discusses the similar loss of identity and social status women experienced on the Overland Trail (4–5).
58. Smith, diary, July 26, 1862.
59. Smith, diary, July 25, 1862.
60. Smith, diary, July 27, 1862.
61. Smith, diary, July 30, August 3, 1862.
62. Smith, diary, August 2–6, 1862.
63. Smith, diary, August 1–2, 1862.
64. Smith, diary, August 1–3, 1862.
65. Smith, diary, August 6, 1862.
66. Smith, diary, July 30, 1862.
67. Smith, diary, July 23, 1862. Jeremy Neely, *The Border Between Them: Violence and Reconciliation on the Kansas-Missouri Line* (Columbia: University of Missouri Press, 2007), 114; Fellman, 52, 97–98, 194; Richard S. Brownlee, *Gray Ghosts of the Confederacy: Guerrilla Warfare in the West, 1861–1865* (Baton Rouge: Louisiana State University Press, 1958), 77–79, 83–84, 159; David T. Holstead, "Guerrilla War in 'Little Dixie': Understanding Conflict Escalation in Missouri During the American Civil War" (Fort Leavenworth, Kansas: US Army Command and General Staff College, 2014), 43–46.
68. Smith, diary, July 31, 1862.
69. Smith, diary, August 1, 1862. Union Colonel Odum Guitar defeated Colonel Joseph Porter, who was recruiting under the Confederate Partisan Ranger Act, at Moore's Mill, Callaway County, on July 31. Sixty-five men were killed and over 150 wounded. Brownlee, 81–87; Holstead, 46.
70. Smith, diary, August 5, 1862. Porter had moved north, but Montgomery County guerrillas who had fought with him returned eastward (Brownlee, 87–88).
71. Nelson notes that many Americans were familiar with the aesthetic categories of the sublime and the picturesque as ways to understand the natural landscape and its artistic depiction (5, 130–33). See also Wink, 18–19.
72. Smith, diary, July 31, 1862.
73. Smith, diary, August 7, 1862.
74. Smith, diary, August 8, 1862.
75. Smith, diary, August 10, 1862.
76. "Seneca Falls" pocket notebook, Account Books of HP Smith 1847–1853, Box 3, SBSC.
77. "Reminiscences," 51.

78. Smith, diary, August 10, 1862.

79. Smith, diary, August 11, 1862.

80. Smith, diary, August 16, 1862.

81. Smith, diary, August 17, 1862.

82. Smith, diary, October 3, 1862.

83. Hattie and Henrie to Father and Mother, October 5, 1862, in Harriet Smith Journal, transcribed by Stanley Barney Smith (unpublished typescript, 1955), 170–74, SBSC.

84. Smith, diary, October 10, 1862.

85. Smith, diary, October 18, 1862. Discord often arose between refugees and hosts as families stretched their living space, food, and other resources to support relatives suffering emotional and financial losses. Rable, *Civil*, 190; Kimberly Harrison, *The Rhetoric of Rebel Women: Civil War Diaries and Confederate Persuasion* (Carbondale: Southern Illinois University Press, 2013), 90–95.

86. Isa H. Smith, Addendum to Harriet Smith Journal, transcribed by Stanley Barney Smith (unpublished typescript, 1955), 174, SBSC.

87. Smith, diary, November 15, 1862.

88. Smith, diary, November 16, 1862.

89. Brownlee, 92–93.

90. *HVC*, 305–9. Colonel Clark Wright reported that in addition to the men killed or captured in combat by the Sixth Missouri Cavalry, seven were "unaccounted for, except by General Orders No. 18" (309). General Schofield had ordered that "robbers and assassins" actively engaged in "unlawful warfare" be "shot down upon the spot." General Orders 18, Headquarters, Missouri State Militia, May 29, 1862, *OR*, vol. 13: 402–3.

91. M. A. Page to Smith and Family, February 2, 1863, SBSC.

92. Isaiah 8: 6, 12, 15.

93. M. A. Page to Smith and Family, February 2, 1863, SBSC.

94. Brownlee, 94–99; *HVC*, 307, 310.

95. M. A. Page to Smith and Family, February 2, 1863, SBSC. A Sixth Kansas soldier killed Brice and Crack Mayfield near Neosho December 26, 1862 (*HVC*, 336–37).

96. [M. A. Page] to "Friend Smith & Family," March 23, 1863, SBSC. *HVC* reports that Cedar County militia killed Tapp, Amos, Clendenin, and William Wood one night and that Kansas troops killed John Brown, Sr., when he refused to obey an order to halt while hunting cattle on the prairie (856). On Union troops targeting fathers of guerrillas, see Beilein, 22–23.

97. Marion M. Page to Hattie, January 25, 1863, SBSC.

98. [Marion Page] to Hattie, March 23, 1863, SBSC. John Brown married Syntha in 1860. Henry Smith diary, November 25, 1860; Vernon County Marriage Book A, 67 (https://vernon.mogenweb.org/marriages/bookA.pdf); US Census (Population), 1860, Montevallo Township, Vernon County, Missouri.

99. M. A. Page to Smith and Family, February 2, 1863, SBSC. In autumn 1862, many farms burned when federal troops pursuing Coffee set fire to the prairie accidentally or intentionally (*HVC*, 343).

100. [M. A. Page] to "Friend Smith & Family," March 23, 1863, SBSC.

101. M. A. Page to H. P. Smith, August 13, October 29, 1863, SBSC; [Marion Page] to Hattie, December 15, 1863, SBSC.

102. M. A. Page to H. P. Smith, October 29, 1863, SBSC.

103. [Marion Page] to Hattie, December 15, 1863, SBSC.

104. [Marion Page] to Hattie, September 20, 1863, SBSC.

105. M. A. Page to H. P. Smith, October 29, 1863, SBSC. William Andrew Steward was killed in Dade County May 22, 1864 (ancestors.familysearch.org). His father, Jesse Steward, and uncle, Charley Robinson, died a few years later. See monument for unmarked burials in Oldham Cemetery, Cedar County, Missouri (findagrave.com).

106. M. M. Page to Hatty, April 21, 1864, SBSC.

107. M. M. Page to Hattie, February 1, 1865, SBSC.

108. [Marion Page] to Hattie, June 25, 1865, SBSC.

109. M. A. Page to H. P. Smith and Lady, April 10, 1865, SBSC.

110. M. M. Page to Hattie, September 8, 1865, SBSC.

111. *HVC*, 343, 859.

112. W. G. Johnson to Hattie, December 12, 1862; [Joseph] to Father, December 2, 1862; W. G. Johnson to Henrie and Hattie, January 23, July 17, October 6, 1863 and March 11, 1864; Volney to Parents, February 7, 1863; Edelia to Hattie, March 2, 1863; W. G. J. to Henry and Hattie, July 30, 1863; J. C. Johnson to Father and All, August 2, 1863; all SBSC. Joseph C Johnson and Volney C Johnson, Illinois Civil War Muster and Descriptive Rolls Detail Report (https://apps.ilsos.gov/isaveterans/civilmustersrch.jsp) and Illinois Civil War Regimental and Unit Histories (https://www.ilsos.gov/departments/archives/databases/reghist.pdf), Illinois State Archives, Springfield, Illinois. On Turchin's court-martial, see William A. Blair, *With Malice Toward Some: Treason and Loyalty in the Civil War Era* (Chapel Hill: University of North Carolina), 134–37, and Mark Grimsley, *The Hard Hand of War: Union Military Policy Toward Southern Civilians, 1861–1865* (New York: Cambridge University Press, 1995), 81–85.

113. W. G. Johnson to "children," July 5, October 26, 1864; Edelia to Hattie, November 27, 1864; Joseph to Edelia and Hattie and Cynthia and Archy and Henry, January 15, 1865; R. F. Steele to W. G. Johnson, April 8, 1865; E. S. Johnson to "children," October 4, 1865; all SBSC.

114. "A Copy of the Original Military Records written by Colonel Orlando Hurley Moore, United States Army, 1856–1865," undated typescript, Orlando H. Moore papers, 1856–1894, BHL. (http://name.umdl.umich.edu/2011398.0001.001); Kristopher A. Teters, *Practical Liberators: Union Officers in the Western Theater during the Civil War* (Chapel Hill: University of North Carolina Press, 2018), 129; Robert R. Mackey, *The Uncivil War: Irregular Warfare in the Upper South, 1861–1865* (Norman: University of Oklahoma Press, 2004), 180–85; ST Allen to Hattie, May 26, 1861, SBSC.

115. US Draft Registration, Class II, Compiled List, Schoolcraft, Kalamazoo County, Michigan, Provost Marshal n. 338 (ancestry.com); Sewell, 88–89.

116. Smith, diary, February 23, March 2, May 15, 1863.

117. Smith, diary, May 15, 1864.

118. Smith, diary, March 19, 22, and 26, 1864.

119. M. A. Page to H. P. Smith, June 12, 1864, SBSC.

120. Smith, diary, December 3, 1864.

121. Smith, diary, January 26, 1865.

122. Smith, diary, April 15, 1865.

123. Aaron Astor, *Rebels on the Border: Civil War, Emancipation, and the Reconstruction of Kentucky and Missouri* (Baton Rouge: Louisiana State University Press, 2012), 5.

Conclusion

1. Hattie to Cynthia, January 20, September 3, 1867, Stanley Barney Smith Collection (SBSC), A-88, Archives and Regional History Collections, Zhang Legacy Collections Center, Western Michigan University.

2. Isa to Cynthia, April 5, 1868, SBSC; *Portrait and Biographical Record of Kalamazoo, Allegan and Van Buren Counties, Michigan* (Chicago, 1892), 567.

3. Hattie to Cynthia, [January] 1869, SBSC; Carole Elizabeth Nowicke, *Not Built by Jack—But by You and Me: The Schoolcraft Ladies' Library Association, 1879–1920: A Study of Women's Reading Culture in Rural Southwestern Michigan* (PhD dissertation, Indiana University, 1998), 178–79, 214–15.

4. Samuel W. Durant, *History of Kalamazoo County, Michigan with Illustrations and Biographical Sketches of Its Prominent Men and Women* (Philadelphia, 1880), 514, 521.

5. Henry Smith diary, December 14, 1867; May 30, July 4, 1868, Henry Parker Smith Papers, Bentley Historical Library (BHL).

6. H. P. Smith Call Book, 1869, Box 6B, SBSC; Square Dance Calls, Box 5, SBSC; Elias Howe, *American Dancing Master and Ballroom Prompter* (Boston, 1862), Box 11, SBSC.

7. Jeremy Neely, *The Border Between Them: Violence and Reconciliation on the Kansas-Missouri Line* (Columbia: University of Missouri Press, 2007), 136–37.

8. W. S. Hall to Henry P. Smith, February 18, 1866; Hattie to Cynthia, August 5, 1866; Henrie to Cynthia, September 23, 1866; Harriet to Cynthia, April 14, 1867; all SBSC.

9. In 1878, Henry P. Smith was plaintiff in a Vernon County foreclosure suit against Brown and three others. Case 3765, Roll C60673, Missouri Judicial Records Historical Database (MDH: https://s1.sos.mo.gov/Records/ArchivesDb/JudicialRecords/Results.aspx). An 1886 plat map shows Brown remained. William Bracher, *Map of Vernon Co. Missouri* (Stockton: 1886), LC: https://www.loc.gov/resource/g4163v.la000409/. Brown told of accompanying Quantrill on the 1863 raids on Lawrence and Baxter Springs, Kansas. See obituary, *Kansas City Star*, 21 Sep 1940, p. 3, for MSGT John Brown (1844–1940) at findagrave.com.

10. US Census (Agriculture), 1870, Montevallo Township, Vernon County, Missouri; *HVC*, 859–60.

11. *HVC*, 851.

12. Babbs and Stoddard, *Map of Cedar County, Missouri* (Philadelphia, 1879), 9, Missouri County Platbooks Collection, State Historical Society of Missouri (MDH: https://mdh.contentdm.oclc.org/digital/collection/mocoplats/id/2717/rec/1); US Census (Agriculture), 1870 and 1880, Benton Township, Cedar County, Missouri; US Census (Population), 1870, Montevallo Township, Vernon County, Missouri; *HVC* 616, 860; Matilda Upton to Mrs. Smith, August 17, 1868, SBSC.

13. *HVC*, 343–48, 442, 613–14, 647, 873–74.

14. US Census (Population), 1880, Schoolcraft Village, Kalamazoo County, Michigan.

15. H. P. Smith, Milk Business Account Book, 1887–1891, Box 6A, SBSC; *Portrait*, 567. In 1879, the Smiths sold 225 gallons of milk, 210 pounds of butter, and the eggs from seventy-five hens. The farm produced 460 bushels of wheat, three hundred bushels of oats, and four hundred bushels of corn. A flock of forty-two sheep yielded 180 pounds of fleece. US Census (Agriculture), 1880, Schoolcraft Township, Kalamazoo County, Michigan.

16. Nowicke, *Not*, 156.

17. Nowicke, *Not*, 210.

18. Nowicke, *Not*, 155-6; *Kalamazoo Daily Telegraph* (December 19, 1882): 3; Keith Howard, "Social Music in 19th Century Kalamazoo: Tripping the Light Fantastic," Kalamazoo History, Kalamazoo Public Library website (kpl.gov).

19. C. Elizabeth Nowicke, "Walter F. Smith: The Marine Band's Original Second Leader," *Fortitude* (Spring/Summer 1982): 19–20, Box 10, SBSC.

20. Smith, diary, February 27, March 1, April 19–21, May 4, 1892.

21. Smith, diary, March 26, April 9 and 23, May 7 and 20, June 24, 1892.

22. Smith, diary, April 9, 1892.

23. Nowicke, "Walter," 20.

24. *Portrait*, 567.

25. Stanley Barney Smith, "Notes on the Village of Schoolcraft in the 1850's," *Michigan History* 40, no. 2 (June 1956): 133, n. 12.

26. Smith, "Notes," 129, n. 1.

27. Hattie and Henrie to Father and Mother, October 5, 1862, in Harriet Smith Journal, transcribed by Stanley Barney Smith (unpublished typescript, 1955), 173, SBSC.

28. Smith, diary, May 15, 1864, Henry Parker Smith Papers (BHL).

29. *Portrait*, 567.

30. *HVC*, 203, 272, 855–58.

31. See Matthew C. Hurlbert, "How to Remember 'This Damnable Guerrilla Warfare': Four Vignettes from Civil War Missouri," *Civil War History* 59, no. 2 (2013): 143–68.

INDEX

Page numbers in *italics* indicate images.

abolitionists: blamed for instigating war, 175; called fanatic, 68, 193; lectures by, 53; in Republican Party, 68; in Schoolcraft, 241n125; violence against, 101, 113. *See also* Douglass, Frederick; Kelley, Abby

agriculture: horses used in, 26; in Kalamazoo County, Michigan, 4, 35; magazine, 85, 94–95, 102–3; in Vernon County, Missouri, 83–84, 115–17. *See also* Corn Belt; farm: Smith family; farmer; *Moore's Rural New Yorker*

Ainsworth, Cynthia, 28–29, 68–69, 218n91

Allen, Jo, 197, 253n53

Allen, Jonas, 60, 71, 76

Allen, S. T., 110–11

Alton, Illinois, 155, 181, 200, 257

American Phrenological Journal, 104

Anderson, Frank, 131, 138–39, 154, 204, 253n39

Arthur, T. S., 41–43, 223n59, 224n65

Astor, Aaron, 149, 202, 211n3, 255n106, 263n20, 267n123

Austin, Thomas H., 117, 119, 126, 131, 138–39, 151, 200, 204

Badger, Albert, 117, 119, 138–39, 151, 200, 204, 253nn38–39

Bailey, Phillip, 47, 227n119

Bales, Bob, 138, 140, 144, 150, 182–84

Balltown, Missouri, 117, 119

bands: cotillion, 51; presidential campaign (1856), 71; serenade, 51–52. *See also* individual names

Baptist churches: American Baptist Home Mission Society, 22; beliefs of, 16–18, 29–30, 37–40, 42, 55, 174–75; Cedar Falls Academy, 22, 42; Johnson family in, 22–23; Madison University, 22; Montevallo congregation, 138, 204; network, 22–23

Barney, Agnes, 205

Barney, Mary, 104, 203

Barnum, P. T., 4, 52, 89

Battle of Dry Wood Creek, 126

Battle of Lone Jack, 196

Battle of Moore's Mill, 190

Battle of Pea Ridge, 142

Battle of Wilson's Creek, 126

Beilein, Joseph, 10, 213n18

Bennett, Emerson, 43, 225n82

"black Republican," 120–21, 123

Blair, Frank, 101

Blair, William, 136, 247n97

Blann, Charlie, 132, 137, 143, 152, 165, 173

Bloomer, Amelia, 53

Bloss, C. A., 42, 224n73

"border ruffian," 99, 122, 194

Bowery B'hoy, 49

Boyd, Mark, 116–17, 137, 163, 167–68, 180, 184

Boyd, Mrs., 116, 124, 167

Boyd family, 99, 113, 116, 138, 189, 191, 259n46
Brazier, John, 154–55, 203–4, 257n142, 257n146
Bremer, Frederika, 47, 227n119
Brim, John, 137
Bronte, Charlotte (Currer Bell), 104, 242nn146–47
Brown, E. Lakin, 48, 63, 75, 215n37, 228n129
Brown, George, 185, 203
Brown, John (Old John Brown), 98–100, 115–16, 137, 151–53, 163, 170, 185, 197
Brown, John (Young John Brown), 137, 203, 268n9
Bulwer-Lytton, Edward, 46–47, 226n115
Burke, Diane Mutti, 80, 235n3, 241n126
Bushman, Richard L., 88, 236n35
bushwackers. *See* guerrillas
"Butternuts," 152, 171

Carrico, Parson Joseph, 138, 141, 155, 169, 182, 184, 197, 199, 204
Cavicchi, Daniel, 52, 223n44
Cedar County, Missouri, 83, 118, 137, 141, 155, 182, 204
Cedar County Militia (Union), 197, 266n96
Certeau, Michel de, 6, 211n6, 212n7
Chase, Capt., 153–54
childrearing: and discipline, 16, 178–79; father's participation in, 64, 66, 72–73; and illness, 64–66, 189–90, 194; rewards of, 66, 73
Clark, Colonel, 123
Clark, Lee, 79–82, 96
Clawson, Mary Ann, 138, 252n34
clerks, dry-goods: characteristics of, 26, 52; clothing of, 102; potential for advancement, 25, 61, 76, 93; salary, 24, 61, 63, 65, 68, 93, 117; stigma, 62, 76, 107; working conditions, 67, 76, 93
clothing: of children, 90, 171; of clerk, 102; critique of fashionable, 37–38; of farmers, 102, 242n129; of homespun cloth, 171; as marker of social class, 38–39, 52; sewing of, 39, 185, 203; wartime shortages of, 131, 171
Cobb, M. Rush: farmland search, 77, 79–82; partnership, 82, 85, 96–98, 108, 110–11, 116, 141; saddle and guns, 122, 124, 160; sale of land, 203
Coffee, John, 140, 154, 190, 195–96
Conforti, Joseph A., 88, 237n52
Cooper, James Fenimore, 47, 104, 227n119, 242n144
Corn Belt, 116
corporal punishment, 33, 113, 178–79, 219n129
courtships: economic considerations, 23–24; expectations of marriage, 21, 27, 31, 44–45; gender role negotiation, 23, 31; marriage anxiety, 17–21, 29; romantic love, 17–18, 20, 28–30, 44–45; suitable husband, 16, 23, 28–30, 31; suitable wife, 15, 23, 26–27, 31
credit, financial, 24, 30, 39, 61, 63, 65, 145. *See also* debt
Culvertson, Dr., 152, 169

Dade, Dr. John, 112, 124; Baptist, 138; election (1860), 119; Freemason, 138; fugitive, 143–45, 150–52, 165–66, 169, 254n77; Missouri State Guard, 123, 128, 130, 140
Dade, Mrs., 173, 180, 185, 198, 259n46
dances. *See* balls; bands; fiddlers
debt, 24, 31, 34–35, 61–62, 65–66, 80, 85. *See also* credit, financial
diaries: of Harriet Johnson (Smith), 5, 8–9, 157–59, 206; of Henry Smith, 4–5, 8–9, 144, 206; as historical source, 4–7; shared in courtship, 20; and subjectivity, 7
Dickens, Charles, 47, 53, 108, 227nn120–22
disloyalty, 136, 139, 156, 162–63
Douglass, Frederick, 4, 53–54, 101
Drake, Mr., 143
droughts, 61, 112, 116, 171

Duncan, Delamore, 79–82
Dyer, Thomas G., 138–39, 252n30

Edgeworth, Maria, 47, 226n116
Enrolled Missouri Militia (Union), 190
entertainment: circus, 49, 52, 74; concerts, 52, 125; lectures, 53, 67, 73, 101; theater, 49; touring companies, 49, 52. *See also* leisure activities

farmers: capital required, 24, 61–62; characteristics of, 26; income of, 34–35, 61–62, 65
Farrar, Bernard, 155
Faust, Drew Gilpin, 158, 257n4, 260n77, 261n89, 261n93, 263n7
Federal troops: pursuit of guerrillas, 142–43, 151, 190–91; scouts, 136, 140–41, 143, 154, 161; surveillance, 135–36, 157, 162–64. *See also* Fort Scott, Kansas: troops
Fellman, Michael, 10, 146, 149, 181, 184, 212n7, 238n58
Fialko, Andrew, 10, 213n18
fiddlers: call books, 203–4, *204*; for dancing, 29–30, 50–51, *50*, 59, 74, 203, 205; *Fiddler*, *118*; musical styles, 30, 50–51; social capital, 30, 74, 111, 117; stigma, 17, 29–31, 51, 54–55
Foner, Eric, 67, 233n60
foods: in Missouri, 79–80, 97, 109; of refugees, 185, 188, 192; salt as essential, 161; shortages, 109, 112, 171, 241n111; troops demand for, 127–28
Fort Scott, Kansas: town, 84, 110–11, 118–19, 185, 198, 200; troops, 126, 130, 140, 143, 164, 167, 196; Union garrison, 131–32, 138, 151–52, 154, 170, 177
Frank, Lisa Tendrich, 173, 261
freedom of speech, 176–77
Freemasons: Balltown Masonic lodge, 117, 119, 138, 151; as communication channel, 138, 151, 252n34; Kalamazoo Masonic lodge, 49; obligation of assistance, 128, 145, 151; Vernon County Masonic network, 123, 138
Fremont, John, 4, 69–71, 127–30
Fuller, Metta, 40, 223n49

Gabbert, Eliza, 204
Gabbert, John, 143, 150–51, 196, 254n69
Gabbert, Mrs., 197
Gamble, Hamilton, 124, 130, 190
Garnett, Kansas, 199–200
Gatewood, James, 119–22, 139, 144, 247n93
General Land Office, 81–82
General Orders 1, Department of the Missouri, 141
General Orders 13, Department of the Missouri, 136
General Orders 18, Missouri State Militia, 156, 266n90
General Orders Nineteen, 190
Genius of the West, 46
gentility, 37, 40, 54–55, 88, 92–93, 148, 161, 171–73, 208
Gorn, Elliott J., 49, 228n141
Gorrill, Miss, 36
Gould family (S. S., Hannah, and Amelia), 47, 51, 53, 229n177
Gray, Susan E., 22, 67, 215n32, 233n57, 234n85
Greeno, Captain, 138, 140–41
guerrillas: attacks on judges, courthouses, and records, 131, 182; bands of, 136–37, 141–42, 149, 160–61, 170, 173–74, 182–84, 190, 198; civilian aid to, 141–45, 150–53, 160–61, 165–66, 173–74; creek beds used by, *177*, *178*; difficult to identify, 136, 165; Federal troops kill father of, 197; ideals of manhood, 147–48, 183; punishment of, 136, 141, 145, 156
Guitar, Colonel Odum, 265n69

habeus corpus, 135
Halleck, Henry, 130, 135–36, 141, 145
Harper's New Monthly Magazine, 94, 104–6

Harrison, Kimberly, 158, 258n6, 261n87, 266n85
Henry, Judge, 138, 151, 154, 198, 200
Henry, Mattie, 198, 200
Hepler, Dr., 151, 154
Higonnet, Margaret, 170, 260n63
History of Vernon County, Missouri, 4, 208
home guards (Montevallo), 124–25
homes: abandoned, 155, 185; ideal image of, 61, 65, 77, 94; intrusion, 123, 141, 154, 160–62; in ruins, 155, 186–87; as site of memories, 185; threatened by war, 157, 159, 170
honesty, 20–21, 26, 37, 145–46, 166, 170
Hoosier, stereotype of, 89
horses: hidden from Federal troops, 129, 142–43, 150, 153; racing, 17, 40, 48, 49, 54, 98; ridden by guerrillas, 99, 143, 148; ridden by women, 90, 172, 250n160; theft, 132, 137, *142*, 198
hospitality, 144–46, 153–54, 160–62
household goods: chairs, 92; kitchen utensils, 97; sale of, 180–81
"household war," 159, 161–62, 171–73
Howe, Elias, 203, 268n6
Hudson, John C., 116, 215n32, 245n54
Hull and Arnold's Quadrille Band, 29, *50*, 51, 205
Hunter, DeWitt Clinton, 117–19, 124, 126, 131, 138, 196, 204, 251n174
Hurt, Douglas, 80, 235n8

Independence Day (Fourth of July), 29–30, 51, 118–19
informers, 152, 162–63, 182

Jackson, Claiborne, 120–25, 130
Jayhawkers (Kansas militia), 124–29, 143; burn and loot Missouri homes, 126–27; camp overnight in Montevallo, 130; fear of, 124–27; usages of term, 139–40. *See also* Fort Scott, Kansas; guerrillas
Jefferson City, Missouri, 82, 107, 121–22, 124, 130
Jennison, Charles, 110, 125–26, 128

Johnson, Abigail, 32, 36–37, 41, 43, 46, 221n5
Johnson, Eunice, 16, 101
Johnson, Joseph, 61, 75, 101, 111, 200
Johnson, Lizzie, 192–94
Johnson, Mary, 75, 101
Johnson, Solomon (Harriet's brother), 22, 102, 192, 194, 200, 221n5
Johnson, Solomon (Harriet's grandfather), 22
Johnson, Solomon (Harriet's great-grandfather), 22
Johnson, Solomon (Harriet's uncle), 32, 41–43, 221n5
Johnson, Volney, 200
Johnson, Wakeman, 18, 31, 41, 45, 66, 111, 195; advice from, 16, 30, 74; as Baptist preacher, 16, 22, 175, 215n38
Jones, Mrs., 198, 200

Kalamazoo, Michigan, 79, 195; Republican rally (1856), 69–71
Kalamazoo County, 21–22, 24, 35, 49, 109
Kansas: Jayhawkers, 124–30, 132, 137, 165, 173; Missouri refugees in, 198–200; Quantrill's raid on Lawrence, 198–99; statehood, 120
Kansas Territory: anti-slavery activists in, 67, 87, 109–11; Lecompton Constitution, 110; Missouri border with, 82–84, 102; Missouri fears invasion by, 119; press coverage of, 67, 82, 87, 110; violence in, 82, 110–11, 119
Kansas-Nebraska Act, 63, 67, 70
Kelly, Abby, 53
Kelly, Catherine E., 36, 88, 220n3, 221n6, 222n27, 225n96, 237n48
Knight, James, 155
Know-Nothings (American Party), 63–64, 67
Kulikoff, Allan, 90, 238n55, 239n69

Lane, James, 110, 126–27, 130
leisure activities: backgammon, 54, 93, 117; card games, 40, 49, 54, 74, 117; fishing, 16; horseracing, 40, 48, 49, 54, 98; hunting, 49; parties, 36, 40, 54–55, 74–75, 78. *See also* balls; entertainment; singing

Leslie, Frank, 128, 188
Leslie, William, 109, 113, 137, 141–42, 186, 199
Lily, 53
Lincoln, Abraham, 4, 69–70, 119, 121, 135, 170, 200–201
Lindley, J. Riley, 154–55, 181–82, 203–4, 257n142, 257n146
Lindley, Mrs., 154
literacy: advantages of, 7–8, 45–46, 65, 148–49; as marker of social class, 45, 92–93, 100, 225n96; in Vernon County, Missouri, 98–99, 116, 149. *See also* reading; writing
literature: as conversation topic, 47; dangers of sensational, 43–44; evangelical and reform, 40–43; influence of, 17, 19–20, 22, 43, 47; and literary critics, 43, 46–47. *See also* reading
Little Dixie, 80–81
log houses: building process, 97–98, 106, 109; building techniques, 85–86; dog-trot plan, 85, 94–97, *96*; ideal image of, 85–86, 96–97; stigma of, 55, 103, 105, *106*
Longfellow, Henry Wadsworth, 171, 260n65
loyalty, 112, 120, 136–39, 148, 153–54; conflicting, 9, 138, 145, 155–56, 208–9; shifting, 4–5, 9, 138–39, 163–65, 183
Luskey, Brian P., 76, 235n120
lyceum, 45–46, 176
Lystra, Karen, 23, 28, 214n11, 216n51, 218n96, 231

Maddox, Wilson, 144, 254n73
malaria, 65–66, 112, 124
manliness: ideals of, 23, 25–26, 64, 66–69, 146–48; and independence, 67–68, 77; measures of, 35; and recreation, 48–49; Republican rhetoric on, 67–70, 77–78; rituals of, 233n74; transcending race, 53–54; and the western frontier, 66–67, 77, 107, 146
Mann, Horace, 34, 42, 224n73
Marryat, Frederick, 47, 227n123
Marvell, Ik, 48, 227n124
Maumee, Ohio, 31–34, 36–42, 45–46
Mayfield, Bryce, 138, 153, 182–84, 197, 266n95

Mayfield, Crawford (Crack), 138, 143, 153, 182–84, 197, 266n95
Mayfield, Jennie, 173–74, 252n19
Mayfield, Mrs., 150
Mayfield, Nora, 119, 166, 173–74, 204, 254n69
Mayfield, Sallie, 173–74, 252n19
Melish, Joanne Pope, 87, 237n45
"mental territory," 8
middle class: expectations of success, 77; gender roles in, 23, 40–42; grammar as marker of, 45; house as marker of, 92, *95*, 97; morality standards of, 39–42; poor and immigrants, distinguished from, 38–39; provincial, 36–37, 88; reading practices of, 103–5, 226n111; social calls in, 37; taste of, 37, 39; wealthy, disapproval of, 37–38
Military Bounty Land Warrant, 35, 81, 85, 236n29
military prisons (Union), 151–52, 154–55, 170, 182
Missouri: opinions on secession in, 120–21; provisional state government, 130, 135, 182; secession convention, 121, 124
Missouri General Assembly Extraordinary Session, 121–22
Missouri State Guard (Confederate): camp near Montevallo with fleeing governor, 122–24; confiscate guns and horses, 122–24, 196; forage food in Montevallo, 127, 196; hidden from Union troops, 128, 130; pass through Montevallo, 126–27; recruits killed or captured, 195–96; recruit near Montevallo, 131, 139–40, 195–96. *See also* Hunter, DeWitt Clinton; Montevallo company, Missouri State Guard; Price, Sterling; Taylor, Wm. Henry
Missouri State Militia (Union), 136, 182, 266n90
Montevallo, Missouri: terrain, 83, 85–86, 162–63, 177–78, *178*, 186; township farms, 115–17, 137, 236n24; village, 83–84, 118, 137
Montevallo company, Missouri State Guard, 122, 124, 126, 139–40, 142–44, 154
Montgomery, James, 110–11, 119, 125–26

Moore, Orlando Hurley, 29, 49, 54–55, 68–69, 200–201, 267n114
Moore's Rural New Yorker, 85, 94–95, 102, 104
moral certainty, loss of, 164, 170, 176, 193, 207–8
moral fable, 41–43
More, Hannah, 42–43, 225n75
Morress, Captain, 151, 256n124
Morrissey, Katherine G., 8, 212n15
music. *See* balls; bands; fiddlers; singing

narratives, oral: accounts of atrocities, 167; proverbs, 171; rumors, 166, 190; trickster tales, 168–70, 173–74
Neely, Jeremy, 10, 110, 116, 213n19, 244n18, 245n53
Neosho, Missouri, 84, 127, 130, 266n95
Nevada City, Missouri, 84, 111, 117–19, 121, 131, 138–39, 199–200, 209
New England cultural heritage, 21–23, 36, 39–40, 80, 87–89
New England Emigrant Aid Society, 87
New York Ledger, 104
New York State, 4, 22, 36, 49, 88–89, 103–4, 112. *See also* Seneca Falls, New York
New York Tribune, 104

oaths: of allegiance, 130–31, 136, 138, 141, 152–54, 164; of loyalty, 130, 135, 182
Osage River, 130, 186
Osceola, Missouri, 84, 127, 140, 155

Page, Marion: Maumee, Ohio, 36–37, 40, 42; Michigan, 69; Missouri, 108–9, 112, 124, 137–38, 162, 166, 185–86, 259n46; wartime and postwar letters from, 198–200
Page, Maurice: Maumee, Ohio, 31, 33, 36–37, 42, 221n5; Michigan, 69; Missouri, 108–9, 116, 118, 120–21, 137–38, 150–54, 162–66, 181, 209; wartime and postwar letters from, 195–202
Panic of 1857, 105–6, 108, 111
Parker, John, 68, 105–6, 108, 113, 195
Parsons, General, 123
Partisan Rangers (Confederate), 190

Phelps, Almira Hart, 104, 242n142
Phelps, Elizabeth Stuart (H. Trusta), 41, 223n58
Phillips, Christopher, 129, 139, 211nn3–4, 250n158, 253n41, 256n125, 256n134
political participation, 35, 62–63, 77–78. *See also individual political parties*
Porter, Colonel Joseph, 190, 265nn69–70
Portrait and Biographical Record of Kalamazoo, Allegan and Van Buren Counties, Michigan, 3–4
Potawatomi, 48–49, 53
Pottorf, George, 138
Prairie Ronde, Michigan, 48, 50
prairies: agriculture, 109; fire, 113–14; home, as literary ideal, 86, 93–94, 95, 111–12; landscape, 177, 187; terrain, 80, 83, 108; wildflowers, 178, 186
pregnancy, 60–61, 111–12; childbirth, 60, 64–65, 112, 124; contraception, 60–61, 65
Prentiss, Elder, 42, 104
Price, Sterling, 4, 121–22, 124, 126–27, 140, 142
Probate Judge, Vernon County, 3, 119–21, 130–31, 204, 246n78, 247n93
Provost Marshal, 136, 152–55, *156*, 181
public domain land sales, 81–82
Puke, stereotype of, 89–90, 98–99, 101, 110, 238n58
Purcell, Helen (Smith), 60, 76, 125, 132, 204
Purcell, Isaiah, 116–17, 121, 132

Quantrill, 185, 196; raid on Lawrence, Kansas, 198–99

Rabinowitz, Richard, 28, 218n92, 218n95, 222n31, 264n24
racial identity, 54, 101
Railey, Alek, 197–98
railroads: access to markets and goods, 24–25, 52, 82, 101, 116; impact on land prices, 79–80; lack of, 74, 82, 91, 109, 116, 203; opposition to, 90–91, 100; travel by, 27, 32, 79, 107, 155, 195
Randolph, Mrs., 198
Randolph, W. B., 143–44, 200, 254n73

INDEX

Ransom, Willis, 132, 152, 256n125
Ray, Branch, 125, 131, 143, 198, 204
Ray, James, 83, 126, 130–31, 137, 140–41
Ray, Mrs., 198
reading: aloud, 42–43, 48, 104; communities, 42, 103–5, 203; silently, 43. *See also* literacy; literature; moral fable
reform movements, 5, 34, 40–41, 53, 175
refugee: burden on hosts, 194; loss of social status, 188–89; stigma, 192–95; temporary, 126–27; travel as, 186–92, 195; usages of term, 188, 249n140
Republican Party: appeal to northern men, 67–68, 70, 77; Fremont presidential campaign events, 69–72; Lincoln's Kalamazoo speech, 69–70; Michigan roots, 63; Missouri opposition to, 119
respectability, 30, 39, 45, 52–53, 77, 88, 171, 185, 208
Reynolds family, 36–37, 221n5
rhetorical strategy, 7–9, 17–20, 44–46, 55, 65, 86, 149, 158–59
Robinson, Charlie, 184, 197, 262n105, 267n105
Robinson, Ed, 186
Robinson, Solon, 104, 242n143
Romanticism, 111, 148, 183, 187–88, 190–91
Rothman, Ellen K., 23, 214n11, 217n52
Rotundo, E. Anthony, 25–26, 76, 217nn68–69, 233n74, 235n119
Ryan, Mary, 25, 213n8, 217n66, 237n40

Sagamaw, Chief, 48
salesman, traveling, 4, 26–27, 35, 61
Sandage, Scott, 26, 217n67, 217n72
Schofield, General, 156, 266n90
Schoolcraft, Michigan: brass band, 203; financial prospects in, 24–26, 34–35, 61–62, 93, 107, 201–4; leisure activities, 48–51, 54–55, 73–76; terrain, 83; village, 24, *206*, 209
Schoolcraft Ladies Library Association, 205
Schoolcraft Musical Association, 203
Schoolcraft Republican Wide Awake, 125

Scobey, William, 127, 129–30, 143, 155, 250n160
secession, 120–21, 130, 138, 164, 175, 192, 198; "Union meeting" to oppose, 120; Vernon County support for, 121
Sedalia, Missouri, 117, 155, 180, 182, 184–86
Seneca Falls, New York, 4, 24–27, *25*, 30, 46–47, 51–54, 101, 147–48
Servoss, Archibald, 102, 105, 111–13
Servoss, Edelia (Johnson), 16, 44, 88, 111–12
Shackleford, John, 137
Shakespeare, William, 47, 93, 125, 240n88
Simms, Clay, 144, 182–84, 196
singing: church choir, 51, 54, 73, 125; Glee Club, 51; Jenny Lind, 51–52; parlor music, 51, 54; sheet music, 40, 51; at temperance meetings, 41
Sixth Kansas Cavalry (Union), 138, 140–41
slavery: and Baptist missionaries, 23; in Missouri, 79–81, 98, 101; in Vernon County, 100; and western territories, 63–64, 67–68, 70, 72
Smith, Eliza, 21, 26, 48, 64, 148, 203–4, 227n126
Smith, Gerrit, 53
Smith, Harry, 124, 135, 158, 185–86, 189–90, 194–95, 204–6
Smith, Isa: early childhood, 64–66, 69, 72–73, *73*, 75–76, 97; Montevallo, 108–9, 113–14, 123–24, 162, 172, 178, 248n110; refugee, 185–86, 189–90, 194–95; "Reminiscences of Missouri," 117–19, 126, 142–43, 150, 153, 182, 192, 243n163, 250n171; Schoolcraft (adult years), 205–7, *207*
Smith, Stanley Barney, 5, 205–6, 211n5, 266n83, 266n86
Smith, Thaddeus, 21, 48, 67, 74, 111, 125, 236n29, 242n129
Smith, Walter F.: Montevallo, 112, 124, 135, 141, 158, 161, 172, 178–80; refugee, 185–86, 189–91, 194–95; US Marine Band, 205, 269n19
Smith and Bonfoy dance band, 205

Smith family farm (Montevallo): agricultural production, 115; compared to other township farms, 115–16; equipment, 115; financial aspects of, 85, 108; labor shortage, 98; partnership, 82, 85, *86*, 96, 108, 112; as safe house for guerrillas, 149–50; sale of, 203; water supply, 109, 112, 116

Smith family farm (Schoolcraft): agricultural production, 34–35, 61; as dairy business, 4, 204–6; financial aspects of, 24, 34–35, 61–62, 65

social class distinctions, 51, 55, 65, 92, 172, 188–89

social networks, 5, 7–8, 10–11, 80; of men, 137–39, 149, 184–85; of women, 162, 166, 185, 198

Sousa, John Philip, 205

Sousa's New Marine Band, 205; Southern man, 111, 129, 150, 153; men, 129, 141, 152, 181–84, 190, 193

Springfield, Missouri, 81–82, 84, 118, 122, 126–27, 130–31, 197

St. Louis, Missouri: Federal troops in, 121–22, 130, 154–56; Smith family members in, 61, 79, 107, 155, 171

Stanton, Elizabeth Cady, 4, 53, 229n177

Steward, Jesse, 137, 142, 177, 182, 253n53, 262n105, 267n105

Steward, William, 142, 166, 177, 186, 196, 199, 267n105

Stith, Matthew, 10, 213n19

Stone, Martha Hubble, 43, 225n79

Stott, Richard, 88, 237n49

Stowe, Harriet Beecher, 46

Sue, Eugene, 46, 226n113

survey township, 81–83

"survival lying," 146

Sutherland, Daniel, 140, 251n9, 253n49

Tally, Berry (Old Man Tally), 143, 254n77

Tapp, Sam, 138, 140, 153–54, 161, 197, 266n96

Tapp, Sarah, 198

Taylor, Bayard, 47, 227n119

Taylor, Wm. Henry: Baptist, 138; county sheriff, 117, 119; Freemason, 117, 138; 250n154; marriage, 150; Missouri State Guard, 124, 139–40, 259n48; Union prisoner, 143–44, 151–52, 154–55, 165, 170, 181; postwar, 200, 204

temperance advocacy, 40–41, 206

Thatcher, Judge S. O. (Lawrence, Kansas), 199

Thomas, Dr. Nathan, 209, 241n125

Thomas, Pamela (Brown), 241n125

treason, 121, 136, 153, 200

Tyrell, Mary, 40, 42, 111–12, 244n29

Unionists, 120, 130, 136–39, 141, 150–51, 162, 186, 198–99, 204

United States Marine Band, 205

Upton, Ed, 137–38, 180, 197, 199, 254n74

Upton, George, 137, 197, 199, 200, 204

Upton, Matilda, 198

Vermont, 21–22, 37, 39, 48, 88

Vernon County, Missouri: court, 3–4, 111, 117–19, 124, 130–31, 138–39, 150, 209; government of, 117–21, 124, 130–31, 138–39, 204; location of, 82–84; Order 11, impact on, 199–200, 203; slavery in, 100, 111; Texas cattle blockade in, 117

wagons: covered, 79, 107, 187; lumber, 35, 51

Walter, Scott, 112, 115

Warner, Susan, 104, 242n141

Webster, Dr., 126–27, 129, 155

Webster's Large Dictionary, 92–93

weddings, 38, 59, 150

Wheeler, Charles, 65, 104, 125

Wheeler, Frances (Smith), 125–26, 204, 242n129

Whig Party, 63, 67

whiteness, 21, 77, 100–101

Whites, LeeAnn, 10, 173, 260n82, 261n86, 261n89

Williams, Stephen, 169, 184, 189

Willis, N. Parker, 43, 225n81

Wink, Amy L., 158, 258n5, 264n49

Withers, William, 83, 91, 100, 111

womanhood, 5, 18–19, 23, 37–38, 171–74, 185

Wood, Jo, 139, 143–44, 196, 254n74
Wood, Joseph S., 87, 237n46
Wood, William, 197, 266n96
Woods, Michael E., 167, 259n55
Wright, Wily, 168
writing: discouragement of, 46; lyceum paper, 45; memoir, 206; personal, 4–9, 157–59; petition, 119, 155, 181, 246n78, 250n171; for publication, 3–5, 46, 102–3; resolution, 117, 120, 246n63; skills, 7–8, 45–46, 65. *See also* diaries; literacy; rhetorical strategy
Wyatt-Brown, Bertram, 145, 153, 172, 254nn82–83, 254n86, 256n130, 260n80
Wyrick, Mr., 151, 197, 256n124

Yankees: as comic character, 88–89; described by northern press, 87, 89–90; hostility toward, 101–2, 109; house, 5, 7–8, 91–92, 94–95, 95, 97; identity as, 4–5, 9, 21, 89, 102–3, 202, 207–8; morality, 39–40; New England heritage of, 21–22; peddlers, 89; settlers in Missouri, 91, 100, 102–3, 108–9, 110–11; settlers in Schoolcraft, Michigan, 21–22, 67, 89; stereotype of, 89; usage of term, 88–89; village ideal, 87–88; yard, 5, 87–88. *See also* New England cultural heritage

ABOUT THE AUTHOR

Marilyn Ferris Motz is Emerita Associate Professor of Popular Culture at Bowling Green State University, where she retired in 2015 after serving as Chair of the Department of Popular Culture for eleven years. She holds a PhD in American Culture from the University of Michigan, with concentrations in social history and folklore. She taught courses on topics including material culture, folklore, cultural theory, nineteenth-century popular literature, history of popular entertainments, and amateur/grassroots artistic performance. She is the author of *True Sisterhood: Michigan Women and Their Kin, 1820–1920*, and co-editor of three books, including *Making the American Home: Middle-Class Women and Domestic Material Culture, 1840–1940*. Her articles on nineteenth-century Midwestern American diaries are included in *Inscribing the Daily: Critical Essays on Women's Diaries*, edited by Suzanne Bunker and Cynthia Huff, and *The Diary: The Epic of Everyday Life*, edited by Batsheva Ben-Amos and Dan Ben-Amos. "Folk Expressions of Time and Place: 19th-Century Midwestern Rural Diaries" was published in the *Journal of American Folklore*. Two journal articles examining the strategic use of personal correspondence for family survival appeared in *Turn-of-the-Century Women* and *Southwestern Historical Quarterly*. Other articles on creative expression in everyday life include "Visual Autobiography: Photograph Albums of Turn-of-the-Century Women" in *American Quarterly*, "Garden as Women: Creation of Identity in a Turn-of-the-Century Ohio Town" in *National Women's Studies Association Journal*, "The Practice of Belief" in the *Journal of American Folklore*, and "Material Culture and Heritage" in *A Companion to Popular Culture*, edited by Gary Burns. She lives in Toledo, Ohio, with her husband, Timothy Allen Motz.